Kick Ass

University Press of Florida

Gainesville · Tallahassee · Tampa · Boca Raton · Pensacola · Orlando · Miami · Jacksonville

kick ass

selected columns of

Carl Hiaasen

edited by Diane Stevenson

04 03 02 01 00 99 6 5 4 3 2

All the selections in this work were previously published by the Miami Herald
Publishing Company, a division of Knight Ridder, One Herald Plaza, Miami, Florida.

The author's proceeds from the sale of this work are donated to the Carl A. Hiaasen
Scholarship Fund at the University of Florida College of Journalism.

LIBRARY OF CONGRESS CATALOGING-IN-PUBLICATION DATA
Hiaasen, Carl.
Kick ass: selected columns of Carl Hiaasen / edited by Diane Stevenson.
p. cm.
Columns originally published in the Miami Herald.
ISBN 0-8130-1717-3 (alk. paper)
 1. Florida—Politics and government—1951– . 2. Political corruption—Florida. 3. Florida—Social conditions. 4. Florida—Environmental conditions. 5. United States—Politics and government—1989– . 6. Hiaasen, Carl A. I. Stevenson, Diane, 1947– . II. Title.
F316.2.H49   1999
975.9'063—dc21   99-36655

The University Press of Florida is the scholarly publishing agency for the State
University System of Florida, comprising Florida A & M University, Florida Atlantic
University, Florida International University, Florida State University, University of
Central Florida, University of Florida, University of North Florida, University of
South Florida, and University of West Florida.

University Press of Florida
15 Northwest 15th Street
Gainesville, FL 32611
http://www.upf.com

For all those who care about Florida.

You just cover a lot of territory and you
do it aggressively and you do it fairly and
you don't play favorites and you don't take
any prisoners. It's the old school of slash-
and-burn metropolitan column writing.
You just kick ass. That's what you do.
And that's what they pay you to do.

CARL HIAASEN

Contents

Preface   xi

Acknowledgments   xiii

Introduction   xiv

1. Welcome to South Florida   1
2. Murder and Mayhem   32
3. See It Like a Native   64
4. Rules Are Different Here   83
5. The War on Drugs   104
6. Tourist Season   128
7. A State of Chaos   158
8. Cops, Courts, and Lawyers   173
9. Candidates with Convictions   206
10. Our Leaders on Parade   242
11. Stormy Weather   269
12. Tax Dollars at Work   293
13. Ralph Sanchez and Other Subsidized Sports   313
14. Choked on Growth   335
15. Vanishing Florida   361
16. The Everglades and Big Sugar   380
17. Wild Kingdom   405
18. Small Victories   422

Preface

Since 1985, Carl Hiaasen has written some 1,300 columns for the *Miami Herald*, all of which I've been privileged to read as a single body of work, though choosing among them to create an anthology of reasonable length meant eliminating far more than I would have wished. While many great columns had to be omitted because of limited space, those gathered here represent some of Hiaasen's finest writing as an advocate for realistic growth and decent government in Florida. Taken as a whole, this collection constitutes a history of sorts, chronicling a decade and a half of the issues, struggles, and personalities affecting the development of the state and the welfare of its residents. Individually, each column provides the distinct pleasures associated with reading Carl Hiaasen— inspired outrage, hilarity, incredulity, and passion—in language brilliantly wielded against two targets in particular: hypocrisy and greed.

While fans nationwide can find his novels anywhere, Hiaasen's biweekly columns have thus far been essentially inaccessible after their appearance in the *Herald* or one of the other papers through which his work is syndicated. Even ardent fans would find it difficult to search archives for past columns, especially those from five or ten years ago. This anthology was therefore originally intended to answer the need for a more permanent record of Hiaasen's career as one of the country's most influential and articulate journalists. But what also emerges from the collection, most significantly for those of us who care about Florida's future, is a clear picture of Carl Hiaasen's continuing role as an uncompromising and eloquent defender of this state.

I'm indebted to many people at the *Miami Herald* for their time and generous cooperation—to Lory Reyes and Michael Clark of the research department; Doug Clifton, former executive editor; Sam Terelli, general counsel; Jim Savage, head of the investigations team; Dave Satterfield, former city editor, now business editor; Bob Radziewicz, assistant city editor; Gene Miller, associate editor for reporting.

I must also thank Anthe Hoffman, Janette Johnson, and Melanie Almeder for their help and encouragement throughout this project.

Information concerning Florida's real and projected growth was condensed from Hiaasen columns; various editions of the *Florida Statistical Abstract* (compiled by the Bureau of Economic Research and Development at the University of Florida); *Florida in the Twenty-first Century*, by Leon Bouvier and Bob Weller (Washington, D.C.: Center for Immigration Studies, 1992); and *South Florida: The Winds of Change*, edited by Thomas Boswell (Miami: Association of American Geographers, 1991).

Diane Stevenson

Acknowledgments

For years I resisted the idea of compiling my newspaper columns into a book, because it would have required re-reading each one myself—a columnist's worst nightmare. Most of us can't bear to look at something we wrote last week, much less a decade ago. That's because the nature of daily journalism is fleeting, today's words made instantly stale by tomorrow's headlines. There is simply no time to look back.

This collection would have been impossible without the keen eye, unflagging enthusiasm, and heroic stamina of Diane Stevenson. She pored through many hundreds of columns to find those that best stood the test of time, and also presented a vivid panorama of a confoundingly diverse state. They reflect my own bent view of the place, so whatever wrath these pieces provoke should be directed at me alone. For her brave job of culling and organizing them, Diane deserves nothing less than a medal.

I am also indebted to the many talented reporters and editors at the Miami Herald, past and present. Their guts, ingenuity, and pit-bull persistence produced the news stories that inspired these columns. I feel fortunate, and proud, to be employed by a newspaper that knows what newspapers are supposed to do: Turn over rocks. Dig out the truth. Kick ass.

Carl Hiaasen
Islamorada, Florida

Introduction

In 1953, Carl Hiaasen was born in Plantation, Florida, a tiny suburb of Ft. Lauderdale at the westernmost edge of then-rural Broward County. By 1960, around the time he got his first typewriter, Plantation's population of 4,800 was roughly that of Ft. Lauderdale in 1922, when Hiaasen's grandfather moved down from North Dakota to eventually found the area's first law firm.

While Plantation remained safely fringed by Everglades and swamp, providing the perfect environment for an idyllic boyhood, Broward County's population of 84,000 had almost quadrupled by 1960. By 1960 as well, almost one-third of the state's entire population was concentrated in southeast Florida, which had grown in that same decade by over 113 percent.

In the years since, Florida has absorbed into its population approximately 300,000 people a year, for a relative growth rate almost triple that of the rest of the country. To accommodate the 700–1,000 new residents arriving daily, a minimum of 300 acres of green space must be paved, also daily, for subdivisions, streets, schools, and shopping malls. Added to that has been the considerable development required to house and entertain tourists, 41 million of them in 1990, the year before *Native Tongue*, Hiaasen's satirical novel about theme parks, was published.

During the same years that 75 percent of all currently existing developments were being built, at least five animal species disappeared completely, and a significant number of others were greatly reduced as their habitats either vanished or were poisoned by agricultural runoff or toxins like mercury. Today, the Everglades is half its original size, Florida Bay is endangered, and Broward County (with a population of 1.5 million and recently ranked ninth in the nation for destroyed wetlands and forests) has drawn Plantation into its geographical center. The dirt bike-path Hiaasen and his friends rode into the swamp, where they camped and caught water moccasins, is now University Drive, nine shopping malls lining the same route they once took.

These are the sources of Carl Hiaasen's outrage and satire, the losses beginning even in childhood, when he and his friends would pull up or relocate surveyor's stakes, feeling that such small, futile acts were nevertheless their moral duty. "We were kids," he says. "We didn't know what else to do. We were little and the bulldozers were big." Their memorable roar Hiaasen often compares to "the sound of money," because greed, he says, is "the engine that has run Florida ever since there was a Florida."

Greed and its accompanying corruption, in fact, occupy one side of Hiaasen's clearly articulated system of right and wrong, while unspoiled wilderness lies on the other. The two are separated by what Skink, in Double Whammy, perceives to be "the moral seam of the universe" as he gazes at the dike separating a contaminated development from pristine swampland. Against this backdrop, events play out in Hiaasen's novels and columns, the moral landscape making almost tangible certain basic and universal values: we should be loyal to our friends, behave with civility and decency, earn our paychecks honestly, experience shame if we steal, preserve the world for our children, and never surrender— either our belief in these values, or to anyone who would violate them for personal gain. As Hiaasen says, "You try to be a good citizen wherever you live. Plant mangroves and don't piss in the water."

Hiaasen traces his strong sense of right and wrong back to the losses of the 1960s—the "complete end of innocence" caused by the Kennedy assassinations, two tragic events creating the historical circumstances that placed Richard Nixon in the White House, accelerated the war in Vietnam, and ultimately led to Watergate. "It was a poisonous time to be coming of age," Hiaasen says. "It seemed to me there was so much wrong in the world. I felt such outrage for so many years over those things happening that it wasn't a hard thing to carry into journalism."

When Hiaasen began his Miami Herald column in 1985, however, after having first been a general assignment reporter and then a member of the Herald's prize-winning investigation team, the newspaper hadn't yet established a tradition of commentary written with "ferocity and passion, mordant wit, and moral outrage," as Doug Clifton, former executive editor of the Miami Herald, describes Hiaasen's bi-weekly column. Miami was still a young city, Hiaasen explains, with no voice, even on the editorial page, that expressed strongly held opinions likely to inspire an equally strong response from readers. So when Hiaasen ridiculed the first Cuban American county manager, whose indictment for grand theft was dismissed because of a 1951 ruling on cattle rustling ("a standard of conduct against which all public officials should be tested," Hiaasen dryly observed), Herald editors initially cringed. Interestingly, however, the following year that same county manager forgot to disclose, as required by law, a large profit he made on a land deal, prompting Hiaasen to write that such memory lapses by someone controlling the county budget suggested the need for a brain scan in addition to a lawyer: "If I thought [he] deserved to be fired for lying to the IRS and buying stolen suits and lying about it, I would say that in the column. Gotta get rid of the guy. And it was unheard of at the time."

From the start, it was also clear Hiaasen would not allow himself to be bullied. In 1987, when a city commissioner objected to funding the Sister Cities convention because representatives from communist countries might attend, Hiaasen called his antics "boneheaded." By certified mail, the commission sent a formal, albeit unintelligible, resolution demanding that the Herald retract or clarify Hiaasen's "false and misleading statement," to which Hiaasen replied that since his original column was neither false nor misleading, he couldn't add even "a cheerfully instructive footnote." He did, however, formulate a resolution of his own, which reads, in part:

"Be it resolved: It is hereby demanded that the Miami City Commission quit wasting time on dumb, self-serving resolutions when there are so many more important issues facing the community.

"Regarding the Sister Cities International convention and the alleged Communist menace therein, it is hereby demanded that city commissioners halt such reactionary nonsense immediately, since it exposes all South Florida to national scorn and ridicule. It is further demanded that if the commissioners choose to make fools of themselves, that they do so in the privacy of their homes and not in a public forum."

Now, much of Miami has come to expect a no-holds-barred Hiaasen column that synthesizes news stories and corruption scandals, and makes sense of issues in its own "brilliant fashion, with humor that skewers," according to Jim Savage, head of the Herald's investigations team, who worked with Hiaasen in the mid-1980s on uncovering and ultimately stopping Port Bougainville, one of several illegally sited developments that would have added altogether some 60,000 people to North Key Largo. On this project, and on the Smuggler's Island investigation, which began with a memo about a water main and ended with a series on dope running in Key West, Savage observed firsthand Hiaasen's legendary insight. It was Hiaasen, Savage notes, who quickly recognized the heart of the story—how drug dealing dramatically altered people's lives, especially in Key West, but with implications for the rest of the country. Savage now uses Hiaasen's story-assembling techniques, as well as his accuracy, fairness, and skillful interviewing, as a model of excellence in investigative reporting when he teaches seminars in project writing. "Carl is the most talented journalist I've worked with because he's an outstanding researcher and a world-class writer," Savage says. "It would be great if we could clone Carl Hiaasen, so one could still be working with me."

* * *

At age four, Carl Hiaasen learned to read using the Miami Herald sports page and maps of Florida. Two years later, when he got his first typewriter as a present from his father, he taught himself to hunt and peck well enough to write his own sports page, reporting on neighborhood kickball and softball games in newsletters he handed out to friends. Even then, he knew he wanted to be a journalist, because getting paid to learn about the world and report on it in stories bearing his name seemed the perfect occupation.

Continuing to write for pleasure in high school, Hiaasen again had his own publication, More Trash, an underground newsletter in which he experimented with irreverent commentary by poking fun at the traditions of mainstream adolescent culture, as well as satirizing the teachers and administrators of Plantation High. At Emory University, he ghost-wrote a doctor's memoirs, and within the next two years, had married his high school sweetheart, Connie, become a father, and moved to Gainesville to major in journalism at the University of Florida.

When he graduated in 1974, having just turned twenty-one, Hiaasen was hired by Cocoa Today as a general assignment reporter, and soon after became a feature writer for their Sunday magazine, Sunrise. Two years later, in 1976, he was invited to join the Herald's Broward Bureau, where he remained for about six months before being moved to the news-paper's city desk in Miami as a general assignment reporter. He quickly became a feature writer for the Herald's Sunday magazine, Tropic, and in 1979 joined two-time Pulitzer prize winner Gene Miller, associate editor for reporting, in investigating and writing "Dangerous Doctors," an eight-part series remembered today for its excellence and impact.

During the early 1980s, while still a member of the investigations team, Hiaasen began to write fiction, spending evenings and weekends co-authoring, with the late William Montalbano, three novels—the re-cently reprinted Powder Burn, Trap Line, and A Death in China. In 1985—as he was about halfway through his first solo novel, Tourist Season, one of seven (Double Whammy, Skin Tight, Native Tongue, Strip Tease, Stormy Weather, and Lucky You) that established his national reputation as one of America's best satirists—the Herald asked Hiaasen if he wanted to write a column.

Those at the Herald who knew him during these early years say that even in his twenties Hiaasen was clearly one of a kind, his gifts being distinctly extraordinary. Doug Clifton remembers Hiaasen as "a young man with talents that far surpassed those that you would expect from someone of that age and experience." Immediately evident, Clifton says, were Hiaasen's wit, probing mind, remarkable energy and the "incred-ible ability to handle himself in tough situations, to write with clarity, and to peer into things and catch their essence."

Since working as an investigative reporter with Jim Savage and Gene Miller, Hiaasen has written some 1,300 columns. A very few recount personal anecdotes—about bonefishing, or blowing up frogs as a child, or trying to find his young son's lost snake, Lefty. Others tackle national issues and political candidates or officeholders. Most columns, however, focus on the overdevelopment of crowded South Florida, its immigration inequities, gun- and drug-related violence, its image and scandals and tourists, and its misuse of taxpayers' money by venal or inept public servants.

The most passionate of Hiaasen's columns often concern politics, corruption, and the environment—in Florida, three closely related topics. Many of his colleagues believe, in fact, that Hiaasen's deep-rooted attachment to South Florida enables him to write with genuine lyricism about the Everglades, and with uniquely venomous, wickedly funny satire about those "greedheads," as Hiaasen calls them, whose make-a-buck morality has led to widespread environmental destruction.

Sometimes Hiaasen is brutally direct, calling one well-known Miami politician "a pernicious little ferret," another, a "worthless blowhard," and a third, "an affable, back-slapping, ribbon-snipping blob." Sometimes he chooses images to emphasize venality—certain legislators are, for example, the "favorite slobbering lapdogs" of canegrowers, and Hialeah's government is an "oozing sludge bucket of corruption," where "the air of graft and deception comes from deep in the soil, like radon gas." He skewers local- and state-level candidates as well, during one election referring to them as "a veritable slag heap of mediocrity" and wondering, "What is it about South Florida that compels people barely fit to function in society to go out and run for office?" However, because Hiaasen doesn't play favorites, he also attacks the "rich tradition of voter apathy, rotten judgment and shallow values" allowing corrupt or unqualified candidates to gain office in the first place, so close to taxpayers' money and so indifferent to their interests.

Although Hiaasen never hesitates to use what Clifton refers to as "a cauterizing light," his satire can also be clearly fun-loving and equally effective in its various other forms—spoofs, invented conversations, lists of rules, questionnaires and surveys, predictions for the new year, diary entries, multiple-choice tests, and song lyrics, like these from February 1990, commemorating Governor Martinez's condemnation of the rap group 2 Live Crew. (The group was busted four months later by Broward Sheriff Nick Navarro, who sent a dozen county cars to "capture" the rappers, inspiring Hiaasen to comment, "Liberal wimps have chastised Navarro for using so many deputies on the 2 Live Crew raid. [But] it's not as if crime is a problem in Broward. Last year the county reported a measly 115 murders, 830 sexual assaults, 5,212 robberies, 6,202 aggravated assaults, 25,478 burglaries, 11,190 auto thefts and 59,541 larcenies. . . . No wonder Navarro could spare a fleet of squad cars to pursue an unarmed musician!")

"Let's Do It Till November," by DJ Jazzy Bob

Yo, I'm Governor Bad
And I'm happy to say
Finally got an issue
That breaks my way.
Found some dirty words
In a jive rap song
So I'm takin' the position
That smut is wrong.

*   *   *

Now I ain't heard the music,
And I ain't read the law,
But I read my campaign polls
And I know what I saw.
I'm in real deep doo-doo
So I better act fast,
Gotta get me some headlines,
Gotta save my a—.
Hey, I don't wanna rap
about the D.O.T.
I know it's outta money,
but don't blame me.
And I don't wanna talk
about the H.R.S.
Yo, enough already!
I know it's a mess.

*   *   *

Don't know what's dirty?
Say, leave it to me,
For the final definition

Of obscenity.
Don't need no Constitution
To tell me what to do.
Gonna confiscate some albums,
Maybe videos, too.
*   *   *
Be a music censor,
Just to see how it looks.
If the polls jump up,
Then I'm goin' after books!

At his funniest and most playful, Hiaasen still remains dedicated to what he considers his responsibility to the public—being straightforward and up-front. "A columnist is paid to take a stand. If a reader can't figure out how I feel about something, then I don't deserve to take my paycheck home that week, because I copped out," Hiaasen says. "I feel strongly about the advocacy role of the columnist."

Certainly, he has never shied away from directly tackling issues in the public interest, even when doing so cost the *Herald* money, as in 1994 when the Lennar Corporation, implicated in the construction scandals following Hurricane Andrew, withdrew advertising because Hiaasen lambasted his own newspaper for promoting Lennar's new home giveaway contest. "According to an exciting full-page advertisement," he wrote, "a lucky reader will win Lennar's 'Home of the Future.' This is not to be confused with Lennar's 'homes of the past,' many of which splintered like Popsicle sticks during Hurricane Andrew." Particularly scathing, this column suggests that, as a "marvel of modern engineering," the home of the future might be made of shingles "actually nailed to the roofs," gables "actually anchored to the walls," real plywood in place of "pressed fiber-board," and might therefore remain "vertical, even in 100-mile per hour winds." (Interestingly, two years later, Hiaasen again had occasion to write about Lennar Homes, when sinkholes full of trash opened up behind houses in a Miramar subdivision the company had built. After 250 truckloads of "tires, rotting tree limbs, rusty appliances and construction debris" were hauled away, the remaining pit filled with brown water and had to be fenced.)

Despite its loss of a major advertiser, the *Herald* never told Hiaasen to stop writing about Lennar, even though "at many, many other newspapers there would have been a heel on the back of my neck to lay off," he says. The *Herald* also printed Hiaasen's criticism of the newspaper's then-publisher, Dave Lawrence, when he contemplated running for governor in 1998. While praising Lawrence as a "smart, decent, compassionate fellow who cares about Florida and believes fervently in the innate goodness of mankind," Hiaasen also vigorously objected to the "untenable and queasy position" his candidacy would have created for "this newspaper, the reporters, columnists and editors who produce it." Anything *Herald* staffers wrote about Lawrence or his opponent, Hiaasen pointed out, could have been perceived as coming from "Lawrence's personal campaign machine," and not from the independent voices the public was entitled to hear.

"What would our readers have thought if I stayed silent? I couldn't. The only way I knew to let our readers know it's business as usual was to do the same kind of tough column on Dave I would do on anyone," Hiaasen says. "It put us in a helluva position." The column in which he takes on his own boss (who was less surprised perhaps than others at the *Herald*, Hiaasen says, and who remains to this day a friend) begins with that customary punch:

> It's definitely something in the water. First there was Mayor Loco, now we've got Publisher Loco.
>
> David Lawrence, Jr., the head honcho of this newspaper, is considering a run for the governorship of Florida. Seriously.
>
> Lawrence has never held public office. He has no fund-raising organization, and thus no funds. Most voters in Florida don't have a clue who he is. And the primaries are only five months away.
>
> But that's our Mr. Lawrence, optimist to a fault. Since he's the Big Cheese around the newsroom, I ought to be circumspect about this bizarre situation. So here goes:
>
> Dave, have you completely lost your marbles?

Although Hiaasen claims he took no real risks in criticizing his own publisher, such columns illustrate why former city editor Dave Satterfield likens their impact to "a baseball bat to the forehead." Calling him "one of the strongest voices in Miami," Satterfield says that because Hiaasen looks at issues in terms of right and wrong rather than according to some narrower agenda, he appeals to a wide readership. "He's looked up to throughout the community not only to be the voice of reason, but to deliver," Satterfield says. "You can cross any of those racial, ethnic divides in Miami and everyone agrees, 'Boy, Carl hit the nail on the head.' He has a very good sense of what's right."

Instead of being the voice of conscience, however, Hiaasen believes he articulates the common-sense view of an already existing but previously unrepresented constituency that has grown over the years. "People were fed up with corruption and overdevelopment," he observes, "but nobody said what everybody was thinking." Now, if an elected official is exposed by the Herald as having taken checks from taxpayers and bribes from special interests, Hiaasen weighs in. "Does that person deserve to be ridiculed and shamed? You bet," Hiaasen says. "He deserves to be miserable and wretched and go right off to jail and think about what he's done."

Doug Clifton, who believes Hiaasen's greatest gift is using an "incredible command of the language to translate his raw passion into something that ignites passion in others," maintains that people read Hiaasen to be outraged, to experience the same emotion he directs toward those who have violated the public trust. Such a response in readers, Hiaasen thinks, can help prevent corruption from becoming acceptable. Such passion in Hiaasen himself—outrage composed of disappointment, anger, incredulity, and scorn, always freshly felt—argues that his reputation as a cynic might be based more on his choice of words than on his view of human nature. That he can still be disappointed at all, after having seen and commented on the worst of Miami's graft, suggests in fact an abiding or renewable belief in the possibility of human decency. While his outrage might express a deep sense of betrayal and loss, he refuses, as Jim Savage says, "to be silenced by anybody or anything."

"When you quit trying and you accept it, that's when you're the ultimate cynic," Hiaasen says. "When you don't speak up and when you don't fight back and when you don't raise hell, that's the ultimate act of cynicism, and it's effectively surrender. It's saying, 'Things are so bad that it's now acceptable.' [But] it's not acceptable, it can't be acceptable."

While a true cynic would maintain that nothing will or even can change, over the years Hiaasen has seen what he terms "small victories" brought about by the cumulative effort of many people. Fifteen years ago, for example, candidates ran for office without even mentioning the Everglades, because "they didn't think anybody cared, but the truth is, millions of people cared," Hiaasen says, and now environmentalism and water quality are big agenda items in Florida because writers, journalists, concerned citizens and activist groups spoke as one voice. Ten years ago, the buddy system allowed graft to be punished by a slap on the wrist, but now, Hiaasen says, "You have judges and prosecutors talking very, very tough about corruption."

Some of Hiaasen's colleagues at the Herald, however, would assess his impact and influence as being more individually direct, enough to determine elections in some cases, according to Jim Savage, and enough to make "government officials hold their breath every Thursday and Sunday," according to Bob Radziewicz, assistant city editor. About the quality of his work, his colleagues are in accord: Hiaasen has few, if any, peers but can, according to Gene Miller, be considered "as good as the dead ones. H. L. Mencken, A. J. Liebling, and Izzy Stone."

Always modest, Hiaasen hopes his column will be remembered as sincere, passionate, and consistent. While certainly embodying those qualities, his work over the last thirteen years has contributed to the history and future direction of Florida in a unique way, perhaps best understood in the context of his move to the Keys when others were fleeing. Why, after all, he asks, does one sit with a dying relative?

For Hiaasen, Florida does seem a form of flesh and blood, and his kinship to it as elemental and profound a relationship as there can be, based on love, time, gratitude, and a devotion that tells us something about the meaning of home. Hiaasen wants for us, I think, what he described John D. MacDonald as wanting for his readers: to care about Florida as deeply as he does, to celebrate it, marvel at it, laugh about it, grieve for it, and even fight for it.

Welcome to South Florida

Carl Hiaasen's South Florida stress test
Now you can figure your stress quotient

October 29, 1985

Once again the Guardians of Miami's Image have been stung by a bolt of rotten publicity—the national Urban Stress Test that ranked the city dead last, citing overcrowding, lousy water and rampant crime.

The establishment has resounded with the usual indignation, outrage and silly whining about how darned unfair the whole thing is. (I don't know precisely what the Chamber of Commerce thinks Miami's national image is, but I promise that the rest of the country wasn't exactly stunned to see us at the bottom of this list.)

At the risk of joining the apologist chorus, I have to admit that the stress test was sort of a cheap shot: There's no way to compare Miami with any other city in America. We're a special place and we deserve our own special standards.

So here's the South Florida Stress Test that I'm proposing for next year.

Scoring is simple: 30 points or less means minimum stress—you're doing fine. Forty to 80 points means it's time to restock the Valium.

Anything over 80 points and you'd better pull the kids out of school, call the moving van and start house-hunting in a quieter place.

Say, Beirut.

CARL HIAASEN'S SOUTH FLORIDA STRESS TEST

1. On the average, how many nights a week are you awakened by the sound of gunfire?
   · Every night (10 points)
   · Four nights or fewer (5 pts.)
   · I sleep right through it (1 pt.)
2. Judging by your experience, what kind of gunfire is it?
   · Saturday Night Special (1 pt.)
   · MAC-10 or Uzi (5 pts.)
   · Medium-range artillery (10 pts.)
3. A safe neighborhood means less stress. If you could see over the eight-foot wall around your neighbor's house, you'd discover that he is:
   · A run-of-the-mill drug smuggler (1 pt.)
   · An exiled dictator (5 pts.)
   · An international arms merchant (10 pts.)
4. How many times have you been taken hostage by a deranged lunatic who was not a member of your immediate family?
   · Only once or twice (1 pt.)
   · Three or more times (5 pts.)
   · I am currently a hostage (10 pts.)
5. The last time a pipe bomb went off in your neighborhood, how long did it take the police to respond?
   · Less than 12 minutes (1 pt.)
   · Less than 12 hours (5 pts.)
   · I'm still waiting and the damn Cadillac has burned to the rims (10 pts.)
6. Water quality is vital to the quality of life. When you turn on the faucet, what do you see?
   · A clear fresh liquid (1 pt.)
   · A liquid of some sort (5 pts.)
   · The bouillabaisse scene from The Exorcist (10 pts.)

7. Recreation is one way to relieve stress. What do folks in your neighborhood do in their spare time?
   - Sacrifice live goats to the gods (1 pt.)
   - Work in a clandestine coke lab (5 pts.)
   - Train at a secret Everglades camp for the invasion of Nicaragua (10 pts.)
8. What happened the last time you went to the beach?
   - A college kid got sick all over my sandals (1 pt.)
   - I tripped on a bale of grass and broke my ankle (5 pts.)
   - I got picked up by the Border Patrol (10 pts.)
9. Culture is important to sophisticated urban dwellers. What was the last major cultural event you attended?
   - The taping of ABC's "Battle of the Network Stars" (1 pt.)
   - A dinner-theater production starring Bert Convy (5 pts.)
   - Charo live at the Eden Roc (10 pts.)
10. A summer vacation is one way to beat South Florida stress. Where did you spend yours?
   - Disney World (1 pt.)
   - A military dungeon in Cartagena (5 pts.)
   - The median strip of I-95 (10 pts.)

Etiquette at a crime scene: What to wear, how to act

June 20, 1986

Shoppers at a West Kendall plaza got a special treat this week when a pair of bullet-riddled corpses were found in the trunk of a Lincoln parked in the lot.

Hundreds of spectators gathered in a festive atmosphere around the scene, many waiting up to six hours for the bodies to be extricated. Some onlookers drank lemonade while others took pictures and watched the death sedan through binoculars. A few even belly-crawled under parked cars to gain a closer vantage.

As the crowd grew, traffic actually backed up on Kendall Drive. "It was a nice day, they didn't have anything else to do, I guess," says Dr. Jay Barnhart, the medical examiner sent to the scene.

Look on the bright side. The fact that a routine trunk murder still draws an audience in Dade County proves we're not so desensitized to crime after all. If folks are so hungry for entertainment, maybe pro basketball really does have a chance down here.

Of course it's one thing to gather out of idle curiosity at a gruesome homicide, and quite another to make it a block party. As at all social occasions, there must be rules of etiquette.

Unfortunately the new maven of decorum, Miss Manners, has written virtually nothing about what is proper behavior at a crime scene. Such a guide is overdue in South Florida, where each day seems to offer a new Grisly Discovery.

Q. What should I wear?

A. Always pick out something that won't clash with the yellow police cordons; pastel greens and blues are nice. A sunbonnet can be fashionable, too. And choose sensible footwear—shoes with reinforced toes, so you can stretch and gawk.

Q. Where should I stand?

A. Upwind, always. Be considerate to fellow spectators. If somebody yells, "Down in front!" then sit down. Bring a lawn chair, or one of those portable stools you rent at golf tournaments. And stay off the fenders of the squad cars.

Q. Is it OK to bring the kids?

A. At burglaries, auto thefts, shopliftings—what the heck, unpack those strollers and give the little tykes a thrill! However, parental discretion is advised for most first-degree felony scenes.

Q. What about some helpful photo tips?

A. You'll want to use slide film, of course, so you can put together a carousel show for the neighbors. Bring a basic 35mm with a long lens, in case the police make you stand far away (they can be so fussy). And no need to hurry the focusing—one thing about dead bodies, they tend to hold very still.

Q. What about souvenirs?

A. Usually it's unwise to try to collect souvenirs from a crime scene. Bullet fragments, shell casings, hair samples, ski masks, money satchels, bloody clothing—sure, the stuff would look swell in the rec room next to your bowling trophies. But, please, the crime lab gets first dibs.

Q. Do we have to bring our own food?

A. Meals and munchies are rarely served at major crime scenes, except for the occasional Sno-Cone vendor. If you're packing a picnic basket, finger food is best—chicken wings, ribs, tacos. Stuff you can heat up on the hibachi.

Q. Can we order some drinks?

A. Conveniently, many exciting homicides are committed in bars, and these establishments gladly serve bystanders. However, if the scene of the crime is a street or shopping mall, plan to bring a small Thermos—soft drinks and wine coolers are acceptable, though champagne is considered poor taste. The sound of the cork sets the cops on edge.

Q. What about wagering?

A. It's simply bad manners to make bets on how many days a body has been inside a car, the number of bullet holes, the length of the victim's rap sheet, or the amount of cash and cocaine in his pockets.

Q. How do we know when to applaud?

A. Some say you should clap when the body bags come out, others say hold the ovation until the coroner leaves. In any case, shouting out "Yo, Quincy!" is considered rude, as is coaxing the crowd into doing The Wave.

And please—no boat horns or cowbells. Have some respect.

The mysterious death of Claude, the sheep dog

February 6, 1987

Last summer, Miami lawyer Frank Furci shot and killed a neighbor's dog during an afternoon stroll.

It happened Aug. 8 in an affluent subdivision of Plantation. Furci was walking his Doberman Ginger, when he encountered Claude, a 73-pound French sheep dog with allergies.

Seconds later, for reasons still not clear, Furci pulled a .45-caliber handgun and shot Claude through the jugular vein with a low-velocity exploding bullet.

Jan Bongers, the man who was walking Claude, couldn't believe it. According to the police report, "the victim observed the dog crawling on the roadway . . . with the above [suspect] standing over the dog holding a handgun to the dog's head."

Bongers backed off, he said, when Furci pointed the gun at him.

After Furci went home, Bongers gathered the dying dog in his arms and ran for help. Neighbor Arlene Garren heard Jan shouting: "That guy just shot Claude! I don't believe the crazy bastard shot the dog!"

Bongers raced to a veterinary hospital with Claude comatose in the trunk of the car.

It was a bizarre incident with like repercussions. Furci now is charged with cruelty to animals and aggravated assault with a firearm, a felony for which he could get a mandatory three years—and be disbarred. However, his attorney happens to be his law partner, the one and only Roy Black.

The killing of Claude the sheep dog became a matter so grave that no less than Dr. Ronald K. Wright, Broward's chief medical examiner, performed the postmortem. "God, do I hate autopsying dogs," Dr. Wright testified.

His task was complicated by the fact that Claude had been frozen, and needed to thaw. Still, Wright was able to determine that the fatal shot had been fired with the gun barrel pressed against the dog's fur.

Roy Black said Furci had acted in self-defense, that Claude had attacked first. He suggested that Furci didn't mean to point the gun at Bongers. The Broward State Attorney's Office didn't buy it.

Then Black went to work. He hired a private investigator. He got aerial photos of the crime scene. In 43 separate pleadings and motions, and 17 depositions, he and lawyer Mark Seiden hammered at the character of Claude the sheep dog.

They demanded records of his breeding, birth and pedigree; of any dog shows he'd won; of any previous bites or attacks. Claude's background, they asserted, was "of critical importance in formulating the accused's defense."

Attorney Black noted discrepancies in accounts of Claude's age (somewhere between six and nine years) and exact breed. A police report described the dog as a Bouvier des Flandres while his owner, Olivia Gluckson, said he was a Briard.

The age was important because of the prosecution's contention that an older dog was less likely to attack. The breed was significant, Black explained, because while Briards might be gentle, "the characteristics of a Bouvier des Flandres, on the other hand, could be entirely different."

Unfortunately, Claude was not around to defend his honor. His credentials included work as a professional dog model in magazines.

In a deposition Jan Bongers testified that the sheep dog had approached Ginger "in a very pleasant, playful manner," and that the two dogs had sized each other up the traditional doggy way.

ATTORNEY: "Who did the sniffing?"

WITNESS: "Both."

Olivia Gluckson poignantly testified how Claude had rallied briefly at the veterinary hospital; how he had recognized her and even wagged his tail shortly before the end. "You couldn't help but like Claude, he's a very sweet and gentle dog," she said.

Olivia said she phoned Frank Furci and said, "Did you shoot my dog?" She said the lawyer replied, "I don't know you," and hung up.

Furci declined to discuss the shooting. His wife Joan has said she went outside when she heard their dog Ginger make a "loud, loud cry." She said her husband told her the sheep dog had attacked them.

The case was scheduled for trial this week, but postponed. Apparently Roy Black has done his job—there is talk of a deal that would permit Furci to plead no contest to the animal cruelty charge and avoid the three-year felony.

"Disgusting," Jan Bonger says. "A very frightening kind of case," adds Olivia Gluckson, who says her children are still "devastated" by Claude's violent death.

In all the court records there is no explanation for why anyone walking a Doberman in daylight would need a .45-caliber pistol for anything.

Pistol-packing guards shoot up sense of security

February 11, 1987

Last week a security guard at a local Food Giant grocery store shot and seriously wounded a customer who was arguing over the price of limes.

It's an age-old question for the lawman with a gun—where to draw that fine line for using deadly force. Is it limes, or tangerines? Grapefruits or guavas? Produce or dairy products?

Just when do you pull the trigger?

Now comes the news that the security guard, Hugo Nilo Salazar, has himself been in previous scrapes with the law—a disclosure that seems to come as no shock to state licensing officials.

To see what a crackerjack job Florida is doing to regulate the private security business, I checked our clippings from the last five years. Some of these guys make Barney Fife look like Wyatt Earp:

• August 1986. A security guard shot a man in the back after he allegedly walked out of a South Dade convenience store without paying for a six-pack of beer.

• May 1986. One security guard shot and wounded another security guard in a dispute at a Miami Beach hotel bar.

• March 1986. In Pompano Beach, an ex-security guard allegedly robbed the hotel that had employed him and shot two of his former co-workers.

• December 1985. In Lauderhill, a 21-year-old security guard said he accidentally shot his friend in the head while their car was stopped at a traffic light.

• October 1985. In Miami Beach, a former security guard who was returning his uniform accidentally killed himself while trying to remove his gun from the waistband of his pants.

• June 1985. In North Dade, one security guard shot and fatally wounded another during an argument.

• June 1985. In Palm Beach, a security guard who was not authorized to carry a weapon allegedly used a shotgun to shoot a suspected shoplifter.

• March 1985. A Miami security guard was charged with second-degree murder after shooting an unruly customer at a Church's fried chicken restaurant.

• March 1985. A Pompano Beach security guard was charged with manslaughter after allegedly shooting a suspected burglar with a 20-gauge shotgun.

• January 1984. A security guard at a Miami construction site was charged with second-degree murder after shooting another guard during a quarrel.

• August 1983. A security guard was charged with manslaughter after shooting a suspected shoplifter as he ran through Miami's garment district.

• August 1983. A 73-year-old bank security guard allegedly shot and killed another guard because he thought that the man had put a voodoo hex on him.

• April 1983. Two security guards at a Key Biscayne marina got into an argument and opened fire on each other. One died.

• August 1982. In Miami Beach, a security guard was charged with second-degree murder after fatally shooting a 78-year-old man. The old man allegedly had tried to stop the guard from beating up a woman.

The pattern is unsettling. When security guards aren't shooting each other, they're shooting unarmed civilians, which happens to be a crime. Not even real policemen can shoot shoplifters.

While some firms diligently check a guard applicant's qualifications, others obviously don't care. To make matters more ridiculous, police are not required to report crimes by security guards to state licensing authorities.

To prove conclusively that any bozo can become a security guard, this newspaper sent a reporter out to do just that. In one day he got a gun, a badge, a nifty uniform—and a job.

That was 15 years ago, and not much has changed. Obviously legislators still don't have enough wisdom to keep guns and badges away from clods, loons and hotheads. If there's no other solution, do what Sheriff Taylor did to Barney Fife—take away his bullet.

Horse race would have sloppy track

March 21, 1988

This week, the Florida Cabinet gets to hear about the big plan to put an Arabian horse-racing track on Miami Beach. Literally, on the beach.

Such a bold idea could only come from that special breed known as the "Miami Beach promoter." In this case, two such visionaries announced that November is a swell time to hold the first Arabian Horse Desert Classic.

They're talking about a weeklong jamboree that would include a charity ball, a 26-mile run and—hang onto your cabanas!—a beauty pageant.

The promoters have predicted 100,000 visitors would flock to watch the ponies run on the beach between Fifth and 15th streets. (Presumably, grandstand prices will vary with proximity to the stables, the cheaper seats being downwind.)

The Beach is hoping to attract 2,600 top racehorses from around the world. For authenticity, even the jockeys would be garbed in Arabian-type costumes.

The mere promise of Willie Shoemaker dolled up to look like Valentino is a powerful draw indeed, but toss in a bevy of half-naked beauty queens and you've got class with a capital C.

Not surprisingly, Mayor Alex Daoud has hailed the scheme. The Chamber of Commerce says it will make the media aware that Miami Beach really does have a beach, as its name might suggest.

State agencies are not as keen on the Arabian Classic. Delicate health questions have been raised about the presence of 2,000-plus horses on a public playground.

As one official in Tallahassee put it: "Just like we don't like sanitary landfills in parks, we felt running horses on a beach is incompatible with the beach."

One problem is that the sand on Miami Beach is technically more of a grit—pulverized shells dredged off the ocean floor and packed by bulldozers. If it's too rough or too hot on the hooves, I suppose you could always fit the horses with tiny open-toed sandals.

The other problem is not so simple to solve. As everyone knows, these big animals are not easily housebroken.

Think about it: 2,600 thoroughbreds. Figure 20 pounds of muck per horse, per day, and you get (conservatively) 52,000 pounds. That's 26 tons a day. Now stack that up over a week's time and you're staring at 182 tons—we're talking a Mount Everest of horse puckey.

Skeptics would see cleanup as a messy problem; optimists (and isn't this what the Beach is all about?) would see it as a public-relations challenge.

It's not so big a crisis, really. Tourists on South Florida beaches are used to quick-stepping around all kinds of daunting obstacles, from poisonous jellyfish to gobs of tar, to the occasional human torso. A horse dropping would hardly make them dash for the hotel checkout.

Before allowing such a minor drawback to squelch an otherwise brilliant idea, why not try to turn it around and make something positive?

One obvious solution is to ask the city commissioners themselves to clean up after the horses. They are, after all, vastly experienced in this area.

Another suggestion:

Between races, we stage celebrity "scoop-ups." Line up five famous people, give each a gold shovel and a burlap sack, and tell them to go to it. For the inaugural, we could fly down the entire cast of *The New Hollywood Squares*.

Picture a shovel-wielding Richard Simmons chasing a pack of sleek Arabian steeds along the shimmering sands of Miami Beach—well, you just can't buy that kind of publicity.

And, for the kiddies, a boisterous "Dodge the Muffin" contest. Epcot, eat your heart out.

Some people are saying that thundering horses don't really fit the image of a tropical beach. Neither do Teamsters, yet they're down here every year with their conventions and loud shirts. Talk about a scary stampede.

With more polished extravaganzas like the Arabian Desert Classic, the future of the Beach is shining. No more cheap gimmicks and crackpot promotions. This is the big time now.

Sophistication with a capital S.

Just when you thought it was safe to go to the beach ...

April 6, 1988

Fun and frolics reigned at Haulover Beach again this past weekend, as scores of chowderheads ignored posted warnings and plunged straight into a dangerous riptide.

If that weren't enough excitement, a mob of male high-school kids attacked several teenage girls, ripping off all their clothes, grabbing their breasts and genitals and chasing them down the beach. When one of the Haulover lifeguards tried to shield one of the girls, he was kicked repeatedly.

"She was naked and they were grabbing her. I just wanted to get her out of the crowd," said the lifeguard, Ken Chouinard. "It made me sick, and it also made me fearful for the people who come out here."

Some of these festivities were captured on tape by a WTVJ-Channel 4 news crew and should be recommended viewing for anyone who is considering a leisurely family outing at Haulover.

For years this has been a trouble spot, though the parks department doesn't advertise the fact. Keeping the beach safe apparently is a low priority in the budget, as evidenced by the minimal way in which the county polices the area and staffs its lifeguard crews.

"We get the same consideration as macrame classes and kickball games," says Lt. David Battenfield, a Haulover lifeguard for the past 15 years. "This county is providing people access to this beach, but it's not providing their protection."

For a long time, the lifeguards have been trying to get someone to pay attention. The near-riot this weekend, combined with the perilous surf conditions, portend a disaster in the making—an expensive one.

Currently, Haulover Park has 11 full-time lifeguards on staff. Part-timers are hired to fill out the shifts, though many are not trained as emergency medical technicians, as the full-time lifeguards usually are.

Haulover Beach is about 1.4 miles long, but almost 43 percent is out of immediate range of a lifeguard tower and basically unguarded. The biggest stretch between towers measures 810 yards—a long way to run, if somebody's drowning at the other end.

The last accident took place March 23. Lifeguards got there swiftly and pulled the 42-year-old tourist out of the water, but he died later.

The miracle is that it doesn't happen more often. During the past week or so, strong winds and spring tidal conditions have made Haulover particularly treacherous, with invisible run-out currents sweeping many swimmers out toward the open water. Lifeguards officially closed the beach on three days, but plenty of idiotic showoffs hopped in anyway.

On March 27, Haulover lifeguards logged 10 rescues. On March 29, the number was nine. On March 30, it was 15. Business peaked again this past weekend with 19 rescues on Saturday and 28 more on Sunday.

While the park is much more crowded than it was in 1975, there are five fewer full-time lifeguards now. During last year's budget crunch, the county proposed cutting back even more on the staffs, but the lifeguards successfully argued against it.

Today the lifeguards meet with county parks officials to plead—again—for help in making the beach safer. They aren't asking for salary hikes; they want more lifeguards, more towers and better lifesaving equipment. They also want a regular and visible police presence.

Saturday's clothes-ripping melee took place with a Metro crime suppression team nearby. Still, the teenagers ran wild. "A combat zone," Battenfield said. No arrests were made at the scene; police say they are trying to identify the assailants.

On the bright side, at least nobody took a bullet.

On March 26, startled Haulover beachgoers watched as one man pulled out a machine gun and shot another, while still a third drew his own pistol and popped off a few rounds. A bystander was shot and wounded as he walked his three children out of the park.

Just another day at the beach. If the undertow doesn't get you, the snipers will.

Let's crow for Hialeah cockfighting

April 17, 1989

Let freedom ring!

Three dozen men cradling live chickens appeared at the Metro Justice Building the other day to demonstrate in favor of—don't laugh—cockfighting.

The men were members of a Hialeah "social club" raided last week. Police arrested 186 people, seized 86 birds and grabbed $40,000 in gambling money.

The club offers live music, rides for the kiddies and a restaurant. But the main attraction is a 250-seat fighting pit where grown-ups sit and cheer while two dumb barnyard animals mutilate each other. Can you think of a nobler cause for demonstration? Raise your placards high, boys.

How dare the police shut down such an enriching pastime! My goodness, if they strip us of our right to torture God's hapless creatures, then what next?

Granted, an organized cockfight isn't really an act of nature. Under normal farm conditions, most roosters are too busy chasing the hens to stop and disembowel each other.

But with a little human guidance and just a touch of inbreeding, a rooster becomes a ferocious fighting machine.

I know what you're thinking: chickens. Gamecocks are basically just chickens in drag. And how fierce can a chicken be?

Plenty fierce, especially if you attach razor-sharp spurs to its scrawny yellow legs. These devices are made of honed steel, bone or fiberglass. The purpose is to replace the rooster's natural spur with something slightly more effective.

Otherwise a cockfight is about as thrilling as a Foghorn Leghorn cartoon. Without artificial spurs, the birds just hop and squawk and pull each other's feathers out. Where's the drama in that?

But add those nasty little can-openers, and cockfighting becomes a macho life-or-death spectacle. In fact, matches often do not officially end until one of the two birds expires of its wounds. That's when the big money changes hands.

We're talking rich tradition. Dueling poultry goes back to the days of ancient Persia and Greece, before video games, when people were forced to amuse themselves with whatever was handy. Given the abundance of chickens, and the relative ease with which they could be dragooned, it was only natural that a mindless blood sport would evolve.

Popular among English nobility (what wasn't?), cockfighting was soon introduced in colonial America. Among its ardent fans was the highly cultured Andrew Jackson. Always controversial, cockfighting was outlawed in Great Britain and Canada. Massachusetts banned it in 1836. In recent years, the legality has been debated from Maryland to Louisiana to Key Largo.

In some places, cockfighting remains legal provided that the birds are not fitted with sharpened spurs, and that no gambling is allowed. This, of course, takes all the fun out of it. If the roosters can't slash each other to shreds, and if the spectators can't bet on it, where's the pleasure?

The argument from animal-rights sissies is that cockfighting is cruel, even sadistic. They like to mention that big raid in West Dade a few years ago, when police found live roosters with their eyes missing. It happens, sure, but at least they didn't wind up as fried nuggets in a Col. Sanders box.

Most of those arrested last week at the Hialeah pit were accused of misdemeanors, although a few face felony charges that carry possible five-year prison terms. In Florida, it's illegal to promote, stage, attend or gamble on an animal fight.

Now's the time to take a stand against such government intrusion. Tell those pointy-heads in Tallahassee that enough's enough—what goes on between a man and his chicken, well, that's a sacred and private thing.

And who's to say these gallant birds don't relish the tang of fresh blood on their beaks! Why, you should see their tiny eyes light up when those spurs are strapped to their shins. There is no finer moment in sports.

So cheer those crusaders who carried their killer roosters to the court-house steps, for justice comes to those who crow the loudest. Free the Hialeah 186!

Land snakes! Pythons seem to like it here

October 11, 1989

Finally, some good news about Florida wildlife.

The panthers might be vanishing, but the pythons have arrived.

You know all about Big Mama, the 20-foot beauty that was living comfortably under somebody's house in Fort Lauderdale. The neighborhood kids kept telling their parents that they'd seen this monster subterranean serpent eating raccoons and opossums, and naturally their parents didn't believe a word of it.

Once captured, Big Mama has gone on to become a star of local and national media. If you're in the TV biz, there's no video like snake video.

Then, just when you thought it was safe to be a raccoon again, along comes Junior, another semi-humongous python who turned up last week at a local construction site. Though measuring only about 17 feet, Junior was nonetheless stretched out and posed with every TV reporter in the tri-county area. The next day the poor creature died from internal bleeding. Such is the price of fame.

The authorities want us to believe that these two snakes were freaks in our midst and that their discovery within weeks of each other was just a wild coincidence. They want us to swallow the notion that these pythons were family pets that either escaped or were abandoned. But how many people do you know who own a 20-foot snake? Or even two 10-footers?

No, these carnivorous beasties had been loose for some time, doing what pythons do best—eating, sleeping and making lots of baby pythons (females lay up to 100 eggs).

Wildlife experts say there's nothing to worry about, but they said the same thing about Bufo toads, and look what happened. And parrots—every neighborhood now has its own flock of screeching parrots. Were all these birds somebody's pet? Not unless they staged a mass breakout. More likely, they've simply adopted South Florida as their new home and are merrily reproducing in the tops of our banyan trees.

Same goes for the pythons. They're here to stay. Both Big Mama and Junior were an exotic species called the reticulated python, which happens to be the longest snake in the world. Here are the most commonly asked questions about our newest tropical neighbor:

Where do they come from?

The reticulated python is native to Southeast Asia, Indonesia, Burma and the Philippines.

How big do they get?

Commonly growing to 25 feet, the largest known specimen was killed in 1912 on the north coast of Celebes. The snake measured 32 feet, 9½ inches.

What do they eat?

Pythons prefer to dine on small mammals, although the larger specimens will gobble the occasional deer or goat. In one of the few documented cases of its kind, a 31-foot reticulated python is known to have eaten a 14-year-old boy on the island of Salebabu, in Indonesia. The attack happened several years ago, and there's no reason to suspect that this particular python has migrated to South Florida. Yet.

Are pythons swift, clever and keen-eyed?

No, pythons generally are slow, dull-witted and myopic. In stalking prey, however, they have the considerable advantages of stealth, camouflage and about 300 pounds of sheer muscle. They also love to climb trees and swim rivers. The good news is they're not poisonous. The bad news is they kill by brute constriction.

How do I know if one is living under my house?

If you haven't seen your poodle for a few days, it might be a good idea to check around. Fortunately, a python such as Big Mama only gets hungry every couple of months. The rest of the time they just sort of curl up and grow.

What do I do if I find a 32-foot python in my yard?

The one thing you don't do is try to kill it with a rake. Rakes work fine on pesky little garter snakes, but not pythons. All you do is get them incredibly ticked off, which is a bad idea. As any professional reptile trapper will tell you, the ideal python is an unperturbed python.

You said these things climb trees! So what happens if a giant python falls out of a tree and lands on top of me?

Then you can kiss your sorry asp goodbye.

Send in clowns—and book them, of course

January 9, 1991

Busted again.

Performance artist Kman (no hyphen), AKA Art Kendallman, AKA Monkey Joe, AKA the Missile—collared during the Orange Bowl parade.

Intercepted as an unauthorized clown.

"I was just parading like I do every year," Kman says. "They said the director didn't want me there."

Kman loves a parade. He waits all year for the Orange Bowl. Usually he tags along with the Ringling Brothers clowns, but this year the Ringling clowns didn't participate so Kman was pretty much running solo.

His costume was, well, distinctive. The green jump suit with the red dots wasn't too gaudy, especially for a clown. The sneakers with the flashing lights weren't so peculiar, either. It was the rest of the outfit: "I have a helmet with goggles and a mask. My mask is like a hawk pilot. I'm a hawk! Yeah, and I have a helicopter on my head."

That's what seems to have caught the attention of police.

"It's motorized and everything," Kman says of the helicopter. "It's a great chopper. It's a Huey. I found it at Toys R Us, amazingly enough. A scale-model Huey!" So he was whirlybirding down Biscayne Boulevard toward the grandstand and the network TV lights when a Miami policeman stopped him. Kman didn't have a permit to be there.

He told the cop he hadn't missed an Orange Bowl parade since 1984. He explained how the Ringling clowns always welcomed him into their formation. Kman says the cop told him OK, get with the Ringling guys. But there was no sign of them, so Kman loosely hooked up with some clowns from the phone company.

This is how he describes his act: "Basically I'm flying this helicopter on my head and basically running around. I do different stunts, turns and spins. I'm a dancer, so I dance while I do this."

He was just warming up, revving the chopper, when the same cop spotted him again. "I also was walking really slow, and that had something to do with it," Kman theorizes.

At any rate, he got arrested for trespassing. The police report straightforwardly describes the suspect as a man "adorned with a helicopter" who "did not belong in the show."

As he was hustled out of the parade, some of the spectators booed the cops. Kman spent five hours in custody. "They had great fun with me," he recalls. "They had me posing with officers and taking pictures." Kman relates the story with annoyance but no bitterness. He's been arrested before. Once he was riding the Metrorail as Monkey Joe—that is, dressed as a monkey and squatting on his haunches like a monkey and occasionally making noises like a monkey—when he was busted for wearing a mask in a public place.

On the day the pope visited Miami, Kman was arrested again for refusing to remove his goggle mask. At the time, he was riding a bicycle with the scale model of a Hercules military transport plane mounted on the front. He is uncommonly fond of miniature war toys; he once appeared in public as a nuclear-powered aircraft carrier.

Says his lawyer, Glenn Terry: "He's a harmless guy who's trying to say something, though I don't know what it is."

Police say Kman wasn't causing any problems at the Orange Bowl parade, except that he refused to go away. The parade folks say it's unfortunate that Kman was arrested, but say he should've got a permit like all the other clowns.

"We had Captain Crime Stopper, and the World's Fastest Clown," notes Gene Cokeroft, director of production for the parade. "My gosh, we'd never say no to a clown." He added that Kman's whirling helicopter-on-the-head routine sounded very entertaining.

Next year, Kman promises, he will go through the proper clown channels. As for the theme of his performance, the message of his art: "Fly in peace," he says. "Whatever."

No peace for movie ushers who want quiet

June 26, 1991

AMC Theaters has announced a crackdown on customers who yak during movies: Violators will be ejected after one warning.

This ought to be fun, especially in South Florida. We've got the loudest, surliest, burliest, most well-armed movie audiences in the hemisphere. A verbal warning might only provoke them.

What prompted AMC's new policy was a national survey in which 71 percent of those interviewed named "disruptive behavior" as the reason they don't go to the movies more often. Like AMC, Wometco and General Cinema are attempting to discourage talkers by showing on-screen warnings before every film. The test will be trying to back up those threats with serious muscle.

AMC says it will order its ushers to patrol the aisles vigilantly. I didn't even know they still employed ushers! They've got plenty of uniformed young men whose job is guarding the uniformed young women who make the buttered popcorn, but these fellows are under strict orders never to leave the refreshment stand. You seldom catch them inside the theaters.

Say you scrounge up some ushers crazy enough to take on a South Florida movie audience. Training them will cost a fortune. Start with a basic martial-arts course, then six weeks on the firing range, nightscope training, wilderness survival school, hostage negotiations, and so on. Those who don't wash out of the program still won't be prepared for the teeming hellpit that is your average early-bird matinee in, say, West Broward. There's one sure way to see if an usher is combat-ready. Put him in the aisles during a Woody Allen movie.

Allen is a literate and witty screenwriter. His movies are full of clever lines, exquisitely timed. Enjoying the dialogue, unfortunately, requires that one be able to hear it. That's simply not possible in many local theaters.

The problem is chronic and insurmountable. Woody Allen sets most of his pictures in New York. Many South Florida moviegoers are from New York, or have relatives there, or once visited there on vacation. Thus they cannot restrain from exclaiming, at the most crucial moment of the movie:

"Look, there's the Chrysler Building! We were there with your cousin, remember? Back when she had that terrible gout!"

At which point, the wife is likely to say (in a voice like a diesel): "That wasn't the Chrysler Building, it was the World Trade Center! And it wasn't gout, it was gallstones!"

Other Manhattan landmarks that send moviegoers into clamorous eruptions are Radio City, the Empire State Building, Macy's, the Plaza Hotel, any Broadway marquee, and of course Central Park. Whenever there's a scene in Central Park, you might as well go buy some Raisinets and relax in the lobby, because you won't be able to hear a word of the movie. Audience members will be trading moldy Central Park anecdotes for 15, 20 minutes easy. Another perilous situation for ushers is *Terminator*-type films, which rely on spectacular methods of incineration, dismemberment and organ removal. In other parts of the country, such scenes evoke normal shrieking and groans of disgust. Here in South Florida, though, they inspire long esoteric debates about technique—for example, is a grain thresher more effective than a circular saw? How long do human body parts keep in the refrigerator?

Only the boldest of ushers would interrupt such a conversation with a "Sssshhhh."

Once a customer defies the warning, the challenge is subduing the noisy culprit and removing him or her from the movie. Many of these babblers are quite huge, much bigger than your average usher. Nothing short of a flash fire is going to budge them from their seats.

AMC's solution is to offer a refund if they'll get up and leave peacefully. That'll probably work fine in Tulsa, but extra coaxing may be required here in Miami.

We're talking stun guns and grappling hooks.

Miami politics a sticking point for voodooers

February 20, 1992

Miami City Hall, usually likened to a circus, is now a chamber of the occult. Goodbye, Ringling Brothers. Hello, Addams Family.

Commissioner Victor De Yurre's office is being plagued by eerie happenings. A miniature coffin, containing hair, appeared on an assistant's desk. A door was defaced with a cross drawn in blood. Two of the commissioner's aides recently received anonymous voodoo-style dolls, with pins protruding from the tiny torsos. Each of the dolls wore a noose.

Maybe this stuff goes on at all city halls, but I doubt it. Even by Miami standards, a punctured voodoo doll is worthy of concern. De Yurre has downplayed the creepy incidents and remained calm. However, three veteran aides have abruptly departed his staff for other city jobs.

We don't know if the mystery doll-impaler was aiming his ire at De Yurre personally, but the possibility must be addressed. Criticism of politicians takes many forms, and a miniature coffin undoubtedly deserves more attention than a telegram.

South Florida's multicultured society offers a rich selection of hexes, spells and curses that could be unleashed on local officeholders. I can understand why disgruntled citizens might resort to blood scrawls and the like. Nothing else seems to work. Say Metro approves an ugly shopping center for your quiet suburban neighborhood. Say the swing vote on the zoning change was a commissioner who ignored all even-tempered letters and phone calls. How do you repay such betrayal? You either wait for the next election and vote the rascal out of office—or lay a heavy-duty hex on him now.

Buy a voodoo doll (about $5 at curio shops) and dress it up to resemble the offending politician. For authenticity, you should costume the doll with as much detail as possible. (For instance, if the target of your spell is Mayor Steve Clark, the doll should have a tiny little five-iron in its hands.)

The next step is choosing an appropriate curse. Hexing a governor or senator will require bigger medicine than hexing, say, an assistant city manager in Hialeah Gardens. For dosage information, amateur conjurers can consult many modern texts. A good one is *Voodoo and Hoodoo* by Jim

Haskins, who culled centuries of folklore to document popular hexing customs.

A favored technique is to cut open the voodoo doll and sprinkle cayenne pepper inside. Sew the doll up with black thread. Then you tie its hands and place it in a kneeling position in a remote corner of the house. Says Haskins: "You may subject it to other indignities—kick it, blindfold it. Corresponding problems will befall the victim." More somber rites involve a small coffin, a black cat, a chicken and a glass of whiskey. Details are too gross to mention here, but suffice to say that the chicken and the cat get the worst of the deal.

A word of caution: When attempting black magic, please don't harm any innocent creatures. Not even a slug should lose its life because of Victor De Yurre, or any politician.

Most homespun spells are designed for wicked landlords, wayward spouses and greedy relatives. Improvisation is necessary to make them effective at city hall. Don't waste time sticking pins into your mayor-doll's back. Stick them into its pockets, to discourage graft.

Experts don't know if voodoo will become a potent political force in South Florida, but its use might be more widespread than suspected. Haskins writes of a tested ritual to cause mental confusion and temporary insanity:

"Obtain a piece of the intended victim's hair and singe it lightly over an open flame. Then bury it deep in the ground to cause him to lose his mind."

This one already has been tried, with obvious success. See for yourself. Visit the next Miami commission meeting.

Modern world puts evolution into reverse

July 6, 1995

Scientists are advancing a theory that human beings have stopped evolving because we've interfered with natural selection.

Thousands of years ago, the fittest of the species endured, while the weakest stumbled into tar pits or got eaten by saber-toothed tigers. That doesn't happen much anymore, and consequently—these experts assert—humans are actually devolving, getting dumber and less fit.

The hypothesis is bolstered by the popularity of daytime talk shows and psychic hotlines. More empirical evidence is supplied every Fourth of July, when alcohol and explosives are freely distributed among the populace.

It would've been an ideal day for geneticists and naturalists to have visited Dade County, where a water crisis became a startling biosocial experiment.

Here's what happened. Runoff from recent heavy rains dumped hazardous levels of fecal bacteria and other nasty microbes into the Oleta River and Biscayne Bay. Health officials quickly detected the contamination, and warned people to stay out of the water.

It was not a precipitous announcement. Swimming in sewage is dangerous, especially for children. Bacteria enter the human body through any orifice of convenience, and commence to make you sick as a dog.

A Ph.D. in microbiology is not necessary to grasp the concept: Clean water is good. Poopy water is bad.

Local newscasts aired the pollution warnings for days, and displayed detailed maps showing which areas were unsafe for swimming. By dawn's early light on July 4, it was reasonable to assume that almost everybody was aware of the problem, and had relocated their picnic plans to a safe beach.

Out of fairness, though, let's say a few sheltered souls remained clueless. Perhaps they didn't have a TV or radio.

Fair enough. You pile the family into the car and head across the Rickenbacker Causeway. You park along Hobie Beach, unload the coolers, smear on the sunscreen, dash for the water . . . and there it is.

A sign. DANGER, it says, in English and Spanish. Don't swim here. The water's contaminated!

Now comes the moment of truth. You can almost hear Darwin's ghost. Surely these morons aren't going swimming in THAT crap! Not with their kids! Not with a warning sign right in front of their face!

Wrong, Charlie baby.

Into Biscayne Bay they wade by the score, splashing among the playful *E. coli* germs. TV stations featured the footage as part of their upbeat Independence Day coverage.

To a scientist, the scene would seem irrefutable proof that the new theory is true—the human race is backsliding toward the primordial bog. At the very least, those swimmers should've been dragged from the water to have their chromosomes counted.

Eons ago, when man lived in caves, dumb moves were often fatal moves. The quick and the smart survived, the slow and the dimwitted didn't. If one member of the tribe ate a berry and died, the others henceforth avoided those darn berries.

Over time, humans advanced and grew sturdier.

Not anymore. Now we've got seat belts, air bags, antibiotics and stomach pumps to save fools from their own mistakes. That's all right. Caring for others is one of the nobler traits of our species.

The result, ironically, is that the genetic future of mankind isn't so rosy. Stragglers once culled from the herd now (in the absence of sabertoothed tigers) operate motor vehicles, watch Jerry Springer, cavort in pollution and even breed.

Darwin would be truly worried. The evolutionary gap between the bacteria and us is closing.

Give macho dogfighters real taste of action

January 18, 1996

As this is being written, a group of strangers—scientists, bystanders and tourists—are treading chilly water, trying to save some sick dolphins that beached near Stock Island at Key West.

The urge to help weaker creatures is one of the nobler traits of human beings. Unfortunately, the kindness gene is not omnipresent in mankind. In a few notably stunted specimens, a cruelty gene remains dominant.

Witness the arrests last weekend of 12 men at a filthy, makeshift dogfighting arena in West Dade. Metro-Dade police say the fellows were festively gathered to watch pit bull terriers tear each other to shreds.

"One of the most disgusting things I've seen in my life," said Sgt. Gary Shimminger of the Crime Suppression Team. "Despicable, really horrible. You're looking at these poor helpless dogs, and one of them had no face. Just gums and teeth."

In case you're not aware of how dogfighting is conducted: The animals are turned loose against each other until one is either dead or so mangled it can no longer bite back, at which point the fun apparently goes out of the match.

Bets are placed on the pit bulls before and during the battle, which customarily is accompanied by rousing shouts, heavy alcohol consumption and uncontrolled drooling (by both man and beast).

The longer the fight continues—and the bloodier it becomes—the more cash changes hands. Thus it becomes profitable to prolong the carnage, and the suffering of the dogs.

Although quite illegal, pit-bull fighting remains a popular pastime in certain circles of beetle-browed mutants and mouth-breathers. It's also a markedly masculine affair, torrents of testosterone being needed to get drunk and watch two simple-minded creatures maim each other.

When police raided the dog pit last Friday, they found 11 injured terriers, which had been bred specifically for viciousness and biting tenacity. The animal whose face had been chewed off was euthanized right away. The same sad end awaits the others.

As for the "sportsmen" apprehended at the scene, most face misdemeanor charges. Two of the defendants, allegedly caught holding bloodied dogs in the ring, are accused of baiting or fighting animals, a felony that carries a top fine of $5,000 and five years in the slammer.

Should these fellows be found guilty, let me suggest that our prisons are too crowded with ruthless criminals to accommodate a couple of lowlife dog abusers. Let me also suggest that prison is far too good a place for them.

I propose alternative sentencing—one that would make dogfighting less of a spectator sport and more of a true macho test. As a bonus, very little in the way of taxpayer resources would be required:

1. Upon conviction, immediately put the two defendants in a squad car and return them to the dog pit.
2. On the way, make a brief detour to Pet Warehouse and purchase approximately three dozen cans of Alpo. Either beef or chicken will do fine.
3. Once the sportsmen are back at the pit, tether them to short leashes. Stake the leashes firmly into the ground.
4. Open cans of Alpo.
5. Smear chunks of Alpo on the sportsmen. Baste generously.

6. Now reunite sportsmen with their surviving pets.

7. Leave them in privacy for, say, eight or nine minutes.

8. Return with Hefty bags and a WetVac to clean up.

Oh, I almost forgot: No betting would be permitted on the terriers. However, modest wagers would be accepted on whether or not the defendants will ever again be eager to attend a dogfight.

Dead shark nothing but a sound bite

January 9, 1997

Nothing chums up the media like a big, dead shark.

It happened again this week when a commercial fishing boat hauled in a rare great white in the waters off Key Largo. For nearly two days, Miami TV stations went wild with the story. Some news programs even provided "team coverage."

Team coverage of a dead fish.

Depending on which channel you watched or which newspaper you read, the shark's length was either 16 feet, 17 feet, 18 feet or 20 feet. Its weight was reported variously between 1,000 and 2,000 pounds.

The only facts of which you could be certain were:

1. It was huge.

2. It was deceased.

3. It was a shark.

It's easy to blame Steven Spielberg for the inane frenzy that accompanies the killing of a great white, but it's the media that have turned a fright movie fad into a dockside ritual.

The phenomenon is exaggerated in tropical locales such as Florida, where (with the recent decline of tourist homicides), we're always on the lookout for new things to terrorize winter visitors. I'm all in favor of this, but not at the expense of the beleaguered shark.

There was nothing mythic or Hemingwayesque about the capture of the great white near Pickles Reef. Longline fishermen laid out miles of hooks in deep water. The shark glomped one of the baits and became entangled.

No epic battle occurred between man and beast. The fish was already stuck when the fishermen checked their rigs. A mechanical winch cranked up the line.

The whole episode was no more heroic than a tow truck dragging an Oldsmobile out of a rock pit. Incredibly, the shark still was alive after being pulled back to the mainland, where it soon died. The swarms of gawkers were thicker than the flies.

Traffic snarled. Cameras clicked. The media was alerted.

A giant shark is a spectacular thing, without a doubt. A great white is one of those creatures that stirs in humans the most primitive of fears, even though we are statistically far more likely to die from a lightning bolt, a bee sting or a bowl of bad oysters.

Still, nothing livens a sluggish news day like one of those razor-toothed leviathans, hanging by its tail in a marina. (Photographers adroitly avoided showing the regurgitated stomach.)

Around the dead-shark shrine in Key Largo, the standard media question to wide-eyed onlookers was: "Does this make you afraid to go in the water?"

Correct answer: "No, but I'll think twice about slathering myself in squid blood and dangling off a size 9/0 hook overnight in the Gulf Stream."

As breathtaking as the sight of a dead 16-foot shark might be, the live ones are infinitely more awe-inspiring. They do not, however, hold quite so still for pictures.

Even in the "team coverage" it was seldom mentioned that sharks, an essential marine predator, are disappearing from our oceans. They're being slaughtered disgracefully for their fins, which are sold for big money to Asian markets.

The great white killed off of Key Largo was hoisted into the bed of a truck and hacked into pieces. Its dorsal and pectorals will someday season an expensive bowl of soup, consumed by a wealthy businessman hoping to bolster his sexual stamina.

An even less noble end awaits the remainder of the fish. Its jaws were sold to a collector, and a few hunks of flesh went to bystanders. The carcass had been lying around for so long, without ice, that a seafood house in Tavernier didn't want any part it.

Much of the great shark probably will turn up as chum, or as bait in crab traps.

But you won't see that part of the story on the news. Dead meat doesn't rate, without the jaws.

Corruption: Our growth industry

May 3, 1998

Miami civic leaders seem shellshocked by the announcement that Knight Ridder, parent company of the *Herald*, is moving its headquarters to Northern California.

I say: Adios, corporate weasels. Who needs you?

Oh, we really don't want to go—but we need to be in Silicon Valley with all that nifty, cutting-edge Internet technology.

Yeah, right. The truth is, Knight Ridder's gone soft. Thrown in the towel. Turned yellow. It isn't tough enough to handle Miami anymore.

So good riddance, cyberweenies. Enjoy your vineyards and your "majestic" redwoods and your scenic Pacific Coast Highway. We'll be just fine down here in the oppressive heat and the gunfire.

For too long South Florida has done back flips to impress major firms, only to have them desert the place or go bankrupt (sometimes more than once). It's time to focus more positively on a steady, dependable, homegrown enterprise.

I'm talking about corruption. That's the wave of the future. That's where the jobs are.

Example: The U.S. attorney's office in Miami is doubling the size of its anti-corruption unit. The troop increase comes after a wave of scandals involving the County Commission, the Building Department, the Miami City Commission, the Miami elections and the Port of Miami.

Some say epidemic corruption is bad for our image—in fact, it's cited as a reason many companies won't relocate here. And it's true that almost every institution, from the cops to the courts, has been stained by serious scandal in the past decade.

But why not make the best of it? What's bad for a community's image isn't necessarily bad for the job market.

A proper corruption investigation requires a massive law enforcement infrastructure, which means more employment opportunities—and not only for agents, prosecutors and judges.

Think of each breaking scandal as its own job fair.

Bugging the phones of crooked politicians, for example, will require hiring extra wiretap technicians. That means extra typists to transcribe the wiretaps, and extra clerks to photocopy the transcripts, and extra repairmen to replace the toner in the photocopy machines, and so on—all the way down to the extra process servers and bail bondsmen needed as the indictment draws near.

Unlike newspapers, corruption is a growth industry. Knight Ridder's pullout will cost the area fewer than 150 jobs, a blip compared to what would be lost if there were no bribery and racketeering to fight.

Think of the many millions of dollars trickling into the local economy as a result of every corruption probe—gas for the undercover cars, videotapes for the surveillance cameras, file cabinets for the plea-bargain agreements. And don't forget those hefty hotel and restaurant bills run up by conspirators, co-conspirators and snitches.

Those who winced at the Knight Ridder headline Wednesday probably winced at this one Friday: "Port funds diverted to Democrats." The story: $120,000 mysteriously got funneled from the Port of Miami to the Democratic National Committee. The feds are on the case.

Bad for business? Tell that to the FBI agents flying down to the Caymans to track seaport cash, or to the local travel agent who booked their flights, or to the cabbie who drove them to the airport, or to the local defense attorneys who will represent the accused.

No, don't fret over the departures of Knight Ridder, Southeast Bank and Blockbuster. South Florida can be booming, in spite of them. When you're talking graft, you're talking jobs.

Indicted? Act indignant

August 23, 1998

A new and entertaining South Florida custom is the pre-indictment press conference. The purpose is to declare one's innocence, in advance of arrest.

Last Thursday, such an event was staged by two honchos of the Cuban American National Foundation. They're about to be charged in Botched Plot No. 4,877 to kill Fidel Castro.

CANF President Francisco "Pepe" Hernandez and director Jose Antonio Llama sat before reporters to denounce their pending indictment, and indignantly blame it on pro-Castro sympathizers in the Clinton administration.

(The appearance of indignation is vital to all pre-indictment press conferences. Equally important is cooking up a lurid conspiracy theory to explain why you are being singled out for prosecution.)

Hernandez and Llama are in hot water because of what happened last fall off the coast of Puerto Rico. A 46-foot boat, La Esperanza, was boarded by the Coast Guard after reporting mechanical problems. A search turned up ammunition, bipods and two .50-caliber sniper rifles.

One of the Cuban exiles on the boat reportedly admitted they were on their way to the Venezuelan island of Margarita to shoot Castro. The Cuban president was going there for the Ibero-American Summit.

At first it seemed like just another bungled assassination plan. People are constantly plotting against Castro, and often the schemes end up on some broken-down boat, loaded with incriminating ammo.

What made this one different was that the boat was owned by "Toñin" Llama, and that one of the .50-caliber sniper rifles belonged to Pepe Hernandez. Both men have high-profile roles in CANF, the dominant anti-Castro lobby that claims not to support violence or terrorism.

La Esperanza's fateful voyage began at a private dock in Coral Gables, one of many things that attracted the curiosity of U.S. authorities. Shortly after the exile crew was arrested, a San Juan grand jury began taking testimony. Indictments of Hernandez and Llama are expected Tuesday.

At least that's the word from their attorneys, who did all of the talking at the pre-indictment press conference. One, the ubiquitous Jose Quiñon, said the case against his clients was "politically motivated."

Another lawyer, Manny Vasquez, elaborated: "The enemies of the embargo [against Cuba] are behind this action. When Castro snaps his fingers, our government jumps."

It's a fabulous crock, of course, but even the flimsiest of conspiracy yarns appeals to some Castro haters and talk-radio addicts.

Notably missing from the CANF leaders' pre-indictment press conference was a plausible counter-explanation for the suspicious facts of the case. On matters of evidence, the indignant attorneys and their indignant clients remained mum.

How, for example, did Llama's boat come to be used in this screwball mission? Was he in the habit of loaning it to heavily armed pals for leisurely excursions to South America?

And how did Hernandez's .50-caliber sniper rifle get aboard La Esperanza? Why does he even own such a ridiculous weapon—it's a tad excessive for plugging deer or squirrels, and the bulky bipod makes it impractical for everyday self-defense.

Maybe it's all innocent coincidence—the boat, the sniper guns, the trip timed to Castro's arrival. Or maybe unnamed "enemies of the embargo" somehow orchestrated the whole fiasco-at-sea. But how?

These and other questions that weren't answered at the pre-indictment press conference could be asked at trial—or again even later, if there's a post-conviction press conference, which is also becoming a South Florida custom.

Murder and Mayhem

Can gun laws solve Dade's murder wave?

July 31, 1985

The FBI says Dade County is once again the murder capital of the United States, and we've been swamped with statistics to support the fact.

The new numbers are ugly and they make headlines. Headlines, of course, inspire Civic Leaders to form committees and place blame and offer brilliant solutions.

One says it's just drug dealers killing each other off; another sees a reprise of Mariel violence. Still another says the answer is putting more cops on the street.

They've been saying all this for five years, and one gets the idea they might be missing the big picture. Murder is not just a passing public relations problem; it's here to stay.

"It's too easy for people in public positions to give an easy answer," says Dr. William Wilbanks, criminal justice professor at Florida International University. "In a year in which murders are down, everybody wants credit. When murder goes up, everybody says, 'Don't look at me'."

In the first place, the numbers aren't as bad as they seem. The body count actually has dropped dramatically since the nightmare years of 1980–1981.

Secondly, the numbers aren't always complete. Experts point out that federal per capita murder statistics rely on outdated Dade County population figures that exclude thousands of illegal aliens and winter residents. If the murder rate were recomputed accurately, we'd surely lose our No. 1 national ranking.

Thirdly, the numbers are not always compatible. The FBI reported that 425 people were murdered here in 1984. The Dade County medical examiner's office, where the corpses wound up, counted 462. This is how they were killed: gunshot wound (359), stabbing (40), beating (27), strangulation (8), child abuse (6), drowning (2), fire (7) and others (13).

Wilbanks suggests that this is not a crime wave, but a way of life. His book, Murder in Miami, meticulously charts the fluctuations in Dade County's homicide pattern from 1917 through 1983. It is a sobering document that avoids platitudes and simplistic solutions, which is probably why it's not easily understood by politicians.

"Everybody wants to make it some alien force affecting our community," he says. "But it's not any one factor. My argument is, it's more of a murder culture."

Chilling words, but no cause for panic. Yet.

There are traditional categories of urban murder—domestics, drug feuds, robberies—that always will exist in a volatile, gun-happy community. And while a high murder rate is deplorable, it doesn't always mean that Joe Citizen stands a greater chance of being randomly gunned down on his way to the K mart.

Mike Gonzalez, dean of Miami homicide cops, says that 75 to 90 percent of all murder victims know their assailant. His favorite axiom: "If you're not a dope dealer, and you don't settle your domestic arguments with a gun, and you're halfway sensible about where you go at night, you haven't got a chance in the world of being killed."

I asked Gonzalez what can be done to stop the killing, and he talked about controlling handguns.

"With a gun, it's so easy, so efficient, so impersonal. There are more people killed in Miami than are killed in Great Britain, West Germany and Tokyo put together. And it's because of guns.

"Everybody buys a gun because they're gonna shoot the crooks, right? How many crooks do you think are killed this way?" the detective asked. "Children in back seats get killed with those guns. Ma and Pa get killed. The evidence is, they don't protect themselves with these guns, they kill each other."

And that's half our homicides right there.

Civic Leaders, of course, would much rather rail about drug assassins or crazed Mariels than suggest tough gun laws.

Gonzalez is no politician, but he's investigated about a thousand murders. What that makes him is an expert.

On the beach, reality doesn't take a vacation

August 9, 1985

We beat the ambulance by two minutes.

The emergency room at Mount Sinai was filling with gray-suited men wearing plastic IDs, and out front were the cops—motormen, patrol officers, detectives, SWAT commandos, all with the same haggard look in their eyes. The look of the Grim Wait.

The call had gone out as a hostage situation, then a sniper and then this: "We have two police officers down!"

Racing across the Julia Tuttle Causeway, we'd heard another voice on the radio: "They're on the way to Sinai. We need a trauma team. We need a trauma team!"

And both of us, the photographer and I, thought the worst. Somebody murdered some cops, we thought.

At the emergency room we were told that the number was four. Four police officers shot during—what else—a drug deal.

In the swank Doral Beach Hotel, of all places. In the middle of a dead summer, in the murder capital of America.

What exactly had gone wrong was not clear, but it certainly wasn't Crockett and Tubbs gliding through a TV bust. Four cops down was life gravely mocking art.

It doesn't matter how long you do this sort of thing, the sight of the first ambulance always turns your throat to sandpaper.

Because the first ambulance usually is where they put the one who took the worst shot. The first ambulance tells the story—just how bad it's going to be.

The doors swung open and there lay Detective Jim Mahle. His head was wrapped to cover two bullet holes in the right side of his skull. But one hand was moving. Best of all, he was conscious.

Then came Detective Joe White, bearded and shirtless, his white shorts bloodied. His eyes were open and he was holding his own IV bag. Sgt. Mike Lowe, a crimson smear on his forehead, walked into the emergency room on his own.

Another ambulance delivered undercover man James Scarberry ("I'm OK," he said), and then came the wounded police informant, pale, and moaning into an oxygen mask.

A few minutes later, a woman in a pink outfit gingerly made her way past the police cordon. A reporter asked if she were related to one of the victims. "No, my daughter just had a baby," the woman said, smiling. "I'm here for a happy occasion."

Soon a trauma specialist came out to announce that the policemen were going to make it. Miraculously, none of the injuries was life-threatening.

Over at the Doral, a man with a mop swabbed the front steps. The place was quiet.

"I got to work and I saw all these cop cars," said Rocky Hile, the downstairs bartender. "I thought they were shooting another episode of *MiamiVice*. I saw the blood on the steps and I thought: Boy, they really go all out. Then I come in and turn on the news at six o'clock and that's when I found out . . .

"I had a guy at the bar earlier tonight who was on the 10th floor when it happened. Heard all the shots and thought it was some kind of celebration," Rocky said. "Then the elevator door opens and there's a guy on a stretcher, all covered with blood. It still didn't occur to the guy that somebody had actually been shot.

"Until he got downstairs and saw the SWAT team."

I thought about that poor tourist—gaping at the stretcher in the elevator, finding the elegant lobby taken over by men with automatic weapons. I imagined the fellow turning to his wife and muttering, "You were right. We should've gone to Epcot Center."

Or maybe not. Maybe he knew what to expect from the South Florida vacation package: four days-three nights-one shootout.

That evening, by the hotel pool, Pfizer and Co. threw a private party attended by trim executives with new golf-course tans. There was an open bar and a twirling ice sculpture of a sailfish.

Upstairs, in a suite on the 11th floor, forensic experts hunted for bullet fragments and measured the bloodstains on the carpet.

Appalling gore fails to daunt film audiences

October 16, 1985

Imagine this: It's a sunny holiday afternoon in autumn. Birds sing. Teenagers lounge on Haulover Beach. Joggers trot through the Grove.

Yet in a dark downtown theater, redolent of foul hot dogs, more than 40 people are watching one of the most abominable movies of all time.

The film is called The Mutilator. Its profoundly repugnant newspaper advertisement features a gleaming marlin gaff and promises: "By sword. By ax. By pick. Bye bye."

I have not come to review this motion picture, but rather the audience. I anticipate a cavalcade of geeks, troglodytes and sociopaths—who else would pay $2.50 to watch a bunch of dumb white college kids get hacked into corned beef?

But a quick survey before the action starts offers these demographics: A well-dressed young couple, sharing Polaroid snapshots; a moody guy in a dingy tank top, girlfriend on his lap; several teenagers, slightly rowdy but too muscular to rebuke; up front, an entire family, including a 6-year-old, a toddler and a nursing infant.

And, of course, sitting by himself: the obligatory strange pale man with the baggy pants and bucket of popcorn. You know the one.

The film begins, and even before the opening credits there is a gruesome killing that would send most normal folks scurrying for the door or the restrooms. Not this bunch—a true gore corps.

The titles flash: *The Mutilator.* "Written and directed by Buddy Cooper." Enough said.

Then the actors, none of whose names are remotely familiar (aliases, no doubt).

Then: "Special appearance by Ben Moore."

Who the heck is Ben Moore? No one seems to know, but instinct suggests that he plays the title role.

The plot unfolds:

A group of boisterous, beer-guzzling college kids talks a pal into crashing Dad's beachfront townhouse for the weekend. The father happens to be a demented lunatic who sleeps under some gardening tools in the garage and has a respiratory disorder so severe that his breathing can be heard all the way to Seattle.

Beyond this, *The Mutilator* follows the identical script of *Friday the Thirteenth, Halloween* and all other teen slasher movies:

1. The Trampy Co-Ed is the first to die, but only after the mandatory semi-nude swimming scene.
2. The Dumb Blond Jock is the next to be mangled.
3. The Goofy Comic-Relief Guy is third on the menu (and the only character whose mutilation seems to sadden the audience).
4. Next is the Concerned Cop, who gets beheaded.
5. Then there's quite a tedious Stalking Sequence, with lots of bad camera work and bass violas.
6. The climax is the tired old Car-Won't-Start-Scene, with Mr. Mutilator clumsily hacking his way through the convertible top.
7. Finally the killer is gored, stabbed, burned and run over by the young collegiate heroine, who is (I swear) a self-proclaimed virgin and proud of it. She also is a master of kung fu, as any Southern California virgin must be.

During all this carnage I expect raucous outbursts from the crowd, but the theater is reverently quiet, as if we are watching Olivier do Hamlet.

According to my notes, the only audible exclamation comes during the decapitation scene when a man in the back row cries, "Oh s—!" Which pretty much sums up my sentiments, too.

Sitting one row ahead of me is a handsome gray-haired woman with an embroidered shopping bag. She watches the entire film silently, without a murmur or a flinch. In fact, she is sitting so still that I begin to worry that she might have passed away during the marlin-gaff scene.

But, moments after the final mutilation, the old woman bolts for the exit, understandably eager to escape before the house lights come on. I catch up with her and ask what she thought of *The Mutilator*.

She smiles and says, "It's incredible, yes?"

Oh yes.

Crowd gripped by "real" crime drama

April 12, 1986

One color of death was bright yellow.

Yellow were the police ribbons that stretched from tree to tree, to keep people away. The ribbons fluttered in the morning breeze, and crisscrossed in mock gaiety the Kendall neighborhood. Outside the ribbons, crowds stood and stared. On the inside, men with radios and clipboards and tape measures and cameras moved grimly from one corpse to the next. There were four corpses in all.

Yellow was the color of the plastic sheets that covered the two FBI agents, who lay dead in the shade of a black olive tree. Occasionally the breeze would lift the sheets, and a policeman or federal agent would hurry forward to cloak them again.

The dead killers lay bloody and uncovered.

Incredibly, seven agents had been shot here. It was the bloodiest day in the FBI's history. A federal prosecutor who knew the dead agents watched and wept. He was not alone.

From an elevated parking ramp, reporters, photographers, TV cameramen and dozens of bystanders looked down on the tableau, at the intersection of Southwest 82nd Avenue and 122nd Street. Construction workers drank beer and guessed about how it had happened. A lady shopper with an Instamatic snapped a picture.

It was a bright cloudless day, a day when all the colors of death were vivid.

The broad bloodstain in the middle of the road was already burgundy, turning to brown in the heat.

A shotgun lay nearby, five empty green shells shining like emeralds on the pavement. A few feet away was a black-barreled pistol and, beyond that, what looked like an automatic rifle.

During the chase, two cars had crunched into a bottlebrush tree, its blossoms crimson; beneath its outer branches were two cream-colored FBI Buicks, one pocked by bullet holes. The brake lights were still on.

Once all this had been noted and absorbed, there was little else to see. The shooting had lasted only minutes. It had been quiet for hours now, and still we stood and watched. The wounded were gone, the dead were silent.

Up the ramp came several Palmetto High School students, some skipping class, others taking an extra-long lunch break. None of them was clowning around, but the distance from the bodies made casual talk an easier thing.

A blond teenager in a sleeveless T-shirt watched for a few minutes, then turned to go. "Death in Miami," he said to some friends. "It's nice to know we live in such a nice city."

Another student, Mark Saymon, asked to borrow a photographer's telephoto lens, to get a closer look. He said this was his third shoot-out scene; the others were a bank holdup and a Farm Store robbery. "Nothing like this," Saymon said. "I can't believe they let that dude lie in the sun."

The dude was dead, of course. He was one of the suspects. Pot-bellied guy with black hair. He lay on his back. His left arm was taped where the paramedics had tried to get some fluids going before giving up; the chubby guy's clothes were soaked with too much blood. A man wearing rubber gloves fished through the dead man's pockets.

What grips onlookers at such times is the proximity of recent death. The danger is past, but the aftermath transfixes.

On television, blazing shoot-outs are followed by commercials. Real-life murder scenes do not dissolve so easily; not in the eye, not in the mind. The color of death is unforgettable.

There is also a ponderous ritual to investigation; the more victims, the longer it takes. On Friday the dead men lay where they fell for four hours.

Finally the killers were placed in the back of a light-blue van and hauled off to the medical examiner.

The agents were taken away in separate hearses.

The color of death was jet black.

Gunman, shot 12 times, wouldn't quit

August 6, 1986

The epilogue to the bloodiest shootout in FBI history is a stack of four autopsy reports, numbered 86–966 through 86–969 in the Dade medical examiner's office.

These are detached and clinical accounts, as precise as can be expected considering the mayhem behind the Suniland Shopping Center. Each file has a diagram of where the cars came to rest at 12201 SW 82nd Ave. on the morning of April 11. Drawn next to the automobiles are supine stick-figure bodies, four of them.

Two of the figures represent FBI agents Gerald Dove and Ben Grogan. The others are robbers Michael Lee Platt and William R. Matix.

The files are a collection of tangible and observable facts, some well-publicized and some obscure. For instance, all four of the men had Type O blood. Three wore Nike running shoes; both Dove and his killer took size 10½. The two suspects died wearing empty shoulder holsters. Platt had a black glove on his right hand.

William Matix, the man originally thought to have murdered the two agents, probably didn't kill anybody. He fired his shotgun only once. He was shot in the jaw, the neck, the left cheek, the right forearm, the right side of the head and the right cheek. The last bullet tunneled to his spine.

After the autopsy, Matix's eyes were donated to science.

A trail of bloodstains proved that Michael Platt murdered the two agents. He used a Ruger Mini-14 rifle, serial number 184–95273. The high-speed slugs can make an entry wound scarcely a quarter-inch in diameter and an exit wound as big as a fist.

In barely two minutes more than 100 shots ripped through the South Dade neighborhood. Forty of those came from the Ruger.

Grogan's 9mm Smith & Wesson had been fired nine times and Dove's had been fired 20, which meant the young agent had reloaded during the fight.

Agent Ron Reisner's gun had been shot six times, while agent Gilbert Orrantia's .357 had been fired 12 times. Badly injured, agent Edmundo Mireles had fired a 12-gauge shotgun five times, then heroically staggered to the car in which Matix and Platt were trying to escape. There Mireles shot them both fatally with his .357 revolver.

Investigators did their best to reconstruct the movements—who stood where, who shot whom, who died first—but on paper it's impossible to describe the choreography of terror that morning.

What's obvious is that the shootings didn't happen the way they do on TV shows; there was no script. Nor were the wanted men mere paper silhouettes on the range at Quantico. Probably all the firearms training in the world wouldn't have prepared the FBI agents for the likes of Michael Platt.

They shot him only moments after he slithered from his stolen Monte Carlo and took aim. He was hit again and again, yet he did not fall. Somehow, through an animal reserve of adrenalin or pure fury, Platt kept darting and bobbing and firing the Ruger assault rifle.

In all, seven agents went down in his sights.

A sad irony emerges from the ballistic tests. Of the first bullets that Platt absorbed, the most deadly came from the gun of agent Gerald Dove. The shot exploded Platt's right lung—a killing wound, but it didn't even slow him down. He simply ducked around the car, ambushed Dove and Grogan, and kept on shooting.

To the agents, Platt must have seemed a spectral force.

The man was hit 12 times: once in the forehead, twice in the right arm and chest, once in the right forearm, once in the upper chest 12 inches below the head, once in the right shoulder, once in the thigh, and multiple times in both feet from shotgun blasts.

Like his partner, Platt died with one of Mireles' bullets in his spine. Fifth cervical vertebra.

That was the one that stopped him. Platt and Matix and their weapons were dragged from Grogan's car. A policeman reached into the driver's side, slipped the gearshift to park and turned off the key. Finally it was over.

Machine-gun shortage rattles NRA

September 3, 1986

Some deeply disturbing news from our ever-vigilant friends at the National Rifle Association: America is in the throes of a serious machine-gun shortage. Hard to believe, but apparently true. If you've tried to buy a new machine gun lately or just trade in that rusty old family favorite, you got quite a shock.

That darned liberal Congress has passed a law banning the sale of all new machine guns. Incredibly, President Reagan signed it. The emasculatory effect was to limit the number of machine guns in nationwide circulation to a measly 127,000, most of which are probably in Hialeah. The NRA, whose aim is to guarantee enough guns for every maniac in the country, has launched a new lobbying campaign to persuade Congress to repeal the machine-gun legislation. The effort couldn't be more timely, following the recent slaughter of 14 innocent persons in Oklahoma by a lunatic using three handguns. To think he could have done the whole job with a single Thompson.

Many of you probably hadn't heard about the machine-gun shortage until now, but South Floridians have a special stake in solving the problem.

In recent times the machine gun has become a vibrant and inextricable part of our culture, lending spice and spontaneity to an otherwise dreary drug scene. Thanks to films such as *Scarface* and TV programs such as *Miami Vice*, the Ingram MAC-10 is now as indelible a part of South Florida's image as the palm tree. Are we going to sit still while a bunch of pencil-necks in Washington spoil it? Think of tradition. Remember how the legendary El Loco (the original El Loco—Dade County is probably the only place with more than one) hung from a speeding sedan on the Turnpike and fired away at a drug rival. And who could forget the photograph of the Colombian traveler machine-gunned to death in his wheelchair at Miami International.

Miami just wouldn't be the same without its rat-tat-tat.

True, plenty of machine guns are still out on the streets, but they're getting worn out and junky. We all know what happens when you leave your Gustav M45 lying in the backyard—one lousy rainstorm and the muzzle corrodes, the trigger starts to jam, you name it.

The urgent need for new guns was illustrated a few days ago when police raided a crack house in Broward County. Along with cocaine and the usual cache of handguns, two machine guns were seized in the arrest. Believe me, these were the worst looking machine guns you ever saw; they might as well have been held together with paper clips and masking tape.

I'm sure the coke dealers were embarrassed to be caught with such decrepit weapons, but what choice did they have? Thanks to Congress, no new ones are being produced for the U.S. market. They can blame Rep. Larry Smith of Hollywood, who wrote the offending law. Smith says there's no good reason for private citizens to have machine guns, and challenges the gun lobby to come up with any legitimate uses for the deadly automatic weapon. An obvious answer is hunting. What could match the thrill of bringing down a buck with 96 rounds of Parabellum fire at 100 meters? Saves you the trouble of skinning it, too.

So you're not a sportsman? Fine. The machine gun is still an invaluable urban companion. Next time some jerk sneaks in and steals your parking space, feed him a MAC-10 Popsicle and just watch how fast he backs out. Finally, try to imagine what would add more excitement and variety to a police officer's day than knowing that any two-bit creep could have a loaded Tommy gun under his front seat.

So as the NRA pursues its latest quest, all South Florida awaits the day when it's once again possible to gift wrap a shiny new Uzi for that someone special. Maybe even in time for Christmas.

Miami, a city beset by gun problems? Read on!

March 7, 1988

Tarnished Image Alert: Miami officials are concerned that a new book contains outdated information that gives a wrong impression about the area.

The book, due out in May, is called *Cities of Opportunity*. It lists 42 American cities that are promising and exciting places for young people to relocate. Miami makes the list.

Sounds very positive, except for one glitch. The author, John Tepper Marlin, dares to suggest that we've got a little gun problem down here in South Florida. Now, where would he get a crazy idea like that?

In particular, he mentions the infamous loophole in the state's new handgun law that made it legal to walk around with a six-shooter on your hip. That part of the law was hastily fixed, but not before Marlin had already sent off his manuscript.

The city had a chance to point out this mistake, but was two months late in replying to Marlin's publisher. Consequently, the gun stuff stays in the book.

Some complain that it's not fair to bring up the Dodge City slur again, and fear that the book will present a distorted view of how safe it is to live down here.

If only Mr. Marlin had taken the time to visit in the last week or so, he would have gone back to his typewriter with a completely different outlook about guns in South Florida.

These are some of the stories he would have seen on TV, or read in the papers:

• Someone with an automatic weapon opened fire from a passing car at teenagers on a street corner in Coconut Grove. Three youths, including two high-school football stars, were wounded in the apparently random attack.

• An ex-con robber with a violent past pulled a 9mm Smith & Wesson on a Miami cabbie, who quickly shot him to death with a Colt .45, one of two pistols he was carrying in his taxi under a new concealed-weapons permit.

• A University of Miami law school graduate named Irv Ribler was shot to death while driving down I-95 in North Broward. Police believe the murder stemmed from a brief traffic altercation with strangers.

• In Liberty City, three men were shot on the street when somebody in a white Camaro or Firebird opened fire with a shotgun. As the car roared off, the gunmen kept shooting at bystanders, and wounded a 19-year-old woman.

• As her children watched, a woman upset over a custody battle shot her ex-husband to death with a pistol in the parking lot of Dade's main juvenile court.

- Four friends out cruising in North Miami decided to play Russian roulette with a .38-caliber pistol. Jose Cotto, age 14, lost. He was the third teenager to die this way in Dade County since January.

- Police arrested two men for the robbery-slaying nine months ago of a children's ice-cream vendor near Kelsey Pharr Elementary School. Authorities noted that this murder was not related to the robbery-shooting of another ice-cream vendor near the same school in January.

- A former member of the Yahweh religious sect pleaded guilty to second-degree murder in the shooting deaths of two tenants who refused to leave an Opa-locka apartment when the Yahwehs tried to evict them.

- In Fort Lauderdale, a Canadian tourist was shot to death in his beachfront hotel room while Spring Breakers partied along The Strip.

- Burglars who broke into a Northwest Dade home stole a 9mm handgun, an Uzi semiautomatic machine gun, a .32-caliber pistol, a 12-gauge shotgun and a Beretta of unspecified caliber.

This is only a recent sampler. Yet, anyone can plainly see that not one of these incidents resulted from so-called "loopholes" in Florida's firearms laws.

So maybe next time a Mr. Smartypants Liberal wants to write a book, he'll buckle down and do his homework.

A gun problem? Us? What an imagination, this guy.

Legislators, we're dying for gun law

April 29, 1988

So the madness goes on.

Another policeman falls, while the clowns in Tallahassee argue about whether Key lime or sweet potato should be the state pie. Earlier in the week, they haggled intently over the selection of a state sand.

But don't worry. The true sweat and toil for this legislative session has been saved for the burning issue of repealing a motorcycle helmet law.

Just amazing.

How many cops do we have to lose before somebody up there gets some guts?

How many funerals will it take? How many manhunts? How many pictures of anguished relatives rushing into hospital emergency rooms?

Last year, the Legislature sent a lenient new message about handguns, and this year we got it. The homicide rate is way up, and more cops are down.

Let's hear it for some of the constitutional champions in the Legislature who gave us these murderous laws: Larry Plummer, John Hill and the two Lehtinens; Don Childers of West Palm Beach; Jim Scott and Tom Gustafson of Fort Lauderdale; Arnhilda Gonzalez-Quevedo of Coral Gables; Ron Saunders of Key West; Ray Liberti of West Palm Beach; Anne Mackenzie and Debby Sanderson of Fort Lauderdale; Luis Morse, John Cosgrove, Lincoln Diaz-Balart and Javier Souto of Miami; Roberto Casas of Hialeah; Robert Starks of Homestead; and our very own NRA poster boy, Al Gutman.

Hope to see all of you dropping by Jackson Hospital to wish Officer James Hayden a speedy recovery.

The madness is as uncivilized as it is intolerable. We are past the point of scaring off tourists; we're scaring off good cops. Anyone in his right mind would think twice about putting on a badge in a state that abides such bloodletting.

Officer Hayden was wounded during a routine traffic stop on a busy street—four weeks to the day after fellow officer Victor Estefan was murdered under similar circumstances. In the last month, three Miami policemen and a state trooper have been shot by motorists.

I would not blame Chief Clarence Dickson for telling his officers to treat every traffic violator as a potential killer; to approach every car with guns drawn, anticipating another freak with a Smith & Wesson in his lap. Why not? This is the new code of the street.

Finally, the mayor is talking about a trip to the capital to discuss the gun law. He ought to charter a plane and take a delegation in blue. All of us react more viscerally to the shooting of a law enforcement officer, and we should. If the police aren't safe, nobody is. Yet, at the same time, we shouldn't forget the daily blood bath that doesn't make the front page.

A week ago, J. D. Davis was killed in his front yard when he was hit by a stray bullet from a neighborhood crack dispute. Davis wasn't a cop; he was just an innocent guy with a wife and kids. He could have been your husband, your brother, your son, your father.

Some people say that it's already too late; that once a society arms itself as prolifically as South Florida, there is no disarming it. To some extent, this is true. Once the guns are sold, they only come back as police evidence in robberies, murders, suicides. Even then, they don't always come back.

A few days ago, police say, a man drove out to a South Dade tomato field and killed his wife with a 9mm handgun, then shot himself. By the time officers reached the scene, a passerby had already stolen the dead man's gun.

The answer to this madness is not acceptance, and it's certainly not more handguns. A beginning would be a new set of laws, starting with one that makes it illegal to have a pistol in your car, period.

If you had met Jim Hayden's assailant under more casual circumstances and asked about the handgun in his Malibu, he probably would have told you he was carrying it for protection. He would have told you it was his right, just check the law.

Victor Estefan's killer could have given you the same line.

And God help you if you disagreed.

New NRA ad misses the mark

May 23, 1988

The National Rifle Association has kicked off a frantic counteroffensive in Florida with new radio commercials designed to scare every law-abiding citizen into buying a handgun.

Displaying its usual disregard for facts, the NRA asserts that strict handgun laws will punish only the innocent, because criminals don't apply for gun permits.

Wrong. In Dade County, one out of 15 applicants for a new concealed-weapons license has a felony arrest record. Since the new laws took effect, violent drug dealers, home invasion robbers and mental defectives have gotten legal gun permits—despite the NRA's assurance that no such thing could happen.

Under fire from angry constituents, legislators are fumbling around with a sham response—a whopping three-day waiting period. This won't accomplish anything, except to allow these wimps to slink home from Tallahassee and claim credit for a "tougher" gun law.

Meanwhile, it's been another typical week for handguns in South Florida. A 10-year-old Richmond Heights boy, upset over a bad school performance report, killed himself with a .357 found under his parents' bed. In Coral Springs, an investment counselor shot an ex-employee four times and then himself over a labor grievance.

The NRA ads imply that a pistol in the nightstand is all that stands between a free society and a criminal siege. Fear sells, and nobody sells it better than the NRA.

If you really want to feel safe and secure, consider the number of handguns that enter the criminal underworld every day. The NRA seldom confronts the issue of where these guns come from—the guns used to shoot at cops and store clerks and cashiers.

Guess where they come from. A sample from the last three weeks:

A 45.-caliber handgun was stolen from a truck parked outside the Sunshine Medical Center on Southwest 72nd Street.

A .357 magnum was stolen from a man who was attacked by three assailants in West Dade.

A .38-caliber revolver was stolen out of a Chevy Blazer parked in the 24700 block of Southwest 87th Avenue.

A .38-caliber Smith & Wesson was stolen from an apartment on the 8400 block of Southwest 107th Avenue.

A thief who stole a 1987 Ford Bronco on Southwest 63rd Street also got a .357, which had been left in the truck.

A 9mm handgun was stolen from the glove box of a Buick parked at Westchester Hospital.

A thief who stole a Ford pickup on Northwest 109th Street also got a .38-caliber pistol and .25-caliber handgun, both of which had been left in the truck.

A .38 was stolen from a parked car in the 1100 block of Northwest 128th Street.

A 12-gauge shotgun and a .357 Smith & Wesson were stolen from a home in the 16000 block of Northwest 45th Avenue.

A .38 Smith & Wesson was stolen from under a mattress inside a house trailer in the 6000 block of Southwest Eighth Street.

A .22-caliber semiautomatic Beretta was stolen from a diesel repair shop on Okeechobee Road.

A .44 magnum was stolen from an apartment in the 17200 block of Southwest 95th Avenue.

A .380 was stolen from a home in the 19300 block of Southwest 117th Court.

Another .380 was stolen in a house burglary on Hammond Drive, in Miami Springs.

A .357 was stolen by burglars who broke a sliding door on a house in the 10800 block of Southwest 168th Street.

The big score took place in North Broward, where burglars broke into a tackle shop and swiped a MAC-10, a MAC-11 and eight handguns.

And these are only some of the cases reported to police.

Most of these weapons were purchased with honest intentions, and now they're in the hands of criminals. They will not likely be used for the lawful defense of life or property, but rather for crime.

For those who lost their handguns to crooks, the NRA's solution is simple: Go out and buy more. Call it supply-side gun regulation.

Burglars, thugs and stickup men couldn't be happier about it. Right now, the NRA is the best friend they've got—besides our state Legislature.

Shop closing may trigger gun panic

March 1, 1989

Authorities braced for "a wave of consumer panic" today following the announcement that the Tamiami Gun Shop has closed its doors.

The owner insisted that the closing of the store, South Florida's biggest retail firearms dealer, is only temporary. He said he's planning to sell the place to new investors.

Meanwhile, police and civil defense officials prepared for widespread unrest in the face of a possible gun shortage. Mandatory rationing could be imposed.

"We anticipate panic buying, looting, and hoarding of weapons, particularly handguns," said Sgt. Earl "Bucky" Fuqua of the Metro-Dade police. "We are urging people to stay calm because this is only a temporary situation. There's still plenty of guns out there for everybody. Honest."

Yet by dawn today long lines had begun to form at other South Florida gun shops. Anxious customers brought tents and sleeping bags, waiting all night for the stores to open.

Tensions ran high in some gun lines and several fights broke out, though no serious injuries were reported. "Since they didn't have pistols, they had to use their fists and feet," Fuqua said. "It was pathetic, I'm not kidding."

To avoid a shortage, many gun dealers say they are voluntarily limiting the number of weapons purchased by a single customer. The emergency quota includes one Saturday Night Special, one imported semiautomatic handgun, one domestic shotgun and one unconverted MAC-10.

"Yeah, cutting back is a hardship," admitted one gun dealer, "but at a time like this, we gotta think about what's good for all society, not just what's good for our pocketbooks."

Industry analysts were hard-pressed to explain the sudden closing of Tamiami Gun Shop, a colorful family attraction in Miami. Thanks to Florida's liberal new weapons laws, business at most firearms stores has been booming lately.

The number of handgun homicides—considered a prime economic indicator—showed strong and steady gains last year in the tri-county area. Especially large increases were noted among 13- to 17-year-olds, a sign that handguns were breaking solidly into the lucrative youth market.

In addition, police reported that more handguns were swiped from homes and cars than ever before. This usually is good news for gun dealers, who are swamped with customers wanting to buy new weapons to replace those that were stolen.

Since repeat business is so important to gun shops, some analysts speculate that Tamiami might have simply done its job too well—selling so many guns to so many people that burglars haven't been able to keep pace in stealing them.

Such conditions could conceivably lead to a saturated marketplace.

"Saturated? South Florida? No way," said Sgt. Fuqua. "In fact, just the other day I stopped a guy for speeding over on Flagler Street. When I looked in the trunk of his car—no gun! Checked the glove compartment—empty! Under the front seat—nothing! Hey, you can look it up in the report if you don't believe me."

Other police agencies confirm similar isolated incidents where officers have encountered unarmed civilians—a clear signal that the handgun market has not yet reached its full potential.

Some observers say it's possible that Tamiami didn't change with the times. The store gained national attention for selling a .357 to a disgruntled stock investor (and felon) named Arthur Kane, who immediately used the gun to shoot his broker and kill another man.

But while Tamiami's reputation as a handgun dealership was assured, other gun shops around the country were getting even bigger headlines by diversifying into more exotic weapons, such as AK-47s. Pistols, it seemed, were becoming passe.

Still, most experts believe that a modernized Tamiami Gun Shop will reopen and be as popular as ever. "Hey, if they don't sell another Glock, it won't matter," Sgt. Fuqua said. "In this town you can make a killing off bullets alone."

Sad reality: Armed society means cops die

April 30, 1990

Every time another police officer is murdered, anguished voices rise to ask: When will it stop?

The answer is, it won't.

We live in an armed society where people shoot each other every day for the most mundane and empty-headed reasons. Sometimes they shoot cops.

To us, the murder of any police officer seems senseless, but it's not. Some creep with a pistol in his car decides he doesn't want to get arrested, so he starts shooting. Makes perfect sense to him.

These are not clear-thinking, highly principled, law-abiding citizens. These are dirtbags. They've spent most of their sorry lives doing dumb crimes that got them in trouble, and then repeating their mistakes at every opportunity.

Maybe they come from broken homes. Maybe they've got a drug habit. Maybe they grew up in a bad neighborhood and never had a chance. Whatever the reasons, there are thousands of these losers on the streets of South Florida, and plenty of guns to go around.

Several weeks ago there was the funeral for Broward Sheriff's Deputy John Greeney III. This week it's Metro-Dade Officer Joseph Martin. Inevitably there will be another, and another after that.

Few countries in the world bury so many slain police officers. Such crimes are rare in Great Britain, Japan, even Canada. The only place more dangerous than the United States is Colombia, where drug gangsters slaughter policemen by the carload.

The most telling thing about Officer Martin's murder is how ordinary the suspects are. They're not big-time bank robbers, federal fugitives, or ruthless cocaine assassins. They're burglars and car thieves, 19 and 20 years old; common crooks whose rap sheets show no history of armed violence.

What happens in that frantic millisecond when panic, or rage, or pure cold-bloodedness takes control?

If we could peek into the mind of whoever pulled the trigger on Joseph Martin, we would probably be stunned by the simple, impulsive nature of his decision. There you are in a stolen automobile, late at night, pulled over by a squad car. And there's the gun on the seat . . .

We are raising a generation of young criminals who shoot first and think later. They are fascinated with deadly weapons and casual in their killing. So far this year, the Dade State Attorney's Office has handled 45 cases of murder or attempted murder in which the defendant was age 17, or younger.

Just this weekend, a police gang task force raided two homes in North Dade and seized seven guns, plus a silencer; two juveniles, an 18-year-old and a 19-year-old were arrested. What they intended to do with all these firearms is not known, but they probably weren't planning to start a museum.

It's common to blame the parents, blame the schools, blame society for letting these kids slip away. Some of them can be rehabilitated, some of them can't. The main thing is, they're out there in growing numbers.

Most criminals begin their careers as two-bit house burglars, and in South Florida that means you deal in guns. For sheer terror there's nothing like glancing through a week's worth of burglary reports to get an idea of the arsenal on the streets—AK-47s, AR-15s, Uzis, MAC-11s and every type of handgun imaginable, all stolen from the bedrooms, car trunks and glove compartments of regular citizens.

Some of these weapons will end up killing somebody, maybe even a cop.

This is the terrible irony: In trying to protect ourselves and our families, we've armed the very outlaws whom we fear. Some of them are crazy, some of them are mean and some are just plain stupid. Many are barely old enough to drive.

We should hardly be surprised when one of them snaps, for whatever reason, and takes aim at a badge. The only surprise is that it doesn't happen more often.

Pass all the tough crime laws you want. Build bigger prisons. Heat up the electric chair.

It won't stop the killing. We are too late for that.

In tourist haven, mayor sticks to guns

June 27, 1990

Another reason to plan your family vacation for somewhere else: Miami Beach Mayor Alex Daoud has armed himself with four semiautomatic handguns and a night sight.

The ostensible reason for Daoud's private arsenal is "personal protection." Presumably the night sight is necessary in case the mayor is attacked by bats.

Like many of Daoud's recent dealings, the weapons acquisition raises questions about ethics. The companies from which he received the guns just happened to be competing for a big Miami Beach Police Department firearms contract. The firm that supplied him the most guns—three Sig Sauers—got a $153,000 city contract, with the help of Daoud's vote.

Maybe this is just another weird coincidence in a long string of weird coincidences that have put the mayor at the center of a federal investigation. Maybe he's just a friendly guy who can't say no to a good deal. Or maybe he's a shameless moocher and shakedown artist.

This is something for prosecutors to decide. An equally disturbing question for the public: Does South Florida really want another of its elected officials armed to the teeth?

Tourism officials can't be ecstatic with the revelation that the mayor of one of our major destination cities turns out to be a gun freak. The truth is, Daoud is not alone in his paramilitary passion. Remember when Joe Carollo was investigated for owning an Uzi?

The trend escalated when Rep. Al Gutman posed fetchingly for an NRA advertisement with his beloved .380 Beretta. Finally a South Florida officeholder was honest enough to admit that he didn't feel safe in his own community without a reliable semiautomatic.

Gutman's full-page appearance in national magazines made it respectable for other local politicians and civic leaders to arm themselves, often with unfortunate results.

One night a few years ago, Miami Mayor Xavier Suarez left a handgun inside a briefcase on the front seat of his car. It was stolen by a thief. Acting U.S. Attorney Dexter Lehtinen has a fondness for more powerful weapons, particularly AR-15 assault-type rifles. He has lost two of them to local burglars.

And last year the former chairperson of the Greater Miami Chamber of Commerce, Dorothy Weaver, reported that an Uzi was stolen from her bedroom. I don't know if Uzis are now the standard-issue weapon for all Chamber of Commerce members, but it would be interesting to do a survey.

If South Florida is such a safe and desirable place to live, why are all these big shots packing heat?

A clue, in Mayor Daoud's case, is the special serial number engraved on his new Glock handgun: 007. The man thinks he's a secret agent!

Former Beach police chief Ken Glassman recounted how Daoud frequently asked to practice on the police firing range. When the chief balked, Daoud proudly produced a photograph of himself firing automatic rifles on a gun range in Israel.

The Israelis (at least those who had never visited Dade County) must have been quite amazed that the mayor of an American city would be so proficient in military skills. Watching Daoud in action, they could only conclude that Florida must be a much more exciting place than they had heard.

Let's assume that Daoud imagines himself to be a real secret agent. Why did he get four handguns? Even James Bond carried only one at a time. Maybe the mayor wanted a gun for both ankles and both hips, in case he's ambushed by enemy commandos at Penrod's.

The image of a heavily armed Alex Daoud cruising the streets is unsettling. Current gun laws can't even protect us from known felons and deranged maniacs, much less macho mayors.

Politicians shouldn't be trusted with anything more lethal than a gavel. The way things go, it won't be long before a burglar steals Daoud's heavy artillery, which will then be turned against the innocent citizenry of Miami Beach.

Let's just hope it doesn't happen during a travel agents' convention.

Live or rerun, murder is now mainstream TV

January 31, 1993

Not so long ago, parents were being warned that their kids could sneak out and buy black-market videotapes of people being murdered.

Today, snuff films have gone mainstream. You can watch them on the nightly news.

With a Miami TV crew looking on, Emilio Nuñez Jr. emptied a semi-automatic handgun into his ex-wife. The tape of the killing was broadcast repeatedly by local stations, often accompanied by insightful freeze-frame analysis.

Like everyone else, I sat and watched. Pop, pop, pop. As domestic homicides go, it was noteworthy mainly for the ironic location (a cemetery), and for the forensic convenience of a camera capturing the crime.

Naturally, the Nuñez tape became a hot property. TV stations all over the country picked it up. Some chose not to show the shooting, but many did. This was followed by the usual wrenching debate about violence on television—what's newsworthy, what's gratuitous gore.

Down here, there wasn't much discussion about whether to air the footage. It was a legitimate local story, extreme even by South Florida's diseased standards.

Now the crime is old news, but you can still catch the video almost any evening on local TV. Nuñez's capture, his extradition hearing, his arraignment, an interview with his family—each new event is an excuse to cue the murder tape one more time.

Most stations considerately have cut the part when Nuñez stands over his ex-wife and pumps slug after slug into her body. Yet some stations continue to show the jarring first shot to the head, punctuated by the cries of the interviewer.

More chilling than the murder itself is the fact that most viewers, myself included, are tired of seeing it. The Nuñez tape has been broadcast so often that it no longer shocks. It should, but it doesn't.

Television has given America a unique intimacy with real-life violence. In 1963, Lee Harvey Oswald was shot on live TV. It was the first murder my generation ever saw, and for a long time it was the only one. There was no such thing as Insta-cam.

The Zapruder film of John Kennedy's assassination now has been viewed by practically everybody, but for many years it was kept from the public because it was considered too horrible. These days nothing is too horrible.

Newscasters warned us that the Nuñez video was graphic, but I don't know a soul who didn't watch it. Crime scenes always draw a crowd; hit-and-runs, holdups, lunatic sniper sprees. Video is the next best thing to being there.

Satellites feed the morbid craving. As if there's not enough carnage here in Florida, we now get nightly recaps of the bloodiest mayhem committed across the nation. Inundated visually, our shock threshold rises with each killing we see, whether live or on tape.

Gruesome at the time, the grainy black-and-white footage of Oswald's murder today seems prosaic. By contrast, Emilio Nuñez's graveyard frenzy unfolds vividly, closeup and in living color. Even so, the impact wears off after the 13th or 14th viewing; probably sooner, for our kids.

We've seen so much that we've built up an unhealthy tolerance. Numbness sets in until there's a fresh fix. And we never need to wait too long.

On Thursday, police released the videotape of a Broward store clerk shooting a robber in the head. The incident occurred months ago, but who cares? They showed it on all the channels, again and again. As a bonus they played the 911 call, too.

Exciting stuff, this reality. They're doing it to death.

Great gift ideas for very young snipers-to-be

With all their caterwauling about juvenile violence, wimpy liberals in Washington have succeeded in intimidating toy dealers just in time for Christmas.

The country's largest retailer, Toys R Us, has decided to stop selling a Sega video game called "Night Trap."

I haven't played "Night Trap," but the plot seems fairly routine: Vampire home invaders drain the blood of nubile co-eds by drilling into the veins of their necks.

Fun for the whole family, right?

But after pantywaists in Congress complained about the "graphic" content, Toys R Us yanked the video off the shelves. In an atmosphere of such panic, what'll they ban next—toy guns?

I raced to the nearest Toys R Us outlet to find out. With great relief I can report that the store's arsenal remains fully stocked and ready for action.

For that future cocaine cowboy in your house, several toy Uzis are still available for about $3.99. My favorite is the Neon Uzi Squirter, a "clip loading" water gun that supposedly sounds like an authentic assault rifle.

If that's too much firepower for your trigger-happy tyke, start him out with something smaller—the .357 "Make My Day" Magnum, manufactured by RealTech and sold for $7.99. The Clint Eastwood quip stolen for this toy's promotion actually referred to a .44, but that's quibbling. The "Make My Day" Magnum features "real firing sounds" and a rotating cylinder.

Kids growing up in big cities are much too streetwise to be amused by replicas of dinky Wild West six-shooters or clumsy muzzle-loaders. The shelves of Toys R Us amply reflect the precocious interests of today's urban youngster.

H. T. Toys sells an AK-47 water rifle that's unbeatable at $2.99, while Combat Force offers an adorable M-16 for $4.99.

A word of caution: According to the instructions, the M-16 is unsuitable for children under 3 years old—not because it's morally questionable to let toddlers play with toy weapons, but because they tend to disassemble them and swallow the plastic parts.

Not to worry.

The motto of the toy gun industry is: Safety, safety, safety! So many kids brandishing realistic-looking toy pistols have been shot by police and homeowners that many manufacturers have switched to neon colors, to avoid future confusion.

For example, the venerable Daisy Company offers a Buffalo Bill Rifle with an orange cap on the barrel to make it "easily identified as a toy." The gun promises a "loud bang," but the label warns: "Do not fire it closer to the ear than one foot."

Santa, are you listening?

Strolling the aisles, it's impossible not be tempted by the M-60 Automatic Assault Lazer ("Try Me! Pull Trigger"). For $19.99, your pint-size holiday sniper can hear the same pop-pop-pop that real snipers do.

And the extra ammo belt makes a cool stocking-stuffer.

No armory would be complete without a selection of 9mm semiautomatics. Toys R Us sells a model resembling the one used so successfully by the madman on the Long Island commuter train. Made in Macau ("Loaded—Try me!"), it's a bargain at $5.99 . . . and there's no waiting period. Yet.

But parents seeking the ultimate in toy weaponry should train their sights on "Survivor Shot." For $29.98, Junior gets a high-tech rifle and a battery-operated headset to be worn during simulated firefights.

The toy's major selling point is plastered in bold letters on the box: "When you're hit, you feel it!" That's right—the sting of a bullet, without the permanent brain damage.

Now we're talking fun.

Take pride in hometown arms maker

March 26, 1995

Those sappy bleeding hearts are at it again. I guess they won't be satisfied until they've completely destroyed the free-enterprise system.

Their latest whipping boy is one of South Florida's most prosperous and innovative companies, Navegar Inc., maker of handy low-cost Intratec assault weapons—and my write-in nominee for *Miami Herald* Company of the Year.

Forgive a little hometown cheerleading, but Miami doesn't have much to brag about in the way of light manufacturing. Intratec has put us on the map!

Its Tec 9, Tec-DC9 and Tec-22 were among the most sought-after street guns in the United States, according to the Bureau of Alcohol, Tobacco and Firearms. For legions of budget-minded gang members who couldn't afford a MAC-10 or an Uzi, the Tecs became the ideal travel companion.

"High spirited," according to Navegar chief Carlos M. Garcia, whose business was booming (literally).

But wouldn't you know it—as soon as a hard-working entrepreneur makes the big time, those candy-ass liberals come along and try to ruin him.

Last year's ban on 19 types of assault rifles targeted the Tecs, and forced Navegar into an inconvenient re-engineering of its product line. Lost because of picky new regulations were such helpful features as the threaded barrel, for attaching silencers.

Undaunted, the resourceful Garcia devised a new generation of legal weapons that look and perform much like the old ones, but with fewer bullets.

Then, last week, another ambush: The families of victims murdered in 1993 by a homicidal lunatic sued Navegar for negligence.

OK, so it's true that Gian Luigi Ferri walked into a San Francisco office and shot 15 persons, killing nine. And it's also true he was firing two Tec-DC9s, made right here in Dade County. And, yes, each gun was capable of shooting 32 rounds without being reloaded.

But how was Carlos Garcia to blame? Who could imagine that anyone would ever use a cheap, rapid-fire, easily concealed semiautomatic for violent purposes?

The California families contend that the Intratecs have no sporting use, and are promoted with criminals in mind.

True, sales brochure bragged that the Tec-DC9 was specially coated for "excellent resistance to fingerprints." There's probably a perfectly good explanation—maybe Intratec customers are neatniks who don't like smudges on their grips.

Garcia has patiently explained that his guns are meant for recreational "plinking" at tin cans "or objects like water jugs." He says they also seem popular with survivalists bracing for another world war.

Just as Ford knows that some of its cars will end up in fatal accidents, Navegar has become aware that some of its firearms are not being used to shoot water jugs.

As Garcia once said: "I know some of the guns going out of here end up killing people, but I'm not responsible for that."

Despite serious run-ins with the ATF (for making weapons too easily converted to machine guns), Garcia perseveres. Each fusillade of rotten publicity makes him work even harder.

In 1990 a robber used a Tec-9 to murder Broward Sheriff's Deputy Jack Greeney. A weaker company might have closed shop in shame, but Navegar's assembly line never missed a beat.

From 1991–93, it put more than 125,000 more Intratecs on the streets of America, making Florida nearly as famous for deadly weapons as it is for citrus.

One way to say thanks is to name Navegar as our Company of the Year. Let's show Garcia that we care about him as much as he cares about us.

TV newscasts no more violent than real life

May 8, 1997

A new national study reports that South Florida's TV stations spend 27.5 percent of their evening news broadcasts on crime and criminal justice, prompting the obvious question:

Is that all?

The surprise isn't how much time Miami TV devotes to murder and mayhem, but how little. The average for local 6 P.M. news broadcasts was 29.3 percent—about 30 seconds more than in the blood-spattered Dade-Broward market.

If anything, our stations show uncommon restraint. South Florida being the violent pit it is, TV news directors could easily fill the entire program with local gore. They seldom do.

Yet the University of Miami professor who directed the media study laments the findings. "It's unfortunate," said Joe Angotti, "that body-bag journalism is what local news chooses to focus on at the expense of more important stories."

Hogwash. What is unfortunate is that there's so much violence that it can't be ignored. Sadly, body-bag journalism reflects a body-bag world. We all worry some about crime because it's touched all of us.

Is it not "important" news when a two-bit shoplifter guns down a security guard in broad daylight at one of South Florida's busiest shopping malls?

How about when four members of a family, including two little children, are slaughtered in their Miramar home? Or when a father, his son and a friend are executed by intruders at an electronics warehouse in West Dade?

All that from just a week's worth of police-blotter entries. You see the problem: No other single place can compete with our volume, ferocity and weirdness of crime.

Considering the deluge, Miami's TV stations do a decent job of balancing police news with health, education and politics. Some days, it isn't easy.

Give viewers a choice between an informative story about a new low-cholesterol diet or a grisly tale about sickos stealing human heads out of crypts, and they'll dial up the cadavers every time.

For the crime-content survey, researchers in eight markets studied a half-hour of news broadcasts on four random days. Wow, that's two whole hours of TV in each city—and who's calling whom shallow?

(Incredibly, the most infamous of our local stations, WSVN-Channel 7, finished third in the body-bag derby. No talk yet of a slander suit.)

One hole in the methodology: Only English-speaking TV stations were studied. Another flaw: Only 6 P.M. broadcasts were analyzed. Many stations start the news at 5 P.M., and in-depth features often air that first hour.

That's not to say some crime stories aren't overplayed and exploited on TV, sometimes disgracefully. It's also true that some are underplayed.

In any case, there aren't many news directors who wouldn't love to get more time for school issues, medical breakthroughs, political analysis and I-Team investigations.

The problem is, news keeps happening. You can't keep it off the air.

To insinuate that crime coverage isn't serious journalism is to repudiate one of the media's essential roles. People want to be safe in their communities, and they deserve to know when they're not.

One reason that serious crime fell so sharply in New York is that the media kept a spotlight on it. As for the use of "sensational video" decried by Professor Angotti, Anthony Windes probably isn't complaining.

He's the Sears guard whose shooting was captured by a store camera. The chilling replay, widely broadcast, is what enabled police to identify the shoplifter who allegedly pulled the trigger.

How much more important can TV news be?

A war looms on gun sales

June 18, 1998

If the National Rifle Association gets its way, Florida will hang on to its dubious reputation as America's biggest flea market for illegal firearms.

The NRA has promised to "do whatever it takes" to kill a proposed constitutional amendment that would seal a gaping hole in the state's gun laws, and make it harder for itinerant traffickers to restock their arsenals here.

As it stands, unscrupulous dealers working the Florida circuit can sell practically any type of weapon to anybody, as long as the transaction occurs at a gun show or flea market. Sales by firearms "collectors" at such events currently are exempt from the cooling-off period and background check that apply at retail gun shops.

The result is that outlaw dealers slither from one gun show to the next, falsely claiming to be collectors or one-time sellers. In this way thousands of high-powered weapons are peddled to buyers who haul them out of the state.

It's as easy as buying a Slurpee, and requires the same paperwork: none.

Florida is the prime source of illegal handguns and street weapons confiscated by police in New York and other seaboard cities. Next to orange juice and cocaine, guns are our most lucrative interstate freight.

Law enforcement officials, backed by Gov. Lawton Chiles, lobbied to get the flea-market loophole closed by the Legislature—a lost cause. Most lawmakers are either scared of the NRA, or politically beholden to it.

So prosecutors and police turned instead to the Constitution Revision Commission, which was writing a slate of amendments for next November's ballot. The commission crafted a firearms measure that has provoked a frantic war cry from NRA leaders.

The last time Florida voters were given a voice on a gun control law, it passed by a landslide. That was the 1990 amendment requiring a three-day wait and criminal records check for handgun purchases.

The NRA whined and wailed. It said the law was unnecessary because criminals don't buy guns at gun stores.

Turns out the NRA was wrong again. Since the amendment was adopted, background checks have prevented thousands of convicted felons from purchasing handguns at retail outlets.

But, until now, the law couldn't stop those same felons from buying a suitcase full of Glocks from a friendly "collector" at the weekend gun show.

The new amendment gives counties the power to close that insane loophole by requiring records checks on all gun sales on property "to which the public has the right of access"—a provision strongly supported by law enforcement in Miami-Dade and other urban areas.

The NRA opposes it virulently, saying communities have no right to make or enforce their own firearms laws. The courts say otherwise, and early polls show widespread support for the new ballot measure.

As fall approaches, the gun lobby will launch a media blitz to scare voters away from the gun-show amendment. Don't be surprised if the NRA models its campaign after the one Big Sugar ran to defeat the Everglades cleanup amendment in 1996.

The cane growers spent millions proclaiming that the penny-a-pound proposal was a new tax on consumers—a complete lie, but it worked. Look for the NRA to try the same thing.

We'll hear how the gun amendment is a diabolical step toward mandatory gun licensing, or even government confiscation! Maybe if we're really lucky, they'll trot out Charlton Heston for some doomsday-style TV spots.

It should be quite an act, and if it somehow succeeds Florida will remain the prime shopping mecca for the country's underground gun traffickers.

See It like
a Native

700 more cops will not solve crime problem

September 20, 1985

On Wednesday the Metro Commission wisely snuffed a scheme that would have raised property taxes to put 700 more cops on the streets. The Dragnet Tariff, I call it.

It's hard to imagine how otherwise sane and circumspect members of Miami Citizens Against Crime could have conceived something so lame and simple-minded. Maybe this is what happens when wealthy white folks in the suburbs get a gritty taste of urban crime.

When the corporate VP's wife is too scared to drive to Dadeland, when an executive's home is invaded by thugs, when robbers move from the projects onto the interstate—then we've got ourselves a crime wave.

Suddenly the streets aren't safe. Suddenly we need more cops.

Tell that to the grandmother in Liberty City who's lucky to make it to the Pantry Pride without losing her purse to thieves.

Or the widow on South Beach with triple dead bolts on the door.

Or the Hialeah cabbie who gets a pistol shoved in his ear.

For these people, fear is nothing new. They don't need to see the FBI statistics, and they don't need histrionics from downtown businessmen. And they definitely don't need more police—they need the ones we've already got put to better use.

Since 1980, Metro's police roster has grown 48 percent, from 1,480 to 2,195 officers. At the same time, the city of Miami added 61 percent more police, from 660 to 1,062.

For five years we've been throwing more cops at the criminals and what have we got to show for it? The highest murder rate in America, and the second highest violent crime rate.

Under the Dragnet Tariff, property taxes would have been hiked to generate up to $90 million for expanded police departments, courts and jails.

What's wrong with that? First, the fantasy that more cops mean less crime. Dade County is living proof that it isn't true.

Swamp I-95 with state troopers and the highway robbers simply retreat to neighborhood intersections—where they keep on robbing.

Unleash an army of U.S. drug agents to wage war on smugglers and—five years later—cocaine has never been purer, cheaper or more abundant.

Still, you never hear police brass complaining about too much manpower; they'd take paratroopers if somebody offered.

The truth is, local police departments have all they can do to manage the cops they've got. Metro is investigating some of its own for allegedly peddling cocaine. Two Miami policemen recently were busted for allegedly trying to sell guns and badges to drug dealers, while several others are being investigated for crimes including murder, robbery and, ironically, home invasions. This week a Hialeah officer went on trial for a drug execution.

Obviously it's time for recruiters to stress quality over quantity; one rotten cop negates a hundred good ones.

Both Metro and Miami will be adding some police under the new budgets. In the meantime our restless civic pillars ought to turn their attention to the elements that produce the criminals whom we so fear—the unemployment, poverty, teenaged pregnancies, broken homes and dropout rate. Solving these problems isn't going to happen over cocktails at the Banker's Club.

I wish the MCAC—which has been a leader on the crime issue—could persuade county commissioners to scrape up big money for more first-rate teachers. Plus a few more million for vocational training, or drug education in the schools, or Parole and Probation.

Politically, of course, it's easier to put a prowl car on every corner. Had the Dragnet Tariff passed, we certainly would have seen results: more arrests, more overcrowded prisons, more clogged court dockets, more early paroles. And the streets would have been no safer.

As long as some neighborhoods remain bleak factories of crime, we can put a whole generation in jail and it won't help. There'll always be a bitter new wave, coming of age in the same social misery.

Dilapidated county clinic medical shame

April 30, 1986

The sick children come here, where the roof peels, the pipes leak, the electric wires get wet, the carpet turns moldy.

Where it's so overcrowded that babies' urine samples are taken in the hallways. Where not long ago a pregnant mother tripped over a crawling infant, fell and cut herself. Where there's no room for private consultations, even for gynecological patients.

Where the waiting room is often so packed that the line of youngsters spills outside, all the way to the busy street. "It's a miracle," one nurse says, "that we haven't lost a baby to a car."

This is the South Miami public health clinic, the shame of the county.

For months nurses, patients and administrators have been writing letters, signing petitions and pleading with authorities to do something, because the place is crumbling.

They've received numerous replies—all politely sympathetic—but little help. Meanwhile several veteran nurses have asked for transfers after coming down with respiratory illnesses; another contracted hepatitis. The staff is convinced that the South Miami health clinic is not a healthy place to be.

The one-story building at 5798 SW 68th St. is only 3,170 square feet. It probably was never meant to be a medical clinic, and certainly never meant to serve 3,723 patients.

Those who bother to come out and see it agree: It's a terrible place to bring the children.

From Administrator Ada DeVeaux, who's been with the health department since 1956: "I've never worked in a facility like this in all the years I've been here. It's a fire hazard, the whole place."

From nurse Maureen Orr, who's worked at rustic hospitals in Vietnam and Colombia: "I truly never have worked in such deplorable conditions . . . We keep wondering why, what's happening?"

The county says fixing the South Miami clinic is a job for the state. The state says money is tight. While memos shoot back and forth, the kids keep coming.

Last week the clinic shut down for four days when water gushed through the ceiling into one of the examining rooms. The overhead pipes had rusted out, leaking dangerously all over the electrical connections. After TV stations showed footage of the damage, the pipes got repaired, the ceiling got plastered, and the clinic reopened.

The patients who come here—up to 200 a day—are mostly poor. Many are Mariel and Nicaraguan refugees who travel from as far south as 120th Street, and as far west as the Collier County line. Almost everyone pays a nominal fee for a doctor's exam.

The children wait for tetanus shots, TB vaccines, throat cultures—the sort of things all kids need. Pregnant women and new mothers wait, too—many of them high-risk patients who need special attention.

Hundreds and hundreds of families depend on the South Miami clinic for basic health care that most of us take for granted. If we could help it, we wouldn't take our kids to a place that even the nurses say is hazardous. Some parents have no choice; that they care enough to bring their babies is reason enough for the state to do better.

"A disgrace," agrees state Rep. Betty Metcalf.

Upset by conditions at the clinic, she and Sen. Roberta Fox are trying to pry some money out of the Legislature. Unfortunately, an election year isn't the optimum time to ask for a brand-new clinic.

The staff at South Miami would happily settle for a different location—any empty old building with at least 10,000 square feet, and some funds to fix it up. Metcalf and Fox are shooting for at least $500,000 for repairs and renovations.

The folks in Tallahassee are unfailingly generous when it comes to subsidizing operas and auto races and beauty pageants and tourist promotions. Here's a chance to help out a special interest group that's really special—sick children who've got to wait in the sun, just to see a doctor.

Despair, rage fester in housing projects

July 27, 1987

Seven long summers ago, Northwest 22nd Avenue was afire in July.

People who lived in the James E. Scott housing project lined the sidewalks to throw rocks and bottles and epithets at passing cars. The mood was furious and grieving, an afterburst of the McDuffie riots.

Today, if you visit Scott or just about any project in Liberty City, ask the people what has changed in their lives. The answer is sometimes bitter and sometimes resigned, but always the same: Nothing has changed, they say; not a damn thing.

The *New York Times* could run a 7-year-old photograph of the Scott project and nobody would notice the difference, because there is no difference. Many have tried to do good things, but the lives of most people haven't improved.

It's hard to explain how there is so little money for job training or decent housing or black business loans at the same time $2 million in public funds is being spent on a one-day visit by the pope.

Last week, while some folks were hyperventilating about Miami's image in the newspaper, folks in Liberty City were trying to sweat out the deep heat. While civic leaders flew to Manhattan and got rooms at the Waldorf, activist Georgia Ayers stayed here and tried to keep a few youngsters out of jail. She lost no sleep over the *Times* magazine article.

"I'm not angry about anything they said about Miami," she said. "I hope it shames the hell out of them."

The ugly, malignant truth is that things are worse in Liberty City and Overtown than they were in 1980 or 1983, when riots broke out. Add to the unemployment, lousy housing, high crime and lost promises a new ingredient for despair: crack cocaine.

A block off 62nd Street, lanky dealers hang in pairs on the street corners, with toddlers playing underfoot. Driving through is chilling enough; having to live here is harrowing.

The Rev. Barry Young is a former juvenile court bailiff who is now a counselor with Ayers' Alternative Program, which works with first-time criminal offenders. Rev. Young thinks the peace on the streets is brittle and tense.

"The spark is there," he said as we pulled into Scott.

On a scrubby vacant lot, middle-aged men sat in the shade and watched the cars go by. Counselor Marcia Wallace: "When you get up at 7:30 in the morning and your father's sitting out there, and when you come home after school at 3 o'clock and he's still there . . ."

William Smith: "There's a lot of people out of a job. Like me, I'm out of a job." But he was radiantly proud of his niece, Jarenae, who last year won two trophies and two certificates for scholastic excellence at Drew Junior High.

By contrast, a magenta Cadillac cruised 61st Street—brand-new car, the paper tag still taped to the rear window. The driver wasn't more than 17; his passengers even younger. "Did you see that? Can you believe that?" Rev. Young said.

On a corner across from Gwen Cherry Park, where knee-high kids were running circles in the grass, a young man in a black Jaguar sedan pulled up to do some business with the local retailers. Everyone on the block knew who and what he was; the little ones will, too, someday.

Julia Sullivan, 73, has lived two decades in the same Liberty City apartment. From her front door she sees a world that is not much different for her four great-grandchildren than it was for her 20 grandchildren, or her 11 children before that.

"The children need to get off the streets, they need a job," Mrs. Sullivan said. "Sometimes needing and wanting are two different things."

In the projects, the heat bakes so hard and the air rises so thick that it would seem to leave no strength for picking up a rock or a bottle or a gun. That's what we thought seven years ago, too.

Of a shy young ninth-grader, Rev. Young asked: "What do you want to see change?"

"Everything," the young man said.

For poorest, life only gets worse

The word is riot.

Not melee, or disturbance, or incident. If it makes you feel better, go ahead and say it that way.

But the word is riot.

Whether it lasts five minutes, five hours or five days, the ingredients are the same—the fierce combustion of honest passion, confused fury, frustration and idle thuggery.

A young man is dead in the street with a police bullet in his head, and all you know is what you hear on the corner, and what you hear on the corner is bad.

So there is your spark.

What you saw on television the other night you've seen before. And if you were there, in Overtown, there was only one word for what was happening. And it was happening on Martin Luther King Day, of all days.

Gunshots. Looting. Cars on fire. Cops under siege. What would you call it—a heated dispute?

For, oh, how we yearn to minimize this thing, to calibrate it in some way to reassure the tourists and the national media that it isn't as terrible as it was in 1982 or 1980.

No, it's not nearly as terrible. Not if you merely add up the dead and wounded, count all the rocks and bottles. Take a quick survey of gutted buildings and charred cars.

No, by that measure it's not as terrible as before. Not unless you happen to live there. Then it's worse.

On Monday night, troopers blocked the interstate and sealed off the core of the city. On Tuesday morning, civic types downplayed what this will do to Miami's future as a vacation destination. They hoped that the visiting press wouldn't dwell on this isolated "disturbance" on the eve of the Super Bowl.

Well, screw the football game. This community's problem is slightly more pressing than PR. What good is a shimmering new skyline when the streets below it are bleaker than ever?

We've got neighborhoods that in eight years have edged no closer to becoming humane places to raise a family. Neighborhoods with not enough decent housing and not enough decent jobs. And now we've got a new influx of refugees to add to the tension.

We also have something we didn't have in 1982 or 1980, something to deepen the cycle of despair and futility. Now we have crack cocaine.

In these neighborhoods, some of the first sounds that a child learns to recognize are the flat crack of gunfire and the whine of a police siren.

Nearing midnight: We are on the corner of Northwest Second Avenue and 20th Street. A building has been set aflame and a crowd is gathered outside to watch it go down, and talk about what happened to the young man on the motorcycle, the young man who died.

The intersection is clogged with cops and journalists. The fire gives an orange glow to the smoke roiling skyward, a sight that brings back memories. This time around, the cops know the drill of neighborhood containment. This time around, most of the photographers are wearing bulletproof vests.

Every time a squad car goes by—pump guns bristling from the windows—there is the crackle of broken glass on pavement; glass everywhere, just like the last time. Two dumpsters are on fire. Overhead a police helicopter circles the blaze and aims a piercing white eye on the dismal neighborhood.

On the corners with the women are children, so many of them, and so small. Many of these kids were not yet born when Arthur McDuffie was beaten to death near the expressway. Some were still in diapers when Nevell Johnson Jr. was shot in the head at a video arcade.

Now, barefoot, these children of the new Miami tiptoe around the glass on the street. Gingerly they pick up the small gray cardboard canisters—toys for the little ones, souvenirs for teenagers. The labels on the canister say: No. 2 Riot Agent CS Grenade, Continuous Discharge. Manufactured by the Smith & Wesson Chemical Co.

Riot agent. Gas. A pungent damp cloud of the stuff rolls down 20th Street. This time around, the cops and photographers have brought masks.

The little children rub their eyes and scurry to get upwind. It is their first whiff of tear gas, but they are learning fast. On these streets, they will have no choice.

HRS research project is a study in folly

January 29, 1990

What will those clever minds at HRS think of next?

The newest scheme is to deny job training to thousands of eligible poor people—then pay for a research study to see how they're doing.

Amazing but true.

This spring, about 5,500 indigent Floridians will be purposely shut out of a program that offers job skills and child-care benefits instead of straight welfare. The theory behind the $25 million Project Independence was to train people for jobs so that eventually they can get off public assistance.

Similar welfare-to-work plans have been advocated as a first step toward fixing the nation's paralyzed anti-poverty programs. Many experts now believe that welfare is hopeless unless it's tied positively to employment.

To test the effectiveness of Project Independence, a private research company will create what is known in science as a control group—in this case, 5,500 people who will be denied the job classes and child care, and studied like human guinea pigs.

Their "progress" over a three-year period will be compared to that of the 11,000 luckier souls enrolled in Project Independence.

Gee, I wonder what the findings might be. Do you suppose a person who gets job training stands a slightly better chance of finding work than someone with no skills?

To answer this and other stumpers, The Manpower Demonstration Research Corp. of New York is being paid $2.4 million. The firm has conducted similar studies elsewhere, and claims that the results enable "workfare" programs to become more efficient.

That sounds like promotional hype, but let's assume it isn't. Let's assume the methodology is sound. If hope is snatched from a single destitute family, then the human cost of this experiment is too high.

Several legislators have joined sociologists in condemning the program as cruel and exploitative. HRS says the study is perfectly ethical.

Maybe a white rat wouldn't put up a fuss, but these are human beings chosen without their consent to be Group A—the have-nots. The selection process is supposedly random, a bleak lottery that will affect the lives of needy people from Dade, Broward and seven other counties. Between 15 and 25 percent of all who apply for the jobs program will be shunted to the control group.

Remember that the outcasts are fully eligible under the law to participate in Project Independence. They are being rejected purely because the state wants to see how they fare without this special help.

Wait until the have-nots discover that somebody is being paid $2.4 million to watch them scurry through the urban maze. It works out to about $436 for every man, woman and child in the control group. The Ford Foundation gave $400,000 to bankroll the study, while we taxpayers are providing the remaining $2 million.

There's nothing wrong with reviewing public assistance projects to see if they really work. Given the miserable history of welfare, it makes sense to take a hard look at each program—but not like this.

The HRS plan is misguided, wasteful, coldhearted and just plain dumb. What possible social insight can be gained by randomly denying opportunity to some indigents while rewarding others? And what do you tell the unlucky ones—sorry, folks, maybe next time?

As long as the Legislature is funding deprivation experiments on humans, here's an interesting one:

Make a random selection of state employees (say, the Secretary of HRS and his top staff) and take away their jobs for three years. No salaries, no state cars, no expense accounts, no health insurance, no pensions.

Then hire several thousand poor people (for, say, $2.4 million) to go around studying the dreary new lifestyle of Mr. Gregory Coler and his bureaucrats. Follow them to the grocery and the bank and the doctor's office. See how they're getting along with no money.

Certainly such innovative public servants wouldn't mind taking a turn being poor, in the name of science.

Prostitutes talk of risk—and addiction

May 14, 1990

Nine prostitutes gathered in the library of the Dade Women's Detention Center.

They talked about selling sex in the harrowing age of AIDS and crack cocaine. What they said was: Not much has changed. They carry protection. They get tested for the disease whenever they're in jail. Beyond that, it's business as usual. The johns don't seem too worried. Most of the time, they don't even want to put on a condom.

Victoria Brown, 26, arrested near Biscayne Boulevard: "If you're a heavy crack user, it doesn't matter if you've got AIDS or not. If you get in a car and the guy asks if you've got AIDS, are you gonna tell him the truth? No way. Not if you want to get paid."

By her own count, Victoria has been arrested 95 times on prostitution-related charges. She is 26 years old, a veteran of county jails.

Sun Kelly, a slender South Korean woman, makes $600 to $700 on Saturday nights—a sum envied by the others. Where does all the money go? "Smoke," Sun said. She's been a prostitute for 25 years.

Ask the group who else smokes rock, and they all raise their hands. "Crack cocaine," said one, "is the biggest pimp there ever was."

To explain their dangerous lifestyle, the women tell of enslaving drug habits and, often, a wretchedly brutal family past. Their customers usually have no such excuse. You see these idiots getting nabbed in police sweeps on the nightly news—blue-collar guys, professionals, Yuppies, college kids. Talk about mindless desperation. Talk about stupid.

A sample of what's out there: Of the nine prostitutes interviewed, most had used intravenous drugs. At least two women (one of them three months pregnant) had syphilis, while another had herpes. Most said they had been tested before for the AIDS virus—all negative, they said. But keep in mind: By the time the results of their latest tests are known, they'll be out turning tricks again.

From Victoria Brown: "I've had over 15 tests, and I never once found out the results." She says she'd quit if she were notified that she'd tested positive. That's what they all said. "I would commit suicide," added Linda McArthur. "I would take an OD of heroin and die." Said another: "I'd lock myself in a room and smoke myself to death."

But, tragically, prostitutes with AIDS often continue working. They have no place else to go—even if they're dying, even if they risk infecting others. The justice system keeps them for 30 days, maybe 60 days, that's about it.

Proposed laws that would keep infected prostitutes in custody have failed in the Legislature; it's doubtful such measures would survive a constitutional challenge. While it's a crime to give another person a sexual disease, prosecution is nearly impossible.

It is not a crime to be sick and alone on a street corner.

Roxcy Bolton, an activist who has been counseling abused women for years, says a halfway house is needed, a facility where AIDS-stricken prostitutes can go. It would be, in one sense, a hospice—a quiet place to die.

There's no assurance that all would choose to stay there, but the opportunity should exist. To continue putting these women back on the streets is madness.

"If something is wrong with me, I want to know," said Tina Green. A prostitute since age 13, she still has no plans to quit out of fear. "This is a career for me," she said.

Although statistics indicate the prostitute is more often the recipient than the transmitter of AIDS, the sexual act puts every customer at risk. And there are other victims of the trade, some of them truly innocent.

A year and a half ago, Victoria Brown went into labor while lying in a Miami crack house. She got to the hospital just in time, but didn't stay long.

"I left my baby in Jackson, and I never went back." She said she doesn't know what happened to the child, or where it is today.

Then she began to cry, and all the women—every one—cried with her.

Con artists hit the road to prey on old

May 23, 1990

The criminals we worry most about are crack dealers, armed robbers, rapists and murderers. This fear comes from living in urban America.

There's another kind of crook who is seldom caught, rarely prosecuted and almost never jailed. Yet his brand of crime is particularly cruel and predatory because it targets the elderly who live alone.

Every year gypsy criminals come scouting for victims in the Sun Belt. They knock on doors and offer bargain home repairs, roof sealing and driveway paving—work that's invariably shoddy and overpriced.

A more sinister ruse is the unarmed "home invasion"—one thief talks his way into a house and distracts the owner, while partners loot the place. In this way, hundreds of old people have lost all their money. In one month, 26 such gypsy burglaries were documented in the city of Miami; frequently the thieves pose as utility workers from FPL or Southern Bell.

Because court systems are already clogged, the traveling con artist is a low priority. The crime networks, though, are vast and well-organized webs that take in millions—and are more difficult to penetrate than the Mafia.

This week the Florida attorney general's office is holding a police seminar on Eastern European and American gypsies, as well as the "travelers," vagabond thieves of Irish, Scottish and English descent. (The notorious Williamsons of bogus roofing fame are Scottish travelers.)

Bunco cops know all the sad stories. The driveway paver whose "asphalt" is nothing but motor oil mixed with gravel. The "exterminator" who smuggles a piece of termite-eaten lumber into the attic and offers it as proof of infestation.

On the infrequent occasions that they're caught, gypsies and travelers rarely do time. Typically they offer full restitution in exchange for dropping the charges. "When they're arrested," said investigator John Wood, "they're usually the most polite, courteous people you'd ever want to meet."

Like everything else, it's an act. In addition to swindling the elderly, criminal gypsies go for insurance fraud, welfare cheating and shoplifting. They also excel at "store diversions" in which one family member creates a noisy scene while others empty the cash registers. This scheme netted $42,000 from one Chicago supermarket and has been used all over the country.

But these are the most tragic stories:

• A wheelchair-bound dialysis patient in Pinellas County found his house safe missing after gypsies "worked" on his roof.

• A wealthy 84-year-old widow in Houston was fleeced of $367,000 by Irish travelers who did only $2,500 worth of home repairs over 22 months. Police say the families passed the widow's name from one group to another because she was such an easy mark.

• Four gypsy women traveling through southern Ontario stole more than $500,000 from senior citizens during a three-month crime spree.

It's easy to dismiss the victims as gullible fools, but older folks are often intimidated into paying even if they don't want to. Commonly, gypsy roofers do the "work" first (usually a quick spray of useless paint), then demand an outrageous fee. If the victim balks, the clan members protest loudly and traipse through the home, searching for cash.

The "marks" are selected carefully. Almost always they are old, frail and alone. Because of failing eyesight or weak memories, they make poor witnesses in court. Humiliation and embarrassment discourage many victims from prosecuting. An 84-year-old widow who lost $44,000 in a gypsy burglary wanted to report the theft as only $100— she was afraid her relatives would put her in a nursing home if they learned the truth.

Miami officer Charlie Taylor, who specializes in tracking gypsy and traveler families: "When you talk to an old woman who's lost her entire life savings, it breaks your heart. What do you say to console her?"

Now is the season when the gypsies and traveler families start north, but police say they'll be back. Florida has been very good to them.

Without changes, nursing home neglect will occur

December 3, 1992

Imagine the scandal if 10 small children died, one by one, at the same day-care center.

The press would swarm like hornets, indictments would rain, and the dump would be nailed shut forever. Which is exactly what should happen.

It's different, though, when the dead are not so young.

A recent series in this newspaper exposed an appalling pattern of abuse, neglect and mysterious fatalities at state institutions, nursing homes and boarding homes. The victims were not babies but adults— the weak, the poor, the disabled, the elderly, the mentally impaired.

At one North Dade facility, the Landmark Learning Center, at least 10 patients have died under suspicious circumstances during recent years.

Among the casualties was a retarded paraplegic named Richard Daniels, killed by a blow to the abdomen. In some places that's called murder.

No one has been arrested for Daniels' death. Landmark claims he suffered the fatal injury by falling against the arm of his wheelchair—an explanation not embraced by the family, police or medical examiners. Meanwhile, Landmark remains open.

Administrator Ulysses Davis, who was temporarily relieved of command this week, said his facility had made no mistakes in treating patients, but added (in the understatement of the century): "There's always room for improvement."

More often it's not violence but pure neglect that kills. Earlier this year, a 48-year-old retarded woman died of a bowel obstruction that, according to investigators, wasn't noticed or properly treated by Landmark health workers. Another case: A 27-year-old woman died, riddled with cancer that Landmark doctors somehow failed to discern. Another: An epileptic patient died after a seizure on the floor; Landmark workers said they thought he was only taking a nap.

Unfortunately, such horror stories aren't uncommon. Across the state, old and disabled patients have been found half-starved, consumed by bedsores, crippled by undiagnosed bone fractures. Time and again nothing happens. Nothing changes.

Responsibility is tangled among too many state agencies. Weak laws make it hard to prosecute adult abuse cases, and harder still to shut down shabby nursing homes. Health-care workers, grossly underpaid and sometimes undertrained, are frequently reluctant to report patient abuse for fear of losing their jobs. The system is perfectly designed to perpetuate itself.

Right now, in the great state of Florida, a guy who kicks a dog stands a better chance of going to jail than someone who slugs an invalid in a nursing home.

People moved out of sight are also moved out of our consciousness. Often they are as helpless as children, as trusting as kittens. Yet it's almost as if, because they're grown-ups (not cuddly babies), their deaths are not so tragic or important.

True, people die every day in nursing homes. If it happens to your grandmother or grandfather, you pray that the end was peaceful and natural, that they weren't punched or starved or ignored to death. Because if they were, you stand little chance of getting the truth and virtually no chance of getting justice.

Government tends to react the way society does, with emotions deciding our priorities. When a child under HRS supervision is tortured by a monstrous parent, the reaction is an appropriate convulsion of outrage and cries for dramatic reform.

The death of Richard Daniels, age 43, is no less sickening. And he is but one of the forgotten.

That's why the case of Landmark Learning Center is so disgraceful. With the same track record, a day-care center would've been boarded up a long time ago.

For that matter, so would a kennel.

English-only repeal won't impose Spanish

May 16, 1993

Dade's so-called English-only ordinance will probably be repealed this week. The sky won't fall. The earth won't quake. And the Metro commission won't start conducting its meetings in Spanish.

Yet many will call it a sad day when the law is scrapped. Some warn that its repeal will legitimize ethnic separatism, dual languages dividing dual cultures. But if the English-only law was (as supporters insist) meant to unify Dade, it was a flop.

The ordinance was passed overwhelmingly in 1980 as native entrenchment against a tidal wave of foreign-speaking immigrants: All government meetings and publications were to be in English. So there!

Well, guess what happened in the next 12 years. Hispanics became a majority in Dade. The county's politics, culture and economy transformed—and plenty of folks didn't like it. Thousands packed up and left for Lake City or Ocala. They're still leaving, and it's understandable. Watching one's hometown change so radically is tough, confusing and often painful. Getting out is one solution.

Not all who stayed have adjusted easily. Some of us crackers won't ever get used to hearing Spanish at McDonald's. How come them people don't learn to speak American? In moments of impatience, I've had similar grouchy thoughts.

Then I remember all the money this newspaper spent trying to get some Spanish into my skull, with minimal results. Someone as linguistically stunted as myself is in no position to lecture anybody about learning a second tongue.

The message of the English-only law is that those who come to this country should adopt our language. That sounds fair, but the reality of mass immigration is another story.

Today, 57 percent of Dade residents speak something other than English at home. All those people are touched by government and need to be well-informed. As a practical matter, it would be irresponsible—no, idiotic—to neglect the thousands who haven't yet learned English, or can't. Societies that exclude people pay a terrible price, as we know firsthand.

Judging from the hysteria, some seem to think abolishing English-only is equivalent to imposing Spanish-only. That's absurd. The official language of Dade will always be English. We don't need a law saying so.

The ordinance is a relic of Anglo defiance that offends many Hispanics, bilingual or not. Citizens of Dade United says it's simply intended to save taxpayers money. Yet there's no mistaking the resentment from CODU's Enos Schera, who told the New York Times: "They have already established another Cuba inside Dade County, and now they are forcing Spanish down our throats."

Nobody's forcing Spanish down mine, nor would I force English down theirs. You can't. Assimilation happens at its own pace—and, believe it or not, it is happening here.

Bob Joffe, a well-known pollster, writes that "Spanish is dying among Hispanic voters" in Dade. What he means is that bilingualism is rising significantly. More than half of foreign-born Hispanic voters surveyed said they didn't care if they were interviewed in English or Spanish.

Such increasing fluency suggests that, 20 years from now, language won't be such a burning issue. Let's hope not, because it's the least of our troubles. Runaway growth, runaway crime, the water crisis, government waste—you want something heavy to worry about, take your pick.

Find people who can solve those problems, and it won't matter if they speak English, Spanish or Mandarin Chinese. We'll find an interpreter. It's not the language that counts, it's the ideas.

Safe parks act worthy of a vote

October 27, 1996

In a political season that can charitably be described as uninspiring, there is actually something worth voting for.

It's called the Safe Neighborhood Parks Act, one of the most promising crime-fighting ideas to reach a ballot in Dade County.

It won't build a single new prison cell, or put one more police officer on the beat. What it might do is take thousands of at-risk kids off the street and give them places to play.

Working with the nationally recognized Trust for Public Land, a grassroots citizens' coalition proposes to raise $200 million for improving about 170 county and neighborhood parks.

The money would come from a sale of general obligation bonds. Cost to the average Dade property owner: about $8 a year. "The price of a pizza," says Hank Adorno, a former prosecutor who is helping to lead the campaign.

State Attorney Katherine Fernandez Rundle and others believe the Safe Parks Act will cut juvenile crime, which is exploding in Dade at a chilling, almost inconceivable pace. They say more kids can be saved if they've got somewhere else to go, and something else to do.

No matter where you live, the parks program would touch your family: in Northwest Dade, soccer and softball fields at Amelia Earhart; in the Grove, refurbishment of the Virrick Gym; in South Dade, lights for the athletic field at Benito Juarez.

There's also money for the Haulover pier, the Crandon beaches, the campground at Greynolds and select purchases of open and threatened green space.

Each project is described on the Nov. 5 ballot—reading through the list would be worth a few minutes of your time.

It sounds almost too good to be true. And if you've been reading the headlines the last few months, the obvious question is: How much of the $200 million really will go to the parks, and how much will be diverted or stolen?

Says Adorno: "I think we've made it politician-proof."

The ordinance provides that the bond money can be used only for capital projects, not for operating costs, debts or exigencies. If a municipality doesn't budget enough funds to maintain a park, it won't receive anything for improvements.

An oversight committee of citizens will be appointed by the Metro Commission, to make sure that the monies are spent only on voter-approved projects, and that beachfront cabanas don't get priority over inner-city gyms.

The ordinance also calls for independent audits, and allows taxpayers to sue if the park funds are misused or ripped off.

That's not to say every penny will be safe from thieves and incompetents. It is Dade County, after all. The program is doomed without keen-eyed, fair-handed supervision.

But strong, overriding arguments favor the parks bond. First, it's been done before successfully, almost 25 years ago. A result was Tamiami Park, Tropical Park and Metrozoo, three of the county's most popular recreation sites.

Second, something tangible must be done for a generation of restless urban kids who are, in shocking numbers, turning to crime and gangs. The cost to taxpayers of incarcerating just one is $40,000 a year. The tab for a career felon is stratospheric.

So the Safe Neighborhood Parks Act becomes a community investment, as well as an act of faith.

Of course the juvenile crisis is too complex to be solved simply by lighting a basketball court or building a swimming pool. But if it keeps one kid off the street corners and out of trouble, that's a pretty good start.

Easily worth the price of a pizza.

Rules Are
Different Here

Stowaways ran in pursuit of their destiny

December 4, 1985

This fall, an Australian media tycoon named Rupert Murdoch was granted U.S. citizenship just so he could purchase seven television stations.

Last week, five Haitian stowaways seeking work in America arrived on a freighter in Fort Lauderdale. They weren't offered citizenship. They weren't even allowed off the boat.

In a scene straight from Victor Hugo, the men were left to swelter for days in an airless hellhole aboard the freighter *Alco Trader*.

The Bahamas, where they came from, didn't want them; neither did the United States. As both countries quarreled, the ship sloshed back and forth across the Gulf Stream, the stowaways its wretched prisoners.

This sad scene may be repeated in coming months as the Bahamas conducts a coldhearted purge of as many as 40,000 Haitians, many of whom have lived and worked in the islands for years.

For these Haitians, Florida is the next logical destiny, but there will be no parades for them here, either.

If the *Alco Trader* stowaways had been Cubans, Nicaraguans or Russians, you would have seen mobs of angry pickets and demonstrators. Congressmen would have lunged for the telephone, and the refugees would have been whisked to civilized quarters.

And if the stowaways seeking asylum had been Czechoslovakian tennis stars, you would have seen the red carpet rolling out; accommodations in the Hilton, not a hot box.

But Haitians have scant political clout and, so, are of scant use to those in high office. "They were treated like animals," says Father Tom Wenski of the Haitian Catholic Center. "What are they trying to come here for? For life. For a better life."

This country cannot absorb all the hemisphere's poor, but we also can't afford an immigration policy that is a contradictory mess. We speak in one voice to the rich and white, like Murdoch, and in another voice to the poor and black or brown. Meanwhile Congress remains unable to pass a cogent, equitable and humane law.

Haitians are shunned, yet millions of illegal Mexicans get work because Big Agriculture depends on them. Cubans are admitted as political refugees, while Haitians are rejected as "economic refugees"; in truth, there's little difference.

Haiti's stark poverty results partly from its despotic politics, a fact conveniently overlooked in Washington. President-for-Life Jean-Claude Duvalier is a friend and anti-Communist, and we do not upset our anti-Communist friends with talk of human rights.

But the plight of many Haitians is as pitiable as anything in Castro's Cuba; the poverty is more killing, and political persecution not only real but sometimes violent. This summer three Catholic priests were expelled from Haiti for speaking out against the Duvalier regime. A week ago three student protesters were shot to death by Haitian troops in the town of Gonaives.

If this is not repression, I'd love for someone at the State Department to tell me what is.

We Americans have a strange way of deciding who deserves to be in this country, and who doesn't. Citizen Murdoch wasn't fleeing political persecution in Australia; he came here to multiply his fortune.

Just like the Haitians in the cargo box.

Last Friday, the hot and hungry stowaways escaped from their stinking cell. It is unclear whether a guard looked the other way, or simply made a mistake, but I'd like to think the deed was the work of a compassionate heart.

Who can blame the men for escaping? I would have done the same; so would you. So would anyone with a shred of dignity.

If tradition holds, the refugees will soon find jobs, homes and sanctuary among 90,000 Haitian countrymen now living in South Florida. Much of the money they earn will be mailed home to poor relatives.

Somehow I feel better about the stowaways on the loose than I do about Rupert Murdoch.

Mass murders haunt Mayan asking refuge

June 27, 1986

Her name is Petrona Mateo Esteban. She is from Guatemala. She came to the United States because something horrible happened to her family in the highland village where she lived.

The United States says Petrona should not stay here, that it's safe for her to go home; there is a new government in Guatemala and things are looking up.

This week Petrona's deportation trial began in U.S. Immigration Court in Miami. It was a most unusual proceeding.

Petrona is a Kanjobal Indian, one of about 800 who have resettled in Indiantown as migrants. She is 26, and partially crippled from a childhood disease. She speaks neither English nor Spanish, only the unique Mayan dialect of her village.

The court interpreter, the only one to understand Kanjobal, had learned a language slightly different from Petrona's. Her story, painful to recall under any circumstances, became excruciating in Judge Neale Foster's court.

She wore a beautiful Mayan dress and sat impassively on the witness stand. Often she spoke in little more than a shy whisper. She tried to tell how they had practically skinned her father alive.

In 1982 Petrona's village, El Mul, was caught in Guatemala's vicious civil war. The guerrillas would raid the rural towns for food and chickens; then the army would sweep in, tracking the insurgents and punishing those thought to have aided them.

Defense attorney Peter Upton: "How do you know there was a war?"

Petrona: "Because the helicopters came by."

Q. "What were the helicopters doing?"

A. "They were dropping bombs and shooting bullets."

Later Upton asked: "Did the soldiers ever kill anyone in your family?"

A. "They came and killed my father . . . he was taken by them and beaten by them . . . It was 6 in the morning. We were sleeping at the time. They broke down the door."

Petrona said the army men seized her father and two brothers, Esteban and Alonzo, and dragged them away from the others. Alonzo was only 14. Petrona said the soldiers beat them with rifles and hacked them with machetes. She and her mother ran for their lives.

After the soldiers had gone, Petrona said, she came back and found her home burned to the ground. Her brothers and father lay dead. Her father's features were "destroyed." His hands had been bound behind him; Petrona untied the rope.

In all, 11 men were murdered in El Mul that morning. Petrona said she remembered their names, they were her neighbors: Tomas Augustin, his son Daniel, Miguel Jose, Mateo Martin, Esteban Martin, and so on.

After the massacre Petrona eventually fled to Mexico to pick cotton and coffee. From there she made her way to America.

She does not fully understand the politics of her country, but what she knows is this: Men with guns came from the hills and invaded her village. They stole her family's food. Other men in uniforms arrived and stole more. They also slaughtered her father.

As you might imagine, Petrona does not wish to go home.

Kathy Hersh of the American Friends Service Committee says of the Mayans: "They were really caught in the crossfire. They are apolitical. The government doesn't know what to do with them."

Six months ago Guatemala elected its first civilian government since 1966. The United States says this is a new leaf, that the military is enlisting "civil patrols" to improve its image and help battle insurgents. Unfortunately, more than 700 men and women have been murdered in political violence since the new regime came to power.

Petrona seeks asylum here. Her case, and those of other Mayans, probably won't be settled until early next year. The immigration court must decide if the Kanjobales would be singled out for violence if they returned home, if they have a well-founded fear of persecution.

What Petrona Mateo Esteban has is simply a well-founded fear of death.

You've got to have a racket to get asylum

January 8, 1988

Maybe the answer is tennis rackets.

I was wondering what it takes to convince U.S. immigration authorities that Haitians seeking political asylum in this country now have a legitimate claim.

Massacres of voters in the streets apparently are not sufficient evidence of persecution, nor is the assassination of a presidential candidate and attacks on his supporters.

After all the bloodshed and terror, Haitians fleeing to the United States are still being turned back, and many of those here still face deportation.

So I was wondering what it takes to be considered a political refugee, when along comes the case of Madalina Liliana Voinea. She is a 17-year-old tennis player from the Communist-bloc country of Romania.

You'll remember that, shortly before Christmas, Madalina came to Miami Beach to play in the Rolex International Tennis Championships at Flamingo Park. After a scheduling mix-up, she got in a cab, went to the Miami airport and asked for asylum.

You've never seen our government work so fast.

After a two-hour interview, INS district director Perry Rivkind decided that Madalina would face persecution if she went back to her homeland. Said Rivkind: "If she returned, she would be restricted from playing tennis, from going to college, and maybe she would be jailed."

Asylum was promptly granted, a press conference was called and a new media sweetheart was born. Madalina immediately got on a plane to New York, where, according to United Press International, she "spent the day shopping at Saks Fifth Avenue and strolling down Fifth Avenue admiring the window displays."

Personally, I wouldn't want to go back to Romania either, but the haste and fanfare with which the INS welcomed Madalina to America is puzzling to other applicants.

The usual criterion for granting political asylum is a "well-founded fear" of persecution. As human rights violations go, it's hard to compare a machete murder with somebody nixing a six-figure endorsement deal for Puma tennis sneakers.

Madalina came here courtesy of the Romanian government, which regards its promising young athletes as national assets, and treats them accordingly. Compared to most of her countrymen, she led the charmed life. Compared to Haitians, she lived in a paradise.

Based on the examples of Ivan Lendl and Martina Navratilova, it certainly will be easier for Madalina to become a millionaire as an American. This is true for athletes from practically any other country, Communist or not. Everyone wants to play in the United States because there's more money here.

Haiti doesn't produce many international tennis stars, as most people are too busy trying to find food and avoid getting shot by government-backed goons.

Given Madalina's case, if I were scheming to escape Haiti—and who wouldn't be, with the rigged election coming up?—the first thing I'd do is get myself an inexpensive tennis racket.

As soon as I got stopped by the Coast Guard or Border Patrol, I'd tell them that I was a budding tennis star, trying to make it to Wimbledon. I'd say that I could never go back to Haiti—not because of the gross political atrocities, but because they don't have any good grass courts.

What would the INS say to this? Imagine the scene if the next rickety boat to hit our beach delivered 200 people carrying Wilson tennis rackets and asking where's the next tournament.

Something tells me there would be no big press conferences, no happy feature stories, no trip to New York for a stroll down Fifth Avenue.

Somebody in Washington would come up with a new excuse as to why young Madalina Voinea is welcome, and the Haitians are not.

Maybe it would be the tennis rackets themselves. Maybe only refugees playing with graphite get asylum.

Immigration's double standard is an outrage

July 15, 1991

Sen. Connie Mack has arrived at the startling conclusion that U.S. immigration policy appears unfair in its disparate treatment of Haitian and Cuban refugees.

There's a real shocker. The Haitians have been getting shafted for only about a dozen years now. It's nice that somebody in Washington finally noticed.

Mack's moment of revelation came after two outrageous incidents made the double standard impossible to ignore.

On July 7, a Coast Guard cutter intercepted a wooden sailboat packed with 161 Haitian refugees and two Cuban rafters, whom the Haitians had rescued at sea. The Cubans were brought to Miami, while most of the Haitians were returned to Port-au-Prince.

Even the most cold-hearted bureaucrat could grasp the awful irony. To the Haitians on that creaky sailboat, the Cuban rafters must've seemed like kindred travelers—poor, like themselves, but brave enough to risk an ocean crossing in pursuit of a new life. Of course the Haitians would reach out and help; they shared the same dream.

Then with the interdiction came the bad news, and excuses: The Cubans get to stay because Cuba won't take them back. The Haitians have to go because Haiti will. So much for being good Samaritans. News of the refugees' plight sent a crackle of anger through Miami's Haitian community. This time the discrimination was so flagrant—and the juxtaposition so sad—that politicians had no place to hide. How could one seriously defend a policy that welcomed Cuban refugees but rejected the Haitians who had saved them?

Last week, a new spark erupted. All it took was one stark, indelible image on television: Haitian stowaways, manacled and caged on the hot deck of a freighter.

It could've been a flashback to the 1800s, when slave ships sailed the tropics. But this was 1991 in Miami, Florida. The United States of America.

Where men whose only crime was to seek a better future were being locked in chains.

The five stowaways were removed from the freighter and brought to the Haitian consulate. Arrangements were made to send them home. When immigration officers arrived to take them to the airport, the Haitians cried and struggled and begged to stay. In the scuffle, one managed to escape.

Most of that, too, was captured on television. It was painful to watch.

But if you stayed tuned a little longer, you saw another kind of immigration story, one with a cheerier angle. A young Cuban baseball player named Rene Arocha had defected to the United States, slipping away from his teammates during a stopover in Miami.

Now Arocha was being hailed as a hero, wined and dined and fitted with a new Italian suit and a silk necktie. No manacles on his wrists, no INS agents at his side. Arocha told reporters that he throws a 92 mph fastball. He said he wants to play in the major leagues. One of his former coaches called him "the Dwight Gooden of Cuba."

Back home, Arocha led a more comfortable and privileged life than many of his countrymen. He was not a political activist, just a ballplayer with a good right arm. He didn't leave Cuba to escape persecution, but to seek fortune. He said lots of other players would love to do the same thing.

And why not? In America, a 92 mph fastball is worth millions of dollars. A Wheaties commercial can't be far behind.

That Arocha will be allowed to stay is a foregone conclusion. INS looks favorably on sports celebrities. It matters little that he isn't a true political refugee; neither was Ivan Lendl or Martina Navratilova.

Destitute Haiti, not having an abundance of tennis courts or baseball diamonds, doesn't produce many tennis pros or big-league pitchers. But it is a place that, like Cuba, produces many brave dreamers.

To favor some over others is more than an injustice. It shames this country, and all of us whose ancestors made the same journey.

Racism adds to the pain of repatriations

February 2, 1992

The cutters are on the way, carrying hundreds of heartbroken souls to a place where mad-dog soldiers go on murder sprees.

Our own government admits as much. The U.S. ambassador to Haiti was briefly recalled in protest of bloody thuggery against a political candidate. Last week, for the first time, diplomats mentioned military intervention as a possible option.

Yet the Supreme Court, by a 6-3 vote, says the Haitians can be "repatriated," a sterile euphemism for what's really happening: They're being returned to the bowels of hell.

Many Floridians, though saddened, also feel a secret sense of relief. It's not because they're coldhearted xenophobes— they're not. They are simply weary and worried.

Miami has absorbed more immigrants, in a shorter time, than any city in recent history. The resources here are stretched dangerously beyond their limits. Schools are jammed. The county hospital is overwhelmed. The jails are overflowing. Decent, affordable housing is a fiction.

From a practical view, it's insane to accept thousands more refugees when we can't care for those who are already here. From a moral view, though, it's hard to defend slamming the door.

U.S. immigration laws are disgracefully riddled with double standards. If everyone were treated the same, we wouldn't have the depressing spectacle now unfolding in the Caribbean.

The Haitians' major disadvantage is being Haitian. If they were Mexicans, we'd invite them to pick lettuce in California. If they were Nicaraguans, we'd let them wait here until we're sure Managua is running a democracy. And if they were Cubans, they'd be welcomed the moment they were plucked from the sea.

For years, the INS defended itself with a standard line: Most Haitians trying to enter the United States were fleeing poverty, not political persecution. This made them deportable.

New events have turned U.S. policy inside out. Today Haiti is wracked by bloody turmoil, and Cuba's economy is rotting. Florida is receiving political refugees from Port-au-Prince and economic refugees from Havana. Language is the main difference between them.

You cannot separate tyranny from the despair it produces, whether the tyrant is named Duvalier or Castro. Like Cubans, Haitians are victims of generations of political oppression. It isn't fair for the law to treat them differently, but it does.

Think of the outcry if the Coast Guard began hauling Cuban rafters back to Havana, or shipped them to a sweltering barbed-wire camp! Every politician in South Florida would scream bloody murder.

Haitian refugees have few such powerful supporters. Sen. Connie Mack has spoken most strongly for their cause—but a sad cause it is, because there's no painless, or shameless, solution.

It would be folly to throw open our borders to all who are poor and hungry, or who suffer under a harsh, neglectful regime. We'd be swamped. Given a choice, half the hemisphere would pack up and move to Miami in a heartbeat.

But if we're firm about restricting immigration, then we also must be fair. Racist policies add to the pain of those we shut out, and to the misery of waiting relatives.

Today, U.S. strategy is to gild the double standards and set a stern example that will scare potential refugees. The sight of overcrowded American cutters pulling into Port-au-Prince harbor might deter future voyagers, but not for long. Dreams die hard on the coast of Haiti.

In a dozen tiny inlets, old boats are being patched, sails stitched, provisions hoarded. Men gather with nervous families. A captain arrives, and money changes hands—someone's life savings. Then the journey to Florida begins.

Those who fail the first time will surely try again.

Any sane person would.

Keep goodwill afloat at sea: Sink INS piracy

October 24, 1993

The newest pirate of the high seas doesn't even have a cannon.

It's the U.S. Immigration and Naturalization Service, which is extracting heavy booty from ships that rescue refugees at sea. Blackbeard himself would be envious.

Last week, crew members aboard the cruise liner *Royal Majesty,* sailing between Miami and Cozumel, Mexico, spotted a flare in the night sky. Using searchlights, Capt. Petro Maratos found a raft carrying eight Cuban refugees.

The men had been at sea for five days. Some were dehydrated and hallucinating. The *Royal Majesty* picked them up and took them to Key West.

For its act of kindness, the cruise ship now faces a $24,000 fine. That's $3,000 per rafter. According to INS policy, anybody who brings undocumented immigrants ashore is subject to monetary penalties.

For the *Royal Majesty,* it was the third time in two weeks that it had picked up Cuban refugees near the Florida coast. The first groups totaled 11 persons (including a young child), and the passenger liner was rewarded with a fine of $33,000.

The heavy penalties are meant to discourage alien smugglers, not humanitarians. But the practical effect of the INS action against the *Royal Majesty* is to deter all private American vessels from rushing to the aid of immigrants who face possible death on the water from starvation, sunstroke or drowning.

Whatever one's feelings about this country's screwed-up immigration rules, few would argue that a boat captain should ignore anyone's desperate cry for help, including refugees. Yet that's what is happening. Many rafters have reported that they were spotted—and passed—by several commercial and private vessels before finally being picked up.

It's not surprising, given the harshness of the INS fines. Maybe the cruise companies can afford a few thousand dollars here and there, but many shipowners can't.

Ironically, the oldest of maritime laws require sea captains to assist those in danger or distress. The INS seems to be encouraging just the opposite. It's nuts, like something from a Joseph Heller novel.

The awful consequence is that innocents will probably perish, if they haven't already, because some skippers are afraid to do the right thing. How anyone can turn his back on a child in a drifting raft or a wallowing old sailboat is almost beyond comprehension, but it happens.

The case of the *Royal Majesty* has its own sour irony. For years the cruise lines have been under fire for surreptitiously dumping garbage in the ocean, but the feds have seldom cracked down with the tough fines provided by law. Now comes a cruise ship captain who nobly attempts to save a few lives—and the government instantly hammers him for $57,000. Some message.

Although INS fines can be appealed, many boat owners don't have the time, patience or money to fight the bureaucracy. It seems a simpler matter—and one of basic human compassion—for the Clinton administration to revise immigration policy to allow rescues at sea, without fear of penalty for the rescuer.

A $3,000-a-head fine is certainly justified for alien smugglers who prey on Cubans, Haitians and other poor immigrants. The trade in human cargo is lucrative and sometimes brutal in Florida waters, and we need strict laws.

But it's indecent to punish honest captains and shipowners for undertaking legitimate rescue missions, often at considerable risk and expense. When a man is sick or parched or delirious from the sun, when he's in a sinking raft surrounded by sharks, there's only one thing to do.

You save him. You don't ask to see a visa.

Alpha 66 threats: New theatrics by inept militants

February 27, 1994

"Those who dare ignore our new appeal will tremble with fear at the violence of our actions."

That ominous little valentine was mailed from Alpha 66, the militant anti-Castro group, to an organization that ships humanitarian supplies to Cuba.

Alpha 66 doesn't want food and medicine sent to the island. The letter was a warning. The FBI says it's investigating.

Nothing will come of it. Nothing ever does. Few, least of all Fidel Castro, "tremble with fear" at the mention of Alpha 66. The group is good at threats, but not so good at actual terrorism.

Sincerity isn't the issue; competence is. Alpha 66 is famous for botching missions. If Barney Fife were a freedom fighter, this is the bunch he would join.

On Feb. 6, several Alpha commandos found themselves adrift in an 18-foot outboard off Miami. The boat carried an impressive cache: shotguns, AK-47s, pistols, a .50-caliber machine gun and 25,000 rounds of ammunition.

Everything one would need for a seagoing assault on Cuba—except a boat mechanic.

In a now-familiar scenario, the disabled vessel was towed to port by bemused Coast Guardsmen, who took away the group's weapons. Alpha 66 later provided the press with differing versions of the "mission," all heroic.

Who knows what they were really doing. The notion of loading an arsenal on a puny 18-footer and heading for Cuba is almost too absurd to be believed. Doing it on a Sunday, when the waters off Key Biscayne are full of innocent boaters, is just plain reckless.

Granted, it's tough to maintain credibility after decades of paramilitary actions that could charitably be described as ineffective. Remember the mock invasion of Elliott Key, when armed Alpha 66-ers wound up captured by park rangers?

Episodes like that don't help the cause. The urge to vindicate one's self with new dramatics must be tempting. Plans abound, but the execution remains flawed.

Thirteen months ago, the Coast Guard grabbed a load of arms, including grenade launchers, from an Alpha 66 boat off Cuba. Last May, Customs agents followed another craft with engine trouble to a marina in the Middle Keys, where they confiscated grenades, pipe bombs and heavy weapons.

Perhaps the group needs to invest less on weaponry, and more on boat maintenance.

Another weak spot is public relations. After the embarrassing bust in May, Alpha leaders declared that the boat had been on a "military mission" against targets in Cuba. That would be a major violation of U.S. law.

So, at trial, the story changed from one of patriotic bravery to one of ignorance. Lawyers for the commandos said their clients had no clue how the guns and explosives got stowed aboard their fishing boat. A Key West jury believed them.

Confusion also occurred last fall, after Alpha 66 warned that it would begin taking violent action against foreign tourists in Cuba.

The U.S. State Department condemned the manifesto and threatened federal prosecution. Alpha leaders asserted that attacks against visitors in Havana would be carried out not by Alpha's Miami wing, but by secret sympathizers on the island. As if that made it all right.

That the FBI tolerates such silliness proves that it doesn't take the group too seriously. But suppose a steering cable breaks on an explosive-laden Alpha 66 vessel, sending it crashing into innocent boaters in Government Cut. Given Alpha's checkered history, the scenario is not so far-fetched.

The feds should either prosecute these guys, or buy them brand new Evinrudes.

The other rafters suffer with silence

August 21, 1994

In the torrent of reaction to President Clinton's strict new policy toward Cuban refugees, scarcely a word has been uttered about the Haitians.

The same politicians now bellowing in outrage about the interdiction of Cuban rafters made not a peep of protest when Clinton took the same step to halt the influx of boat people from Haiti.

Today, at the U.S. Navy base in Guantanamo Bay, more than 15,000 Haitians are held in miserable detention. It's essentially one of the world's largest prisons.

Except when there's a riot, as there was recently, the Haitian detainees are mostly forgotten by the press and politicians. That's partly because nobody has a good idea what to do with them, or what to do about Haiti.

Just like the Cubans, the Haitians fled an economic nightmare caused by repression, corruption and a harsh U.S. trade embargo.

Like the Cubans, the Haitians were so desperate that they set out for Florida in flimsy, overcrowded crafts. And, like the Cubans, many perished on the journey.

There are differences. The Haitians have no special immigration law giving them status in the United States. Their exile community is smaller, and much weaker in political clout, than that of Cuban Americans.

And finally, of course, Haitians are black. You will never see, in your lifetime, a coalition of conservative Democrats and Republicans on the floor of Congress demanding automatic asylum for Haitians fleeing the Cedras regime. Never.

Yet most of the same right-wingers who vaguely demand that Clinton take stronger action against Fidel Castro oppose an invasion of Haiti. Why? Because very few votes—or campaign contributions—are to be gained from that position.

Those now blasting the president say he should focus not on the refugees, but on toppling Castro. But they don't say how.

We've already got an embargo—what about a military blockade? Brilliant.

The Haitian blockade has international approval. A blockade of Cuba doesn't, and wouldn't. Not only would it violate the trading rights of neutral nations, it would generate more misplaced sympathy for Fidel.

More importantly, a blockade is an act of war. Not even Bob Dole wants a war with Cuba; too many Americans would die. The truth is that, short of sending troops, only so much can be done to destabilize Castro.

In the meantime, it's insane not to protect our own borders. Stopping refugees at sea is a heartbreaking affair, but the alternative is to throw open the doors to every hungry soul in the Caribbean—not just Cubans and Haitians, but everybody.

Oh, we've got acres of open space . . . in Montana, Wyoming, Utah and Nevada. But Caribbean refugees tend to stay here in South Florida, and we're already jammed to the gills with people.

Another Mariel would be catastrophic. Florida would be swamped, and Castro would get a new lease on life.

Gov. Lawton Chiles was right to demand fast federal action, and Clinton was right to begin intercepting rafters. The word will quickly spread in Cuba, and the number of those taking to the sea will begin to drop.

Among Clinton's most venomous critics is the aptly named Newt Gingrich who, being from Georgia, has no firsthand experience with immigration problems. Newt says the new Cuba policy displays a "mixed morality."

As usual, Newt's confused. Mixed morality is imprisoning one group of economic refugees while welcoming others.

When Rep. Gingrich visits Guantanamo to show support for the Cubans detained there, perhaps he'll find time to chat with some Haitians as well.

They'll be the black ones, Newt. The ones you forgot about.

Protests create anger, gridlock—not friends

May 11, 1995

What a great idea for civil disobedience: Let's block an expressway!

Brilliant. Let's see how many thousands of working people we can tick off on a sweltering afternoon! Won't that help the cause!

The plan is to call attention to the fate of 13 rafters returned to Cuba by the U.S. government. And Monday's mess on State Road 836 did attract all the TV stations, as did Wednesday's multiple street blockades.

What the protesters have failed to anticipate is the fierce backlash. An elementary rule of protest: You don't win public support by antagonizing the public.

Those stuck in a man-made traffic morass aren't thinking about rafters or the implications of U.S. immigration policy.

They're thinking: Where are the cops? Why aren't these yahoos being hauled away?

They're thinking: I'm late for work. I might lose my job.

I'm late for court. I'm late for a sales meeting. I'm late for a doctor's appointment.

My children are waiting at the day-care center. My mother's waiting at home for her medical prescription.

My baby's in the car and it's 95 degrees out here.

What do these people think they're doing?

All over town, small numbers of Cuban-American protesters are staging "spontaneous" traffic blockages. Everyone else is out of patience. The havoc bred rancor, starting at the 836 tollbooth.

The public relations damage from such a brainless, inconsiderate stunt is incalculable. Those protesting President Clinton's new Cuba policy are a minority who ought to be trying to win converts, not alienate those who might otherwise be sympathetic.

I was a long blessed way from the traffic jams, but I know how drivers felt. What a senseless tragedy if some elderly motorist, trapped between exits, had died from a heart attack or a stroke.

Nothing is gained by disrupting the lives and livelihoods of ordinary folks who had nothing to do with the Cuba deal. It's infinitely more logical to hop a bus to Washington, D.C., and block traffic at the White House. Of course, the police there wouldn't be quite so tolerant.

That's the irony. Outside of Miami, hardly anybody in the country cares much about what's happening in Cuba. Polls show that more Americans are upset about the admission of the Guantanamo refugees than about the new repatriation policy.

In fact, a WPLG-Channel 10 poll reveals similar feelings here in Dade, including a sharp division within the Cuban-American community. The last thing that protesters can afford to do is undermine their support here at home, but that's what they do when they block traffic.

It's reckless, pointless and counterproductive.

Civil demonstrations are a core part of American democracy, and of the Miami exile movement. Marches and rallies take place frequently, and are almost always well-organized and nonviolent.

On Tuesday, a couple of local politicians, to show support for the refugees, got themselves peacefully arrested outside the White House. That's a tradition.

Another is the hunger strike, such as the one taking place outside the *Herald*. Equally irresistible to TV cameras, these protests make their point—and they make the 6 o'clock news.

Meanwhile, nobody's day gets snarled. Nobody's welfare is endangered. Nobody gets stuck in the hot sun. Nobody's fuming and cursing. Nobody's worried sick about their kids, their jobs or their doctor's appointments.

There are many ways to keep the passion and anger in political demonstrations without provoking scorn and hostility.

All those motorists stranded by protests were plenty angry, but not at Bill Clinton or Fidel Castro.

Flotilla really empty vessel of exile protest

August 31, 1995

On Saturday, another flotilla sets sail for Cuba.

The best thing that could happen is that nothing will happen. The worst thing that could happen is that somebody decides to be a martyr.

Organizer Ramon Saul Sanchez has promised there will no repeat of July's fiasco-at-sea, when flotilla vessels entered Cuba's territorial waters and defied government patrols.

That confrontation ended when a flotilla craft was intentionally side-swiped by Cuban gunboats—an incident that caused an uproar in Dade County and deafening silence in the court of world opinion.

Scarcely a peep of protest against Fidel Castro was heard outside Miami. Many foreign governments plainly felt the Cuban president showed restraint in not blasting the seafaring intruders out of the water.

World leaders who care nothing for Castro's regime will still defend Cuba's sovereign right to protect its own borders. That's why July's flotilla excursion was an international flop.

This time Castro says he won't be so patient with the exiles. Maybe he's bluffing, maybe not.

Last month, flotilla supporters in private planes buzzed downtown Havana in a deliberate breach of Cuban air space. Since then, anti-aircraft batteries have been placed near the harbor.

I don't care how good a pilot you are, a Cessna will only go so fast. Chuck Yeager himself wouldn't fly one over a machine-gun nest. Then again, Yeager never fantasized about martyrdom.

Whether any would-be martyrs join Saturday's flotilla is a big question. But if any protesters seriously think that getting themselves shot will galvanize the global community against Castro, they're foolishly mistaken.

Ramon Saul Sanchez, who once favored paramilitary action against Havana, now advocates nonviolent strategies in pushing for a democratic Cuba.

Yet his July flotilla, billed as a solemn and peaceable ceremony, disintegrated into a taunt. Its reckless cat-and-mouse tactics nearly provoked Castro's patrol commanders into unsheathing their heavy guns.

This time, Sanchez says, his boats won't cross Cuba's 12-mile territorial limit. But they will be carrying outboard-propelled inflatable rafts.

Twinkling with mischief, Sanchez won't divulge the mission of the little rafts. Presumably, protesters intend to dart into Cuban waters and do something—drop leaflets, shoot off flares, moon the gunboats. Who knows what.

The rest of the world will only shake their heads and wonder what's the point. The only one to gain from petty provocation is Fidel himself, who milks these moments for all they're worth.

Here I am, minding my own business, when those darn Miami exiles show up in planes and boats, picking another fight . . .

But turn on the radio in Dade County and you'll realize that, after 36 years, the mere act of annoying Castro is considered a great moral victory. It's sad, like a little kid who stands outside the window, making faces until he finally gets your attention.

A genuine heartfelt protest is one thing, invigorating in its dignity. But a prank is just a prank.

Nothing that takes place this weekend off Havana will bring Cuba one bit closer to democracy, or push Castro one day closer to exile, or move the suffering Cuban people one step nearer to freedom.

As thrilling as it might be to provoke Fidel's regime face to face, it accomplishes zero. The flotilla simply becomes a floating pep rally for one faction of the exile community and a dangerous pep rally at that.

In a battle against inflatable rafts, Castro's gunboats won't even need bullets. A knitting needle will do the job.

Immigration priorities are warped

January 8, 1998

Every kid who wants to get out of Cuba should be taking batting practice, because baseball is their best ticket to the United States.

Cuban pitcher Livan Hernandez defected and became a World Series hero. His half-brother Orlando escaped by boat to the Bahamas last week, and was promptly offered a humanitarian visa by U.S. officials. Soon he'll be playing in the majors.

No other country can match our mania for professional sports and the way we idolize athletes. It's an obsession that warps our immigration priorities, among others.

A Cuban jock has a better chance of getting into the United States than a Cuban doctor, engineer or schoolteacher does. That's hard to justify, and one reason for the mixed reaction in South Florida to the special way Orlando Hernandez was treated.

No one disputes that El Duque, as he is known, was persecuted in Cuba—kicked off the national baseball team after Livan's defection. Likewise, no one doubts that Orlando would have faced prison or other retribution from the Castro government had he been sent back.

That's exactly what has happened to others who were not blessed with a 90 mph fastball.

Three years ago, the United States began repatriating Cuban rafters intercepted on their way to Florida, a move designed to deter another chaotic Mariel exodus. The policy shift was necessary and overdue.

For a long time the United States had used a double standard for Caribbean refugees, routinely turning away Haitian boat people while accepting most Cubans without question. Yet the dream they carried on their journeys was the same: to escape economic hardship caused by political repression.

The world is full of people in similar grim predicaments. The United States cannot absorb them all, but it makes room each year for a fixed number from each country.

Exceptions to the rules are commonly made for sports stars. Ballplayers are always welcome. So are tennis prodigies and ice dancers and champion weight lifters.

These aren't political activists; they're jocks looking for a payday. Nothing wrong with that. Unfortunately, the same opportunity cannot be promised to everyone who wants to come here. It's just not possible.

Every year, 20,000 U.S. entry visas are offered in Havana, and the demand far outstrips the supply. El Duque turned down his special visa and is instead headed for Costa Rica, a move that allows him to negotiate more fruitfully with American baseball clubs. Soon he'll be rich, and good for him.

But I can't help thinking of a woman I met near Havana a few years ago. She lived in a small apartment with her husband, children and mother. Though she expressed no interest in moving to Miami, the woman had big-league credentials.

She couldn't throw a slider, but she was as valuable as any athlete for whom we've rolled out the red carpet.

This woman was an eye surgeon. She specialized in caring for children and the elderly. For her skill and dedication, she was rewarded by the Cuban government with a salary equivalent to about $5 a month.

In this country the woman would be wealthy, of course. In this country she could afford $5 for a daiquiri.

Still, she didn't speak of leaving Havana; she had her family and patients to think about.

But I'm wondering what would happen if she changed her mind; if she and her relatives ended up stranded on a Bahamian island, like Hernandez and his friends. I wonder whether anyone in Washington would make a fuss, or even notice.

I know visas are scarce, but maybe they'd let her use El Duque's. If not her, then maybe somebody like her. Somebody without a sports agent leading them to freedom.

The War on Drugs

Justice deposes the ruling king of cocaine wars

June 4, 1985

Say farewell to one of Dade County's most treacherous outlaws. His name is Conrado Valencia Zalgado, but he is better known as El Loco.

He was the original cocaine cowboy—a drug runner, machine gunner, bond jumper, high roller, master of disguise. In his prime, he made Pacino's Scarface look like Tommy Tune, but now Conrado's day is passed, his luck evaporated.

On May 22, a Dade County judge ordered El Loco to prison for the next century or so, thus closing a wild saga in our cavalcade of crime. For once, the good guys actually won.

Valencia was the bullet-headed, bare-chested maniac who hung from a speeding Audi and fired a submachine gun at rival coke peddlers on the Florida Turnpike Extension six years ago. When the cops caught up with the car, they found a dead Colombian named Jaime in the trunk.

Conrado, of course, professed total surprise.

Three months later, the late Jaime's friends retaliated, blasting two of El Loco's soldiers in the infamous Dadeland Massacre.

South Florida's image never fully recovered from that summer of 1979, and the torrent of national publicity that followed. Those of us who covered the cocaine wars imagined Dodge City reborn—each day seemed to bring a new atrocity, a new corpse (35 drug killings in one six-month stretch).

Along with their precious powder, the Colombians imported an astounding brand of violence. The crimes were almost impossible to solve—suspects and victims alike possessed an impenetrable array of fake names and phony passports. Among these alien gangsters, El Loco was a king.

After the turnpike shootout, he was charged with attempted murder and tossed in jail, but not for long. Conrado came up with the proverbial cash in a briefcase—$105,000 to be exact—posted bond and immediately disappeared.

He moved his family and his cocaine network to Los Angeles, where he became a laid-back Valley guy. He began calling himself Max, and cruised the Topanga Hills in a red 1948 DeSoto convertible (vanity tags, of course). He was having a swell time until some smart cops went through his garbage and found a phone bill with lots of calls to Miami.

From then on, El Loco's days were numbered. One summer night in 1982, Conrado Valencia opened the door to a girlfriend's apartment and wound up sucking on a gun barrel. A Los Angeles policeman was on the other end.

A few days later Metro-Dade detective Al Lopez and I went to California to see the legendary Loco. He was clanging around the Los Angeles County Jail in body manacles, and he was in a crummy mood. The cops out there had thrown the book at him; the cops back in Dade County were waiting their turn. El Loco didn't want to talk. Not to me, not to Lopez, not to anybody.

A California judge gave Conrado 30 years in prison, and last month he returned to Miami to face, at long last, the charges from the Turnpike shootout. He was convicted swiftly and on May 22, acting Circuit Judge Norman Gerstein sentenced "Jose Ramon Ruiz" (one of Conrado's many aliases) to 125 years.

Even if Loco escapes, which is always a possibility, he will find a different world awaiting him. The bloodiest era of the cocaine cowboys seems to be over, and flamboyant enforcers are less in demand. The word's gotten back to South America: Low profile means more profit.

True, cocaine is more plentiful now than in the summer of 1979, but at least the malls and highways are a little safer. These days most drug killers are polite enough to do their work in private.

Maybe that's the best we can hope for.

Adios, Conrado. Don't bother to write.

Dade's latest drug fight all wet—pass it around

November 5, 1985

Everybody sing: Ninety-nine bottles of — on the wall, ninety-nine bottles of —. Take one down, pass it around . . .

Congratulations, Dade County. No longer are we merely the Murder Capital of America; now we're the Specimen Capital, too.

First it was a couple hundred Miami police, proudly lining up to give samples to prove they're drug free. Not to be outdone, the Hialeah police followed suit. Next came the idea to test firefighters and even garbage collectors.

If they keep going at this rate, they're going to need a tanker truck to haul all this stuff away.

Lester Freeman of the Miami Citizens Against Crime has come up with the nuttiest scheme of all: All 52 MCAC members—staid bankers, lawyers, civic leaders, media honchos—are to have their exalted urine screened for drugs this week.

Curiously, the results will be reported anonymously, no names attached.

So much for this week's bizarre contribution to the national news: Miami's most prominent citizens cheerfully urinating into a cup to prove they're not whacked out on dope.

The point of this distasteful little charade? "A leadership demonstration," they say.

This isn't leadership, it's vaudeville. Is there another place in the civilized world where the Catholic archbishop has to urinate into a cup to prove he's clean?

As a member of MCAC, that's what the Rev. Edward McCarthy is going to do this week. Talk about trying the Lord's patience.

Who'd have expected such embarrassing publicity from the same folks so obsessed with purifying South Florida's image? Welcome to Miami. Give us your tired, your poor, your huddled masses—and how about some urine, while you're at it.

True, this kind of drug testing has become quite the national rage. The military uses it, and major league baseball wants to make it mandatory.

But a preplanned mass urinalysis is nothing but a gross publicity stunt. It doesn't prove you're honest. It doesn't prove you're competent. It doesn't even prove you're drug-free.

All it proves is that you know how to hit a cup.

Experts have contended that this kind of assembly-line testing can be unreliable, error-prone and unfair.

"The issue has become preposterous," says Dr. John P. Morgan of the Mount Sinai School of Medicine in New York. "It's like hunting Communists."

Dr. Morgan, who has written and testified extensively on mass urinalysis, says the most common type of test is flawed by "stunningly high false-positive results." The odds of a mistake are frequently compounded, he says, by incompetent lab work.

"God forbid you take the sample and mix it up with somebody else's. Or suppose you mismark one of the cups," adds Erich Gressmann, a toxicologist at the Dade County Medical Examiner's Office.

No wonder the MCAC doesn't want its members' names on these jars. There'd be hell to pay if Frank Borman's specimen somehow got mixed up with that of, say, rock musician David Crosby.

Even if the urine test is done correctly, it might show that you haven't snorted cocaine during the last 48 hours, or smoked a joint in a couple weeks, or dropped diazepam since yesterday morning. And that's all it shows.

And nobody in their right minds (Chuck Muncie being the possible exception) is going to voluntarily give a urine sample while he's flying high.

Mass urine testing is no way to get rid of crooked cops, and it's certainly no way for South Florida's civic pillars to demonstrate "leadership."

If they're so darn proud, maybe they ought to take the test in public. They could rent the Miami Beach Convention Hall, charge admission, maybe auction off a few celebrity specimens.

Call it Bladder-Mania.

Everybody sing . . .

'Cocaine' tea has bitter taste of controversy

January 13, 1986

As I write this, I'm wired to the gills on cocaine. Speeding like a bug-eyed banshee. Flying first-class on the David Crosby Express.

That's what urinalysis shows.

The only trouble is, I haven't touched any cocaine. Not a single toot. Is the test wrong? Technically, no.

But it's not right, either. Here's what happened and why it illustrates a hazard of drug-testing mania.

Last week you probably heard about Health Inca Tea, a Peruvian product sold in health food stores. Health Inca is an herbal tea made from coca leaves. "Just one cup leaves you feeling up," the box promises. The leaves are purportedly "decocainized" to remove the cocaine—the same process used for Coca-Cola.

However, the *Journal of the American Medical Association* recently reported that Health Inca Tea was not cocaine-free, and that traces of the drug turned up in urine samples of 36 tea drinkers.

The amount was quite small and not considered harmful for normal persons (Andean dwellers have been chewing coca leaves for centuries with no ill effects). But, as you might expect, some stooge in California drank 80 tea bags' worth of Health Inca and complained of "severe agitation." Surprise, surprise.

The reaction to the journal article was predictable. The DEA and FDA immediately announced plans to reassess the legality of Health Inca Tea, and wholesalers yanked crateloads out of circulation. Meanwhile, health food stores were inundated by consumers who generously offered to buy up all remaining coca tea bags (no doubt to keep them from the hands of impressionable youngsters).

The controversy was too crazy to pass up. The other day I bought one of the last boxes of Health Inca Tea from Beehive Natural Foods in South Miami. Dr. Lee Hearn, a well-known Miami toxicologist and drug expert, offered to test my urine after I drank the tea.

Honestly, this is not great stuff. My sister remarked that it smells like old lawn cuttings, and the taste is not dissimilar. The only way to choke it down is with honey.

Last Tuesday I drank less than two ounces. A day later I stopped by Dr. Hearn's lab to give a urine sample—sure enough, the test revealed minute but detectable traces of a cocaine metabolite.

The big experiment began: On Wednesday I drank five cups between 8:30 P.M. and 11:30 P.M. That's 35 ounces of tea. God hasn't invented the bladder that can hold 35 ounces of hot tea, so it was a long night.

According to the journal report, each tea bag contains 4.8 milligrams of cocaine. Five tea bags are roughly equivalent to one line of street cocaine.

After the first cup, I felt slightly peppy and that's all. Pulse: normal. Frankly, I get more of a buzz from a can of Pepsi.

Even after five cups I wasn't exactly hanging from the ceiling by my fingernails. I wasn't grinding my teeth. I wasn't paranoid and I wasn't euphoric. I wasn't even doing my party impression of Robin Leach.

What I was, was bloated. Slept like a log. Pulse: normal.

The experiment continued: Thursday, 6 A.M. Groggily I aimed for the little bottle. Then the ultimate etiquette question of the 1980s: Exactly how does one carry a urine sample?

I tried an inside pocket of my coat, but then I thought: What if I get in a messy car accident? People will think I'm bleeding this stuff.

Next I tried the glove compartment, but then I thought: What if the top of the bottle comes unscrewed? It would ruin my new ZZ Top tape, not to mention the auto warranty.

So I put the sample in my briefcase, which contains nothing of value, and drove to Toxicology Testing Service. On Friday Dr. Hearn called with the news: "A good strong positive."

Under both the common EMIT drug screen and the more sophisticated gas chromatography mass spectrometry, my urine tested positive. It showed cocaine and two related substances, benzoylecgonine and methylecgonine, the latter in such concentration that the test went off the scale, Dr. Hearn said.

"There was a bunch of cocaine," he said. "We found a complete pattern of someone who uses cocaine . . . a very high positive."

Except that all I had was coca tea, a legal product, purchased and consumed legally.

"It's not decocainized," Dr. Hearn asserted. The amount of cocaine in Health Inca Tea probably isn't enough to get you high, he said, adding, "The only thing it can do is get you in trouble."

Why? Because many companies and branches of the military automatically fire, discharge or refuse to hire anyone whose urine shows benzoylecgonine. Courts, employers and DUI prosecutors have long recognized this as proof that someone has used illicit cocaine.

But, as shown, that's not necessarily so.

An expert witness in many drug trials, Dr. Hearn had never heard of Health Inca Tea before last week. Most drug labs hadn't. It isn't known how many other such products are floating around.

Dr. Hearn plans more tests on the Health Inca brand. When he called the health food store to order a box, the price had jumped from $7 to $24—the true spirit of free enterprise!

I told my boss that I failed the drug test but he refused to fire me, even though it would have made a better ending to the column.

The real ending is not so funny.

With consternation Dr. Hearn described the current case of a U.S. Air Force man in Panama. The Air Force wants to dump him because his urine tested positive for cocaine. All along, the serviceman has insisted that he's never used the drug.

What he has done, he says, is drink a blend of coca tea, purchased regularly (and legally) at a small Panama shop.

Last week Dr. Hearn called Air Force investigators and told them to go find a box of that tea.

This time it's not a lark. This time a man's career is at stake.

TV drug raids rated a 'G'—for goofy

December 5, 1986

The other night, while watching Geraldo Rivera attempt his now-famous undercover TV drug deal, I found myself sort of wishing that some crazed doper would do us all a favor and shoot him.

Not kill him or anything truly serious—maybe just a flesh wound to the buttocks, though the irony of such an injury would have been lost on most viewers.

In case you missed the action, Rivera hosted a two-hour documentary that included live drug busts from several cities, including Pompano Beach and Miami. The audience got to see real-life footage of cops pulling their guns, busting down crack-house doors, handcuffing squirming suspects and seizing relatively minuscule amounts of dope.

I can't say it wasn't exciting—drug raids are. Whether staging one for a national television audience is smart law enforcement or self-serving hokum is another matter.

In Houston, for example, the big take was less than a gram of cocaine and an ounce of grass; on the positive side, a reporter there says it was the first time in recent memory that the sheriff had bothered to show up at a crime scene.

As expected, Rivera's toughest critics were those most intimate with the narcotics business. Lou Garcia, a retired smuggler I've known for several years, tuned in to Geraldo's performance Tuesday night and quickly became disgusted. "It was a joke," he said. "I didn't finish. I switched over to HBO."

The problem wasn't the subject matter, but the show biz approach. Rivera gets so excited by the sight of his own face on camera that he darn near hyperventilates. You want to put a cold compress on his forehead and make him lie down for a while.

The program's goofiest moment came when Geraldo announced that he was going undercover to do a drug deal himself. The first time, he looked like he was on his way to a casting call for Pirates of Penzance. You had to see this getup to appreciate it. As luck would have it, the drugs turned out to be fake, too.

The next time, Geraldo waited alone in a "plush" Fort Lauderdale hotel, where he posed as a cocaine customer from New York.

(Of all the police departments in the country, leave it to the Broward Sheriff's Office to go along with this nutty scheme. Imagine how they must have explained it to their liability lawyers: "OK, guys, what we thought we'd do is get one of the most recognizable TV journalists in America and let him go into a room to buy a kilo of coke from a bunch of armed criminals, just for fun . . .")

So guess what happened. The bad guy recognized Geraldo. And why not, since this time his entire disguise consisted of Brylcreem and a pair of sunglasses. He might as well have worn an ABC blazer and had Barbara Walters on his arm.

Anyway, after a bit of bluster the deal gets done, the cops burst in and Geraldo gets the last laugh. Afterward, a Broward detective chortles at the hapless coke peddler: "You're now the most famous dope dealer in America." Make that the dumbest dope dealer in America.

The apparent message of this little escapade is that any media yahoo can do a drug agent's job, though I'm not too sure. Last week a coke dealer opened fire on three DEA agents in Miami, and I'm kind of sorry Geraldo wasn't there to see how the part is really played.

Maybe *Media Vice Cops* will become an exciting new weekly series. I'm sure that Nick (Prime-Time) Navarro, the Broward sheriff, would happily sign on as celebrity technical adviser.

Personally, I'd tune in anytime to see Jane Pauley try an undercover drug deal. Granted, it would have to be an unusually perky drug deal, but I bet the Nielsens would be monstrous. Likewise Dan Rather could probably be persuaded to score a dime of black-tar heroin, if he were careful not to get beat up.

Pretty soon they'd all be lined up to take a turn undercover in the fast lane—Peter Jennings, Tom Brokaw, all the big shots, with the possible exception of Irving R. Levine. I don't think smugglers go for bow ties.

From Michigan, direct to you: drug-free urine

March 27, 1987

The job of a U.S. postal carrier grows more perilous every day.

A bottle of urine arrived in Wednesday's mail. The package was open; fortunately, the bottle was not.

I don't know whose urine it was, but I know whose it is now.

Mine. I paid for it—more precisely, the newspaper paid for it. And with all due modesty, I think this little gem belongs in the Expense Account Hall of Fame: "Two ounces of urine—$19.95."

People all over the country are buying other people's urine. The reason is to decoy drug tests, implemented by many companies to identify employees who have recently used marijuana, cocaine or other substances.

As the urinalysis craze grew, it was only a matter of time before somebody cashed in. In recent months several companies have sprung up offering "clean" urine to anyone who wants to pay for it.

The bottle that I ordered came in a brown envelope from a Michigan firm called Insurine Labs, a pioneer in this exciting new field. The urine-by-mail business is going so swimmingly that Insurine's founders say they've expanded the operation.

"It's a growth industry," says business manager Al Robinson. "We started it. We're No. 1. We send out a good product."

Since *Consumer Reports* has yet to test mail-order urine, and since I wasn't about to attempt any comparisons myself, I had to take Al's word on the quality issue.

"We've got distributors in 33 states," he went on. "We're franchising in Canada. We're in London."

I asked him where the stuff comes from. More to the point, who it comes from. "We've got two labs in California that hire donors," Al said. He described the donors as normal, healthy persons trying to make a little extra money. He said they get $5 a shot, but they don't get paid until the urine sample tests clean.

Each bottle arrives with a piece of paper stating that the urine contains no detectable amounts of amphetamines, barbiturates, methadone, opiates, metabolized cocaine, benzodiazepine or THC, the active ingredient in marijuana.

And at the bottom of the chart, highlighted (fittingly) in yellow magic marker, is this disclaimer: "THIS PRODUCT IS SOLD AS ADVERTISED AS A SPECIMEN ONLY. INSURINE LABS DOES NOT IMPLY OR SUGGEST THAT IT BE USED IN ANY UNLAWFUL OR IMPROPER MANNER."

I asked Al Robinson what his product might be used for, other than rigging a drug test. "People use it for what they want to use it for," he said. "They can wash their small car with it, you know what I mean?"

A second warning on the Insurine urine chart says: "NOT TO BE TAKEN INTERNALLY UNDER ANY CIRCUMSTANCES WHAT SO EVER [sic]."

So Al isn't taking any chances.

At first, he said, he and Insurine founder Meryl Podden considered the urine-selling scheme "a novelty." Originally they sold the samples for $49.95 "and there was no sales resistance at all. None."

The price came down with the competition. After Insurine was mentioned in U.S. News and World Report, orders shot through the roof. Al says the company is doing so well that he and Meryl decided to franchise, so they'd no longer have to do the shipping.

I said this sounded like the ideal set-up, not having to handle the stuff yourself.

Al said there have been no problems, no complaints from unsuspecting postmen. He said the packages must be sturdy to withstand the frigid Michigan winters. Each sample is sent in a clear plastic bottle with a screw top.

"They don't leak," Al added. "And there's no law against it. Nowhere in the country."

Customers who don't intend to use the sample for a drug test might have trouble deciding what else to do with it. As a gift idea it leaves something to be desired, though the bottle itself is attractive enough. A mischievous sort might be tempted to leave it on the cologne counter in a big department store, but of course this would be wrong.

Yacht-pot policy makes zero sense

May 11, 1988

Sleep well, America. Your borders are safe.

Last Saturday, the Coast Guard cutter *Tampa* seized a luxury yacht in the Yucatan Channel after a search turned up 1/10th of an ounce of marijuana, scarcely enough to roll a joint.

The capture of the 133-foot *Ark Royal* was executed under Operation Zero Tolerance, a new policy that encourages the Coast Guard to probe the crannies of private boats. Guardsmen spent the weekend stopping vessels in South Florida; eight have been seized locally, including a shrimp boat carrying a misdemeanor amount of pot.

This isn't Zero Tolerance, it's zero intelligence.

Of all the idiotic ways to waste money and manpower, this is one of the all-time tops. It ranks with the infamous Florida City Roadblock of 1982, when hundreds of cars northbound from the Keys were stopped and randomly searched for drugs and illegal aliens.

The roadblock resulted in only a few seizures, and the State Attorney's Office refused to prosecute because of constitutional questions. Out of pure embarrassment, the debacle was not repeated.

Now comes Zero Tolerance, which permits the confiscation of any vessel carrying even minuscule amounts of drugs. Forget the fundamental questions of guilt or innocence: Who had possession of the stuff? Who carried it on the boat? Did the owner even know?

The ostensible point is to punish recreational drug consumers for their role in the nation's hellish narcotics problem.

On Sunday the *Ark Royal* was towed to Key West amid much fanfare and many mini-cams. What a blow against the drug cartels: a swank $2.5 million yacht in tow, all because of 1/10th of an ounce of pot!

Before you start cheering, consider this: The *Ark Royal*'s owner was far away in California when his boat was seized. Not a shred of evidence connected him to the teaspoon of marijuana, or to any narcotics involvement. Yet he's the one who had to pay.

The Coast Guard returned the *Ark Royal* Tuesday, but what of the other Zero Tolerance cases? The U.S. government (meaning taxpayers) will spend a small fortune pursuing the seizures, only to get pounded in court.

The policy is rotten with holes: indiscriminate, inequitable, ineffective. Do charter captains now have to strip-search their customers before heading out for a day of deep-sea fishing? And what about the big cruise liners—why isn't the Coast Guard boarding the S.S. *Norway* for a cabin-by-cabin shakedown?

Taking Zero Tolerance to its logical extreme, perhaps we'll see a day when the Coasties confiscate one of our own aircraft carriers because some dumb sailor stashed a joint in his bunk. Think of what the U.S.S. *Nimitz* would bring at public auction!

The very idea of using the Coast Guard for this headline-grabbing nonsense is an insult to the men and women who serve in the agency. If search-and-rescue has been officially replaced by search-and-seizure, then at least let them go for tonnage, not tokers.

All this year we've heard the Coast Guard brass complaining about the $100 million shortfall in the current budget—a deficit that's forcing cutbacks in the agency's interdiction efforts.

But if this is what they wanted the money for, then their budget deserves to be hacked. Give the extra millions to the DEA, or to local police. Shut down some crack houses. Put some real smugglers in jail.

There's no question that casual drug users fuel the underground narcotics economy, but confiscating private boats—whether it's the Ark Royal or a leaky dinghy—won't change a thing. It certainly won't change anyone's mind about using grass or cocaine. That takes education, and education isn't as splashy as a fancy yacht.

Zero Tolerance is a stunt that displays the sinking desperation, and hypocrisy, of the so-called war on drugs. While Reagan's boys secretly negotiate a cushy exit for a dope-dealing tyrant in Panama, the Coast Guard is snooping after ski boats off Crandon Beach.

Drug czar would scare any pusher

June 24, 1988

Pablo Escobar and the rest of the South American drug barons are undoubtedly quaking in their Guccis, following the announcement that Florida soon will have a full-time "drug czar."

This promises to be a thrilling mission, at least the way Gov. Bob Martinez describes it.

He promises that the new czar will have broad responsibility for fighting narcotics on all fronts. The governor went so far as to say that the drug czar will have his very own task force, and that this task force will actually have the power to make "recommendations."

I can already hear those lily-livered liberals crying whoa, let's not get carried away! A task force is so . . . extreme—why not start with a committee, or maybe a small advisory board?

But I say bravo, Governor! Throw down the gauntlet. Take off the gloves. When the going gets tough, the tough make recommendations.

Martinez proposes urine testing for bus drivers and the death penalty for drug kingpins, and he stands the same chance of achieving either one. One of the governor's boldest ideas is to unleash the National Guard to do battle against the cocaine titans. This should certainly liven up those long weekends at the armory.

The governor was not terribly specific about exactly what the National Guard is supposed to do, but this is why you need a drug czar, to nail down the details.

Another important priority of the $60,000-a-year drug czar should be thinking up snazzy code names for investigations.

You've noticed that every major drug bust has a clever-sounding name to go with it—Operation Grouper, Operation Black Tuna, and so on. Unfortunately, after so many years and so many big cases, we're running short of catchy code words. Now you hear things like Operation Dead Flounder, or Zero Tolerance.

We desperately need a drug czar to make sure that all future nicknames sound good on TV and fit neatly into newspaper headlines.

"Czar" itself is a word that newspapers love because it's short, and it has a "z" in it. Headline writers almost never get to use the letter z, so in the months ahead you'll be seeing many news items such as: "Drug Czar Says Crack is Very Bad."

Or: "Czar to Smugglers: Stay Out of Florida!"

One of the czar's most vital jobs will be to call press conferences in order to "put the drug smugglers of the world on notice." This should be done at least twice every year.

One problem facing the new czar is that so many different law enforcement agencies are fighting Florida's drug war, it's hard to know who should get the praise for a big seizure.

To avoid having Customs and DEA and FDLE and the Coast Guard and the FBI and OCB and ATF trample each other dashing for the microphones at press conferences, we need a drug czar who can claim credit for each and every kilogram, and do the speaking for everybody.

We also need someone who knows something about camera angles, so that the contraband can be displayed in a fashion that is dramatic, without being garish.

To show that he means business, Gov. Martinez gave his new task force exactly seven months to come up with its first batch of recommendations. You can bet that Escobar and his pals are marking that time on their calendars, knowing that the clock is finally running out.

Of course, they should be careful not to confuse the Governor's Drug Czar's Task Force with the Vice President's South Florida Task Force, or the Blue Lightning Strike Force, or the Congressional Task Force, or the joint DEA-FBI Task Force, or the Joint Legislative-Executive Task Force, or any of the other nine jillion task forces already deployed in the war on drugs.

The usual cynics have implied that the czar/task force idea is nothing but a naked grab for publicity, but I don't buy it.

Ask any expert and he'll tell you that Gov. Martinez is so right. Winning the war on drugs is easier than any of us dreamed. All we really need is more bureaucracy.

Mason jars won't make roads safer

February 17, 1989

Great Moments in Urinalysis (continued):

Now Gov. Bob Martinez has proposed drug-testing for all first-time applicants for a Florida driver license. The screening would cost each driver an extra $30 and would be conducted one month before applying.

Again Bladder-Buster Bob has come up with an idea that commands headlines but defies logic and common sense. Our current driver system is hardly a triumph for public safety. Ask any state trooper about the thousands of licensed motorists who are hopelessly impaired without the influence of narcotics. They are simply inept.

Up at Emission Control, Martinez insists that urine tests for Florida drivers will deter drug use and weed out the serious abusers. Yet in its present form, his plan would do neither.

The flaws reflect either ignorance or naivete by two panels, one an "advisory council" and the other a "task force" assigned by the governor to tackle the drug problem. The gaps in the urine-testing program are bad enough, but the premise is based on a fantasy.

There's not a shred of good evidence—medical, sociological, criminal or otherwise—that mandatory preannounced drug screening either discourages or prevents abuse. Only a half-wit or a hapless addict is going to get loaded on the day before his urine test—and most users don't fall into either category.

Martinez is correct when he says that driving is a privilege, not a right. But he's daft if he thinks urinalysis of driver applicants is going to make for safer streets—not unless they invent a car with a spectrometer built into the dashboard; a car that won't start until the driver fills a specimen jar.

By far the most lethal drug is alcohol, but I didn't hear the governor explain how his new plan was going to keep drunks off the road. If Martinez is serious, why stop with a urine test? When a driver goes for his license, give him a Breathalyzer, too. It would make about as much as sense as what he's suggesting now.

In fact, the governor's urine screen for drivers is not a drug test so much as an intelligence test. Anybody who couldn't beat it is certainly too stupid to get behind the wheel of a car.

It's so simple. Lay off the coke for a couple days and your specimen will be as pure as a mountain stream. A month later, when you go for your driver license, your nostrils can sparkle like the valleys of Aspen but it won't matter, as long as you can parallel park.

And consider the estimated $30 that each driver will pay to get his urine analyzed. Under the most rigid clinical conditions, urinalysis is never error-free. Imagine the quality of the lab work when the state starts handing out contracts to hacks and phonies looking to cash in on the new gold rush.

The governor's plan to test new drivers means more than a million urine samples a year. At $30 a clip, that adds up to serious money. And in Florida, serious money attracts serious sleaze.

Don't be surprised if the same guys who used to peddle time shares and oil leases suddenly turn up in Tallahassee with white coats and a van full of Mason jars. And don't be surprised if they get a piece of the action.

A most mystifying aspect of Martinez's urine manifesto is that it applies only to first-time applicants for a driver license.

Though the governor exhibits grave concern about our drug-riddled workplaces and neighborhoods, notice that he doesn't suggest urine testing as a condition of license renewal for Florida's current 10 million drivers—which would include, coincidentally, most legislators, Cabinet members and Supreme Court justices, not to mention major campaign contributors.

Rather, Martinez's bold new attack on the drug plague focuses on two nefarious groups of would-be motorists—retirees moving to Florida and teenagers just turning 16.

For years lawmen have been scheming for a way to outwit these dope-crazed renegades, and now they've got the break they need.

So you wanna drive, huh? Then line up and tinkle, Gramps.

Cops making crack makes little sense

April 26, 1989

"It's sort of like making fudge."
—Lab director of the Broward Sheriff's Office, explaining his recipe for crack cocaine.

So Broward County is manufacturing its own crack. Why not? Nothing better illustrates the misguided, haphazard state of the so-called war on drugs.

Talk about mixed-up priorities. Talk about headline-grabbing. Talk about a Keystone Kops mentality. Naturally you're talking about Nick Navarro, Sheriff Willie Wonka himself.

Of all the goofball stunts he's tried (including his comical TV partnership with Geraldo Rivera), a crack factory is the screwiest of all.

In a seventh-floor lab of the Broward Sheriff's Office, a county chemist cooks up a plate of fresh crack cocaine. The crack is cut into $20 rocks, packaged in tiny plastic baggies and sold on the streets. Sold by cops. When people come up to buy, they get busted.

You might wonder why no other law enforcement agency in the country has tried this clever scheme. There are plenty of reasons, starting with common sense.

The technique by which undercover cops "sell" drugs is known as a reverse sting, tricky enough under the best of circumstances. Typically, police officers posing as drug sellers must display or "flash" a package of real dope to the prospective buyers. Once the deal is made and money changes hands, the cops can make the arrests.

The danger is obvious: rip-offs. The bad guys arrive not with cash, but with guns. The plan is to steal the cocaine and take off. This is what happened when Miami Beach officer Scott Rakow was murdered—a reverse sting gone bad. Years ago, DEA agents nearly lost a truckload of marijuana when a reverse sting turned into a bloody rip-off at a South Dade warehouse.

Suppose a Broward Sheriff's Office deputy trying to sell dope gets robbed, and suddenly some dirtbag is loose on the street, peddling Navarro-brand crack to school kids—crack manufactured by the same people who are supposed to be taking it off the streets.

Why is Broward cooking its own? Officers say they aren't confiscating enough crack to use in big drug stings. Not enough crack? Other urban police departments have no trouble seizing plenty. There's not exactly a shortage of the stuff, especially in South Florida.

Another problem is honesty. The Broward crack lab relies on the assumption that every officer who comes in contact with the cocaine will be straight and pure. In a dream world this might be true, but virtually every local law enforcement agency—from the DEA to the Sweetwater police—has suffered the scandal of drug corruption.

All it takes is one crooked cop and you've got more dope on the streets. Grade-A government dope.

An experienced DEA agent voices a different concern about cops making their own crack: What will happen when these cases go to court? If a fed-up judge trashes the Navarro scheme, it could affect all reverse-sting operations. Such a court decision—over a lousy $20 rock—could cripple many multimillion dollar cocaine investigations.

A second-year law student could have a field day attacking the crack lab: "And where did these drugs come from, Deputy Smith?"

"Uh, we made it ourselves."

"Really? So you manufactured the cocaine. You took it out on the street. You offered it to my client for sale. Yet my client is the one who gets arrested!"

The question that inevitably will be raised in court: By creating the drugs, are the cops creating the crime? Have they crossed the line between enforcement and entrapment? And for what—15 seconds of glory on the local news.

Imagine, in the days of Prohibition, if the government decided to open its own distillery. Brewed up a batch of hooch, bottled it, parked a truck on the streets of Chicago and offered everybody a snoot. You don't think the jails would have overflowed in two hours?

Blockbuster statistics, sure, and big headlines—but absolutely no dent in the problem.

Everybody expects cops to seize dope. Nobody expects them to make the stuff. Just try to convince a South Florida jury that there isn't enough crack out there already.

U.S. murder of drug lords invites chaos

June 12, 1989

Your Tax Dollars at Work (continued):

Last week, it was revealed that U.S. authorities are considering the launching of hit squads to assassinate drug kingpins in foreign countries.

A day later, the U.S. Customs Service announced that it had foiled an assassination attempt on the life of Colombian cocaine lord Pablo Escobar Gaviria.

I wish they'd make up their minds. Either it's all right to murder these guys, or it isn't.

In the first case, a couple of fine upstanding South Floridians were arrested on the turnpike with 23 MAC-11s, 18 AR-15 assault rifles, five machine guns and assorted other party favors, recently purchased from a Palm Beach County arms dealer.

The government says the weapons were on their way to Colombia to be used in an elaborate plot to snuff the elusive Mr. Escobar, a leader of the Medellin cocaine cartel. The killing was allegedly ordered by the rival Cali cartel, with whom Escobar has had long-running business disputes.

In announcing the weapons seizure, Customs officials conceded that a larger public service might have been achieved had the assassins been allowed to carry out their mission. However, there are still a few gun laws left in this country, and Customs felt morally compelled to enforce a couple.

In the meantime, U.S. Attorney Dexter Lehtinen (who had called his own press conference to announce the capture of another alleged cocaine gangster) went out of his way to chastise Customs for "leaking" the details of the Escobar escapade. This snippy exchange typifies the sort of selfless commitment and close interagency cooperation that has helped make the drug war the raging success that it is.

The joke of the week, though, belongs to those geniuses at the National Security Council who are now mapping plans to sneak into South America and murder suspected drug leaders. This ought to be a riot.

The idea is that by knocking off a couple of Escobars and Ochoas, we throw the cartels into chaos and disrupt the flow of cocaine. Absolute nonsense—but exactly the sort of James Bond theatrics that would appeal to desperate bureaucrats who don't know any better.

Certainly the cartels are led by evil, violent men, and certainly they have inflicted unfathomable misery on this country, as well as their own. But killing them will achieve nothing except to bring vicious retaliation against U.S. drug agents, diplomats and civilians in Colombia, Peru and Bolivia.

A man such as Escobar already lives in constant fear of being murdered by his own colleagues. He is protected by armed bodyguards, as well as by crooked cops and soldiers. Assuming a U.S.-backed hit squad could even get to him, it would almost inevitably cost American lives.

And for what? Within days of Escobar's death, there would be a new face at the top of cocaine's corporate ladder. The crops would still grow, the labs would still cook, the planes would still fly.

Look at the infamous Carlos Lehder. He was captured, extradited to America, tried, convicted, locked up forever—all without causing even the slightest dip in the supply of cocaine. Shooting him wouldn't have been any more effective. To the cartel, he was totally disposable.

Beyond the practical problems of a U.S. drug assassination are the diplomatic ones. In Bogota, sovereignty remains a passionate cause among lawmakers—if the overnight extradition of Lehder caused an uproar, imagine the reaction to the arrival of American killer commandos. Indeed, how would we react if the Colombian president sent undercover assassins to Florida?

William Bennett, the new drug czar, favors U.S. military strikes against foreign "narcoterrorists." If he thinks a hit squad in Medellin is going to solve the crack problem in Washington, he is sadly, pathetically deluded.

To put it in perspective: If Lee Iacocca dropped dead tomorrow, the Chryslers would keep on rolling off the assembly lines. The same holds true for Pablo Escobar and the busy cocaine factories of South America.

Bush fails to pay price of drug war

September 8, 1989

The good news is, we've finally got a president who seems to comprehend that cocaine poses a greater threat to this country than communism ever will.

The bad news is, we still don't have a president willing to pay for a real war on drugs.

Most of the $8 billion pledged by George Bush this week was already in the new budget. He asked for about $716 million in additional funds—peanuts, really, if you're seriously talking war.

Amazingly, Bush's budget director, Richard Darman, has suggested most of the new money should come out of social programs: aid to immigrants, grants for juvenile justice programs and subsidies for federal housing projects.

Brilliant thinking, Dick. Of all the places to scrounge for drug-fighting money, pilfer it from those most brutalized by crack: the young, the poor and minorities.

It's not like we don't have the funds for an all-out drug war; the money is there, and in sums greater than you can scarcely imagine. Billions and billions of dollars—$290 billion, as a matter of fact. Easy to find, too, right across the Potomac from the Capitol. Huge building called the Pentagon.

They've got one little program over there called the Strategic Defense Initiative, otherwise known as Star Wars—space lasers that are supposed to shield us from a nuclear attack. Lots of top-notch scientists don't think SDI can ever be made to work; others say it will be obsolete by the time it's ready to be implemented, well into the next century.

President Bush wants to spend $4.6 billion on Star Wars in the coming year, an increase of $600 million over the 1988 budget. What would happen if we put this program on hold for 12 months and used that money for the drug war?

Any way you cut it, $4.6 billion represents a substantial commitment. Think of all the prosecutors you could hire, all the prison cells you could build, all the rehab counselors you could train, all the children you could reach through new educational programs.

For the sake of argument, let's say Bush wants to leave Star Wars alone. Let's say a 12-month hiatus would disrupt research and development. Then let's look at another system that's supposedly finished, researched to perfection: the B-2 Stealth bomber.

Despite serious doubts by military experts as to whether this aircraft will be able to fool Soviet radar, the Pentagon wants to build 132 of them at a total price tag of about $70 billion. Each new plane supposedly will cost about $550 million.

Although defense contractors are notorious for underestimating, let's give them the benefit of the doubt. What if you took the money from just 10 new Stealths (say two a year, over the next five years) and applied it to the federal anti-drug budget? That's more than $1 billion a year that we aren't using now.

Given the choice, most Americans would want their tax dollars fighting crime on the streets, not floating around in outer space. There's no clear and present danger to compare with having a crack house on your block.

Money alone isn't going to end the cocaine wars, and many reasonable critics wonder if we haven't already squandered too many billions on a law enforcement strategy that has failed dismally. Yet there are signs that increased funding does make a difference, especially in the classroom. To claim that we simply don't have the money is nonsense; worse than that, it's hypocritical.

The money is there, if Congress and the president can find the courage to use it.

George Bush is smart enough to know that the political stakes have changed since Reagan, Carter and Nixon declared their wars on drugs. Today the streets are so frightening and cocaine crime is so prevalent that American voters are ready to blame somebody if things don't improve— and that somebody is likely to be the president.

Four years isn't enough time to stamp out crack, but it's enough to learn if George Bush means business. Judging by this week's announcement, war is heck.

BSO strikes again in battle of the bulge

December 17, 1990

Another true chronicle in America's War on Drugs:

An appeals court has rebuked the Broward Sheriff's Office for permitting female undercover officers to randomly search the crotches of airport travelers.

And you thought the Hare Krishnas were annoying.

For years now, eagle-eyed BSO deputies have been scouting for suspicious trouser bulges on the theory that drug smugglers often hide the booty between their legs. When a likely lump is located, the suspect is pulled aside and an official grope is conducted.

That's what happened to one Anthony Lewis Tognaci in 1987 while he waited for a USAir flight at Fort Lauderdale-Hollywood International Airport. Unknown to Tognaci, the dimensions of his groin had caught the eye of BSO Lt. Vicki Cutcliffe.

According to court records, Cutcliffe approached Tognaci after noticing an unusual prominence in his pants. Tognaci consented to a search, and while patting him down Cutcliffe felt something "crinkly" located "a little bit higher than where his male organs would be, normally."

The possibilities seemed limited.

The young man was taken away and strip-searched. Police found 112 grams of cocaine, and charged Tognaci with drug trafficking. He pleaded no contest and was sentenced to 3½ years.

He appealed the case, arguing that Lt. Cutcliffe's search "exceeded its scope." In a ruling handed down last week, the Fourth District Court of Appeal upheld Tognaci's conviction, saying "it is not clear from the evidence that the officer actually touched appellant's genitals."

However, the court expressed serious concerns about the BSO's crotch patrol, because travelers who consent to being searched aren't informed that it will focus on "this most private area of the body."

The judges also questioned the value of such methods in drug enforcement. They cited Lt. Cutcliffe's testimony that she had searched "hundreds of men's crotches without discovering any contraband."

Said the court: "We emphasize that these encounters are random, not generated by any articulable suspicion of wrongdoing, not by a drug courier profile, nor by a fear of the officer's safety."

Rather, the searches are motivated only by the contour of a suspect's pants. Sternly the judges added: "And at least based upon the hundreds of searches which not do not produce any drugs, we conclude from the testimony that the genital search is not a very effective investigative tool [the court's word, not mine] . . ."

For her part, Lt. Cutcliffe doesn't seem to mind below-the-belt surveillance. She said it's easier for her to do it because most male deputies are reluctant to search a male suspect so intimately.

Nonsmugglers seldom complain—flattered, perhaps, that the natural topography of their trousers made someone think they were carrying something extra.

Still, problems extend beyond the appellate court's Fourth Amendment concerns. Now that the BSO strategy has been publicized, lots of very lonely guys are probably heading for the Fort Lauderdale airport in the hopes of being frisked, and frisked slowly, by Lt. Cutcliffe.

Then there's the more delicate public-relations challenge. Some tourists who come to South Florida might not wish to be groped as they disembark. Should we warn them to wear baggy pants? To avoid crinkly underwear? To carry their cellular phones in a back pocket?

It's an unusual welcome, that's for sure. When you get off the plane in Hawaii, you get a lei around your neck. Here in Florida you get a hand on your zipper.

In spite of the court's warning, Sheriff Nick Navarro has announced no plans to terminate the crotch patrol. So if you're passing through the airport, don't be shocked if a female cop stops you and whispers: "Is that a kilo in your pants, or are you just glad to see me?"

Tourist Season

Only a fool fails to follow these rules

September 19, 1986

Florida's new tourism jingle is catching some flak, and this is too bad. The $4 million slogan, unveiled this week, is: "FLORIDA—The Rules Are Different Here."

This is the first honest tourist slogan we've had in a long time, and it's a shame that a few naysayers are picking on it. The rap against the new jingle is that people in the country's heartland might misconstrue the part about how "the rules are different here."

What's to misconstrue? Accept the phrase exactly for what it says and you have a public service announcement; a friendly warning, if you will. We should be delighted that our tourism promoters finally are taking a responsible approach.

Fort Lauderdale Police Chief Ron Cochran says the new tourist pitch is "about the dumbest thing I ever heard." He says it promotes an image of rampant lawlessness. I say it merely informs.

By way of counterattack, Beber, Silverstein, the agency that developed the Rules campaign, hired a big research company to go out and interview 11 New Yorkers to see if they were scared off by the jingle. Why it required a big research company to find 11 talkative New Yorkers I'm not sure. Naturally the New Yorkers said no, the slogan didn't scare them away from Florida. These people had all taken the subway to Yankee Stadium and obviously were not scared by anything.

The problem with the new go-Florida campaign is not the slogan, but some of the rules they dreamed up to go along with it. For instance: "You must remove your wingtips before going swimming."

Or: "You must get suntanned in a place you've never been tan before." Or: "You are required to watch at least one sunrise."

These rules are sort of cute—maybe not 4 million bucks worth of cute, but medium cute. Collectively, however, they hardly present the exotic, *Vice*-ish image of Florida that Yuppie travelers all over America are hungering for.

What potential tourists really need is some useful advice, because the rules down here are definitely different.

RULE NO. 1: You must remove your Beretta shoulder holster before going swimming.

RULE NO. 2: You must get wounded in a place you've never been wounded before.

RULE NO. 3: At spring break you must never stand for too long beneath a hotel full of drunken college kids.

RULE NO. 4: You must never stop on Interstate 95 to ask directions from a teenager holding a cinderblock.

RULE NO. 5: You are required to watch at least one sunrise, because that's what time the 10 P.M. Metrobus finally shows up.

RULE NO. 6: You must never light a cigar with 12 drums of pure ether in the back of your car.

RULE NO. 7: You must never wear your beeper into the sauna.

RULE NO. 8: You are required to take home at least a dozen giant Bufo toads as souvenir doorstops.

RULE NO. 9: You must stand in line for three hours outside Joe's Stone Crab, only to be mistakenly rounded up in a Border Patrol sweep of South Beach.

RULE NO. 10: You must never wear a tie to your arraignment.

RULE NO. 11: You must never, ever use your turn signal while changing lanes.

RULE NO. 12: You must never open your front door to a gang of armed men wearing police badges, black Raybans and rubber Ed Meese masks. You must never believe them if they tell you all Florida cops drive unmarked Maseratis.

RULE NO. 13: You must never carry correct change when going through a busy tollbooth, and always spend as much time as possible chatting with the cashier about which way Sea World is.

RULE NO. 14: At the first sight of an actual Florida alligator you must pull off the road and feed it enormous bags of Toll House cookies until it grows so tame that it eats your dachshund.

RULE NO. 15: You must not be alarmed to discover that two entire floors of your hotel have been rented out to the federal Witness Protection Program.

Auto trunks are no place to park bodies

January 21, 1987

Bust our buttons! This week's crime news brings another unique distinction to Dade County: The Car-Trunk Murder Capital of the United States.

Last year local automobile trunks yielded a record number of homicide victims (12), a statistic provoking comment from no less an authority than Dr. Joseph Davis, the unflappable chief medical examiner.

"Years ago," he reflected, "if you found somebody dead in a trunk, it was unusual. There was a great deal of interest. Now it's a ho-hum thing."

Your basic car-trunk case goes like this: Some poor soul is out walking his poodle or pulling into the shopping mall when he notices a Foul Odor emanating from another car.

Next the police are summoned, the trunk of the offending vehicle (usually a late-model, luxury sedan) is pried open and therein discovered one or more extremely dead persons who, more likely than not, have had a passing attachment to the narcotics trade.

A seamy spectacle, to be sure. "Not a pleasant scene to go to," says Metro-Dade detective Al Singleton.

"It's a bother," Dr. Davis agrees. "Another thing that's annoying . . . now you find a car parked at the airport—stinks to high heaven—and for some reason you have to wait six hours while they go find a judge to get a court order to open the thing up! Everybody knows there's a body inside."

Twelve car-trunkers out of 438 homicides is scarcely an epidemic, but for 1986 it certainly puts us at the head of the pack, per capita. (Admittedly, national statistics are somewhat elusive in this area. Believe it or not, most large metropolitan areas don't keep a separate category for car-trunk murders.)

Assuming that the illicit drug business will be with us for a long time, and assuming that a natural by-product of the business is murder, we can only conclude that the problem of corpse disposal will also persist.

On behalf of all hard-working homicide cops and coroners, I'd like to make a public plea for a moratorium on car-trunk murders.

1. It's a lazy and unimaginative method of getting rid of dead drug dealers. Granted, a few old Mafia traditionalists still use car trunks, but only because New York has so little open space for regular dumping.
2. The car-trunk method is rude and very annoying to everyone else in the neighborhood. It is the homicidal equivalent of not picking up after one's self.
3. It ruins a perfectly good car. A dead body in the trunk destroys the resale value of any automobile, with the possible exception of a Ford Pinto.

At the risk of sounding heartless, I really don't give a hoot how many dope dealers are killed by other dope dealers, as long as the deed occurs in private and poses no threat to the innocent.

Dade County had its famous spate of public machine-gunnings a few years back, but lately the bad guys have been more considerate about where they settle their disputes. A common preference is the remote dirt-road executions that my police friends so sensitively refer to as "Krome Avenue Specials."

For one unseemly stretch we also had a run on drug-related dismemberments in Biscayne Bay. Fortunately for the beach tourist industry, this trend abated quietly.

Experts are at a loss to explain the resurgence of the car-trunk method, but part of the blame belongs in Detroit. Back in the mid-'70s, when the gas crunch and Japanese imports forced U.S. automakers to go compact, you almost never read about dead bodies found in trunks. The trunks were just too darn small.

However, in the oil-glutted '80s, Ford, GM and Chrysler all increased production of mid- and full-sized cars—cars with roomy trunks. Drug assassins responded enthusiastically.

Says Dr. Davis: "It sure shows they have a lot of cars to spare."

Another good reason to ride the Metrorail.

Local leaders need to foster pride, not panic

July 20, 1987

Someone please administer heavy sedatives to certain downtown types so they will quit convulsing about the New York Times.

As everybody knows, the Times magazine published a cover story yesterday that asked the musical question: "Can Miami Save Itself?" The article was subtitled "A City Beset by Drugs and Violence."

Actually the headlines had little to do with the text of the article, but it was enough to provoke the usual gnashing of teeth among the Guardians of Our Sacred Tropical Image.

Indignantly they declared that the Times piece was "grossly exaggerated," a perfect description of their own reaction. They also whined that author Robert Sherrill downplayed the wonderfulness of Dade County while dredging up all that nasty old stuff about cocaine cowboys, Mariel murders and racial tensions.

This criticism is not only inaccurate, it's ludicrous. In assessing Miami's current national image, it is impossible not to discuss the indelible traumas of the early 1980s. If anything, Sherrill was merciful for not dwelling on more current events.

Consider a few everyday news items:

• The statewide prosecutor has publicly apologized for unknowingly buying stolen suits, which he said he needed to look nice for an upcoming corruption trial.

• The so-called River Cops case has swelled into the worst police scandal in local history—you now need a calculator to add up all the former city cops implicated in drug-rip-off-murder schemes.

• Meanwhile, a new group of international narco-assassins—these from Jamaica—has relocated its headquarters in Dade and Broward counties, where it's easy to get parts and servicing for their MAC-10s.

• To ensure that our Dodge City reputation never ebbs, many South Florida legislators backed a new state gun law that enables practically any glassy-eyed psychopath to arm himself on a whim.

• And, oh yes, the state attorney general recently was asked to give an opinion on whether animal sacrifices were permissible in Hialeah.

Image problem? What image problem? How could the *Times* suggest such a thing?

Face it, things get bizarre in these latitudes. Consequently, every magazine that strives for hipness has taken a crack at Miami—*Esquire*, *Vogue*, the *Village Voice*, the *New York Review of Books*, the *New Yorker*, and there will be more. Writers come down here because it's interesting, in the best and worst sense.

By now you'd think the Civic Pillars would have the brains to shrug it off, but no. The county manager, who had not yet read the *Times* article, boldly announced that "we're going to take a public stand." (Quick—call the networks. A public stand!)

Then, two days before the magazine actually appeared, an emergency meeting was convened at the Grand Bay Hotel to plot counterpublicity.

The session was closed to the public, so God only knows what was dreamed up. Perhaps it was a list of alternative headlines for submission to the *Times* corrections department: "Miami—We're Doing Our Best, So Lay Off!" Or: "A City Beset By Snotty Press Articles." Something mature like that.

In critiquing the *Times*' presentation, it should be noted that the magazine used a photograph of a mock drug bust staged by U.S. Customs. This was undeniably sloppy, but would a picture of the real thing have made the Chamber of Commerce any happier? Probably not.

The publicized summit at the Grand Bay Hotel accomplished at least one thing: It sold a heap of Sunday newspapers for the *New York Times*. If I were Publisher Sulzberger, I'd send citrus-scented thank-you notes to the whole Beacon Council.

For the record, Bob Sherrill's article does not portray Dade County as the sludge pit of the universe, so take your medicine and calm down. There's nothing wrong with civic pride, but civic panic is embarrassing.

Newsweek story glitz-wraps same old city

January 20, 1988

You probably noticed the restraint with which this paper greeted the current *Newsweek* cover story, bannering it across the front page like a new Soviet arms treaty. The reason is simple: Anytime anyone anywhere says anything nice about Dade County, it's front-page news.

Still shell-shocked from last summer's *New York Times* profile, local tourism honchos had huddled heavily sedated in underground bunkers to await the *Newsweek* piece, predictably titled: "Miami—America's Casablanca."

After a quick review, the boosters proclaimed the portrait to be darned near positive, and called off plans to mewl, sulk and fly to New York in protest.

The fact is, the content of the *Newsweek* story is not much different from what stirred up a storm last July in the *Times*. The real difference is the tropical caption and the pretty pictures.

Let's begin with the cover: There's the glorious new skyline (photographed at such a distance where you can't see all the vacant office space), set behind a tranquil Miami River (photographed at such an angle that the water somehow appears blue).

And no wonder everybody's celebrating! In three years this is the first nationally published picture of the Miami River that did not feature dead drug dealers on the end of a coroner's gaff.

Most of the other *Newsweek* photography is equally flattering—more skyline, a sunset, the Fontainebleau Hilton, a parade through Little Havana. As for dramatic photos of cocaine busts, there's just one teensy-weensy shot of a crack arrest. Big deal.

By contrast, the text itself mentions the C word no less than 12 times, including this passage: "You cannot understand Miami without understanding cocaine, either. Miami is supersaturated with cocaine and cocaine money."

Whoa there, Beacon Council, no need to panic. The very next sentence puts an upbeat spin on the drug climate: "The point many tourists overlook, however, is that the core of Miami's cocaine problem is on the wholesale, not retail level."

So bring the kiddies on down!

Any national story about Dade County must also be rated by the PAN factor—the ratio of positive to negative adjectives. My friend Tom Morganthau, who wrote the main Newsweek story, obviously plundered Roget's in search of superlatives.

At one point he calls Miami an "almost lunatic concatenation of ethnicity, glitz and restless energy." Since Tom is one of only three persons in the whole universe who know what "concatenation" means, he might be forced to defend himself solely on the "lunatic" issue.

A sample of the positive adjectives used to depict Dade County include "unique," "bustling," "prosperous," "newfangled," "proud," "jazzy," "cocky," "mellow," "multicultural," "exciting," "exotic" and "sensuous."

The only thoroughly negative adjective: "dangerous."

Unfortunately, according to the South Florida PAN factor, one lousy "dangerous" in a big magazine article wipes out "unique" and "bustling" and even "exciting"—but that still leaves "exotic" and "sensuous."

Which brings up this Casablanca business.

Miami is everything Newsweek says it is, but if I read one more story calling it America's Casablanca, I'm going to start a petition drive.

In fact, Miami is not at all like Casablanca. For one thing, the handgun laws are much tougher there.

Despite the glow, Newsweek did not overlook our poverty, discrimination, culture clashes or crime. While noting a decline in the homicide rate, the magazine observed that "no sane Dade County resident leaves his door unlocked."

Though true, this comment will not inspire cartwheels among our local image shepherds, nor will the sub-headline characterizing Miami as a "city of wheelers, dealers and refugees."

That's the bad news.

The good news is, they put in a map.

Super Bowl boosters in taxi tizzy

November 21, 1988

Pre-Super Bowl panic has already set in among the custodians of Miami's national image. The first targets of reform are taxi drivers, who are being coached, cajoled and strong-armed into a show of manners.

The dread of tourism officials is that a vulnerable visitor (and we all know how sensitive football fans can be) might encounter a gruff or opportunistic cabbie.

In truth, the odds of this happening are no greater than that of being gouged for a hotel room, gouged for game tickets, gouged for lousy food and, finally, gouged for dopey souvenirs such as official Super Bowl ashtrays and official Super Bowl kazoos.

Which is to say that the prime mission of Super Bowl Week is to separate the tourist from as much of his money as can be pried from his pale little paws.

It is demonstrably easier to accomplish this gentle larceny if one is courteous to the victim during the act. Thus, the urgency of the Miami Nice campaign.

If you wondered why no special courtesy classes for taxi drivers are held in the off-season, the answer is simple: There's no reason to impress the locals.

If you live here and have to call a cab, it's probably because your car was stolen, the bus broke down, you're miles from the Metrorail and you desperately need to get away from some place (say, the scene of a major felony). At this point, you don't really care whether the taxi driver is nice or not, as long as he knows the accelerator from the brake.

As any airport traveler can attest, Dade County has some excellent cabbies, and it also has some cretinous loons. With the Super Bowl blitz bearing down on us, the Metro Commission is considering a schedule of fines to penalize taxi drivers for sins against tourists.

These are absolutely real:

- $50 for failure to maintain neat appearance.
- $200 for smoking without the customer's permission.
- $200 for soliciting tips.
- $200 for abusive language.
- $50 if the cab has a broken air conditioner.
- $50 for a dirty trunk.
- $200 for taking the longest route in order to hike up the fare.
- (my personal favorite) $200 if the driver is carrying a deadly weapon.

Currently, taxi industry officials are negotiating the amounts of these fines with the Metro staff. The preliminary plan is all right, as far as it goes. However, the commission needs to expand the list of fines to include other possible taxi-tourist confrontations:

- $200 for charging passengers "per kilo" of luggage.
- $150 for having a body in the trunk.
- $75 for soliciting tips with a deadly weapon.
- $200 for abusing customers in two or more languages.
- $100 for taking the "Homestead By-Pass" to Miami Beach.
- $50 for cleaning livestock on the dashboard without the passenger's permission.
- $75 for asking the customer to give you a back rub and a quick pedicure.
- $50 for hanging more than one soiled undershirt from the antenna.
- $100 for forcing riders to stand up in the back seat so you can "play Popemobile" along Biscayne Boulevard.
- $150 for bragging to passengers about the results of your latest urinalysis.
- $75 for failure to scrape slow-footed windshield washers off your grille.

The civil penalties suggested by Metro sound tough, but they won't make our streets any nicer. No sane tourist is going to hang around South Florida long enough (or return at a later date) to testify against a rude cabbie—especially a rude cabbie who carries a gun.

Besides, smart taxi drivers know that they don't have to fleece out-of-town passengers or hustle big tips to make a fortune during Super Bowl Week.

All they've got to do is pick up their customer on game day and head out to Joe Robbie Stadium. It's a gold mine, stuck in that wretched quagmire of traffic, watching the meter run and run and run.

Sometimes, dolphins get wrong idea

February 9, 1990

Add this to the list of bizarre things that South Florida tourists can worry about: getting goosed by Flipper.

Strange but true. It has happened at Florida Keys attractions where customers are allowed to get into the water with captive bottlenose dolphins. Usually the dolphins are well-behaved, but occasionally adult males become sexually aroused and make their intentions known.

This is one reason that Florida's Department of Natural Resources has recommended banning swim-with-the-dolphin programs. In a controversial report to the National Marine Fisheries Service, the DNR says that closing the swim shows will prevent injuries to humans, protect the dolphins from catching human diseases and discourage the taking of the marine mammals from the wild.

Operators of Florida's three attractions—Dolphin Plus in Key Largo, Theater of the Sea in Islamorada and the Dolphin Research Center on Grassy Key—say the swim programs are educational and harmless.

They are also profitable. Theater of the Sea charges $50 to swim with the dolphins. For another $50 you can buy a videotape of your dolphin encounter.

If you're not careful, that video could be rated X.

Alan Huff of the state marine lab in St. Petersburg says there are no reliable statistics about "negative incidents" at the dolphin parks, but adds: "We do know that older male dolphins become less trainable and exhibit behavior that is undesirable for a swim program." This includes physical aggression as well as sexual overtures.

A Miami legal secretary who was recently accosted said trainers had warned her of the possibility. In the dolphin mating ritual, it's known as an "erection roll." The male flips the female over and . . . well, you can guess the rest.

Soon after entering the water, the secretary noticed that one of the dolphins was rubbing against her in an unmistakably amorous way. "He liked me a lot," she recalled. Suddenly the animal spun her in the water and swam across her back.

"The guy's yelling, 'Roll with it! Roll with it!' I'm going, 'What the hell's going on? Get him away from me!' I was really scared." It's not easy to say no to 700 pounds of tumescent porpoise.

The swim shows in the Keys forbid customers from grabbing or bothering the dolphins, but sometimes the animals get ideas of their own. They can be aloof, or extremely sociable.

Some animal rights advocates say the mammals are being exploited, which is nothing new. Porpoise shows have been a staple of Florida tourism for decades. Is swimming with a tourist any worse than jumping through a Hula Hoop for a hunk of dead mullet? Probably not.

What's more, doctors have reported great progress among disabled and retarded children who've been allowed to interact with the Keys porpoises.

Getting in the water with these magnificent animals is a thrill, but usually more for the humans than the dolphins. If you were to jump into Biscayne Bay near a wild school, it would most likely head for Bimini. Porpoises remain far less fascinated by us than we are by them.

While there are only four dolphin swim attractions in the country, some experts fear they will proliferate because of the money. Imagine the disaster if every tacky oceanside motel decided to buy a Flipper and invite tourists in for $50 a dip. Fortunately, regulations on the capture and display of marine mammals are fairly strict.

Within a few weeks, the U.S. government will decide what to do about the swim programs. Many feel the DNR's position is too harsh.

For example, Dr. Gregory Bossart, a veterinary pathologist at the Miami Seaquarium, says there is no evidence that diseases can be easily transmitted between dolphins and humans. But he also believes that swim programs must be rigidly controlled and each dolphin carefully selected for participation.

"Some are real friendly, some aren't," he says. "Personally, I would be hesitant about getting in the water with some of the male dolphins I know."

Will we end up swallowing this new tax?

April 2, 1990

Everything you need to know about the latest version of Metro's proposed 2 percent food-and-beverage tax:

Q. Where does the money go?

A. The estimated $3.5 million in annual revenue will go to tourism.

Q. Wait a second. Wasn't part of the tax supposed to pay for a new drug treatment center, and economic redevelopment in the black community?

A. You're thinking of the old tax, the one they screwed up last time. The new tax is just for the tourism industry.

Q. Why do we need a tax to promote that?

A. The Greater Miami Convention and Visitors Bureau says the money is necessary to finance a national advertising campaign to attract more tourists to South Florida . . .

Q. Wait a second. The convention bureau—isn't that the same bunch who spent $500,000 moving into lavish new offices?

A. Well, yeah—

Q. The same bunch who spent $270,000 on a fish-tank display at a travel convention in Budapest?

A. Hey, it was a very impressive fish tank—

Q. The same bunch who was literally going broke this time last year, borrowing $1 million to cover their red ink? And the top guy, George Kirkland—wasn't he the one who charged the bureau for $1,000-a-night hotel rooms in Europe?

A. Yeah, but—

Q. Well, no wonder they need the dough.

A. Hold on, now. Mr. Kirkland recently left to take another job . . .

Q. What—gone already? Boy, he really fell head-over-heels in love with Miami, huh?

A. The point is, it's a new day with bold new leadership. The tourism people say we need this tax money to promote South Florida in a competitive national market.

Q. What's the big problem with our image?

A. Oh, the usual. Crime, drugs, poverty, corruption, chronic racial and ethnic tensions. Nothing that a catchy new slogan won't obscure.

Q. Other big cities such as New York and Chicago have similar social problems. How do these places attract so many tourists?

A. One word: sophistication. For example, in other major cities, civic leaders rarely have their semiautomatic assault rifles stolen from their bedrooms. Also, they tend not to name public streets after cocaine dealers. In Dade County, such recurring incidents have created an undesirable kind of national publicity.

Q. Say the tax passes. What if they waste the money on some really goofy advertising campaign, like: "Come to Miami! Sun, Surf—and DEA on Every Corner!"

A. Hey, that's not half-bad. Let me get a pencil.

Q. Seriously, how do we know they aren't going to spend the $3.5 million on more fish tanks in Budapest?

A. Don't worry. They'd never take a great idea like that and beat it into the ground.

Q. So, how does this new food tax differ from all the others that were proposed?

A. Apparently somebody's actually read this one.

Q. What businesses will be affected by the tax?

A. The new tax should apply only to hotels and motels, though you can never be sure. Last time we were told that only large restaurants would be affected, when in fact all establishments with liquor licenses would have been taxed.

Q. How did such a monumental fiasco happen?

A. No one seems to know. The Metro commissioners say they were never told precisely what the food tax would do. The lobbyists who were paid big bucks to push for the tax said they were too darn busy to examine it closely. Meanwhile the county attorney swears that he knew what it said all along, but no one ever asked him to explain—

Q. Whoa, back up. Do you mean to say that these geniuses were going to vote on a tax they didn't even understand?

A. That's about the size of it.

Q. So, how do we know they aren't pulling the same stunt again?

A. Hmmmm. That's a good question.

Q. Well?

A. I'm thinking, I'm thinking.

Santeria ritual not quite to tourists' tastes

On a recent drug raid in Northwest Dade, police discovered the messy remains of chickens, turtles and a headless goat. "I don't know what all this represents," mused a police spokesman, "but I know it's alarming."

A few days later, at the other end of the county, a policeman heard screams from a suburban house. He rushed inside to find a woman allegedly decapitating a chicken and drinking its blood.

In both cases, the cops had interrupted a Santeria ceremony in which live animals were being sacrificed to appease Afro-Cuban saints. Each saint is said to have its own preferred menu. Yemaya, for instance, favors ducks, turtles and goats. Ogun, a saint of iron, has a thing for red and white roosters. Oshun, the maiden of the river, prefers white hens.

By now, practically everyone in South Florida is aware of Santeria. The occasional dead chicken in a back yard canal scarcely merits a second glance. Not long ago, my son went fishing for peacock bass near the Miami airport. He caught no bass, but reeled in a hefty headless chicken wrapped in men's underwear, which he sportingly released to fight again another day.

For locals, it's nothing new. Visitors are something else. Many have no knowledge of Santeria and are confused and even revulsed by random encounters with gutted livestock. Image-wise, South Florida has enough to worry about without trying to explain the prevalence of animal sacrifices. The most ingenious advertising agency in the world couldn't put a positive spin on decapitated turtles.

Recently one of those true-life TV cop shows assigned a camera crew to ride with a Dade County animal-control officer. Almost immediately the officer came upon a sacrificed goat, whose body segments had been arranged on a railroad crossing, along with some blood and pennies. As the video rolled, the officer calmly explained the meaning of the grisly scene—a Santeria offering to Ogun, of course.

Just one more thing for South Florida tourists to fret about. Martha, call Hertz. See if our collision insurance covers dead goats.

Once I visited a young santera, a practitioner of the rites. She was thoughtful and, by all appearances, sane and normal. When she described the technique by which barnyard animals were sacrificed in her kitchen, she spoke of it as matter-of-factly as if recounting the family recipe for meat loaf.

Unfortunately, what appeals most to Santeria followers—the ability to practice the religion in the privacy of their homes—is what bothers many of their neighbors. The praying and prostrating before statues is no problem. It's the business with animals, which can get sloppy and noisy and (if overpublicized) can play hell with property values. For most of us, the killing of chickens is tolerable as a distant abstraction. When we buy a bucket of Extra Crispy, we really don't mourn the dead fryers who gave their legs, breasts and thighs for our lunch.

On the other hand—call it hypocrisy, call it a cultural gap—most of us aren't too thrilled when one of our kids bursts through the door and says, "Can I spend the night at Billy's? His mom's going to kill a rooster and drink its blood!"

Many of the creatures used in Santeria are eaten, but some are not. The leftovers often turn up in public places. This can be bad for neighborhood relations. What we need down here is a new category of zoning: AS-residential. Animal sacrifices would be permitted there, and no place else. Every home would have its own incinerator.

It would be no comfort to the poor animals, of course. As long as people believe in Santeria, critters will die. For what, I'm not sure.

Years ago, a mad-dog drug killer and fugitive named Miguel Miranda built a Santeria shrine in his back yard in South Miami. There he sacrificed animals, drank their blood and prayed for the gods to protect him from police.

Miguel must've been using defective chickens. The DEA shot him in the head.

Tourists: Be alert for crime Miami-style

August 19, 1991

The Greater Miami Chamber of Commerce needs $40,000 for a project that might save lives: a new brochure that will advise tourists how not to become the victims of crime.

This is a milestone in the annals of South Florida promotion. Finally the chamber is admitting, in writing, that there is a crime problem. It's a small brave step, and let's hope it gets done. Forty grand is peanuts compared to the millions spent to subsidize auto races, tennis tournaments and Super Bowls.

A few weeks ago, Hertz and other rental companies began unbolting the logos from their cars because so many customers had been attacked by smash-and-grab robbers. Tourists, unfortunately, make prime targets.

"Don't leave your common sense at home!" the new brochure tells visitors. Keep your car doors locked and your windows up at all times. Don't pick up hitchhikers. Be careful when using ATM machines. If confronted by an armed robber, don't resist. If a suspicious person approaches you at an intersection, look both ways before running the red light.

It's solid generic advice that applies to traveling in any big American city. Miami, though, is different from other big cities. Before the new pamphlet goes to press, some of the warnings should be modified to fit our unique style of crime.

From the moment a tourist steps off the plane at Miami International, he or she must be vigilant and alert:

• If someone offers you $5,000 to carry his "grandmother's suitcase" through Customs, don't do it.

• When renting a car, check the trunk for dead bodies. If you find one, tell the rental agent immediately—not only are you entitled to a different car, but also to a free upgrade from compact to midsize.

• If you're taking a taxi, beware of drivers who speak fluent English. They're obviously novices who couldn't find Coconut Grove with a cruise missile. Once you select a taxi, though, be courteous and tip generously. Recently a local cabbie was convicted of beating a customer to death in a dispute over a fare.

• Choose a hotel carefully, and remember: Location isn't everything. If the block is cordoned off with bright yellow tape, ask your driver to recommend another place.

• When checking in, ask the desk clerk to put your belongings in the safe—not just your valuables, everything. Underwear, dental floss, sunblock . . . gone when you get back. (A friend recently had his shoes stolen from his room at a very famous Miami Beach hotel. He was told that it happens all the time; apparently there's a booming underground market for used footwear.)

• When going outdoors, try not to dress like a typical hayseed tourist. For instance, don't wear black socks under your sandals, and don't tape one of those tiny plastic sun shields over your nose. And that $800 Nikon dangling from your neck might as well be a neon sign that says, "Mug Me!"

• When playing on the beach, don't leave cash hidden in your tennis shoes. As noted before, shoes get stolen.

• Be wary of roadside peddlers, common at South Florida intersections. If you're really in the mood for fresh guavas, fine. But if a guy comes at your car with a cinderblock, assume he's not trying to sell it to you. Step on the gas.

• If you must carry a purse or wallet during your visit to Miami, experts recommend securing it to your torso with a sturdy 42-inch length of galvanized chain and a single-action Master padlock. Arc welding is an optional precaution.

• No Rolexes, even fakes. Among thieves, these are almost as popular as secondhand shoes.

• When boating in the Atlantic, don't pick up any bales, floating duffel bags or plastic packages. These are often marked, "Made in Medellin."

• On the highway, be careful of police impersonators. Even with a blue flashing light on the dashboard, it's unlikely that a 1968 Fairlane with no hubcaps is being driven by a real cop. Don't stop until you find one.

Finally, when asking strangers for directions, don't ever begin the conversation with the words, "Hi, we're from out-of-town . . ."

Tourist crime not too bad—(just ignore facts)

February 28, 1993

An emergency panel convened last week to tackle the problem of crime against tourists. The topic wasn't just the shootings, beatings, robberies and carjackings committed daily on visitors, but the resulting international uproar.

Contrary to the harsh publicity, law enforcement officials insisted that less than 4 percent of all crimes target "nonresidents" of Florida. That means the overwhelming majority of victims are folks who live here full-time. That comforting statistic is seldom mentioned in the local and foreign news media, which the governor chastised for "hyping" the crime situation, scaring potential tourists away.

The criticism is well-aimed and overdue. For too long we journalists have thoughtlessly put our obligation to report the facts ahead of our larger civic duty to promote Florida as a carefree vacation paradise, regardless of its homicidal perils.

What were we thinking! What possible good can come from telling the whole darn world that innocent visitors are being stalked like stray zebras on the Serengeti?

OK, maybe a few tourists who read these stories will be more careful and alert. Maybe a few watchful ones will avert a mugging, or a trip to the E.R. But what about those timorous souls who see the grisly headlines and bolt for the airport? Whether they're from Berlin or Biloxi, we should make them feel welcome and safe, even if it means "rethinking" the way we cover crime.

Good journalism isn't always good boosterism. We must strive for a balance. No reporter should sleep easily, knowing that he or she might be responsible for a single vacant hotel room, an unrented LeBaron, an empty table at the Strand. We shouldn't be scaring tourists away, even if it saves their lives.

I'm not proud to admit it, but only weeks ago I wrote a column describing a number of gruesome attacks committed against tourists this year. Never mind that the stories were true; it was hyping, pure and simple. I realize that now.

In the future, the watchword is restraint. It's possible to convey even the most harrowing events in a manner that won't stampede our tourist trade. Call it reverse sensationalism.

The old cheap hype: A couple visiting from Germany was the target of a violent carjacking in Fort Lauderdale on Saturday . . .

The new slick hype: A couple visiting from Germany was stranded Saturday when they involuntarily loaned their rental car to several armed strangers, who forgot to return it.

The old cheap hype: Two British tourists were attacked by a gang of smash-and-grab robbers Saturday after stopping at a downtown Miami intersection . . .

The new slick hype: Two nonresidents were shaken but unharmed Saturday after a 13-pound cinder block mysteriously fell from the sky and crashed through the windshield of their rental car at a downtown Miami intersection. After hearing the noise, several neighborhood youths climbed into the car, apparently to make certain that no one was injured. In the confusion, the two startled visitors misplaced their wallets, credit cards, jewelry and camera . . .

The old cheap hype: A vacationing Ontario businessman was shot and wounded Saturday night during an attempted robbery outside a Miami Beach nightclub.

The new slick hype: A plucky Ontario haberdasher was recovering at Mount Sinai Hospital late Saturday after a minor flesh wound interrupted a night of dancing on South Beach.

Police quickly pointed out that of all the victims shot countywide this weekend, 96 percent were not tourists, and almost all were more seriously injured than the visiting Canadian.

Now, isn't that better? Don't you feel safer already?

Fish tales fly in face of logic, but pass 'em on

July 22, 1993

Recent news stories have exposed another harrowing menace to tourists. Giant rogue barracudas are leaping from the sea to mangle unsuspecting boaters, then flopping back into the water to resume their diabolical stalk.

Could it be true!

The first attack happened July 9 in Islamorada. A 46-year-old Tampa woman was badly lacerated after a barracuda rocketed from the depths of Florida Bay and knocked her to the deck of a houseboat.

Anecdotal evidence suggests that the fish was probably jumping, as barracudas often do, in an attempt to rid itself of an angler's hook. That somewhat pertinent possibility escaped mention in the first news accounts, which depicted the incident as a bizarre and premeditated assault.

Best of all, the length of the deranged barracuda was soberly reported as eight feet—the supernatural equivalent of, say, a 90-pound squirrel.

By the time this newspaper delved into the fish story, it was too late to stem the hype. The barracuda's victim had granted an exclusive interview to ABC's *Good Morning America*, so an entire breakfasting nation got to hear the terrifying tale and view the actual sutures.

For those of us who have devoted our lives to scaring people away from Florida, it was a magic moment.

In the past, periodic creature attacks—sharks, gators, snakes, etc.—rated attention mainly from breathless local TV anchors and junky tabloid shows. But this was the big time! This was a legitimate network program embracing the legend of the mutant barracuda and beaming it into millions of households. You can't put a price on that kind of publicity.

And almost immediately the phones began to jangle with reports of other horrifying attacks. An Alabama man, fishing in Bradenton, was said to have incurred minor wounds when struck by a leaping 'cuda. A wire-service account quoted a "shark expert" in Gainesville as saying the incident was "an amazing fluke. I've never even heard of [barracudas] jumping out of the water."

Not in Gainesville, anyway.

The fact is, barracudas are adroit jumpers, especially in pursuit of bait fish. The theory that they would utilize this talent to terrorize tourists is intriguing, but far-fetched. Seasoned fishermen and charter captains crack up at the notion of a killer 'cuda, stealthily circling a boatload of pink-skinned visitors who peer innocently into the brine, adjusting their rented snorkels for that first, fateful dive . . .

Yet I would urge native Floridians not to rush forward and punch holes in such a valuable myth. If people choose to believe that a primordial genetic code has gone haywire, and that a normally indifferent ocean species has turned savagely against humans (particularly those visiting from out-of-town), then by all means let them believe it.

To intervene with dull facts would only squander a prime opportunity. The appetite for weird Florida news is obviously so insatiable that the national media is ready to jump on any story, no matter how flimsy. We must ride the momentum, and keep the barracuda panic alive. Keep the calls and letters coming.

It's been years since *Jaws* was a hit, but lots of people still carry a phobia about sharks. The 'cuda scare has even greater potential because the "attacks" occur out of the water.

No one would be safe from flying barracudas. A splash, a gleam of silver—and suddenly a volleyballer on South Beach is scalped, mid-spike. Two lovers, minced beyond recognition during a midnight stroll on the jetty. A tawny young rollerblader, brutally truncated while skating along a seawall.

Would it ever end? For God's sake, somebody do something. Somebody call Spielberg.

Crime coverage based on how far tourist traveled

January 16, 1994

The new tourist season brings anxiety and trepidation, as South Florida braces for more rotten publicity about crime.

During the past week, visitors from Chile, Bolivia and Switzerland were assaulted by robbers in the Miami area. Although nobody was killed or seriously injured, the incidents received exhaustive news coverage.

Many Floridians are perplexed by the sensational attention these robberies are getting. Smash-and-grabs have been happening for years, and ordinarily they don't make the news. These days it's a lead story.

We in the media should come clean and explain our new guidelines for covering crime. Simply put: If it happens to a tourist, it's a major story. If it happens to a local . . . well, tough luck.

As victims, tourists draw more sympathy. Locals get mugged and shot on a nightly basis; the presumption is that we ought to expect it. Tourists, however, arrive in Florida with a certain sunny innocence. The presumption is that criminals ought to cut them a break.

In fact, that seems to be happening. Metro-Dade Police report that robberies of tourists have declined sharply since last spring. The figures have drawn media notice and applause from the chambers of commerce.

Buried in the stories was the fact that the total number of robberies in Dade has actually increased, meaning the thugs are merely redirecting their felonious energies toward local residents. No one seems terribly concerned. The coverage of tourist crime offers a revealing lesson in competitive journalism.

Not all tourists are equal in the eyes of the media. Foreign tourists are more valuable than domestic tourists, news-wise. The more exotic the tourist, the bigger the story.

One rule is: The farther a person travels to come here, the more significant it is when he or she gets mugged. For example, the robbery of a British couple is automatically more newsworthy than the robbery of, say, golfers from Atlanta.

The accepted method of rating tourist crime is the well-established Fitz-Sanchez Scale, which relies on both geographic and cultural disparities:

• Category One Tourists are those from Great Britain, France, Germany, Spain, Scandinavia, Brazil, Chile, Australia, Japan and the Falkland Islands.

• Category Two Tourists are from Canada, the Bahamas, Colombia, Bolivia, Peru, Panama, Mexico and Jamaica.

• Category Three Tourists are from Nebraska, Kansas, Iowa, North Dakota, South Dakota, Maine and the Amish country of western Pennsylvania.

• Category Four Tourists are from the Sunbelt.

• Category Five Tourists are from New York, which means they're practically local.

• Category Six Tourists are from elsewhere in Florida, and of marginal news value.

In our quest to report every single offense committed against tourists, we have conveniently broadened definitions. A "tourist" is no longer just a person who comes for vacation; it can also be somebody who's down here to see relatives, or make airplane connections.

When we're not really sure why they're in Florida, we refer to them as "visitors." This catch-all term suggests the same innocence as "tourists," and generates the same public outrage.

Some locals complain that the new obsession with tourist crime is rooted mainly in economic panic. True, robbers tend to steal from our winter visitors the thing we Floridians cherish most—their money.

But only a hard-core cynic would insinuate that our interest in protecting tourists stems from anything but true compassion. Someday, if we've got any left over, we'll show the same concern for the folks who live here year-round.

Blacking out Channel 7 unplugs the local color

June 5, 1994

Thousands of tourists are being deprived of one of South Florida's greatest cultural treasures, the nightly newscast on WSVN-Channel 7.

To protest the station's preoccupation with crime, some hotels have begun blocking WSVN's news from their guests' rooms. This stringent step is being taken to guard the tender sensibilities of visitors, in the same way that grown-ups lock the cable box so the kids won't sneak a peek at the Playboy Channel.

The Continental Cos., which owns several local hotels, declared that it was fed up with WSVN's nightly dose of violent video. Another hotelier complained that tourists "look at Channel 7, and they're afraid to go out on the street."

So what? Many folks who live here are afraid to go out on the streets, and it's got nothing to do with Channel 7. It's that evening lullaby of semiautomatic gunfire and police sirens that tends to discourage social excursions in some neighborhoods.

True, on a slow news day, anchor Rick Sanchez can make a routine domestic shooting sound like a sniper attack on an orphanage. But any out-of-towner who doesn't recognize silly hype when he sees it deserves to be scared out of his trousers.

Queasy tourists we don't need. Give us the tough ones. The wily and the battle-hardened. The adventurers.

The hotels' contention that one reckless TV station can frighten off business is a backhanded compliment to Channel 7's cold-blooded programming strategy; people do watch. On the other hand, there are nights when even MacNeil-Lehrer scares the hell out of me. The world can be a scary place.

Whether they're from Oshkosh or Oslo, most of our tourists aren't easily intimidated. Gun battle on South Beach? No problem. Tonight we'll go to the Grove.

Whatever horrors might appear on the TV screen at six and eleven, these intrepid travelers won't waste their precious vacations cowering in a $150 hotel room. They will put on bright telltale clothes. They will go outdoors. They will spend money.

Unless they've been living in a cave for the last 15 years, would-be tourists are well aware that Florida has guns, drugs, nuts and social unrest. To shield them completely from the daily flow, hotels would be forced to zap all local news off the cable.

Channel 7 merely offers a more elaborate smorgasbord than the others. Sure, it's everything the critics say it is—sensationalistic, lubricious and irresponsibly gruesome. If Jeffrey Dahmer lived here, Channel 7 undoubtedly would be his favorite station.

Yet its hard-gore news format has drawn good ratings, worldwide press attention and imitators around the country. Like it or not, Channel 7 is famous.

That's why hotels such as the Grand Bay in the Grove and the Pier House in Key West shoot themselves in the cash register by yanking Rick Sanchez off the cable: Channel 7 itself has become an exotic tourist attraction, to be mentioned in the same breath as Parrot Jungle or Everglades National Park.

People who come to South Florida expect to see blood, and Channel 7 is often the only place they can find it. Take that away, and you've got some mighty disappointed tourists.

Forget the cheap souvenirs. They want lurid anecdotes of shopping-mall shootouts and Dumpster dismemberments to take back home. Otherwise, what's the point of risking a vacation in Miami?

If hotel owners were smart, they wouldn't take the Channel 7 newscast off the tube. They'd put it on Spectravision and charge $7.50 to see it, just like they do with slasher movies.

Perfectly seasoned? Half-baked

August 20, 1995

Miami's new tourist slogan was unveiled last week, to mixed reviews.

If you haven't yet heard it, here goes: "Greater Miami & the Beaches: Perfectly Seasoned."

The image will emblazon T-shirts, novelties and a fortune's worth of worldwide advertising.

Lots of readers have phoned the newspaper to offer comments, half of them rather unflattering. Much of the criticism is aimed at the clunkiness and redundancy of the phrase "Greater Miami & the Beaches."

Evidently the slogan's authors are striving to reach the most feeble-minded of potential visitors—those who might come to Miami and not know there's a beach, and those who might come to the beach and not know there's a mainland.

I submit that we shouldn't be trying to lure travelers who cannot independently deduce, from the names, that "Miami" and "Miami Beach" are in the same general locale. These are folks who'd be much safer in the firm, watchful custody of a bus line tour guide.

Another problem with the new ad slogan: Why must it say Greater Miami? The purpose of such a distinction is puzzling. Is there a "Lesser" Miami that we don't know about? And, if so, why doesn't it want tourism?

Perhaps the origin of the logo's wordiness can be traced to the title of the agency that commissioned it—the Greater Miami Convention & Visitors Bureau. (Note the "Greater" and, of course, the ampersand.)

It's very possible the advertising firm that wrote the slogan—Turkel Schwartz & Partners!—was instructed to repeat the "greater," no matter how awkward and pointless.

Don't underestimate the civic pressure put on these harried, though well-paid, copy writers. Past tourist slogans became memorable for the wrong reasons.

Miami's "See It Like a Native" campaign provoked a huffy reaction because the poster featured a beautiful snorkeler who had misplaced her bikini top. In hindsight, those were the days of innocence.

Later came Florida's unintentionally ironic "The Rules Are Different Here"—presented in the wake of riots, soaring homicide, immigration chaos, and open debate about animal sacrifice. While that particular slogan was quickly put to rest, it took years to recover from the snide jokes.

This time, clearly, the ad agency was under orders to be very, very careful. Puns, quips and metaphors undoubtedly were screened with an eye toward avoiding controversy.

The result was "Perfectly Seasoned," which (although it evokes pot roast more than it does Ocean Drive) could've been worse.

Think about it. Once the agency decided to use cooking jargon in the tourism pitch, many less palatable expressions could have bubbled to the top:

Miami—Marinated in Magic!

Or: Miami—Sauteed With Excitement!

Or even: Miami—Naw, That's Just the Shrimp You're Smelling . . .

Well, you get the idea. And while "Perfectly Seasoned" might sound half-baked, I understand what tourism promoters wanted in their new slogan—something different enough to be noticed, yet bland enough that it couldn't possibly frighten people away.

Forget tourists, residents need crime warning

March 20, 1997

A Florida sheriff is in hot water for telling tourists to stay away because "it's very dangerous" down here.

As if this is big news. As if anyone who hasn't been living in a sinkhole doesn't already know we're the nation's premier sun-gun-and-psycho destination.

Yet, judging from the harsh feedback, Lee County Sheriff John McDougall might as well have stomped on the state flag. For a public officeholder in Florida, spooking tourists is a mortal sin. It's considered much worse than taking bribes.

"I would tell them not to come," McDougall said last week on the *Today* show. "I wouldn't tell anyone in my family to come to Florida right now. I think it's very dangerous."

The sheriff was referring to the ongoing release of hundreds of career felons from state prisons. He advised visitors to steer clear until the convicts committed new crimes and got rounded up again by lawmen.

No sooner had McDougall uttered the words than tourism-industry honchos launched a dyspeptic counterattack. The question is why.

Tourists are notoriously difficult to scare off, and it's unlikely that the sheriff's melodramatic sound bite will have a big impact. After all, this isn't a new rash of rental-car attacks—it's just another politician hungry for a headline.

The felons being released from prison were getting out anyway. The reason they're being freed en masse is because other politicians kept them behind bars by retroactively applying tough new sentencing rules.

You can't legally do that, as any second-year law student would know. So (to nobody's surprise) the U.S. Supreme Court ordered the timely release of those prisoners finishing their terms under the old guidelines.

That was Sheriff McDougall's excuse to rant. He wants a state amendment requiring inmates to serve 85 percent of their sentences—exactly what the new law already requires.

Oh well. A headline's a headline.

The chamber-of-commerce types would've been wise to ignore McDougall's TV performance. Those who ought to be concerned are the folks in Fort Myers—they've got a sheriff who's implying that the life and property of a tourist is more valuable than that of a local.

Because whatever random perils face somebody who visits the Sunshine State for a week or two, violent crime statistically poses a much greater menace to those who live here.

If McDougall honestly meant what he said, then why warn only the tourists? He could save many more lives by encouraging his constituents to pack up their belongings and move out of this "very dangerous" place as soon as possible.

Save yourselves, people! Get out while you can!

The sheriff can quit worrying so much about the tourists. They come and they go, leaving behind billions of useful dollars.

Residents are by far the more frequent victims of homicides, assaults and robberies. Serious felonies have soared with the state's exploding population, and few places are growing faster or more recklessly than McDougall's own county.

You'll know he is sincere about cutting crime when he speaks out in favor of capping growth. Scaring away visitors is a waste of time. Try scaring away the hordes of people who keep moving here to stay.

Not all of them—a couple hundred thousand a year would be a start.

But the sheriff probably won't do that. No politician is honest enough to tell potential voters to run for their lives.

Florida would be a more attractive place if they did. Less gridlock and urban stress. Much safer.

And the tourists? They'd keep coming in droves.

At Disney, it's a wild, wild world

April 23, 1998

Good morning, bwanas! Today's the day we finally open Disney's new Animal Kingdom theme park for the world.

As tour guides, it's your job to make sure all visitors have fun. Many of you have never worked with real live critters, so let's go over the guidelines again.

Number one: If your safari bus should encounter our wild animals acting like, well, wild animals, do not under any circumstances attempt to disconnect them, deprogram them or try to locate the "off" button.

Remember, these are not the dancing country bears—and they're probably not just dancing, anyway.

I know it's a big adjustment for all of us here at Walt Disney World. In the old days, when a jungle beast went haywire we'd just replace a transistor. Not anymore.

The wildlife here at Animal Kingdom sometimes will engage in public behavior that our guests might find puzzling or even disturbing—behavior for which (I'm ashamed to say) a few of our human "cast members" have been occasionally reprimanded.

As tour guides, it's your duty not to let our visitors be distracted. Turning to page 17 of the manual, you'll find a detailed list of embarrassing animal antics, next to the officially scripted Disney explanations.

Scratching, for instance. As you've undoubtedly noticed, our primates can be indiscreet in their personal scratching habits. Please try not to bring this to the attention of your safari guests.

If, however, a guest observes this behavior and inquires, always refer to it as "grooming." Same goes for the licking—those lions, I swear, they never give it a rest . . . Just remember: "Grooming" is the operative word.

Several of you asked about the poop issue. I passed along your concerns directly to Mr. Eisner's office, and I've been told there's not a darn thing to be done. We've got 1,000 animals roaming here and unless the folks in Imagineering come up with some amazing new gadget, there's going to be lots of poop.

Hey, I'm on your side. Sixteen years I worked the Main Street Parade and we never had this problem, except for that one really obnoxious Pluto.

And, yes, I'm well aware how much a full-grown elephant eats—but try to deal with it, OK? "Droppings." That's the approved Disney term, whether it's from a hippo or a hummingbird.

The next item is, sadly, animal mortality. As you know, we've already lost two rhinos, some rare birds, four cheetah cubs. It's made for a few unpleasant headlines, to be sure.

But this is straight from the lawyers: Never use the terms "die" or "dead" on your Disney safari. If the tour bus passes an animal that appears not to be breathing, you may describe it as "lethargic," "inactive," "dormant" or (for the youngsters) "napping."

Finally, let's review the rules on animal sex. I don't know what genius decided to open this park in the springtime, but our animals are in quite the mood.

Some of you heard what happened on Media Day—a little problem with the Barbara Walters crew and that horny pair of wildebeests in quadrant seven. Without going into gory details, let's just say that ABC eventually was "persuaded" to give up the videotape.

As safari guides, it's imperative to remember that this is a family attraction. Animals do not mate here. They "wrestle." They "clench." They "frolic." They "romp." They "nuzzle." And of course they "groom" each other, sometimes intimately.

But they don't mate. They don't hump. They don't "do the nasty." Is that understood?

Good. Now go out there and give these wonderful folks an authentic true-life jungle adventure, droppings and all!

A State
of Chaos

Why not study the brains of top Florida officials?

October 9, 1985

A true news item: State medical examiners have acknowledged secretly removing parts of the brains of executed prisoners for use in laboratory studies of aberrant behavior.

GAINESVILLE—Researchers today announced the expansion of the state's Involuntary Brain Donor Program to include members of the Florida Cabinet, the state Legislature and other qualified public officials.

"This is a tremendous opportunity for a scientific breakthrough," proclaimed Dr. Igor Hans of the University of Florida. "For years people have been wondering what makes politicians act the way they do. Studying their brain cells may unlock this terrible secret."

But several top Florida political figures immediately objected to the plan, calling it "coldhearted, barbaric and just plain icky."

"They're not getting my brain unless they get the governor's," vowed Agriculture Commissioner Doyle Conner.

"Don't worry, they're not getting the governor's," said a spokesman for the governor. "We keep a darn close eye on it."

Scientists argue that the benefits of brain experiments will far outweigh concerns for the privacy and dignity of the deceased. They say it makes more sense to study politicians than convicted murderers.

"Serial killers are a dime a dozen," Dr. Hans said, "but how many Claude Kirks are there in this world?"

Pathologists said that politicians' brains will be preserved in a mixture of formaldehyde and Johnnie Walker Red. Afterward the tissue will be microscopically photographed and dissected, then injected with powerful enzymes made from aspirin and Maxwell House coffee grounds.

To make the brains feel at home, the tests will be conducted in a $150-a-night suite on the top floor of the Tallahassee Hilton.

Dr. Hans said he expects to find striking differences between the brains of politicians and those of other humans.

"They'll be slightly smaller, of course," the famed neurologist said, "but this'll save us a fortune on storage space."

Behavioral scientists have speculated that many officeholders suffer from a cerebral condition known as Milhous Syndrome—a disorder causing the part of the brain that controls modesty, truthfulness and frugality to shrink to the size of a subway token.

Dr. Hans said he will test the theory on his first subject, preferably either a former Margate city commissioner or a Monroe County zoning board member.

Ironically, the donor team is having trouble recruiting experts to work on the landmark project.

"Doctors who wouldn't think twice about examining a bank robber's brain won't set foot in the same lab with a state senator's," Dr. Hans said. "People fear most what they don't understand."

Nationwide, there has been only one documented case of experimentation on the neurons of a political officeholder—a former U.S. congressman who had willed his cerebrum to science.

As part of the experiment, neurologists at Johns Hopkins University placed the congressman's brain on a laboratory table next to a stack of $50 bills. Within seconds, the organ quivered and began inching closer to the money, a phenomenon for which scientists could offer no explanation.

Dr. Hans said he would not attempt to duplicate the controversial Johns Hopkins studies.

"We already know what motivates a brain like that," he shrugged. "We're much more curious about the twisted pathology behind it."

Some ex-officeholders, including several former Florida Cabinet members, expressed "grave concern" that part of their brains already might have been removed without their permission.

However, scientists say that they're doing their best to ascertain that brain donors are actually dead before the organs are taken.

"Sometimes it's a close call," Dr. Hans conceded.

Beer and pizza for everyone, Mr. Governor

June 8, 1987

The Mole People finally adjourned in Tallahassee, emerging squinty-eyed into the sunshine where they are now posing, partying and nearly wrenching their arms patting themselves on the back.

Having committed their largest deeds behind closed doors, the legislators of the great state of Florida would now like you to know what a valiant effort they've made on your behalf.

They passed the biggest tax increase in state history, set up a lottery, and agreed to spend millions more on prisons, indigent health care and water cleanup.

They also passed laws that will legally put handguns into the fists of more drunks, half-wits and fruitcakes than ever before. Despite so-called "safeguards," the Legislature will have no more success keeping licensed pistols from lunatics than it does keeping bad drivers off the highways.

In other ways it was a progressive session because—like them or not—new taxes are the only way to start paying for Florida's explosive growth. The scary part is that the average voter has practically no say in how these revenues will be spent, or who'll get their paws on the money.

Years ago Florida passed its famous Sunshine Laws, ostensibly to take the business of government out of the cloakrooms and corridors. At the time a reform-minded Legislature boldly voted that all meetings of public bodies be held in the open—except, naturally, those of the Legislature itself.

The law that makes it illegal for members of a city council or a school board or a county commission to meet secretly doesn't apply to your faithful representatives in Tallahassee, who this year had their way with $18.7 billion of your money.

How did they do it? We're not exactly sure, since they wouldn't let us in.

True, floor sessions and regular committee meeting are wide open to the press and public, but the real lawmaking doesn't happen there. It happens in private.

Take the controversial new sales tax on services, for instance. It wasn't negotiated on the floor in view of the gallery. It was drafted over beer and pizza at the Tallahassee townhouse of Bob Coker, a lobbyist for a Big Sugar firm. Among those joining the House and Senate leaders in the late-night festivities were key aides to Gov. Bob Martinez.

You remember Bob Martinez, that fellow who campaigned vigorously on a promise of no secret meetings? Remember his indignant TV ads, showing arrogant cracker legislators slamming the door in the public's face? Apparently the governor is not so indignant now.

For a brief moment this session a few senators rebelled. They proposed an amendment that would have required legislators to meet in the open at all times, even when jawboning with the governor.

You can imagine the rapture with which this idea was greeted. Senate Rules Chairman Dempsey Barron and Senate President John Vogt (the King and Crown Prince of the Mole People) snuffed the Sunshine amendment as quickly as possible.

Later Sen. Larry Plummer of South Miami pointedly offered a new version that would have opened all governmental sessions, including "midnight meetings over pepperoni pizza or anything else."

This, too, was flattened by Vogt's gavel.

Think about what it means. These are people who work for you, and whose salaries you pay—yet they won't let you watch what they're doing. It's like having the Maytag repairman lock you out of your own house until he's finished fiddling with your appliances.

Admittedly, cutting deals is a part of the legislative process that's easier done in a tunnel than on TV. But if nothing sleazy is going on, then what's the harm in letting the public see?

Martinez says gee whiz, he'd just love to open all the meetings, really he would—but those darn legislators just won't go along.

It sounds like the governor's eyes have already adjusted to the dark.

Foul odors get worse in legislature

December 12, 1990

The Legislature is like a dead skunk. No matter how bad you think it's going to stink, it stinks even worse.

Few stomachs remain unturned after this week's *Herald* series about pet projects that give away millions of taxpayer dollars. Although everybody was aware that this stuff goes on, many people had no idea that the pilfering is so flagrant.

It's hard to decide which is more outrageous—the way the money was blown, or the lame excuses now being made by those who blew it. Some of my favorites:

• Lottery funds, designated for education, were used to send a bunch of state legislators to Israel as part of an "agricultural research project." Among those who took the free trip were Sen. Gwen Margolis (representing those rolling farmlands of North Miami), and Rep. Jack Tobin of Margate, where almost all the supermarkets do sell fresh produce.

Margolis apparently was too busy tending her crops to respond to inquiries about the Israel trip, while Tobin insisted that the lottery couldn't have paid for the whole thing. It did.

• Last year, the Legislature gave $1 million to fund an "amateur" athletic facility. Instead, the money was sent to the Ladies Professional Golf Association. This year, lawmakers spent another $2 million for a new road to the LPGA's headquarters in Daytona Beach.

Now legislators say the word "amateur" was "inadvertently" added to the funding proposal. They say the grant was meant for the city of Daytona Beach, which needed the funds to help the LPGA move there. Now isn't that better? Three million bucks of "economic development" money for needy professional golfers—who said government doesn't have a heart!

• Metro Commissioner Sherman Winn campaigned for a $400,000 state grant to something called the American International Exhibition for Travel, a firm that staged tourism-promotion shows. By eerie coincidence, Winn's son Steve just happened to be the Tallahassee lobbyist for that company—and got $52,000 for his work. Months later, the owner of American International disappeared, and so did the state's $400,000.

Sherman Winn now prefers not to discuss the matter. Explained an aide: "He doesn't want to be implicated with something he had nothing to do with."

Guess what, Sherm. You're implicated.

• The Beacon Council, guiding light of Dade's business community, hired two lobbyists to pry $150,000 in grant money from the state Legislature. After the funding arrived, the Beacon Council kicked back $15,000 to the lobbyists. The state comptroller's office said that's an improper use of taxpayers' dollars.

The kicker: It was lottery money.

• Rep. Luis Rojas of Hialeah weaseled $100,000 for the Hialeah Latin Chamber of Commerce to fund a "productivity improvement center." The chamber used the dough to hire Rojas' former legislative aide, Carlos Manrique.

Rojas insists that the state money spawned new commerce in Hialeah, and he's right: His buddy Manrique later went into business with a company owner he'd met through the grant program. Hey, if you can't help your friends, who can you help?

• Wooed by lobbyists, the Legislature gave the Greater Miami Opera almost $1 million. Later, some of the lawmakers who voted for the money asked the opera for free tickets.

One of those, Rep. Susan Guber, says—and this is priceless—it's important for her to attend the shows to make sure taxpayer dollars are being put to good use. Bravo!

To her credit, Guber is one of the few legislators who wants to change things so that "turkey" items aren't so easily sneaked into the appropriations bill. There's not a moment to waste, either—Florida is in worse fiscal shape than most had predicted. The crisis is forcing $270 million in emergency cuts next month. Education, social services and law enforcement will suffer.

If the new governor is searching for a popular agenda, he doesn't need to go far. All he's got to do is put his nose in the air and take a whiff of this year's budget.

Junkets show politics isn't a thankless job

May 1, 1991

Whoever said politics is a thankless job ought to read the latest report from the Leon County grand jury.

It describes how some state legislators have accepted free vacations provided by lobbyists from major utilities, auto dealers, the hotel industry, Big Agriculture and insurance firms. In many cases, the trips were not reported as gifts, although the law requires it.

Not surprisingly, the globe-trotting tourists have been reticent to share the highlights of their travels—not even a postcard for the voters back home. In fact, it's almost as if lawmakers wanted to keep it a secret. It's almost as if they were ashamed.

The juiciest details came from the lobbyists themselves, summoned before the grand jury. Much of the testimony focused on hunting trips, a popular escape from Tallahassee's pressures.

Judging from what the lobbyists said, lawmakers find hunting much more enjoyable when they don't have to pay for it themselves. Shooting a high-flying mallard requires total concentration, and who can concentrate when you're worrying about some danged hotel bill?

Friendly special interests arranged for legislators to go on free hunting expeditions to El Campo and Corpus Christi, Texas; Monterrey and Ciudad Victoria, Mexico; Norwood, Colo.; Casper and Thermopolis, Wyo.; the Blue Ridge Hunting Lodge in LaPine, Ala.; the Riverview Plantation, Foxfire Hunting Preserve and Quail Ridge, all in Georgia.

For lawmakers who preferred fish over fowl, lobbyists lined up angling excursions to the wilds of Colorado, Alaska and Nice, France. Not to be outdone, a few nonsporting types in the Legislature took pleasure jaunts to Paris—and Zurich, Monte Carlo, Vail, Lake Tahoe, New Orleans, Breckenridge, Treasure Cay and St. Tropez.

When the scandal first broke, some lawmakers insisted they did nothing wrong because a free trip isn't really a "gift." The grand jury found this argument just as ludicrous as everyone else did. The law, it said, is "plain and unambiguous." A free plane ticket must be reported as a contribution.

The tone of the grand jury's findings was one of barely concealed disgust. And it wasn't only the trips, but the other shameless mooching:

"Several legislators routinely solicited free plane charters/rentals from certain lobbyists solely for personal use."

The report went on: "During a legislative session it is possible for legislators to be furnished breakfast, lunch and dinner by lobbyists while still drawing per diem." No! Who would do such a thing? The grand jurors called for a tougher law that would make it a crime to take anything worth more than $50. Predictably, that's way too radical for this Legislature. A bill imposing a $50 limit on gifts will probably pass this session, but violators won't face criminal charges.

The strongest deterrent to a freeloading politician is the threat of public exposure, and here the grand jury missed the boat. In what seems an act of misguided mercy, the names of the peripatetic lawmakers were deliberately withheld from the report.

Voters then were left to guess, for instance, which sneaky weasel took a free trip and then tried to conceal the fact by paying with his own credit card. Later the legislator approached the lobbyist and demanded full reimbursement for the junket—in cash.

Leon County State Attorney Willie Meggs knows the identities of the alleged perpetrators, and is considering prosecution. Most of the crimes would be misdemeanors, and the penalties would be laughably light.

Nonetheless, a trial would be useful to document the snug relationships between powerful lobbyists and elected officials. Next time the insurance industry flies your local senator to a Paris vacation, you shouldn't have to read about it in a grand jury report.

You deserve a slide show.

Senate remap effort on road to disaster

April 2, 1992

One way to save Florida tons of money, and loads of embarrassment, would be to abolish the Senate.

No one would miss these bunglers, who are stinking up Tallahassee with their rotten, self-serving politics. While the state rapidly goes broke, senators remain pathologically obsessed with redistricting. Translation: saving their own sorry butts.

Republicans want more Republican districts, Democrats want to cling to what they've got. The logjam has paralyzed government. On Tuesday, the Senate froze 20-20 on a vote to adjourn. That's how bad things are.

Voters aren't the only ones to be nauseated. Last week, a panel of federal judges intervened to snatch redistricting powers from the Legislature. Barring a last-minute miracle at the Capitol, boundaries for new legislative and congressional districts will be drawn by a nonpartisan expert, and ratified by the judges in late May.

That's the best news Floridians could get. It's painfully clear that politicians can't be trusted with such important matters.

To appreciate the Senate's miserably irresponsible performance, look no farther than its president, Gwen Margolis, a Democrat from North Dade.

Margolis is full of ambition. She wants to run for Congress in one of two new districts that will be mostly Hispanic. At the same time, she doesn't want to give up her power base in North Dade and Miami Beach. So what does she do? She tailors a new congressional district to fit her desired demographics.

To an untrained eye, the proposed boundaries look like the etchings of a mapmaker on heavy pharmaceuticals. In reality, it's a masterpiece of diabolical gerrymandering.

The Margolis Magical Mystery Tour starts in South Beach and steamrolls up the coast to Hallandale. There it shrinks weirdly to a one-block-wide corridor, sneaks up to Dania, darts back down to Pembroke Park, hopscotches west to Miramar, slithers south to Hialeah, then angles sharply toward Sweetwater. From there the boundary meanders east, grazing Little Havana and parts of Overtown on its journey back to the Miami River.

Nobody said the road to Congress was easy, but this is ridiculous. Some of Margolis' colleagues don't like the map, and now it's a bargaining point: Republicans won't approve the new congressional boundaries unless she approves more GOP seats in the Legislature. The Senate has fought to an impasse.

Seeking compromise, seven Democrats recently endorsed a congressional map drawn by Common Cause, a citizens' lobby. Margolis rejected the plan because it put her in the same district with Dante Fascell, who's not about to surrender his seat.

Margolis isn't the only one playing games. Members of both parties are consumed by fear that redistricting will put them out of office, or stack them against a formidable opponent. They all want a clear, breezy path to re-election.

If only they'd spend half as much time, energy and imagination trying to fix the budget. Instead it's the raw, greedy politics of self-preservation.

While the Senate snivels and stalls, our schools run out of money. New prisons remain unopened. Hospitals cut back vital services to the poor. It's a disgrace, but neither Margolis nor the others seem the least bit ashamed.

With the feds drawing up the new districts, she probably won't be getting that free ride to Congress in November. That means her amazing psychedelic map will go to waste. Perhaps voters can think of a suitable place for her to put it.

State lobbyists may be pulled out of shadows

February 18, 1993

Some of the most powerful people in Florida are also the most anonymous, and they want to keep it that way.

They aren't elected to public office, they hold no position in government and their only loyalty is to the clients who sign their paychecks. Yet they probably have more impact on Florida's future than do all the state's voters.

They're the lobbyists who swarm Tallahassee each year like fragrant, blow-dried locusts. They are thick and they are fast, and nothing escapes their attention. They know how the machinery of lawmaking works, and how to lubricate it in their own interest. You don't know them by name, but most legislators do.

In an age of so-called open government, lobbyists thrive in one of the last dark crevices of privacy. Gov. Lawton Chiles is trying to shine a light in there, and the reaction, as one might expect, is furious and insectile. In an ethics package proposed this month, the governor has asked the Legislature to make lobbyists disclose their incomes, their expenditures and all political donations. He also wants to ban contingency fees, and campaign contributions made during legislative sessions.

Many states have adopted such regulations, but they stand scant chance of survival here. While some lobbyists support reforms, many will resist forcefully. They've got a good deal, and they know it.

• Full disclosure. Put yourself in a lobbyist's position. If you're taking a hundred grand to shill for the tobacco industry, you wouldn't want the whole world to know, would you? It's so embarrassing that your kids would probably disown you. Confidentiality is preferable because it preserves one's pride and respectability.

• Contingency fees. Some lobbyists get paid only if they succeed in their mission to get a bill passed, or to get one killed. The lobbyist who secures a fat grant for his client often grabs his or her cut out of the booty, meaning the taxpayer's pocket.

Last year, an appellate court in Dade County ruled that lobbyists can't take contingency fees or bonuses out of public appropriations. Chiles wants a law that says the same thing. Lobbyists who work on a bounty are screaming bloody murder.

• Campaign contributions. The way it stands, lobbyists can give money to a legislator's campaign at any time—even as that legislator prepares to vote on their pet project.

It's nothing more than legalized bribery. Lobbyists use political donations to lean on lawmakers, and lawmakers use their vote to solicit donations. Both sides get what they want, so there's no incentive to pass a law against it.

"A shakedown," says Bill Jones of Common Cause, the citizen's lobby. He and others are disgusted by the freewheeling bazaar. "I don't think it would hurt to adopt the governor's [reforms]," adds lawyer Steve Uhlfelder, who lobbies for private clients as well as for the American Heart Association, from which he takes no fee.

The job of lobbyist is as old as the republic, and it's not inherently wicked or sneaky. Almost everybody with a stake in the law has lobbyists at work in Tallahassee—not just wealthy phosphate barons and liquor distributors and utility companies, but teachers and conservation groups and the handicapped.

And don't forget the press; we've got our own hired guns prowling the Capitol. When Gov. Bob Martinez included an advertising tariff in his special-services tax, media lobbyists hollered and hectored. (The tax, you'll remember, was squashed.)

No act of mortal man will interrupt the intimate waltz between lobbyists and legislators, but at least Chiles' plan would bring the dance out of the shadows and into the sunshine, where we can all watch.

Pass your law? First, pass me the stone crabs

March 21, 1996

Mooching free food and booze is an old tradition of Florida legislators, and efforts to curb the annual gluttony in Tallahassee usually fall short.

This year, Senate President Jim Scott wants a rule prohibiting members from accepting free meals and liquor from paid lobbyists.

As expected, the proposal isn't sitting well with the restaurateurs who host the backroom bacchanalia, or with the special-interest groups who pay for it.

Scott and other legislators say reforms are necessary to improve the image of the Legislature, which is still regarded by many Floridians as a springtime gathering of slackers, pickpockets and whores.

Defenders of the old way say they're insulted at the insinuation that their vote can be bought for a steak supper and a bottle of wine. Even really fine wine.

They contend that socializing is important to the contentious process of lawmaking, and that a private dinner is sometimes the best way to hear one side of a controversy.

Nobody is suggesting that legislators stop eating with lobbyists, only that they pay for their own meals and cocktails. It's hardly a radical notion, but you should hear the griping.

Perhaps serving the public's needs requires such intense concentration that politicians can't afford any distractions, such as worrying about picking up the check.

Or perhaps they just love free food.

Unless you've spent time in Tallahassee during the legislative session, you cannot possibly envision what goes on during the off-hours—parties, receptions, banquets, barbecues, hoedowns, hayrides, you name it.

For lobbyists seeking an audience with lawmakers, the theory is time-proven: If you give it away free, they will come.

A well-crafted position paper is fine and dandy, but nothing catches a recalcitrant senator's eye faster than a gleaming platter of jumbo stone-crab claws.

And, since every vote can be crucial, every legislator finds himself treated like a star. On a given night, it's possible to eat your way into a deep coma, courtesy of the citrus lobby or the phosphate lobby or the schoolteacher union's lobby—or anybody else who's throwing a bash.

Little wonder that many lawmakers are glad the state capital is Talla-hassee, far from the eyes of their constituents.

In politics, appearance is paramount. And gorging at the trough of high-paid lobbyists gives the appearance of gross impropriety, if not gross stupidity.

That's why Scott wants his colleagues to stop taking free food and drinks. The measure comes up for a vote this week, but already it has been weakened by significant exceptions.

For instance, the free-food ban won't apply if the senator is at a "spe-cial event" with 250 or more people. He or she will also be free to pig out at campaign fund-raising wingdings that are paid for by lobbyists.

Supporters say the new rule is still important because it eliminates extravagant wooing of legislators by individual lobbyists. Others say hungry senators won't have trouble finding loopholes.

Meanwhile, the state House shows little interest in cracking down on the annual Tallahassee foodfest. Its members remain free to eat, drink and be merry—and put it on somebody else's tab.

Lawmakers who indulge will deny that they let it affect their votes. Yet if that's true, why do lobbyists keep paying for all that free food and booze, year after year?

Obviously the influence brokers believe they're getting something valuable in return, beyond the sparkling company of so many legislators.

And they would know better than anyone.

Dave who? Please say it isn't so

April 16, 1998

It's definitely something in the water. First there was Mayor Loco, now we've got Publisher Loco.

David Lawrence Jr., the head honcho of this newspaper, is consider
a run for the governorship of Florida. Seriously.

Lawrence has never held public office. He has no fund-raising organization, and thus no funds. Most voters in Florida don't have a clue who
he is. And the primaries are only five months away.

But that's our Mr. Lawrence, optimist to a fault. Since he's the Big
Cheese around the newsroom, I ought to be circumspect about this
bizarre situation. So here goes:

Dave, have you completely lost your marbles?

Not long ago, a San Francisco newspaper executive went off and married the actress Sharon Stone. That makes sense, at least on one basic level.
But politics?

True, one doesn't get to be a big-city publisher without honing some
political skills. But outmuscling a rival in the corporate boardroom isn't
the same as running for governor.

Lawrence is a smart, decent, compassionate fellow who cares about
Florida and believes fervently in the innate goodness of mankind. Tallahassee would eat him alive. It would be dreadful to watch.

How did this gonzo notion ever take root in his head? It came from
the Democrats, of course. Fearing a November steamrolling by Jeb
Bush and the GOP, Buddy MacKay, the Democratic gubernatorial front-
runner, recently asked Lawrence (a registered independent) to consider
joining the ticket as lieutenant governor.

At the time Lawrence apparently was still in possession of his facul-
ties, because he said no. Later he was approached by a fat-cat Democratic
donor urging him to make a maverick run for the top spot. On Saturday
he will meet with prominent party leaders to discuss his prospects.

Earth to Dave: There are no prospects. Nada. You can't possibly win.

The Jebster has never held elected office, either, but he's already raised
$6.3 million. Also, he's been running for governor since puberty, so
everybody in Florida knows his name. Same for Buddy MacKay, longtime legislator and currently lieutenant governor.

Lawrence is a heavy-hitter among the state's power elite, but few voters outside Miami know his name. Nor is his connection to the *Herald*
likely to boost his chances; in fact, it'll hurt him. Good or bad, journalists
don't win popularity contests—nor should they aspire to.

Which leads to a disturbing aspect of the Lawrence-for-governor story: the untenable and queasy position in which it has put this newspaper, and the reporters, columnists and editors who produce it.

The fact our publisher openly is considering a political candidacy contaminates our credibility in the eyes of some readers. No matter what we do, many will choose to believe (and the other candidates will aver) that the Herald is Lawrence's personal campaign machine, and all of us his conscripted flacks.

There's no way to deflate such suspicions, even if we give Lawrence the same tough scrutiny—even tougher scrutiny—than we do his opponents. Which is exactly what should happen if he resigns to run for governor. Some days he won't be very pleased by what he reads in these pages.

When the announcement of a possible Lawrence candidacy was posted in our newsroom Tuesday, the first reaction was incredulity. Lots of folks thought it was a practical joke. Later, two reporters—inspired by Miami's recent election scandal—facetiously volunteered to collect absentee ballots on Dave's behalf.

Newsrooms are cynical, wary, irreverent places. But to those unfamiliar with the culture of journalism, it's inconceivable that an ex-publisher won't be coddled in print by his former staff. That's the rap we're facing today, and every day until Lawrence makes up his mind.

In his defense, being asked by serious people to run for governor would flatter anybody's ego. No one who knows Lawrence questions his guts or his sincerity; it's his common sense that has deserted him.

No campaign experience. No money. No statewide visibility. And almost no time left to get things rolling.

Meanwhile, the paper to which he has devoted so much of his heart and energy is left to defend itself, fruitlessly, against charges of being used as a partisan rag. What can Dave be thinking?

I saw him in the newsroom Tuesday. He was alert and cogent. His pupils looked normal. His speech wasn't slurred. He seemed in all respects a completely healthy, rational, well-grounded person.

Then again, I'm no doctor. The true test comes this weekend when he chats with the Democrats.

Cops, Courts, and Lawyers

Latest arrests close out bad year for police

January 1, 1986

I watched them on TV the other night, the beefcake cops charged with murder. As they capered and grinned and blew kisses at the courtroom cameras, I couldn't help but wonder if steroids destroy brain tissue.

Imagine: You're a young policeman.

You are hauled out of your home in the wee hours, handcuffed, fingerprinted and hustled bleary-eyed into the Dade County Jail like a bum.

You are accused of a triple homicide, of racketeering, of stealing cocaine and selling it on the street, of using your badge and oath as instruments of crime. You are accused of being the worst thing that a cop can be—crooked.

Yet when you and your weightlifter pals go to court the next morning, what emotion do you display while the whole city is watching?

Arrogance. You mug for the cameras, laughing and joking while every good and decent cop on the streets feels a hot knot tightening in the gut. The feeling is shame.

But you don't have any.

So you and your buddies cling to the macho routine. Hire a big-shot lawyer and wait for bail. Act like it's no sweat. Act like you're not afraid. Disco all the way to the slammer.

What a way for 1985 to end. It really was a rotten year for integrity.

Don't let anyone try to say South Florida's police corruption is no worse than any other metropolis, because they're wrong. No place else comes close.

Consider the local cavalcade of stars this past 12 months:

A DEA agent goes to jail for peddling computer secrets to dopers; three Customs agents are indicted in a pot smuggling ring; an FBI man pleads guilty to accepting cocaine kickbacks; a Metro-Dade officer is charged as a home-invasion robber; a Hialeah cop plea-bargains a seven-year term for his role in a cold-blooded drug execution; a Miami officer awaits trial for allegedly offering to sell badges and guns to drug dealers.

Now this latest milestone: Eight current or former Miami policemen busted in the past week for a smorgasbord of drug crimes, including the ever-popular trafficking of cocaine. One of them, his pockets stuffed with $1,180 cash, fled from fellow officers in a red Porsche, thus ratifying every cheap Miami cliche.

Police Chief Clarence Dickson called the arrests "a total positive," and city leaders were quick to praise the department's housecleaning.

"Housecleaning" seems a polite term for what's going on.

This is not some teensy boo-boo, but a scandal of monstrous dimensions. Arrests were overdue and welcome, but they were not the result of Miami police simply washing their own dirty laundry. The pressure was external and intense: Investigators from Metro-Dade homicide, the Florida Department of Law Enforcement and DEA have been swarming all over the place for weeks. Something was bound to break.

Still, Dickson's cooperation and determination to help solve the Miami River murders are encouraging. I know some cities where it never would have happened, where outside investigators would have hit a wall of hostility. The Key West police force, once a rat's nest of corruption, was famous for this kind of obstruction.

So now a few Miami cops are in jail, but a celebration is premature. Much more is yet to unravel. The full story of what happened last July 27 at the dock of the *Mary C* is bound to be chilling. No one there was a Boy Scout. Three of them wound up floaters, snagged on a gaff.

Unfortunately, the criminal charges go beyond this one midnight episode. They portray a violent network of cocaine thuggery, a mob in blue. The upcoming testimony will not likely calm the nerves next time you see a flashing light in the rearview mirror.

The trial process will be tedious, and feature some of Miami's top defense lawyers. We'll be hearing a lot about how the three dead guys in the river were nothing but low-life drug dealers, how the witnesses against the police are nothing but liars and scoundrels, how Messrs. Estrada, Garcia, Rodriguez and Co. are nothing but innocent scapegoats.

In dope cases such strategy is predictable, and sometimes effective. It can also be justified. In any event, you can bet that the Merry Weight-lifters will be the picture of restraint in the jury's presence.

Convicting a policeman of any crime is difficult, and there are precious few prosecutors who can't be eaten alive by defense attorneys of Roy Black's caliber. Don't be surprised if some of the cops are acquitted.

River cops tell unique tales of acquiring cash

January 12, 1987

As the jury resumes deliberations today in the Miami River Cops case, it's a good time to review some of the most amazing testimony from the last few months.

I'm referring to the various accounts of how some of the seven defendants suddenly came up with so much cash. As U.S. prosecutors have pointed out, it's somewhat peculiar for a young fellow on a city patrolman's salary to all at once start buying new cars, houses, bedroom suites, Caribbean vacations, all kinds of goodies.

To explain the officers' timely good fortune, defense lawyers summoned friends and relatives to present an intriguing look at the family finances. Give credit to the jurors for not falling out of their chairs.

Great Moments in Money Management, Miami-style:

• Officer Armando "Scarface" Garcia testified he removed his family's jewelry from a safe-deposit box because going to the bank was too inconvenient. Instead, Garcia said, he put the jewelry inside a pouch along with $7,000 cash, and cleverly concealed it in a crawl space beneath his parents' home.

• The uncle of indicted patrolman Armando Estrada claimed that over 23 years he scrimped and saved $19,000 in cash, which he stashed in a box in his house. He testified that he used the nest egg to buy a 1985 Trans Am (without even test-driving it), and then decided to give the car to his nephew the policeman to use around town.

• Officer Garcia's girlfriend said she bought a spiffy Datsun 300 ZX with $13,000 cash from a metal box on her dresser. She testified that she earned part of the money as a seamstress, while $8,000 was a gift from her father, who kept it hidden in the family piano.

• The mother of accused officer Arturo De La Vega testified that her dying father had given her $25,000 cash, most of which she later gave to her son the policeman—who supposedly used the inheritance to buy furniture and stocks.

• Admitted drug dirtbag Armando Un Roque said that he sometimes stuffed $40,000 to $50,000 cash into his socks. Then, just to be extra safe, he would hide the socks inside a wall.

Whatever happened to banks? Or savings bonds? Or how about wall safes—with real locks and everything?

See, the U.S. government tends to get curious when it discovers that you've got sacks of loose cash stuffed under your waterbed. The government tends to wonder if the money is profit from some questionable enterprise of the type that goes down on a semi-hourly basis on the streets of South Florida.

True, stacks of cash are pleasant to count, fondle and gaze upon—but they can also bring heartache and remorse. The second worst thing that can happen is that some lucky burglar will discover your secret cubbyhole and make off with your entire life's fortune.

The first worst thing that can happen is that you'll be hauled into court and questioned relentlessly about where all the dough came from.

When that dreadful day comes, this is what you do:

1. Don't say a word about stashing the cash in shoe boxes. Shoe boxes are out. Same goes for cookie jars, suitcases, socks, sofas and pianos. Be creative. Tell the jury you hid the money in a tuba.
2. Be careful when identifying which beloved relative gave you all

that cash. For example, don't get up on the witness stand and say you got $50,000 from your great-uncle Louie, who makes $3.75 an hour scraping chewing gum off the Metrorail stations.

3. When asked what you planned to do with the cash (besides blowing it on giant-screen TVs and gaudy sports cars), tell them you intended to donate half to the Oliver North Legal Defense Fund and half to the Rev. Oral Roberts, so he won't keel over dead in March like he promised.

A Miami jury just might buy this. What happens to you is up to them.

What happens to the remainder of your precious nest egg is obvious. No matter how large, it will still fit nicely into your lawyer's briefcase.

Here's a quiz for potential federal jurors

January 23, 1987

Snide jokes overheard in the wake of the big mistrial: "What's the difference between the Miami River Cops jury and a sack of rocks?"

"Rocks don't snore."

Or: "How many Miami River jurors does it take to change a light bulb?"

"All of them, plus a bailiff to read the directions."

To avoid this sort of embarrassment, all potential jurors in Miami federal court should henceforth be required to take the following quiz. To pass, a score of 100 percent is required.

In other words, no wrong answers are allowed.

In other words, every question must be answered correctly.

In other words, NO MISTAKES ARE PERMITTED. GOT IT??? Sure you do.

1. Billy has 12 apples. He gives four apples to Susan. How many apples does Billy have now?
   a) Eight.
   b) None.
   c) Four—no, seven! Did we say seven? No . . . wait . . . OK, you said apples, right? So . . . what was the question?

2. In a courtroom, the person wearing the long black robe is called:

a) The judge.

b) Zorro.

c) Overdressed.

3. When the person in the black robe asks for a well-reasoned verdict, he is:

a) Talking to the bailiff.

b) Talking to the jury.

c) Wasting his time.

4. All citizens should consider their jury duty as:

a) An integral part of the judicial system.

b) A paid vacation from work.

c) A chance to get your portrait sketched free by a courtroom artist.

5. While sequestered during a long trial, jurors are often cautioned:

a) Not to read the newspapers.

b) Not to discuss the case among themselves.

c) Not to communicate with the psychic spirit of Shirley MacLaine.

6. The word "unanimous" means:

a) All in agreement.

b) All in the same language.

c) All in the same time zone.

7. During the trial, jurors should never:

a) Speak directly to the witnesses.

b) Speak rudely to the judge.

c) Take bets as to which of them can spit the farthest.

8. Which of the following is considered a legitimate excuse to be dismissed from a jury:

a) "My mother has the flu."

b) "My Rottweiler has the mange."

c) "I'm missing all my soaps."

9. The best way to break a jury deadlock is:

a) By a careful and thoughtful review of the evidence.

b) By listening to the tapes over and over.

c) By doing one-potato, two-potato.

10. If a jury wishes to communicate with the judge, the proper method is:

a) Writing a brief and simple note.

b) Raising your hand and asking permission to speak.

c) Slapping yourself in the face and shouting "whoop-whoop-whoop!" like Curly of the Three Stooges.

11. When writing a note to the judge, it is advisable to:

a) Print neatly.

b) Try to use at least one verb in each sentence.

c) Try not to refer to the defendants as "slithering vermin." /

12. As the trial progresses, most jurors are:

a) Absorbed with the seriousness of their responsibilities.

b) Impressed that lawyers for both sides can be so persuasive.

c) Surprised that they don't really get to meet Judge Wapner in person.

13. When selecting a foreman, the jury should always pick the member who:

a) Is the most reasonable and articulate.

b) Has the keenest grasp of both arguments in the case.

c) Can spit the farthest.

Mob desire backfires on longtime cop

August 30, 1989

Today's Episode: Ralph Joins The Mob.

Not Ralph Kramden, but Ralph Finno. He's the former Fort Lauderdale police captain who last year ran for Broward sheriff, and lost. This year, authorities say, Ralph chose a different line of work.

The scene: a typically tacky office on Commercial Boulevard. Hidden TV cameras are rolling (Ralph doesn't know it). Two other guys in the room aren't real mobsters, they're police informants (Ralph doesn't know this, either).

Bogus Mob Guy #1: "To swear an oath to us, that your allegiance is with our family, I ask you to bite this bullet. With this bullet, you are now a part of us."

Bogus Mob Guy #2: "That's the bullet that's got your name on it."

Bogus Mob Guy #1: "Right, that's your bullet. Capisce?"

Ralph Finno: "Capisce." (Uneasily.) "Want me to bite the bullet?"

Bogus Mob Guy #1: "Just bite it. That's good."

Ralph bites. Gingerly he hands the bullet back to the phony mob guy, who then kisses Ralph on both cheeks.

Unfortunately for Ralph, the bullet later reappeared in an evidence bag after Ralph was arrested for loan sharking, racketeering and running a house of prostitution. Today Ralph says he did nothing wrong.

Over months he'd been videotaped discussing alleged crimes with the phony mob guys. His "initiation" into the Family was to be the climax of these friendships. As silly as it looked, Ralph's ceremony went smoother than his brother Tony's.

In a blood oath, Tony and the phony mobster tried to nick each other with a dagger. The dagger was too dull. "Why don't you get me something, for Chrissake's, that can cut!" complained the phony mobster.

Tony took out his own knife. This time the two men sliced themselves so deeply that they wouldn't stop bleeding. The hidden camera recorded them sitting on the sofa, trying to discuss alleged Mafia business while sucking their own fingers.

When Ralph is on camera, the favorite topic is his old rival, Nick Navarro. The phony mob guys say they can arrange for Ralph to be named acting sheriff, if only something happens to Navarro. Ralph loves the idea of being sheriff ("When the time is right, I've got to get my suit pressed!") but appears nervous at the suggestion of foul play: "If anything happens to this guy [Navarro] . . . this town'll be turned upside down by all these young investigative reporters."

At one point Ralph asks if the mob is influential enough to get the governor to remove Nick from office. The phony mob guy makes a noise like a gun, and says that's the only way to get rid of Navarro. Ralph looks queasy. "It's a very touchy, touchy, touchy situation," he says.

The phony mobster, doing a swell Luca Brazi: "You want him gone with the fishes? Fine."

Ralph doesn't look thrilled with the idea of knocking off Navarro, but notes, "He did have threats by Colombians."

The phony mobster asks if Ralph has any ethical qualms about jumping to the other side of the law. No, Ralph says, "I always respected a guy who had talent, could make money and not get caught."

There will be criminal activity, the bad guy warns. "It's a business," Ralph replies. "It's like anything else . . . Even when I was on the job, I had no problem with prostitution, I really don't. Open up 20,000 places, go ahead . . . You want to run some traffic in gambling? Fine. You want to have some loan sharking? Fine. These things never bothered me."

The phony mobster says there might be times when knees must be broken. Says Ralph: "It's very easy to go out and smack somebody around. At the same time . . . can we use this person? Why burn bridges?"

In a prelude to the bullet-biting ritual, Ralph expresses one reservation about his pending career change. He wonders if joining the Mafia might tarnish his 27-year record in law enforcement: "I have extensive, extensive—and I'm not trying to blow my own horn—extensive credentials . . . I don't want this decision to hurt that."

Today Ralph is in jail, no bond. His credentials are in serious jeopardy.

Spotlight on Nick Navarro becoming hot

July 1, 1991

It was many months ago that 60 Minutes arrived to do a segment on Broward Sheriff Nick Navarro.

The sheriff reacted as he always does at the prospect of seeing himself on TV—with joyous gusto. Navarro is a publicity junkie, and the idea of appearing on America's most popular (and serious) news show must've sent him into ecstasy.

Sure, he's bosom buddies with Geraldo Rivera, but nobody takes Geraldo seriously. 60 Minutes is the big leagues. A prime-time puff piece would guarantee Navarro's re-election.

But now the picture's gone bad. The Broward Sheriff's Office is the target of a federal investigation into corruption and influence-peddling. The press, which has given Slick Nick such a sweet ride for so long, now snarls at his throat.

Even worse for Navarro, the 60 Minutes producers are reshaping, if not reconsidering, their profile of the dapper sheriff. By the time it's over, the 2 Live Crew fiasco will look like comic relief. Ironically, Navarro's own pathological itch for self-promotion is what caused some of his problems. Back in 1986, the sheriff was too eager to help Geraldo Rivera find a target for a prime-time drug bust. BSO chose a coke dealer named Nelson Scott.

After complaining for years about Scott's activities, neighbors were glad to see him finally arrested. Why it took so long was something of a mystery, until Scott started talking. He testified that he'd been paying off deputies with cash, dope and hookers. A BSO investigation discounted Scott's charges, but the feds are listening to him now.

The scandal has other dimensions. Agents are exploring the lifestyles of some of the sheriff's top guys. One, Ron Cacciatore, managed to build a $695,000 home on a captain's salary. Cacciatore has said his family inherited some money and invested wisely. He was seen socializing with a fugitive smuggler in the Bahamas, but has insisted he didn't know the man's true identity.

Another focal point is Navarro's friendship with auto dealer Jim Moran, the sheriff's most generous campaign contributor. Recently Moran sold BSO a fleet of used cars at new-car prices. Once Navarro hired one of Moran's security men as a BSO commander, even though the man, James Burkett, had failed a polygraph when asked about drug crimes.

Burkett recently was convicted of lying to U.S. agents about a marijuana operation. He was sentenced to 21 months.

The rain of subpoenas is enough to make Navarro's hair turn from white to black. All involved have denied any wrongdoing, while the sheriff clings to the Nixon defense: Bad things might've happened, but I sure didn't know about 'em.

No, Mr. Tough Guy Sheriff was too busy busting rap musicians to pay attention to what was going on inside his own department. Now he's got a mess that will not stop stinking before the '92 election. The media, which had been Navarro's pliant co-conspirators for so long, are now lambasted for their "feeding frenzy."

To scoff at Navarro's past grandstanding is to underestimate his shrewdness. Over the years he has hyped himself into a national personality; he is far more widely known and recognized than his low-key Dade counterpart, Police Director Fred Taylor.

Even Broward commissioners have been intimidated by Navarro's silky celebrity—they've inflated the BSO budget to an outlandish $197 million a year. For reasons still unclear to taxpayers, the sheriff now employs about 3,200 people.

As much as he'd love to duck responsibility for the BSO scandal, Navarro can't. It's his own top, hand-picked men who are in trouble—not the rank-and-file deputies.

These days, the sheriff's moth-like frenzy for the kleig lights has abated. The true test will come if 60 Minutes calls again. Can Nick resist the urge to face the cameras, to beam his suave visage into 20 million American homes?

Probably not. He who lives by the tube, dies by the tube.

Personal-injury lawyers back in chase—by mail

May 12, 1994

A U.S. appeals court says Florida lawyers don't have to wait 30 days to send advertising material to accident victims. Now solicitations can begin almost as quickly as CPR.

That's great news for starving personal-injury attorneys, since ambulance-chasing by direct mail is more fuel efficient and less hectic than the old way.

Your secretary simply drives to the police station and copies the day's accident reports, which conveniently include the names and addresses of all parties. Soon you've got yourself a lengthy (and potentially lucrative) mailing list.

Disapproval of such tactics caused the Florida Bar to impose the 30-day rule in 1991. Softhearted regulators decided that accident victims should be given a few weeks to collect their wits before being peppered with brochures from lawyers.

The problem was, some accident victims actually got better during that time, and thus had no interest in suing anyone.

It was a sad period for personal-injury attorneys. Some turned to probate law, or even real estate. Others simply went broke. Before long, they were living under the interstate and collecting aluminum.

Fortunately, one brave fellow fought back. His name was G. Stewart McHenry, a disbarred Tampa lawyer with justice on his mind and time on his hands. He hired a non-disbarred lawyer and sued.

McHenry argued it was unconstitutional for the Bar to curb a lawyer's use of the postal system. On Tuesday the 11th U.S. Circuit Court of Appeals agreed, tossing out the 30-day waiting rule.

Once again, lawyers may write to crash victims immediately after the mishap. In composing those letters, the tricky part is to avoid coming off as a cold-blooded mercenary. Voracity should always be glossed with compassion:

Dear Mr. Doe,

It has come to our professional attention that you were recently involved in an unfortunate (plane, bus, train, boat, moped or automobile) accident. We sincerely hope that you and your (wife, children or co-workers) were unharmed and have no cause to take legal action, despite the many millions of dollars you might be able to collect.

However, in the tragic event that you now find yourself (maimed, dismembered, bruised, stiff, achy, queasy, sneezy, dizzy or sexually lethargic), we advise you to visit our office for a free legal consultation.

We apologize for contacting you so soon after your accident. Seeing our postal carrier at the hospital must have been quite a surprise! We sincerely hope his presence did not interfere with any emergency medical procedures.

But experience has taught us that the sooner we can reach victims and inform them of their rights, the more assistance we can give. That's why our firm communicates only by registered mail.

We understand that, under the circumstances, it might be impossible for you to personally sign for our important correspondence—your writing arm might be fractured, sprained or attached to an intravenous tube.

In that case, any licensed (paramedic, nurse, doctor or physical therapist) may accept our mail on your behalf.

We also realize that you might be unable to read this letter and make a timely decision regarding your legal representation. Don't worry. Some of our most loyal clients were heavily sedated at the time we contacted them. Some were even in deep comas.

If that's your situation, a member of our staff will gladly visit you in Intensive Care to explain your options. We're specially trained to interpret your feeblest sigh, moan or tremor.

Your pain is our pain, Mr. Doe. Only a (five-, six-, seven-) figure settlement will truly ease it. Please let us help.

Judicial race is an exercise in extortion

February 28, 1990

The billboards and bus benches shout the news: Soon it will be time to go to the polls and elect our judges.

What a joke.

All around Florida, circuit and county judges already are out pressing the flesh, leeching campaign contributions from the very attorneys who bring cases before them. It's as close to naked extortion as you can get, but don't blame the judges.

It takes loads of money to run a political race. If you're a candidate for a judgeship, the logical place to solicit is law firms because (a) lawyers have the dough and (b) they're the only ones who have the remotest idea who you are.

The public, in most instances, hasn't got a clue.

The average voter walks into the booth and picks a name that looks distinguished or vaguely familiar. He hasn't the vaguest notion of whether or not the candidate is qualified to sit on the bench. Without reading the small print, he couldn't even tell you whether the vacancy is in criminal or civil court, county or circuit.

Unless a judge recently has been involved in a steamy scandal or a high-profile criminal trial, he or she remains largely anonymous to everyone but courthouse regulars. By the time the primary rolls around in September, most people will be taxed even to recall the name of the man who sentenced Miami policeman William Lozano.

You can't blame the voters for not knowing who's who. In Dade County alone, 97 county and circuit judges must run for office. Broward has 62 judges; Palm Beach County, a mere 39. Says Florida Bar President Steve Zack: "Walk up to your favorite lawyer and ask him to name all the judges. It's an impossibility."

The election process is not only shallow but tainted. It rewards the candidates who can afford the best billboards—in other words, those able to squeeze the most money out of lawyers. When the same lawyers later appear in that judge's courtroom, we are supposed to believe that the judge's actions will not be swayed by the memory of political generosities, or lack thereof.

The concept of "selling" judges is tricky because they don't campaign like county commissioners or congressmen; the nuances of someone's judicial record can't be compressed into a snappy 10-second sound bite. Judges can't even take a public stand on issues; they are forbidden by a code of ethics.

So what can they talk about on the political trail? Absolutely nothing of substance. Name recognition is everything; billboards, balloons, blarney. Typically we are better informed about our choice of stick deodorant than our choice of judges.

The Florida Bar and many in the judiciary want reform. Several bills have been filed in Tallahassee that could lead to a change in the way we pick circuit and county judges. Merit selection is the most logical option.

Under this method—currently used in 34 states and our own appellate courts—panels composed of lawyers, appointees and lay people submit lists of qualified candidates to the governor, who then chooses the judge. Every few years, voters get a chance to decide whether to keep or remove that judge.

Those who support the present charade wave the flag and beat their breasts. They warn that merit appointments could be spoiled by politics—yet what's more political than the current spectacle of judges out hustling support from law firms?

Critics also wail that merit selection robs the public of the right to choose. It's nonsense. By voting yes-no on retention, the public will hold the ultimate power to replace any judge.

To argue patriotically in favor of judicial elections is fatuous, because the vast majority of incumbent judges run unopposed. It is no accident. Many of them find campaigning so distasteful that they hire "consultants" to steer potential opponents into other races, or discourage them altogether from running.

It is a loathsome and smelly enterprise, but the hacks who manage these campaigns want to keep things just the way they are.

Judges think fast to explain needles, money

June 17, 1991

Wouldn't you love to have the Maalox concession at the Metro Justice Building?

"Operation Court Broom" already has ensnared four judges and one well-known defense lawyer. The mood at the courthouse is one of acute gastric distress. Everybody's wondering who's next.

Federal raids have turned up wads of $100 bills, as well as other suspicious items. Attorneys are talking openly of shakedowns and kickback schemes. A grand jury is following the trail of slime, and indictments certainly will come.

When the going gets tough, the tough get lawyers. And the lawyers get creative.

So far, my favorite line comes from Ron Guralnick, who represents Circuit Judge Phillip Davis. Agents found a metal box of syringes and aluminum foil in Davis' chambers. Many defense lawyers would've been stumped for an explanation, but Guralnick gave it a shot (so to speak). He claimed the material was "evidence" left over from a long-ago case when Davis was a private defense attorney.

It seems like a prudent man moving to a prestigious judgeship wouldn't bring any syringes, regardless of their origin. Maybe these items held some sentimental value for Davis—a reminder of some memorable courtroom battle. Or maybe he collects old drug paraphernalia, the way other guys collect baseball cards ("Here, I'll trade you three needles for a bong!"). A few other Dade judges would gladly trade Davis' metal box for what was found in their own homes and offices, namely cash.

The FBI loves to spread it around, and Operation Court Broom was a windfall. Documents show that undercover agents paid out $266,000 in $100 bills between August 1989 and May 1991. It was a simple but time-tested scam: Bribes allegedly were funneled to judges in exchange for reducing criminal bonds, suppressing evidence and divulging confidential police information.

Later the feds went looking for their money. Agents found $1,800 in the home of Circuit Judge Roy Gelber. They discovered $5,100 in a dresser drawer at the home of Circuit Judge Al Sepe. Another $14,000 turned up in County Judge Harvey Shenberg's bedroom. And at the law office of ex-judge David Goodhart, agents grabbed an envelope containing $3,500.

OK, imagine you're one of the lawyers for these guys. The first thing you say, with rigid indignation, is, "Hey, it's not against the law to carry cash!"

No, but here's the problem. Every printed currency has a unique serial number. No two are alike. Consequently, it doesn't take Sherlock Holmes to trace a certain $100 bill from the hands of an FBI man to the paws of a judge. Numbers don't lie. On April 2, the feds allegedly handed out a cash payoff to Judge Shenberg. At least $1,200 of those bills allegedly turned up in the raid on Judge Gelber's home. In legal vernacular, this is known as being in deep doo-doo.

If it wasn't marked money, he'd have a dozen passable alibis. The judge cashed some traveler's checks. Or he won the money in the lottery. Or better yet, he was on his way over to Camillus House to make a generous cash donation to the needy!

Not with marked money, he wasn't. Judge Gelber's attorney will be doing some fancy dancing on this one. Perhaps he could argue that Judge Shenberg secretly broke into Judge Gelber's house in the middle of the night and planted the cash. Or maybe Judge Gelber was conducting his own top-secret investigation of courthouse corruption, and had seized the Shenberg money as "evidence."

There's more out there, too—as much as $241,600 in payoffs, still unaccounted for. That's 2,416 $100 bills hidden in shoeboxes, sugar bowls, mattresses, kitty litters, you name it.

If you're one of the shmucks sitting on that dirty money, waiting for the FBI to crash down your door, you've got to be wondering two things. One, how could I have been so greedy? And two, when's the next flight to Nassau?

Court Broom menu includes well-fed judge

February 16, 1992

The most disheartening revelation of Operation Court Broom is how cheaply some of our judges were bought.

Bribery usually means cash packed in a briefcase, wire transfers to a secret Nassau bank account, or a hidden interest in some juicy real estate deal. Those are the types of payoffs that crooked public officials customarily accept.

The last thing that comes to mind is squid. In this case, fried squid—which is served in fancy Italian restaurants under the deceptively lyrical alias of "calamari."

I know what you're thinking: How much corruption can you buy with a plate of squid? The answer: a whole judge, allegedly.

A federal grand jury has heard evidence that Dade Circuit Judge Al Sepe regularly feasted on calamari and other delicacies at a fancy restaurant called Buccione, in Coconut Grove. According to testimony, the judge's lunch tabs were paid by a local lawyer named Arthur Massey, who was seldom in attendance to enjoy the squidfest.

However, Massey frequently appeared in Judge Sepe's courtroom because Sepe frequently gave him court-appointed cases. In fact, the judge assigned Massey to 42 criminal cases that brought the lawyer more than $57,000 in fees. Interestingly, during that same 18-month period, Massey allegedly picked up about $10,000 worth of lunch and dinner tabs for the judge.

Now indicted and suspended on other matters, the well-fed Sepe vehemently denies any wrongdoing at the Buccione bistro. He insists there was no squid pro quo.

Massey, who is under investigation, remains silent. Perhaps his lunchtime largess was heartfelt, and in no way meant as a kickback for receiving those 42 cases. Perhaps he bought fried squid for all his favorite judges, so they wouldn't have to order from the courthouse cafeteria.

Feeding Sepe might have been an act of pure charity. After all, poor Al was barely scraping by on his $90,399 judge's salary. A man's gotta eat, right?

Still, prosecutors suspect a bribe. If so, it's an ingenious scheme—

slimy and pathetic, but ingenious. What better way to get rid of incriminating evidence than to eat it!

I'm not sure how Massey and Sepe would've worked out the specifics. Say the judge got a free meal for every armed-robbery case that he steered to Massey. What were the precise terms of the arrangement—did Sepe order only a la carte? Was wine included? And, most importantly, who left the tip?

The other Operation Court Broom crimes aren't nearly so complex, and the bribes not nearly so tasty. For instance, when Judge Roy Gelber assigned cases to a sleazoid lawyer buddy, the judge's kickback was a flat percentage of the fee—either one-fourth or one-third of the total, depending on how greedy Gelber was feeling that morning.

Taking cash is worse than taking calamari, but it's still graft and taxpayers still pay for it. Besides, $10,000 is a heap of squid. If it was an outright bribe, Sepe has set a cheesy precedent for future corrupt judges and those who seek to enlist them.

Even the dumbest criminal understands the concept of bribing with cash. Bribing with food is much harder. It requires a certain minimum level of savvy and sophistication. Not every case is worthy of Buccione cuisine, but pity the poor shlub who tries to fix a traffic ticket by offering the judge a Big Mac, a large Coke and a side of McNuggets.

Now that the Sepe-squid allegations are public, some defendants will assume the worst about the justice system. Their lawyers will creep into court with brown bags full of menus instead of money. Those facing serious felonies will rely on the Michelin restaurant guide for five-star selections, and hope that their judge is hungry.

The good ones aren't. After a long day on the bench, they don't have much of an appetite. Neither would you.

Borrowing lines from Brando won't help judge

February 4, 1993

Soap-opera time at the Operation Court Broom corruption trial: Confessions of a Newly Reformed Junkie, starring Judge Phillip Davis.

Sure, I took payoffs, he said. But, see, I was hooked on liquor, cocaine and Demerol! The drugs made me crazy.

"I let you down," Davis lamented in court. "I could have been somebody, I could have been somebody!"

Stop, Phil, you're breaking our hearts. I could have been somebody? Now you're swiping lines from Brando.

Here's the sorry truth: The judge is a crook. He took $30,000 in bribes from an FBI informant. He sold his robe and his honor.

What did Davis say as he grabbed a bundle of dirty cash? "Beautiful." It was a Kodak moment, preserved on video by the FBI.

Months later, midtrial, Davis suddenly comes clean about the dope and the booze. Turned him into a monster, he says. Made him nutso, fogged his normally impeccable judgment. That's why he lunged so hungrily for that bribe money—it was those darn evil drugs, taking over.

A sad tale, all right, accompanied by genuine tears. Maybe jurors bought it, maybe they didn't.

For the longest time, Davis has denied using drugs. He denied it to friends before his arrest, denied it to cops afterward. When agents found syringes in his office, the judge made up a silly story about how they got there. He gave TV interviews promoting his deception. Months after allegedly entering therapy, he continued to lie publicly about his drug problem. His own lawyer didn't know the truth.

And exactly when did Judge Davis decide to become an honest man? After sitting through weeks of devastating testimony, seeing the clarity of the FBI videotape, realizing the full weight of the government's case.

Staring at a possible 100-year prison sentence, the judge experienced a moral awakening. Time to tell the truth. Why? Because he was out of options. All that remained was to play the pity card.

I don't doubt that Davis was royally screwed up on drugs. Unfortunately, that's no excuse for being crooked. If it were, you'd have to throw open the doors of the county jail.

In every cell are men and women with wretched drug addictions: the crack head who robbed a Mini-Mart, the drunk who shot his neighbor during an argument, the auto thief who ate amphetamines for breakfast.

Most of them never had the opportunity and good fortune that Phil Davis has. They didn't have a shot at college or law school, and they didn't make judge at age 34. Maybe they were offered drug treatment along the way, but most likely not. And when the time came to answer for their crimes, these men went to jail.

Judge Davis wants the jury to think he's different, special, worthy of forgiveness—as if fixing court cases isn't as bad as stealing car stereos or knocking over ATMs.

The strategy might backfire. Some people, especially those with family members who've struggled with drugs, would say Davis is worse than your average junkie. He wasted chances that most people never get, and he did it for greed.

He had risen to the most honored and powerful position in the justice system. Then, between cases, he'd retreat to his chambers, pack his nose and arrange shakedowns.

A student of drama, Davis poured out his heart on the witness stand: I could have been somebody!

Finish the scene, Phil. You know the rest . . .

You coulda had class. You coulda been a contender. You coulda been somebody.

Instead of a bum, which is what you are.

Court Broom's final score warrants Lysol

April 29, 1993

Fumigate the courthouse. It's finally over.

The Operation Court Broom corruption trial ended messily this week, and the stench lingers. Even by local standards, it was one maggot-gagging parade of sleaze, and one expensive botch job. Too much time, too many charges and a jury that was (putting it kindly) too easily confused—it added up to bad news for the government.

Start with the key prosecution witnesses: Ray Takiff, a phenomenally crooked lawyer who went undercover to pass out FBI bribes, and Circuit Judge Roy Gelber, a phenomenally crooked judge who brokered corrupt schemes with other judges. Leaving a double-wide trail of slime in court, these guys were so odious that the defendants looked almost harmless by comparison.

Almost, but not quite. The defendants: three judges and a former judge, all accused of taking bribes to fix cases. The FBI had a helluva case, too—videotapes, phone taps, marked money. It looked like a cinch.

Final score: 53 charges, 37 acquittals, three convictions and numerous deadlocks. What happened? Lewis Carroll couldn't have hallucinated it.

The weird, warped verdict pleased Judge Phillip Davis and nobody else. The only defendant to be acquitted of all charges, Davis was also the only one to admit his crookedness. After he told jurors how he packed his nose with cocaine and packed his pockets with bribe money, they let him go.

Afterward, one juror said that Davis was clearly guilty of all charges. But, he added, jurors didn't believe they could convict Davis because the judge claimed to have been impaired by drugs. Really? Blowing coke is a legal excuse for committing crimes? Well, by golly, throw open those prison doors! Every inmate with a drug habit, shoo on outta here!

One juror said the judges deserved leniency because they were "first offenders." Like they'd been spraying graffiti instead of selling their oath.

The panel did manage to convict Judge Harvey Shenberg and ex-judge David Goodhart, while painfully acquitting Judge Al Sepe of most charges and deadlocking on others. Any verdict was a miracle, considering the tension in the jury room. Most jurors felt all the defendants were guilty of something, but one holdout—Gloria Varas—didn't want to convict any of them.

Varas says the other jurors badgered her and made her cry. The others say Varas stubbornly refused to consider the overwhelming evidence of guilt. Video of payoffs and bribery plotting failed to impress her. For instance, Varas discounted a surveillance tape of Shenberg taken moments after he stuffed cash in his trousers because, she said, she couldn't tell if the money was really green.

How did this person get on the jury? Before the trial, Varas revealed her belief that her ex-husband had once wiretapped her laundry room. That statement suggests, among other things, that Varas might think unfavorably of electronic evidence. For some strange reason, prosecutors kept her on the panel.

Varas remained adamant during deliberations, and the partial verdict was a lame compromise. Most of the jurors weren't satisfied with the outcome, and some flatly said the system failed.

While Davis rejoices, Sepe is considering a return to his old job. Why not? Voters blithely put him back on the bench after a previous scandal in which he allegedly solicited sex from a defendant's wife. This time, the snag is a mere $5,000 in marked FBI bills that turned up in the judge's nightstand. Voters will eagerly await his explanation.

Meanwhile, the feds intend to retry Sepe, Shenberg and Goodhart on the unresolved Court Broom charges. Let's hope more attention will be paid to jury selection. Next time, no space cadets.

A floating jail: Flotsam of the Schreiber mind

December 10, 1986

Maybe Barry Schreiber's right. Maybe the thing that has been missing from Biscayne Bay all these years is a really nice floating jail.

Sure, we've got porpoises and tarpon, manatees and pelicans—big deal. You can find the same critters at Sebastian Inlet or Marco Island or Key Largo.

But where else except Miami in the modern 20th century would you be able to sail past a shipload of actual hard-core jailbirds? The thought is enough to make you wish Herman Melville or Victor Hugo were alive to write about it. If this had happened years ago, prison lore wouldn't be the same—Steve McQueen would've made his great escape on a jet ski instead of a motorcycle.

Ostensibly the purpose of a Seagoing Slammer would be to temporarily alleviate the well-documented overcrowding in Dade County's landlocked penal institutions. A clever smokescreen, Admiral Schreiber, but we all know the truth: This will be the tourist attraction to end all tourist attractions.

Imagine combining the romance of the Love Boat with the charm of Alcatraz. Even the warden could wear Ocean Pacific.

Think of the headlines, the national publicity, the renewed interest in South Florida's notorious crime rate. And it couldn't come at a better time—the start of the winter season!

If I had the tour boat franchise, I'd already be jacking up the fares and installing extra seats ("On your left, ladies and gentlemen, the home of international singing sensation Julio Iglesias. And on your right, a sweaty boatload of convicted burglars, purse snatchers and sex maniacs . . .")

To be fair, Commissioner Schreiber can't take all the credit for the idea of a prison barge. New York City is already converting an old Staten Island Ferry into a floating lockup. It will be anchored off Riker's Island in the scenic East River, an angler's paradise that seasonally yields its share of three-headed mutant carp and trophy-sized dead mobsters.

For all its riches, the East River is no Biscayne Bay. As you might expect, a few of South Florida's know-it-all environmentalists are raising a ruckus about Schreiber's plan. A floating jail, they say, would be nothing but a floating toilet. They say it would degrade, pollute and poison the crystal waters. Last week, the Biscayne Bay Management Committee even passed a resolution condemning Admiral Schreiber's scheme.

Nobody seems willing to acknowledge some obvious advantages, such as mobility. In the past, Metro commissioners have been unable to select a few acres on which to build a new conventional jail. Every time they come up with a site, dozens of nearby and not-so-nearby residents storm the commission to complain.

With a floating jail, the location is no problem. You simply tow it around late at night, when everybody's sleeping. One week you might tie up off Turnberry, the next maybe Star Island, and the week after that, the Cricket Club. When the neighbors start to gripe, you quietly weigh anchor and sail on.

And can you think of a more festive and fitting entry in the annual winter boat parade?

Admittedly, there might be a few problems with the S.S. *Minimum Mandatory*. The cost, for one—a projected $4.5 million. For that kind of money you could probably lease the *Norway* for a year.

The next item is deciding who gets to be incarcerated on the jail barge. Certainly not just any old convicts—not with all those tourists gawking. Image-wise, it makes sense to pick only the inmates with the deepest tans and best disciplinary records. It also makes sense to pick those who can't swim very fast.

Security on the floating pokey could pose a challenge, but it's nothing that a trained school of ravenous lemon sharks couldn't solve.

As for the aesthetics, there's no denying that many jails are bleak, fetid, dispiriting hellholes.

Our Hoosegow-on-the-Bay doesn't have to look that way. We'll just get Christo to wrap it in pink.

Mathematician needed to sort prison guidelines

January 23, 1994

Florida's new prison-sentencing guidelines are supposed to tell prosecutors which bad guys are the worst, and how long to lock them up.

A prosecutor with many years of trial experience sent me the new rules, along with a gloomy note: "Other than the fact that categories 1-6 do not go to prison, and (categories) 7-9 go for a short time, I have no idea what's going on."

Neither do I. The new method of computing a criminal's sentence is so insanely confusing that Einstein himself would be pulling out his hair.

Crimes are ranked according to seriousness. For instance, passing a bad check or carrying marijuana is Level One. Kidnapping with bodily harm or violent sexual battery on a child is Level 10. Prison time is calculated using points.

Under the rules, 40 points or less means the judge can't send you to state prison. Between 40 and 52 points, the judge may send you to prison. Anything above 52 points is automatic state time. Sound simple? Just wait.

Here's an example from an actual "score sheet" used to train prosecutors. I wish I was making this up:

A bad guy is arrested for aggravated battery—a Level Seven crime worth 42 points. Add another 40 because the victim was severely injured. Plus 2.4 points because the defendant has a prior conviction for auto theft. (Why 2.4 points? Don't ask.) Bottom line: The guy's up to 84.4 points.

Now add four more from a previous prison escape. Add another six because he violated parole. Total points: 94.4. Converted to months, that's almost eight years in the slammer—but hold on.

To finish calculating, take the guy's 94.4 and subtract 28 months off the top. (This innovation replaces "basic gain time," assuring early release.) New answer: 66.4 months. That's 5½ years, right? Guess again.

On a Level Seven felony, a judge may increase or decrease prison time by up to 15 percent. So, our bad guy faces a minimum term of 4.15 years and a maximum of 6.9 years.

Normally he'd get out much sooner, thanks to "incentive" time off for good behavior (for each month served, up to 25 days are cut from a sentence). However, our bad guy is bad enough to earn a mandatory three years, under a separate law.

There. Wasn't that easy? And that's a simple case. It's no wonder that prosecutors are going batty.

Worse, the convoluted new sentencing guidelines don't accomplish what tough-talking lawmakers promised. "Nobody is doing more time," says Assistant State Attorney Michael Band. "It's basically a shell game. Passing the buck."

It's true. Some violent crimes that once earned a trip upstate no longer do: aggravated assault, strong-arm robbery, even battery on a police officer while possessing a gun. Instead of riding a prison bus to Starke, some offenders will serve no more than 364 days in a county jail.

That's because the Legislature is too gutless to raise taxes to build enough new prisons. Under pressure to appear alarmed about crime, lawmakers jiggle a few numbers and call it sentencing reform.

Unfortunately, there are still not enough cells for the most dangerous criminals. "The reality of it is," says Band, "there's no space out there."

Meanwhile, a prosecutor with 100-odd felony cases will spend untold extra hours struggling through the math maze of the new law. When Assistant State Attorney Monica Hofheinz briefed her colleagues on the sentencing changes, she instructed them to bring a calculator and a pencil "with a LARGE eraser."

Wisely, she also recommended Extra-Strength Tylenol.

Miami: No. 1 destination for crooks

September 1, 1994

Now the rest of us know what thieves, robbers and rapists have known for a long time.

Miami is the best place in America to be a criminal. It is to hard-core felons what Disneyland is to Michael Jackson.

In a series being published this week, the Herald used computers to study the effectiveness of Dade's justice system. The results are shocking, scary and disgraceful.

Dade has the worst crime rate in the country, and does the laziest job of putting bad criminals behind bars. Unless you shoot a tourist or rob the mayor, the odds of beating the rap are hugely in your favor.

Only 15 of 100 convicted Dade felons go to state prison; the national average is 46 per 100. Out of 24 major metropolitan areas, Dade is dead last in punishing serious crime.

The customary excuse, swallowed so gullibly by us in the media, turns out to be a myth: There are beds available in Florida prisons, but Dade uses less than half its share.

State Attorney Kathy Rundle insists that crooks often serve more time when sent to county jail rather than state prison. Statistics show that's not true.

Moreover, since 1990, inmates in state prisons are serving increasingly longer stretches of their sentences (44.2 percent today, compared with 33.1 percent four years ago).

To appreciate Dade's marshmallow-softness on crime, consider that a robber arrested in neighboring Broward is three times more likely to go to prison.

What's going on? An incredible jamboree of plea-bargaining.

All big-city prosecutors and judges are snowed under by cases, but dumping them has become an art here in Dade. Of 162 felony defendants—one day's worth last spring—only 12 got prison.

Most of the rest got deals. They had the charges dropped, were put on probation, or were sent through pretrial diversion. One such program, the much-hyped Drug Court, was designed to help first offenders. It's now used as a prison-dodging scam by career crooks. One recent enrollee: a burglar with 28 prior convictions.

Much of the blame falls on prosecutors, and the judges who routinely accept (and encourage) outlandish deals for the sake of expediency.

At the State Attorney's Office, a legacy of leniency began under Janet Reno. Back in 1981, the *Herald* studied a week's worth of Dade felony arrests: Of 407 defendants, 38 went to prison.

Reno lobbied for a bigger budget and more prosecutors, and got both. Nevertheless, benevolent plea-bargaining has continued at a breakneck pace, sometimes with tragic consequences.

Many judges are content to help spin the revolving door, to thin their heavy calendars. The result: plea deals that gladden a mugger's heart.

It's true that Dade's justice system hasn't kept pace with the crime boom. Prosecutors and judges here labor with heavier caseloads than their counterparts in many cities.

But that doesn't account for the outrageous discrepancy in the imprisonment rate. Dade isn't merely the worst, it's the worst by a mile. Obviously there's an institutional philosophy by which prison is the least desirable of prosecutorial options.

Pretrial diversion might make sense for first timers, but it's a ridiculous approach toward a sleazebag with 28 felony raps. What else are prison cells for?

What the Dade courthouse needs is radical attitude adjustment, or an infusion of aggressive new talent. Forget who's governor or attorney general; it's prosecutors and judges who have the power and responsibility to lock up thugs.

That's a rare event in Miami, now a national playground for felons. The rules are different here.

Death penalty should be fair, certain, swift

March 27, 1997

Well, they don't call it Old Sparky for nothing.

Florida's infamous electric chair went haywire again Tuesday, and Pedro Medina caught fire.

No big deal, according to Gov. Lawton Chiles and other God-fearing leaders. They say the convicted killer was already unconscious when his hot-wired skullcap lit up like a Roman candle.

The governor cited the account of the prison's medical director, who declared:

"I saw no evidence of pain or suffering by the inmate . . . . In my professional opinion, he died a very quick, humane death."

Thank you, Dr. Quentin Tarantino. (Did he say "humane"? Yeah, sign me up for this guy's HMO.)

But nobody put a rosier spin on the grisly mishap than Attorney General Bob Butterworth, who mused that a faulty electric chair might prove a stronger deterrent to crime.

And, while you're at it, how about a squirt of lighter fluid as they strap the guy in? Just in case he hasn't figured out the program.

That flames shot from Medina's head and the death chamber filled with smoke was politically incidental to the outcome: The man definitely died. No argument there.

But, once again, the state of Florida looks like it's being run by a bunch of dumb-ass rednecks who couldn't fix a toaster, much less an electric chair.

The last time Old Sparky malfunctioned, cop killer Jesse Tafero ignited not once, not twice but three times. That's because some genius decided to substitute a synthetic household sponge for the real thing.

(See, when a sea sponge is moistened and placed under the death cap, it absorbs some of the scorching heat generated by the 2,000-volt surges. Without a buffer, the condemned man tends to catch fire, which is an unsavory advertisement for capital punishment.)

To avert such ghoulish fiascos, many states long ago switched to lethal injections. Typically, the inmate is reclined on a table and hooked to an intravenous tube. Toxic chemicals drip into his veins, and he basically goes to sleep.

Humane it's not. The death penalty isn't supposed to be.

But injection is the most painless method, and it avoids the Gothic grotesqueries of the electric chair: the shaving and lubricating of the doomed man's scalp; the leather bonds; the death mask; the hooded executioner.

So primitive is the ritual of electrocution that even those who advocate capital punishment often are appalled when they finally witness it. I was.

There's no practical reason for keeping Old Sparky plugged in, but state legislators are a nostalgic lot. Some of those Gomers would bring back public lynching, if they thought there were enough votes in it.

Polls show that most people want the death penalty to be fair, certain and swift. It's none of that now—a failure as a crime deterrent, and a stupendously expensive one. It costs millions more to execute a man than it does to lock him away forever.

But the one thing capital punishment does accomplish is this: It takes a life for a life. That's all it does—but that's often enough for those who've lost loved ones to murderers.

So the question for modern society becomes, how do we carry out this grave and ultimate act?

Answer: Here in Florida, we use a 74-year-old wooden contraption so crudely engineered that its efficiency depends on a sponge.

But don't think we're just a bunch of ignorant, unenlightened hicks down here. We didn't mean for Pedro to flame up the way he did.

It won't happen again, either. Next time, by God, the warden's bringing a fire extinguisher.

Dade attorney batting zero against graft

October 23, 1997

Dade's reputation as the crookedest place in America is secure, thanks to Dade State Attorney Kathy Fernandez Rundle.

On Monday, she declared that no criminal investigation of county paving contracts should begin until an independent audit is done.

And, since Dade commissioners are probably too yellow to order an audit, it's possible that any thieves who skimmed hundreds of thousands of taxpayer dollars will be safe from prosecution.

So what else is new?

When it comes to pursuing corruption, Rundle's record is even more pathetic than that of her see-no-evil, hear-no-evil predecessor, Janet Reno. That's one reason so many crooks flock to public office here—they know that nobody's watching.

The bribery epidemic at Miami City Hall.

Missing and misspent millions at the Port of Miami.

Hundreds of computer-forged housing inspections at the county building department.

All these recent scandals have one thing in common: The State Attorney's Office had virtually nothing to do with exposing them. A perfect batting average of .000.

In some places, prosecutors would be embarrassed if their communities were so visibly a-rot with corruption. In some places, prosecutors actually send out investigators to hunt for dishonest public officials.

And in some places, when wrongdoing is uncovered, indictments are drawn, trials are held and an actual attempt is made to punish the crooks. Can you imagine?

Here in Dade, the task of ferreting out graft is left to the FBI or the media. It's an icky little business, and the state attorney would prefer not to get involved.

The paving scandal is a prime example. In a random examination of three dozen repair jobs, this newspaper documented truckloads of missing materials, projects paid for but never done, and hundreds of thousands of dollars in overcharges.

Sidewalk repairs that should have cost $20,000 were billed (and paid) at $166,024. One homeowner's driveway was replaced for $19,500—six times more than what his own contractor had offered. Another minor patch job cost $9,004 when the price should have been $750.

All the work was done for the water and sewer department as part of a huge county contract with Church & Tower, the firm headed by the loud and politically influential exile leader, Jorge Mas Canosa.

The company says it's "surprised" by the size of the paving bills, and promises to conduct its own investigation, which I'm sure will be relentless, unsparing and thorough. I'm also sure that Chihuahuas can be taught to translate Proust.

Church & Tower's attorney says all the disputed work was performed by subcontractors, and that the county will receive "an appropriate credit" if overcharging occurred.

There is no "if." It happened, and it's no wonder the Church & Tower gravy train has bloated from $21 million to $58 million in 21 months. The tab for "special" concrete repairs alone has soared from $420,000 to $2.3 million.

Perhaps the company is experimenting with a new type of concrete made from diamonds. Or perhaps somebody is simply robbing taxpayers blind.

The county supervisors who approved the outlandish overpayments have been reassigned. (After being questioned by reporters, both men complained of chest pains and hurried to the hospital—a wise move.)

Facing these fresh revelations of money-squandering, the commission has grudgingly agreed to reconsider an audit of the paving contract. Two weeks ago it voted down the idea, after ferocious lobbying by Church & Tower.

The same could happen again, as many commissioners fear antagonizing the Mas family or the Cuban American National Foundation, headed by Mas Canosa.

This would seem an ideal opportunity for a diligent prosecutor, unswayed by politics and suitably appalled by such a massive rip-off, to launch a criminal probe.

Dream on, folks. Kathy Rundle says she wants to see an audit first.

Apparently not quite enough of your money is known to be missing. Oh well. Perhaps her enthusiasm for finding it will be better stoked when the sum exceeds seven figures.

Unfortunately, we might never know how much has vanished in the Church & Tower fiasco. That's because Rundle is leaving the decision to the same knucklehead politicians who approved the contract originally, politicians who've taken plenty of campaign donations from Mas family interests,

And if that doesn't kill the investigation, Rundle has plenty of other options.

Chest pain, for example. I hear that's going around.

State haggles over the cost of stolen days

April 26, 1998

What is a day of your life worth?

The answer is $79.46, if you're Freddie Pitts or Wilbert Lee. That's the amount that the Florida House proposes to give the two men, who spent more than 12 years—exactly 4,405 days—in prison for murders they didn't commit.

Pitts and Lee were pardoned two decades ago, and ever since then have been seeking compensation for their time behind bars. And every spring they've been rebuffed by the Legislature, to the everlasting shame of this state.

This year, finally, Pitts and Lee will be paid.

The debate churns around the choice of an appropriate sum. What monetary value can be placed on four thousand days of freedom lost; four thousand days apart from family; four thousand days blanked off a calendar because somebody made a horrendous mistake?

Pitts and Lee had asked for $1.5 million each. House Speaker Dan Webster countered with a degrading offer of $150,000. Last week, the House settled on $350,000, or $79.46 for every day wrongly spent behind bars.

Some would still call that disgraceful. Others would say Pitts and Lee should be grateful to receive anything.

In 1963, the two black men went on trial for murdering two white gas station attendants in the Panhandle town of Port St. Joe, which in those days was segregated. Wilbert Lee was 27 and Freddie Pitts was 19.

They were convicted by an all-white jury, and sentenced to die. Later, somebody else (imprisoned for killing another gas station attendant) confessed to the Port St. Joe murders, and his account was supported by a girlfriend.

Pitts and Lee were granted a new trial in 1972, but a judge wouldn't let the jury hear about the other man's confession.

Again Pitts and Lee were found guilty. Freedom didn't come until three years later, when they were pardoned by then-Gov. Reubin Askew.

The case remains controversial in the Panhandle, where some folks still say Pitts and Lee are guilty. That it's taken Florida so long to compensate the men can be explained by old Dixie politics.

But this year finds a Republican-controlled Legislature that's avidly courting black voters. It's also a year of great bounty in Tallahassee, so lawmakers have been throwing hundreds of millions of dollars at all kinds of pet projects, causes and schemes.

There's money for jellyfish farming, and for special trucks to haul catfish; money for fairs and zoos and farmers' markets; money for the International Swimming Hall of Fame and even the Palatka Armory ($300,000!).

And at long last there's also some money for Freddie Pitts and Wilbert Lee, 35 years after being sent to Death Row for something they didn't do.

What's right? What's fair? The Senate will decide Monday.

Reparation might be based on the accumulated weight of a dozen productive years gone—the youth of both men, really. Or it could be calculated day-by-day—4,405 of them excised forever from two lives.

A $350,000 lump certainly sounds more generous than $79.46 a day, but it's the same number. Not an insignificant number, either, considering how Pitts and Lee have gotten stiffed in the past.

I don't know what one day in your life is worth in dollars and cents, but $79.46 still seems cheap to me.

Especially considering how lawmakers quietly have set aside $2.5 million for "transition" expenses for Florida's new governor next January—$2.2 million more than what was spent on Lawton Chiles' taking office.

For $2.5 million, it should be quite an arrival. They ought to hold it at the Palatka Armory, and give the rest of the money to Freddie Pitts and Wilbert Lee.

Candidates
with
Convictions

Forget diplomacy, try Joaquin Andujar for mayor

November 1, 1985

First, let's get this ridiculous mayor's race out of the way.

The best man for the job isn't even running, so you'll have to write his name on Tuesday's ballot.

I'm speaking, of course, of Joaquin Andujar.

If you saw the seventh game of the World Series, you know what I'm talking about. The score's about a zillion to nothing when the Cards call Andujar in from the bullpen. He throws a couple of fast balls, then goes berserk and starts chasing the umpires. He gets thrown out of the game but still won't quit: In the clubhouse he grabs a bat and beats one of the toilets to death.

As I watched them drag Joaquin, thrashing and foaming, off the field the other night, I thought: This man would make a great mayor of Miami. He's perfect—more decisive than Maurice Ferre, more stable than Joe Carollo, more intelligible than Demetrio Perez and more energetic than Miller Dawkins and J. L. Plummer put together.

In no time Andujar would mop up the City Commission. Forget diplomacy—we're talking a 93-mile-an-hour brushback pitch.

It's not such a bad idea, when you review this year's crop of political hopefuls, a veritable slag-heap of mediocrity. What is it about South Florida that compels people barely fit to function in society to go out and run for public office? Be grateful that Thomas Jefferson's dead so he doesn't have to witness our peculiar version of the democratic process.

A few stars:

• Miami mayoral candidate Evelio Estrella, who blames the Anglos and blacks for ruining the city. He also refuses to speak English during candidate forums. This guy doesn't belong in City Hall; he belongs in a Mel Brooks movie.

• Miami Beach mayoral contender Alex Daoud, who actually took out an advertisement boasting of an endorsement by Barry Gibb of the Bee Gees. We can only assume Boy George is stumping for Malcolm Fromberg.

• Hialeah city councilman Paulino Nuñez, up for re-election, who allegedly pulled a handgun on one of his enemies during a city meeting. Despite witnesses' accounts, Nuñez denies it happened. He says he owns several guns, but left them home that night. There, doesn't that you make feel better?

• Hialeah City Council candidate Roy Leon, who was arrested for soliciting prostitution, possession of marijuana and carrying a concealed machete. Of all the charges, it's that darn machete business that nags at me, though I'm sure Mr. Leon has a splendid explanation. When does the cane crop come in this year anyway?

• Harvey MacArthur, the socialist running for Miami mayor, who wants to fly in both Daniel Ortega and Louis Farrakhan for advice on city government. All they need is Moammar Khadafy and they'd have a fourth for bridge.

• Frederick Bryant, who is running for Miami mayor but initially refused to let the Miami News take his photograph like the other candidates. Something tells me Mr. Bryant's a bit too shy to be mayor.

• Maurice Ferre, whose bilious campaign advisers make G. Gordon Liddy look like Mother Teresa. How can a man who dresses so snappy behave like such a clod? Think about it: We're getting ethics lectures from a guy who's transferred all his assets into his wife's name. I love it.

As for the contenders for Ferre's job, none fits the bill. Raul Masvidal is a banker—never trust anyone who makes a living playing with other people's money. Xavier Suarez is a lawyer, and this town's already knee-deep in lawyers. Marvin Dunn's a bright guy, but much too even-tempered to be mayor.

Which leaves No. 47, the big right-hander from the Dominican Republic.

Andujar for Mayor—it rolls right off the tongue.

Tough, talented, unpredictable. Just the kind of leadership this city needs—somebody's who's not afraid of a little random violence.

Think about it Tuesday at the polls.

Remember, this isn't just democracy. This is damage control.

Local campaigns masquerade as serious politics

November 2, 1987

If you thought Halloween ended Saturday, you were wrong. The real night of terror is tomorrow, when local elections results are tabulated.

In Hialeah, the most investigated city in South Florida, real estate wizard Raul Martinez is favored to win re-election as mayor. To oust him would be a tragedy, putting dozens of FBI agents out of work.

In Miami Beach, incumbent Mayor Alex Daoud is so confident of re-election that he didn't even bother to show up for a televised debate the other night.

And, finally, the city of Miami—where does one begin?

Political observers are calling it the quietest campaign in years. Many big-time contributors decided to save their money this time around, which meant that the candidates couldn't afford many TV spots. What a loss.

The most vocal campaigner has been former City Manager Howard Gary, who's not even running for office. Gary has been buying radio time to urge blacks not to vote for mayoral candidates Maurice Ferre and Arthur Teele, as well as Commissioner Joe Carollo.

For those of you new to the city, here's a brief history to explain what's going on:

Howard Gary doesn't like Maurice Ferre because, back when Ferre was mayor, he voted to fire Gary, who is black. Carollo voted the same way.

Ferre doesn't like Carollo because Carollo once staged a big press conference supposedly to endorse Ferre, but double-crossed him instead. With the cameras rolling, Carollo announced that Ferre was basically a waste of protoplasm, and that he wouldn't support him if he were the last person on earth.

Mayor Xavier Suarez recently decided that he doesn't like Carollo, either, because the Cuban American National Foundation told him it was OK not to.

The Cuban American National Foundation, a small bunch of rich Republicans, doesn't like Carollo because he's an embarrassment to the human race. Also, he tends to vote against some of their members' pet business projects.

For a long time Carollo and the foundation have argued about who hates communism more. The head of CANF, Jorge Mas Canosa, once challenged Carollo to a duel, but Joe was busy that day.

Back in July, both Carollo and Mas showed up outside the Columbus Hotel to help scare some retarded Cuban teenagers out of town. Both men deserve credit for this brave patriotic gesture.

How does all this relate back to Howard Gary?

Carollo claims—get ready—that his main challenger, Victor DeYurre, is secretly supported by Gary at the guidance of CANF. Herein lies the latest Communist conspiracy.

Gary once served on the board of directors of a bank bought by a drug smuggler, who once said he knew other smugglers were using Cuba in their travels.

The bank must have known, therefore Gary must have known. Therefore, DeYurre must have known. Therefore, DeYurre is obviously a close personal friend of Fidel Castro.

This is the big picture, according to Joe Carollo. People have been institutionalized for less.

The only mayoral candidate who's had anything nice to say about Carollo is Arthur Teele, who is a black Republican.

If you took all the black Republicans in South Florida and put them in Joe Robbie Stadium, you'd probably still have about 73,000 empty seats.

Teele has had a tough campaign. In Overtown he doesn't dare mention that he's Republican, while in Little Havana he's handing out pictures of himself with President Reagan.

Howard Gary has figured out that this is nothing but a diabolical scheme to get Maurice Ferre elected.

If none of this makes sense, don't worry—leadership is an elusive quality. When you go to the voting booth tomorrow, trust your instincts. And try to keep your breakfast down.

A motto for Metro: The check's in the mail

September 2, 1988

Next week, Dade voters get to decide who will sit on the Metro-Dade Commission, that body of government (and we use the term loosely) whose task is to chart the future of the county.

This is the year that commissioners have brought new dimensions to the word craven. Zoning fiascoes aside, the sorriest episode was the debate over what to do about County Manager Sergio Pereira—he of the hot suits boutique, the secret land trust, the forgotten $127,000 windfall and other memory lapses.

As a public service, local television stations should rerun the highlights of the commission's Pereira discussions. That way, voters can be reminded of the moral vacuum in which Steve Clark, Clara Oesterle, Bev Phillips and Jim Redford operate so comfortably.

The fact that the county manager was caught in a bald-faced lie about his own finances, the fact that he violated state disclosure laws—no big deal to the commissioners. They blubbered their fealty even as new revelations were forcing Pereira to head for the hills.

Who could be happy with such a vapid bunch? Take a wild guess.

Judging by the weight of their campaign contributions, those who are most delighted by the commissioners' performance are developers, lawyers and bankers.

Because that's who really runs this county government.

They love the status quo. They depend on its mediocrity. The last thing they want on the County Commission are thinkers, leaders and visionaries; they want people who will be manipulated. Puppets.

Take Steve Clark, who has perfected the invisible-mayor form of government. He has raised nearly $500,000 in campaign funds to keep a "job" that pays $6,000 a year.

Here's a man for whom executive action is deciding whether to play a driver or a two-iron off the 17th tee; a man so flummoxed by the Pereira controversy that private lobbyists had to write his comments for him.

Yet builders, developers, contractors, real estate salesmen and architects think so highly of Mayor Clark's leadership skills that they've given more than $176,000 to help get him re-elected. Lawyers have rewarded the mayor with more than $51,000, while financial interests have coughed up a modest $35,500.

Another incumbent whose campaign has benefited handsomely from development interests is Commissioner Clara Oesterle. Approximately 45 percent of her $403,000 war chest comes from the folks who are busy turning West Dade into a parking lot.

Having accepted such embarrassing sums from special interests, the commissioners naturally denounce the system as flawed. If only it didn't cost so much to run a political campaign these days, they say, then we wouldn't have to take this money.

If that argument isn't obsequious enough, their next line is enough to choke a goat: We don't go out and solicit these contributions, they say, the checks just come in the mail.

So the half-a-million dollars in campaign moola that Mayor Clark has collected is merely a spontaneous outpouring of public support. Yeah, right. And Elvis is still alive, too.

You can bet that whoever shells out this kind of dough wants more than a thank-you note in return. When a nest of zoning lawyers and their wives all give the legal limit of $1,000 each to a candidate, they are purchasing influence, pure and simple. And it works.

Developers love the direction that the commission is taking Dade County because that direction is due west, all the way to the Everglades. Rat-warren condos and strip-shopping malls as far as the eye can see. Go look for yourself.

This, and a ghostway transit system, are the twin legacies of this outstanding batch of public servants.

Little will change after Tuesday's election. Voters who choose their commissioners from bus benches and billboards will again be duped, and it's their own fault. At least the developers know enough about basic civics to learn something important about their candidates.

Like where to send the checks.

Our own Joe shines again in Miami race

October 2, 1989

Somebody Up There must love newspaper columnists because an amazing thing has happened.

He's baaaaaaack.

Joe Carollo. Popping out of his manhole like a jack-in-the-box. To run for the Miami City Commission again!

Thank you, God. Things had gotten so dull lately—we needed to be reminded of the bad old days, when city government was a circus and Joe was the head clown. Sure, there's still back-alley politics, but today it's all so tame and . . . civilized.

In a sick way, we missed Carollo. He was such great copy, guaranteed to say something indefensibly dumb, paranoid or just plain crass.

Joe claims he's mellowed, but don't bet on it. In this new campaign he's challenging the city's only elected black commissioner, and already Carollo has gone on Spanish-language radio likening his opponent to a common street looter.

Vintage Joe. This is the same sensitive fellow who once compared a black city manager to Idi Amin.

Ah, what memories.

Carollo saw spies and counterspies and Communists everywhere, and claimed to have a dashboard bomb detector in his car. He once offered to tell a Senate committee how Fidel Castro's agents had infiltrated the Miami Police Department.

Another time, Joe torpedoed a big Sister Cities convention planned for Miami after learning that a few of the participants came from Eastern bloc countries. Reds!

Not that Carollo didn't have a warm spot for some foreign visitors. Miss Universe contestants, for example. Joe nearly tripped over his agenda in a rush to pose for snapshots with visiting beauty queens.

And when Sheik Mohammed al-Fassi and his wealthy entourage blew into town, Joe tagged along like a drooling puppy, offering the key to the city and (not incidentally) the services of his own private security firm. Any normal person would have been embarrassed, but not Joe.

Who can forget that gloriously despicable double cross of Maurice Ferre during the 1983 mayor's race—Ferre, calling a press conference to trumpet Carollo's endorsement, only to watch Joe trash him mercilessly in front of the assembled media. Poor old Maurice looked like he'd swallowed a bad clam.

Some politicians can legitimately claim stupidity as an excuse, but not Carollo. His reckless words were unforgivable because he knew exactly what he was doing—appealing to the most primitive of voters' fears and biases. He once said: "Sometimes when people are trying to divert attention, they create ridiculous situations and allegations."

People finally figured out that Joe was talking about himself. By the end of his miserable tenure, he had offended, slandered and nauseated the multitudes and gained a statewide reputation as a venal backwater McCarthy—or worse, a parody of one. Even the staunchest of anti-Communist organizations repudiated his tactics.

Carollo's name was such political poison that people who didn't even live in Miami wanted to move here, just so they could vote against him. In 1987, he lost in a muckslide.

Ironically, the only commissioner in recent years to act as preposterously as Joe is the man he's running against, Miller Dawkins.

It was Dawkins who declared that Ronald Reagan created the plight of the homeless "when he fired the air traffic controllers." It was Dawkins who asked if it was legal to build a tall fence around the Camillus House to protect downtown Miami from the poor and the hungry who stay there.

And it was Dawkins who vowed to prevent an AIDS counseling center from opening near Overtown—"if I have to break the law and get the brothers out there and burn it down."

At these moments it seemed like Dawkins was striving to fill the void of crudity left by Carollo, or perhaps trying to eclipse the legend himself.

But, of course, that's impossible. There's only one Joe and he's ours again, at least until November—back in the headlines, back on the talk shows, back in the glare of the TV lights.

Our own little media monster, back from the bogs.

Candidates can't hide true colors

November 13, 1989

Miami poll workers ought to hand out antidepressants at the voting booths Tuesday morning.

What a lame collection of would-be commissioners on the ballot. You could toss a mullet net over any bus bench on Biscayne Boulevard and come up with four more distinguished candidates.

Thank God there were only six days between the general election and the runoff; to subject the public to any further campaigning would be an act of sadism.

First you've got Joe "I Hear Voices Again!" Carollo. Until last week, he had doggedly avoided the English-language media and confined his ramblings to Hispanic talk shows. Then he realized he would need the Anglo vote to win, and instantly he became garrulous and cooperative.

Suddenly Carollo was aiming that pained frozen smile at TV cameras and trying to sound like Mr. Let's-Unify-Miami instead of George Wallace (for whom he once campaigned).

Before long, though, the old Joe resurfaced. You just knew he couldn't go a whole week without unveiling some screwy conspiracy theory, and he didn't disappoint us.

On Friday, Carollo produced a laughably vague affidavit (with all the names conveniently blacked out) alleging a sinister vote-buying scheme in the 1987 election.

Considering the margin by which Carollo got stomped that year, the only person rich enough to buy that many votes was Victor Posner, and he was busy with other charitable matters.

This year Carollo's chances are bolstered by the performance of his opponent, incumbent Miller Dawkins, who once threatened to burn down an AIDS counseling center.

No one on the City Commission has a keener aptitude for uttering dumb things at the worst possible times. For this reason, Dawkins' advisers have urged him to run a low-key race, and to say as little as possible.

This isn't easy when a notorious drug dealer such as Isaac Hicks is announcing that he gave thousands in cash to previous Dawkins campaigns. The candidate has carefully responded that he never engaged in such a slimy transaction, which was (for once) exactly what any smart person would say.

Next we have Rosario Kennedy seeking a commission seat for which she earnestly promised not to run.

Having lost the Democratic congressional primary, the ex-commissioner faces some old uncomfortable questions. Voters are still ticked off about the $111,000 refurbishing of her city office, and they're still curious about her friendship with celebrity tax swindler Monty Trainer.

On the bright side, Kennedy has always been honest when giving her street address, which is more than you can say for her opponent, Miriam "Have Zip Code, Will Travel" Alonso.

Alonso is best known for lying about where she lived in order to run for a Metro Commission seat. The falsely sworn election document was apparently insufficient evidence for the state attorney to prosecute, but it was enough for a judge to kick her off the ballot.

This time around, Alonso promised that she wouldn't try that kind of stunt. Still, you've got to wonder about the force of her ambitions.

She changed party affiliations three times in less than two years—evidence of either crass political opportunism, or a multiple-personality disorder. Most normal people don't switch record clubs three times in two years, not even for a dozen free albums.

So this is the roster from which Miami voters must choose new leadership. It's a shame that not one of the candidates comes without a history of having done or said something profoundly stupid, or downright dishonest.

It's also a shame that only a small number of eligible voters will make the selection for the majority. If those who stay home Tuesday are waiting for a candidate who inspires them, they could die of old age first.

Unfortunately, democracy in these times is less a quest for new heroes than an obstacle course through stale mediocrity. As disheartening as it is, sometimes you've got to choke down your feelings and vote for the lesser of two feebles.

Gersten vote to test savvy of metro voters

March 11, 1993

Sometimes an election is a community IQ test.

The city of Sunrise had one this week. Next Tuesday, it's Miami Beach's turn.

Sunrise did itself proud. An impressive 73 percent of voters decided that they didn't want a convicted extortionist as mayor. The shameless John Lomelo got tromped at the polls.

On Tuesday, a scandalized Joe Gersten runs for Metro Commission in District 5, which includes Miami Beach and part of downtown Miami. For Gersten to be elected would be a big upset—and a profound commentary on the collective intelligence of those voters.

For 11 months, Clueless Joe has been dodging prosecutors seeking to ask him about the curious events of last April 29, when the commissioner's now-legendary Mercedes-Benz was stolen. The car turned up in the hands of Biscayne Boulevard lowlifes, who said they'd swiped it while Gersten smoked dope and had sex with a hooker in a downtown crack house.

Gersten claimed the car was taken from his gated driveway in Coral Gables. For weeks he toured Europe and avoided questions about the incident. When he finally returned, he unsuccessfully resisted taking a drug test. The results didn't rule out the possibility that Gersten had smoked cocaine, but they indicated that he wasn't a regular user.

Joey declared vindication, a bit too soon.

Prosecutors collected the logs from his car phones, and tapes of conversations between the commissioner and the dirtbags who had his car. They took statements from Gersten's maid and fiancee that raised more questions about Joey's wanderings on April 29. And they found a cab driver who swore that he'd picked up a man resembling Gersten on Biscayne Boulevard that night, and drove him to Gersten's neighborhood in the Gables.

Only the hurricane kept the Gersten follies from becoming a running feature on the evening news. To this day, Joey refuses to give a sworn statement about what happened, refuses to disclose how he spent the evening. He says the sneaky State Attorney's Office is trying to trap him in a perjury rap, and he's hired a high-powered defense lawyer to fight the subpoena.

It's been quite a spectacle—an elected public official, desperately ducking his civic duty to take a simple oath and tell the truth.

Clueless Joe blames ruthless prosecutors and bloodthirsty reporters for his troubles, but it was he who called police about the missing Mercedes. It was he who provided the porous yarn about leaving his keys (and his briefcase and his gun) in the unlocked car while he strolled into the house to make a phone call.

But don't count Gersten out. Scandalized or not, he's been able to squeeze an amazing $250,000 in campaign donations out of bond brokers, builders and others who do business with the county, and who want to stay on Gersten's good side in the unlikely event that he wins.

Residents of District 5 recently got a letter from "The Friends of Joe Gersten," extolling the commissioner's virtues while reminding voters that he hasn't yet been charged with any crimes. The letter carried the names of such well-known political and community figures as state Rep. Mike Abrams, Simon Ferro, Jesse McCrary, Barry Kutun, Georgia Ayers, Luis Sabines and Alan Potamkin.

Unfortunately, the letter tells you more about Gersten's "friends" than it does about Gersten. It's interesting that such civic pillars aren't sufficiently appalled by Joey's evasive conduct to make them set aside their political loyalties.

Maybe the voters will be suckered, maybe not. They've got 12 other choices, none of whom are hiding from prosecutors.

Ferre also owes voters an explanation

April 11, 1993

Tales from the crypt: Maurice Ferre is back.

He is risen from the land of political losers to run for Metro Commission. Lucky for him, there's no law against deadbeats holding elected office in Florida.

If bad debts were pit bulls, the former Miami mayor would have lost his most crucial appendages a long time ago. No one but Ferre knows precisely how much he owes, because he conveniently neglected to report it on his campaign disclosure form, as required by the state.

Ferre is no stranger to noncompliance. When he launched this most recent campaign, he still owed $65,000 of a $70,000 fine for campaign-law violations dating to 1981. The debt recently was trimmed to $62,000 after Ferre kicked in a whopping $3,000 of his wife's dough.

He hasn't taken the fine too seriously, and for good reason. In 1983, the Dade state attorney sued for the money, but soon gave up the hunt. Janet Reno says she put the case aside because her investigators couldn't find any funds listed in the ex-mayor's name. Everything had been transferred to Ferre's wife, Mercedes.

Ferre says he did it when the family concrete business, Maule Industries, went belly up in the late 1970s. At the time, the company's liabilities were reported at $23 million. Knowing creditors would be looking for him, Ferre basically gave all assets to his wife—an old dodger's trick, and a legal one.

It wouldn't even be noteworthy if Ferre was some private schlump who'd botched up a few business deals. He's more than that. He's running for a Metro Commission seat that will put him within lunging distance of a combined $3 billion budget.

It's perfectly proper for voters to demand details of a candidate's finances, no matter how muddled. A man who can't balance his own checkbook, and doesn't pay his debts, is a poor choice for handling taxpayer dollars. Ferre's wife, in fact, would seem a more sensible selection.

The ex-mayor solemnly claims to have no assets. He describes himself as an international businessman, but insists he's earned no money—not a dime—since Maule dissolved about 15 years ago. So what's he been up to?

He travels regularly to Puerto Rico and Latin America, where he supposedly assembles complicated mega-deals for other companies. Are we to believe he does it just for the sport? "I put deals together," Ferre explained to a reporter, "and will be paid in the future." What a curious arrangement.

In the meantime, he enjoys a "very nice lifestyle" supported by a "very substantial income" from his wife's family holdings. This, while continuing to stiff the good citizens of Florida for $62,000.

If Mercedes Ferre doesn't wish to cover the balance of her husband's court-ordered fine, that's her business. But it's hard to understand why Ferre himself has made no serious effort to make good on the debt. He's a bright, able-bodied, well-spoken fellow. Why doesn't he get a paying job?

By now, he could have settled the entire matter for a measly six grand a year. Bagboys at Publix do better than that. Of course, even part-time work might interfere with the "very nice lifestyle" to which the ex-mayor is accustomed.

Under fire in the District 7 Metro race, Ferre vows to obey the law and pay off the outstanding 62 grand . . . gradually. The state attorney has made no move to collect.

Too bad it's not a Visa bill. At 18 percent annually, Ferre's 12-year slide would have compounded to a robust $473,686. And those people, like some voters, never ever forget.

Campaigns for mayoral race, so far, so bad

August 22, 1993

The best way for voters to endure the dismal Miami mayoral race is to think of it not merely as another parade of fools, but as a vaudeville audition.

With the election more than two months away, the campaign has already degenerated into a promising orgy of mudslinging and petty sabotage. The three major candidates—Miami Commissioner Miriam Alonso, former Metro Mayor Steve Clark and T. Willard Fair, head of the Urban League—all allege slimeball behavior by their opponents.

The question for Miami voters isn't whether the candidates engage in dirty tricks. It's a given that most of them do. The issue is the quality of these new dirty tricks. Are they personal enough, vicious enough, deceptive enough and craven enough to uphold the city's sewer-rat tradition of scummy politics?

So far, so bad.

Now appearing on many cars are fluorescent bumper stickers that proclaim: "Miriam Alonso is a Communist." Well, Alonso is not a Communist, and every self-respecting Communist ought to be offended at the suggestion. The party's got enough headaches in Miami without having the shrill and conniving Alonso as a member.

On the question of temperament, tabloid newspapers now circulating in Little Havana enigmatically describe the commissioner as "erratic and crazy." Is this propaganda intended to be anti-Alonso, or pro-Alonso? In some precincts, being erratic and crazy would make you the odds-on favorite.

Alonso says the nasty bumper stickers and newspapers can be traced to Steve Clark and his main supporter on the Miami commission, Victor de Yurre. The reason that Clark needs a pal on the commission is (in his own words): "I don't know exactly what's going on down at City Hall because I haven't been there for 20 years."

In fact, Clark has made a career of claiming not to know what's going on, and not being there when it was. Still, he is justifiably irked by insinuations from the Alonso camp that, at 69, he's too old to be a forceful mayor. To be fair, Clark never claimed to be a forceful mayor. Hundreds of weekday golfing partners can attest to his devotion to leisure.

Raising questions about Clark's age and alertness is a risky proposition for Alonso. After all, it was she who completely forgot where she lived—and in fact, gave the wrong address—when running for office a few years ago. Perhaps both she and Clark would consent to mutual CAT scans to allay constituent concerns about possible impairment.

A new face in the political cross fire is T. Willard Fair, although he's not unacquainted with controversy. Writing in the Miami Times, Fair (who is black) has attacked other black leaders by naming them "nigger of the year." No fine trophy or plaque accompanies this dubious award.

Fair's opponents have been reminding black voters of his bluntness and have suggested that such coarse tendencies are potentially dangerous in a city where racial tensions lie close to the surface. Fair is also being slammed for failing to support Dade's black tourism boycott. To note that Clark and Alonso didn't support the boycott either would only spoil a perfectly bad dirty trick.

For all his bombast, Fair is easily the smartest of the three mayoral candidates, which automatically makes him the long shot. Alonso, the loudest of the trio, is presumed the front-runner. Clark, heavily bankrolled by developers, is running a strong and defiantly lackluster second.

While the race is off to a truly disgraceful start, it will require all the candidates' energy to stay gutter-bound between now and Nov. 2. I have every confidence they'll sink to the occasion.

Wacko factor gives city voters a tough choice

October 30, 1993

On Tuesday, thousands of South Floridians can drop to their knees and quietly give thanks that they don't live in the city of Miami.

Nov. 2 is Election Day, and it appears likely that Steve Clark and Miriam Alonso will be in a runoff for mayor. The campaign, as reprehensible as predicted, leaves nauseated voters to ponder the question: Which of these characters will embarrass us the least? Four categories should be considered:

1. General nutty behavior.

Say what you will about Steve Clark, he's not a volatile guy. It takes energy to be volatile.

Miriam Alonso, on the other hand, is frequently shrill, abrasive and emotional. Her 911 call after a routine burglary took the form of wild raving against the police. The potential for future wacko antics seems boundless.

2. Saying dumb things.

This one's a toss-up. Both candidates say dumb things all the time. For instance, Clark still insists that corruption and shoddy construction had nothing to do with the massive damage by Hurricane Andrew.

Meanwhile, Alonso babbles about secret Anglo conspiracies to purge Cuban Americans from office, exhorting supporters: "Whip in hand, we have to expel those who come to destroy our people!"

The image of Miriam Alonso going after Steve Clark with a whip . . . well, it's enough to give S-and-M a bad name.

3. Doing dumb things.

Again, Clark has the advantage here. In order to do something dumb, one must do something. Clark seldom does.

As Metro mayor, he rarely cast a vote without consulting the zoning lawyers, lobbyists and developers who put him in office. Freed from the burden of independent thinking, Clark was able to hurl himself into the task of signing proclamations and snipping ribbons—low-risk assignments that were virtually impossible to screw up.

As Miami commissioner, Alonso has done a few dumb things. After a German tourist was murdered, Alonso announced that she was jetting overseas to assure folks that Miami was a sane and normal place. Tourist officials urged her not to go, but the commissioner went anyway, an exceptionally stupid stunt. There is little evidence that the Germans were charmed.

4. Likelihood of indictment and/or arrest.

This category is crucial everywhere but Hialeah. In most cities, voters prefer that mayors not be busted for major felonies until their term of office is over. It's not just humiliating, it's costly—changing all the stationery from "Mayor's Office" to "Suspended Mayor's Office."

It's hard to say which Miami front-runner is most likely to get nabbed in office. As Metro mayor, Clark was secretly recorded during an FBI bribery probe and called to testify in Alcee Hastings' impeachment hearings. The entire U.S. Senate decided Clark's testimony was not credible, but he wasn't charged with a crime.

Alonso was equally lucky. She flat-out lied about where she lived in order to qualify for a Metro commission race. The law says you can't do that, but the State Attorney's Office let it slide.

Having survived close calls, both candidates are cautious. Neither is likely to get indicted for the first few months, at least.

There are other ways to embarrass the city, and either Clark or Alonso is eminently capable of breaking new ground. Who'd be worse? The choice is so repugnant that many voters yearn for alternatives.

Four other mayoral candidates do appear on Tuesday's ballot. None could bring more ridicule to Miami than the front-runners already have. It's not humanly possible.

Hialeah's new convict-mayor government

November 11, 1993

The good people of Hialeah have spoken. As incredible as it seems to the outside world, they want a convicted extortionist to be their mayor again.

Go ahead and laugh; Lawton Chiles isn't. The governor announced Wednesday that he won't attempt to suspend Raul Martinez for a second time.

For Chiles, it was a no-win situation. Yanking Martinez from office would have subverted the will of many Hialeah voters. Yet leaving him in City Hall gives the impression that Florida tolerates crooks in high places, particularly crooks with the same political affiliation as the governor. It's a messy dilemma.

Most normal cities would be deeply ashamed to have a felon as mayor, but on Tuesday, Hialeah declared—if by the slimmest of margins—that it is beyond shame.

So give the people what they want. Those 14,540 stalwarts who cast their ballots for Martinez surely gave thought to the consequences. Some obviously believe he is innocent, and some obviously don't care. Either way, they've decided that the advantages of having a convict-mayor outweigh the disadvantages.

By allowing Martinez to take office, Chiles establishes Hialeah as a unique sociopolitical experiment of the 1990s—a sort of biosphere of sleaze. The rest of Florida can watch and learn.

What exactly is the mandate for an elected racketeer? Is he expected to continue extorting? If so, how much and from whom? Can he successfully bridge the ideological chasm between his criminal and noncriminal constituents? These questions are seldom confronted in American politics, and here's a rare opportunity to get them answered.

Because of its checkered history, Hialeah is a logical place to experiment with the convicted-mayor form of government. After 40 years of uninhibited corruption, the undeveloped land is mostly gone and, with it, the opportunities for easy graft.

The city is already an aesthetic ruin, one zoning atrocity stacked shoulder to shoulder against another. Even if Martinez went hog-wild, what difference would it really make? How much worse could it get?

In a sense, the Hialeah mayoral race was the purest test of democracy—the frank exercise of electoral choice in the face of civic pride, conscience and common sense. The people wanted a convicted crook, and they elected him.

Does government have a constitutional right to intervene? What would Thomas Jefferson say?

Voters sometimes do confounding things. Candidates who die on the campaign trail occasionally get elected anyway, but at least dead guys can't steal. The election of a shakedown artist is a riskier proposition.

Although Chiles is staying out of it for now, the Hialeah biosphere could be punctured by other forces. Martinez's conviction on six corruption charges is being appealed to the 11th U.S. Circuit Court of Appeals. If the verdict is upheld, the governor has no choice but to jerk Martinez from office.

That's the law. It was conceived on the premise that voters would never tolerate criminals in office and would demand their instant removal. In most places, that's true. Hialeah is a special case, though, and perhaps an exception should be made.

Certainly those who voted for Raul Martinez on Tuesday were aware that he might soon be sent away to serve his 10-year sentence. So deep is their loyalty that many Hialeans would like him to remain their mayor, regardless.

In fact, there's no reason why Raul couldn't take care of the city's business from a prison cell in Eglin or Talladega. All he'd need is a telephone and some privacy.

Heck, it works just fine for John Gotti.

Hialeah vote 2: This time hide the cheating

November 10, 1994

Across the land, weary voters groan in relief: Another insulting, infuriating campaign season finally ends.

Unless you happen to live in Hialeah.

Residents of Florida's crookedest city are gritting their teeth for an ugly new mayoral election. A judge threw out the old one after a trial confirmed "substantial"—how shall we say?—irregularities.

Mayor Raul Martinez won the 1993 contest by only 273 votes, a margin achieved by a timely but statistically improbable influx of absentee ballots.

To the shock of no one, it was revealed that scores of those ballots arrived with forged signatures, witnessed by some of the Democratic mayor's loyal supporters. Bunches of those votes were gathered in a sweep of convalescent homes for the mentally and emotionally disturbed.

Martinez, awaiting a new (and unrelated) trial for bribery, professed no involvement in any skullduggery. His defiant assertion brought giggles not only from cynical Hialeah citizens, but from the battalion of FBI agents assigned to keep track of corruption in the city.

While the feds added electoral fraud to their list of recent crimes, Dade Circuit Judge Sidney Shapiro this week ordered a new mayoral vote to be held within 30 days.

It's hard to steal an election on such short notice. Martinez's supporters will have their work cut out for them. Here are a few tips to avoid another fiasco:

• Don't cut it so close.

If you're taking all the trouble to rig a vote, do it convincingly. Arrange a victory margin wide enough that the result won't hinge on validating a paltry 200-odd ballots. Why make the FBI's job any easier?

• Get better forgers.

The forgery techniques used on many ballots were so bad that even the city's own hired handwriting expert had to admit the signatures looked phony.

Microscopic examination revealed that some of the names had been penned in erasable ink, and even showed signs of erasure smudges. There's no excuse for such sloppiness.

Hasn't anyone in Hialeah heard of tracing paper?

• Get better witnesses.

When bogus absentee ballots are being prepared, it's important to maintain at least the appearance of objectivity. That's tough when many of those "witnessing" the signatures are the mayor's cronies, campaign workers or—in 13 instances—the sister of his own wife.

Another unfortunate choice was Hialeah policeman Glenn Rice, a Martinez campaign volunteer who signed 20 absentee ballots as a witness. When questioned under oath about forgeries, officer Rice crawled safely behind the Fifth Amendment and shut up.

For the upcoming election, the Martinez camp should make an earnest effort to find ballot witnesses who won't get laughed out of court, or require their own defense attorneys.

• Get undetectable voters.

Signing up the infirm and mentally disturbed must have seemed like a clever idea, but it backfired on the mayor's goon squad.

Equally ill-advised was the scheme of putting nonresidents on Hialeah voter rolls. For example, ballots were mysteriously cast in the names of two North Dade people who've never lived in Hialeah. Another woman claimed to have been a legal resident of the city, but she couldn't recall her home address.

Where election riggers made their big mistake was by using living and breathing humans in the fraud. That's not only risky, it's dumb. Dead people make better phantom voters, because they won't blab to federal agents, and they can't be subpoenaed.

The cemeteries of Hialeah are full of potential Raul Martinez supporters, absentee in the largest sense of the word.

Older, yet not wiser, Miami deserves Carollo as mayor

July 28, 1996

So it's your birthday, Miami.

A hundred-year journey ends with three stunning words: Mayor Joe Carollo.

It's perfect, really. Absolutely splendid.

In many ways, the man epitomizes the character of Miami—crafty, combustible and doggedly opportunistic.

Never mind that he would have scared the bloomers off Julia Tuttle and sent cranky Henry Flagler cursing all the way back to St. Augustine, yanking out the railroad ties behind him.

Carollo truly deserves to be mayor. He deserves it because he went to the bother of running, and because he knew that—despite a reputation as a pernicious little ferret—he could gnaw his way out of political purgatory and win.

More than most local office-seekers, Joe seems to understand South Florida's rich tradition of voter apathy, rotten judgment and shallow values.

The hype surrounding Miami's 100th birthday has sparked absolutely zero interest in how the city will be governed entering its second century, or by whom. Joe counted on the fact that folks would get much more excited about the chili dogs and free concerts than the mayoral race. He was right.

Up to 250,000 people are predicted to show up for today's huge centennial birthday bash in Bayfront Park. Less than 22,000 showed up for last Tuesday's special election.

Carollo was elected with a preposterous 16,556 votes—even fewer souls than attend an average Marlins game. Joe deserves to be mayor because an astounding 81 percent of registered voters stayed home, sat on their butts and let it happen.

Too bad for them. Good for him.

Even as modern-day Miami puts on its glossy birthday face, it continues to revel in a checkered history full of rogues, hustlers and blowhards. More than a few of them were elected to public office.

Sure, the city can do better than Joe Carollo, but it must also be said that there's not exactly a sterling legacy for him to sully. Local politics has produced plenty of colorful characters, but few truly memorable leaders.

It's impossible to predict what kind of mayor Carollo will be, but one thing he won't be is dull. Where Steve Clark was happy as long as he had a five-iron or a cocktail in his hand, Carollo isn't content without tumult and controversy.

Forget all the media baloney about a "new" Joe, mellow and matured—that's wishful thinking by jittery old enemies, hoping he'll forget old affronts. He won't. Carollo is as ruthless and nakedly ambitious as he was eight years ago; he's just smoother now.

Besides, Miami (of all places) shouldn't begrudge him either ambition or egomania—basic ingredients, going back to the hairy days of Fort Dallas.

It's fun watching Carollo jerk Wayne Huizenga's chain over the arena lease for the soon-departing Panthers. The sports tycoon deserves a dose of his own petulance, and it's refreshing to see a politician brash enough to stick it to him.

Ever since Miami was born, its so-called leaders rolled over like puppies for anybody who showed up at City Hall with a nice suit, the right lawyer and a fat wad of dough. Nobody asked where the money came from because they were too busy asking for favors.

Land developers always got the red-carpet treatment, but occasionally so did gangsters, gamblers, bootleggers, bank swindlers and cocaine smugglers. Miami became known as a very friendly and gullible town.

The last thing it needs at this point in history is another glad-handing, ribbon-cutting, look-the-other-way mayor. Joe is capable of all that, but he's clearly more comfortable in the role of doubting Thomas.

He doesn't mind infuriating the rich and powerful, and he has always had a pretty good instinct for sniffing out dirty laundry. One of his first acts as city commissioner was to disrupt the cozy downtown parking monopoly around the arena, something that should have been done long ago.

If we're judged by the enemies we make, Joe's got an impressive list. It's encouraging, for example, that he is despised by Jorge Mas Canosa. Perhaps now we'll see a decline in the undue influence of the Cuban American National Foundation upon the city manager, and the police department.

Of course, the potential for fiasco follows Carollo like a hungry bear. He has a knack for the half-baked, half-cocked and insensitive remark, and the black community especially has reason to be wary.

Time will reveal Joe's true self. Sixteen months from now Miami will get a chance to re-elect him, or once again banish him to obscurity.

It's entirely possible that (as his enemies have muttered) Joe Carollo is a sneaky crook, or a nut case. Miami has had its share of both. It's also possible that he's in it just for the glory and honor.

In any case, he is the mayor—and 81 percent of the city's voters have no room to bitch. Enjoy the birthday party and pray, between chili dogs, that history will judge you kindly.

It won't be hard to fill Miami's 'Crooked' seat

July 31, 1997

The long-anticipated indictment of Commissioner Humberto Hernandez leaves open, once again, the designated crooked seat on the Miami Commission.

Long held by Miller Dawkins, now imprisoned for taking payoffs, the post was won by the controversial Hernandez last fall. The lawyer's lopsided margin carried a message from voters:

We'll always hold a place for sleaze in our hearts, and in our government.

Hernandez was hardly an unknown commodity by Election Day. It had been well publicized that he'd been canned as an assistant city attorney for basically operating a private legal practice out of City Hall.

Much had also been written about the buzzardly antics of his law firm following the ValuJet crash, and the complaints lodged by heartsick families of victims.

Similar hard-to-miss headlines had been devoted to Hernandez's prominence in an FBI investigation, and to the fact that agents had visited his office to confiscate files.

So it shouldn't have surprised a soul when the commissioner was formally charged Tuesday in a 27-count indictment involving ambitiously devious bank fraud.

Prosecutors say the plot centered around a Key Biscayne condo, The Pyramids. Phony condominium sales allegedly were set up as a means of securing inflated mortgages, often never repaid. Agents say some of the bogus deals were used to launder millions in dirty Medicare money.

Future-commissioner Hernandez served as an attorney in some Pyramids transactions, and as a buyer in others. (Under oath he once asserted he didn't know the name of a client for whom he was holding almost $1 million of real estate.)

In subsequent testimony, Hernandez developed a fondness for taking the Fifth Amendment.

If convicted on all charges, the commissioner could be sentenced to several lifetimes in prison. His political career will now be put on hold while he strives to avoid joining his predecessor behind bars.

The governor suspended Hernandez on Wednesday, which means the crooked seat on the commission must be filled temporarily. The challenge is to find a suitable replacement, someone who brings to the task an equally shady cloud over his head.

Potential candidates could be chosen from FBI wiretaps and videotapes, but the screening process would take months. Why wait when there's such an obvious choice:

Carmen Lunetta. He's local, he's experienced, he's tainted by scandal—and, best of all, he's available!

The former boss of the Port of Miami, who retires today, could be a worthy successor to the Dawkins-Hernandez legacy. He quit under fire, leaving the port owing taxpayers $22 million.

The heaping debt had piled up as Lunetta spent thousands on golf outings, travel and other goodies. Many thousands more were funneled through a port-contracted company to political candidates.

Lunetta left port finances in such a mess that the new pro basketball arena is in jeopardy, as is the cruise-ship expansion known as Maritime Park.

Although Lunetta is the only person with a clue how the seaport runs, Metro-Dade Mayor Alex "Mister No Fun" Penelas is leery of hiring him as a consultant to help sort out the books.

That leaves Lunetta with loads of free time, at least on those days he's not meeting with his lawyers. A Miami Commission seat would keep him near his beloved port, and intimately involved in the high-stakes Maritime Park negotiations.

It's the worst place imaginable for a man at the center of a major federal investigation, which is all that Miami voters need to hear. Come next fall, it'll be Carmen by a landslide!

Dead men voting couldn't do any worse

November 30, 1997

Miami's laughingstock mayoral race is in the hands of a judge, who eventually could decide to order a new laughingstock election.

Defeated incumbent Joe Carollo and the newly chosen mayor, Xavier Suarez, are battling over the mishandling and forgery of absentee ballots, which resulted in at least one verified dead person, Manuel Yip, casting a vote.

In many U.S. cities, this would qualify as an embarrassing scandal, one worthy of vigorous prosecution. But in Miami the term "tainted election" is a whimsical redundancy, and nobody ever goes to jail for stealing votes.

Moreover, judging by the outcome of this fall's political races, you can make a pretty strong case that dead people in Miami ought to be allowed to vote. How could they possibly make worse choices than the living?

Example: 6,063 persons, all allegedly alive and conscious, overwhelmingly re-elected Humberto Hernandez to the City Commission.

Humberto is the adorable young shyster once fired from the city attorney's office for doing outside legal work on taxpayer time. Later he got in trouble for chasing grief-stricken relatives of the ValuJet crash victims, a squalid little hustle that Humberto blamed on overzealous staff members at his law firm.

Most recently he was indicted by the feds on multiple counts of bank fraud and money laundering. The governor dutifully suspended Hernandez from the City Commission. On Nov. 4, Miami citizens enthusiastically returned him to office with 65 percent of the vote.

Fittingly, it was Hernandez's support that later pushed Suarez to victory in the mayoral playoffs!

Which raises the obvious question: Is there really much difference between a brain-dead voter and a physically dead voter?

Consider: Miami has spent a year reeling from a bribery scandal and teetering on the brink of fiscal ruin. Nobody in their right minds would, amid such turmoil, willingly put the city's fragile budget within reach of an accused swindler—yet that's exactly what living, breathing voters did.

It's a persuasive argument for throwing elections open to everyone, regardless of pulse rate.

Usually when ballots of long-dead residents turn up, forgery is the presumed explanation. I'm not sure that's automatically true in a place as occult as Miami.

Here it's remotely possible that some dead citizens are so appalled by what's happening that they supernaturally find a way to vote from the afterlife, if we give them a chance.

And maybe we should, because I'll bet there aren't 6,063 dead people who would have been caught . . . well, dead voting for a guy like Humberto Hernandez.

Admittedly, the plan has a few problems. Since deceased persons would by necessity use absentee ballots—they are, after all, the ultimate absentees—the possibility of fraud cannot be ignored. (Perhaps signatures could be checked against those on their Last Wills and Testaments.)

Political purists might contend that even if the dead would vote, they aren't as constitutionally qualified as live people. That position is hard to defend, given what happened here at the polls.

Turnout among living voters was so disgracefully low that participation by the deceased should be welcomed. And no voter is less susceptible than a dead one to a politician's grandiose promises, smear campaigns or cheap scare tactics.

Which brings us to the late Manuel Yip. Perhaps his name was, as alleged, forged on that absentee ballot. But suppose it was the real deal. What if it was an impassioned voice from The Beyond, a voice of conscience pleading: "What are you bozos doing to my city?"

Miami politics has caused lots of good, decent folks to roll over in their graves. Next time, let them cast a ballot. At this point, what could it hurt?

Miami 'voters' create new kind of open election

December 14, 1997

Miami's election scandal has taken an intriguing twist, with the revelation that scores of people who "voted" on Nov. 4 don't even live in the city.

Some didn't know they'd voted at all.

Investigators call it fraud, but there's a more positive interpretation. Think of Miami elections as the ultimate in participatory democracy, accessible to anyone—living, dead, residents, nonresidents . . . even those who don't particularly want to participate.

It might be crooked, but it's also an ingenious remedy for the problem of low voter turnout.

If authorities allow the results of last month's election to stand, we could soon see a day when Miami boasts more registered voters than live human beings—a democracy flush beyond the wildest dreams of Jefferson or Paine.

Many of Miami's questionable ballots were filed in support of Commissioner Humberto ("I'll Take the Fifth") Hernandez and Mayor-to-be Xavier ("I'm Not Deranged!") Suarez.

When the scandal broke, Suarez appointed none other than Hernandez to counter-investigate the state's investigation. This was highly humorous for two reasons:

1) Hernandez is awaiting trial for alleged bank fraud and money laundering.

2) His own campaign manager, Jorge Luis De Goti, figures largely in one of the city's most dubious voting patterns.

Records show several "voters" switching their registrations to addresses in Hernandez's district, just in time for the election. At least nine of those supporters registered at homes owned or occupied by family of De Goti.

When reporters tried to find some of the new Hernandez voters, they found them dwelling at other locations, miles outside the city. (Hernandez himself said he'd never condone such a thing.)

Equally peculiar were absentee ballots filed on behalf of Francisca Brice, Cipriano Alvarez and Gloria Alvarez. Since they live in Hialeah and Hialeah Gardens, they hadn't thought about voting in the Miami elections.

They were surprised to find out they had. Their ballots were "witnessed" by 92-year-old Alberto Russi, another campaign worker for you-know-who.

Russi had been arrested for other alleged voter fraud, including signing a ballot for a dead man. Russi said he didn't intentionally do anything illegal on behalf of candidate Hernandez.

Cynics see the unfolding scandal as yet another sleazy chapter of Miami-style corruption. Others might regard it as a historic opportunity to broaden the political process to include those who customarily have been shut out—the dead, distant or otherwise ineligible voter.

A strong democracy depends on citizen involvement, and what was Alberto Russi allegedly doing but striving to involve as many citizens as possible?

Talk about open elections—Miami has a chance to redefine the term. What a bold experiment it would be to unlock the polls not just for the sneaky pals of candidates, but for anyone, anywhere.

Because Miami's image reflects upon that of the whole state, an argument could be made that all Floridians should be entitled to vote here. And because Florida's image reflects upon that of the whole country, a case likewise could be made that all Americans should be able to take part.

Indeed, every U.S. taxpayer has a substantial stake in Miami's future, based on the FBI's investment of time and manpower here.

Theoretically, a ballot cast from Nome, Alaska, is every bit as relevant as a ballot cast from Hialeah Gardens. And with millions of absentee ballots pouring in, it would be hard for our local scammers to steal an election.

The prospect of voting in Miami without actually having to reside here (and constantly worry about commissioners going to prison or the city going bankrupt) could have national appeal. Get registered now!

Or perhaps you already are, and just don't know it.

Strike a blow for democracy: Sell your vote

January 15, 1998

Ten bucks a vote.

That's what some Overtown residents got paid to cast absentee ballots for Xavier Suarez before the Nov. 12 mayoral runoff.

Suarez, who won the election, says neither he nor his campaign staff was involved in any votes-for-cash scheme. Then who was paying off those people in the parking lot of the St. John Baptist Church?

A patriot, that's who! Overzealous perhaps, but still a red-blooded American patriot.

Everybody complains about low voter turnout in Miami but nobody does anything about it. Now, finally, here's a guy who put his money where his mouth was.

Oh sure, we all say we love democracy, but how many of us are willing to dig into our pockets and pay cash for it? How many of us value the electoral process so highly that we'd spend a long hot day rounding up total strangers, then haul them downtown to cast their absentee ballots?

Mayor Suarez should be proud to have a secret supporter who cares enough to make such a financial sacrifice, yet is so modest that he won't come forward to take credit for his bold deeds.

I see this anonymous Angel of Overtown, whoever he might be, as a rock-ribbed Citizen Doe who simply got fed up with voter apathy.

He resolved to do whatever it took to get voters to the polls, and what it took was moola. He probably didn't think of it as a bribe, but as a $10 voucher to a civics lesson.

Maybe he went a bit too far, but such was his fervent concern for the future of his beloved city. Barry Goldwater, another brave American, said it best: Extremism in the defense of liberty is no vice!

Well, the same goes for vote-buying. It's extreme, for sure; a crime, yeah, if you want to get picky. But a vice? Not so fast.

Yes, hard questions have been raised about the motives of the $10 voters. Is this really the kind of political system Thomas Jefferson envisioned, a system in which people sell their ballot privileges on the streets?

Of course not. But neither could Jefferson nor any of the founding fathers have envisioned a place such as Miami, where pretty much everything and everybody has been up for sale at one time or another.

When Cesar Odio was city manager, he was for sale. When Miller Dawkins was a city commissioner, he was also for sale. And when Manohar Surana was the city's finance chief, he was for sale, too.

So it's understandable why some residents might feel their time has come. If public officials peddle themselves to the highest bidder, why (voters might wonder) shouldn't we do the same?

The sentiment grows with each new scandal. It's possible to foresee a day when every eligible voter in Miami refuses to go to the polls, unless they get paid first. On a positive note, voter turnout could easily soar to 95 percent or higher, depending on how much cash is spread around.

Purists argue that bribing voters can taint the political process. That might be true in other cities, but in Miami the practice actually could lead to cleaner elections.

Look what happened in the Overtown incident. Despite rampant ballot-buying, not a single penny was paid to voters who were already dead. That's a record of which other precincts would be darned proud!

Perhaps we'll never know the identity of the Angel of Overtown, or what brought him and his wad of greenbacks to that church parking lot.

Yet we can still applaud the populist ardor that made him reach out so big-heartedly to his fellow citizens.

He definitely made a difference in the mayor's race. He got lots more citizens interested and involved, if only for a few hours.

Most importantly, he showed us how a participatory democracy can also be a profitable one, for voters and candidates alike.

A patriotic soul won't let death cost him a vote

February 8, 1998

This week, Miami-Dade Circuit Judge Thomas S. Wilson Jr. will begin hearing evidence of widespread vote fraud in the absentee ballots cast in Miami's November general election. One of those disputed ballots bore the signature of a man named Manuel Yip, who submitted the following sworn deposition:

Q: Please state your occupation, Mr. Yip.

A: Well, you could say I'm retired. Seriously retired.

Q: And where do you live?

A: Bad choice of words.

Q: All right, where do you reside?

A: Right here on Second Avenue.

Q: In a house or an apartment?

A: Very funny. It's a graveyard, as any dolt can plainly see.

Q: So you are legally—

A: Dead, that's correct. I'm deader than a doornail. Expired, expunged, departed, checked out, eighty-sixed, sleeping the big sleep, whatever. And I suppose you got a problem with that?

Q: Yet you voted in the city elections on Nov. 4.

A: You betcha I voted, and nobody had to pay me, either. It's my proud duty as a late citizen of this great democracy. Ever since I passed away, I've become much more involved in local politics.

Q: Why is that?

A: Well, for one thing, I've had a lot more free time to study up on the candidates.

Q: And you've voted in how many other elections?

A: Before or after I died?

Q: After.

A: A total of four times.

Q: And always by absentee ballot?

A: No, smart guy, I just hop out of my coffin and hitchhike down to the polls. What're you, a comedian? Of course I vote by absentee ballot. I'm frigging deceased, remember?

Q: Mr. Yip, there's no need to lose your temper.

A: What, you think dead folks don't keep up with the current events? I see the headlines, pal. Newspapers blow through here all the time. My understanding is, anybody can vote in Miami. It's like the Publishers Clearing House—all you gotta do is fill out a form and send it in, no questions asked.

Heck, you don't need to live in your district. You don't even need to live in the city. Me? It just so happens I live in the hereafter.

Q: You've made your point, Mr. Yip.

A: Why shouldn't my vote count the same as the ones from Goulds and Hialeah Gardens? Heck, at least this cemetery is inside the Miami city limits.

Q: Mr. Yip, did anyone representing a candidate encourage you to cast a ballot?

A: I didn't need any encouragement. The corruption scandals, the budget disaster—how could I just lie here in heavenly repose and let the city go down the tubes?

Q: And you feel that, as a nonliving person, you're still entitled to vote.

A: Absolutely. Just because we don't pay taxes anymore doesn't mean we don't have an interest in good government. I mean, look around this place—would it kill 'em to cut the grass? Maybe spritz a little 409 on these grungy old tombstones?

Q: Just out of curiosity, do you know of any other dead persons who voted in Miami?

A: Boy, could I make a joke right now.

Q: Oh, we've heard them all, Mr. Yip. Please answer the question—were there other dead voters or not?

A: Let's just say the election results speak for themselves.

Q: And it's your intention to vote again in the future?

A: Every chance I get. Hey, what can they do to me? I'm already—

Q: Dead. Yes, we know.

Clean election? This is a job for Jimmy Carter

March 5, 1998

The good news is: A judge has ordered a new election to decide who will be mayor of Miami.

The bad news is: The election will again be held in Miami.

So how do you prevent it from being stolen like the last one? That's the predicament facing local officials.

Convicted felons, out-of-towners and even a corpse voted last November. Other citizens cheerfully sold their ballots for $10 apiece. Sleazy history could repeat itself in May unless the voting is more closely supervised.

Believe it or not, there is a "supervisor of elections" office in Miami-Dade—and the staff was hard on the job last fall. The problem was, the law saying who gets to vote was so easily subverted, and the fraud so widespread, that authorities were caught unprepared.

This time ought to be different. One intriguing idea, suggested by my son, is to have Jimmy Carter come down and monitor the new Miami elections, as he did in Nicaragua, Haiti and Panama (where he debunked Gen. Manuel Noriega's farcical victory).

True, the Miami of today is more politically backward than all those places, so Carter would face a steeper challenge. For security the former president would need several crack divisions of U.N. troops encircling the polls just to keep out all the bogus voters.

Carter's past willingness to serve as an elections watchdog stems from his own dismaying experience with voter fraud. In his book *Turning Point*, Carter describes how his first run for the Georgia Senate was nearly upended by flagrant ballot-stuffing and—you guessed it—a mysterious turnout of dead voters.

Surely the former president would sympathize with all those honest Miamians victimized by last fall's electoral larceny.

Yet when I phoned his office in Atlanta, Carter's assistants seemed doubtful he'd be able to fit the Miami crisis into his busy schedule. In their voices one could also detect wariness about sending him into such a messy quagmire.

That's understandable. Carter is well familiar with South Florida's reputation for tolerating skulduggery and graft. After Hurricane Andrew struck, I told him that while entire subdivisions of expensive homes in South Dade blew to pieces, most of his low-cost Habitat for Humanity houses didn't lose so much as a shingle in the storm.

"Well," Carter said with a wry smile, "we use nails in ours."

He was on an airplane Wednesday when I tried to reach him to ask if he'd fly to Miami for the elections. His spokeswoman, Carrie Harmon, was diplomatic but cautious.

"To date, the Carter Center has only monitored elections outside the United States—Africa, Latin America. We've never monitored a U.S. election," she said.

I asked what it usually takes to get the former president involved.

"Normally, when we're dealing with developing countries, we have to be invited by all parties—the current government and the major opposition parties," she explained. "That's the only way it works, if everybody agrees to it."

But what about developing cities? Suppose Xavier Suarez and Joe Carollo, the front-runners for Miami mayor, extended a joint invitation—then would Carter consider monitoring a U.S. election?

There was a good-natured pause on the line, and perhaps the trace of a chuckle. "Well, we've never done it before," Harmon said, "but we wouldn't absolutely rule it out. Definitely not."

Now it's up to the candidates: Pick up the phone, guys. Call Jimmy now. If Noriega could do it, you can, too.

Ex-Mayor lives in own x world

March 26, 1998

Tips for tourists and visiting journalists who are having trouble keeping track of Miami's mayors:

The current mayor and former ex-mayor, Joe Carollo, is fondly known as Crazy Joe. He occupies City Hall. The former mayor and current ex-mayor, Xavier Suarez, is fondly known as Mayor Loco. He occupies a mystic parallel universe.

The current mayor was restored to office after courts agreed that widespread ballot fraud had corrupted the November elections. The current ex-mayor has vowed to regain the post with a multipronged legal assault.

The battle promises to drag on, bitterly dividing Miami. That's why a parallel universe is useful.

While Carollo returns to the lugubrious chore of trying to balance the city's threadbare budget, Suarez's supporters can go on pretending he was wrongly deposed by a sinister cabal that includes the governor, law enforcement, the English-speaking media and the entire judicial system.

Having two different Miamis and two different mayors isn't so weird, when viewed in a psychotherapeutic context.

Experts say fantasizing can be a healthy escape from extreme stress. And these days few places are more extreme or stressed out than Miami—hobbled by debt, humiliated by Wall Street, shamed by graft and scandalized by flagrant thievery at the polls.

Denial is an understandable reaction to such grim reality, though the breadth of Suarez's denial is notable. Imagine a frothy make-believe world in which the city's image glistens, the budget is in rock-solid shape, the elections are honorably conducted and normal behavior includes driving around and surprising people at their homes after dark.

That's the whimsical parallel universe in which the current ex-mayor dwells.

Almost two weeks ago he showed up unexpectedly on the doorstep of the former ex-mayor. Carollo said Suarez came to confront him about charges that furniture had disappeared from City Hall after Suarez's exit. Carollo said Suarez was jabbering away, upsetting the children.

"He made no sense," the former ex-mayor said. "We just wanted to get this man, the best way we could, out of our front door and out of our property."

However, in Suarez's parallel universe the trip to the Carollo homestead went very smoothly. "Cordial," is the way the current ex-mayor recalled it. "A nice, nice discussion." He saw nothing rude or inappropriate about his unannounced visit, which is one of the fringe benefits of living in a fantasy world—there's no such thing as bad manners.

Sometimes the two universes do converge in potentially dangerous ways. A few months before becoming ex-mayor, Suarez made that infamous late-night sojourn to the home of a feisty Little Havana constituent who'd criticized him in a letter.

Alarmed at the knocking on her door, the woman (who obviously did not live in the same world as Suarez) picked up a handgun and peeped outside. Luckily for the future ex-mayor, the woman recognized him and held her fire.

Since then Suarez has made other surprise nocturnal jaunts, not all of them publicized. He is becoming Miami's own midnight rambler, in both the itinerant sense and the verbal sense.

This week an appellate panel declined to reconsider his plea for reinstatement. In a parallel universe, that could mean the judges are part of the secret anti-Suarez conspiracy.

It also could mean that, one of these nights, the judges might hear a stranger at the back door; a stranger who quickly engages them in "cordial" discussion. The only thing to do is nod politely, and pretend it all makes sense.

Because, in some eerie faraway world, it must.

Our Leaders on Parade

County meets for a theater of the absurd

February 3, 1988

For all the working stiffs who couldn't be there, Tuesday's county commission meeting was better than Monty Python's Flying Circus.

Imagine the scene: Your county manager has admitted getting $127,878 in a land deal that he did not report, as required by state law.

To get this money, he invested nothing. On the other end of the deal was a Panamanian company controlled by a lawyer indicted for laundering drug money. The county manager says he had no idea.

One of his partners, Camilo Padreda, was a close friend who later got a contract to run the county gun range. The manager says he had nothing to do with it.

The huge profit on the deal came after the county rezoned the property. Pereira, who was working at the city of Miami then, says he had nothing to do with it.

With phones ringing off the hook from angry voters, you'd think that the commissioners would have had a few questions for Pereira.

Like: Is it customary to get a $127,000 return without investing anything in a deal? Didn't you ask who else was involved? If your role wasn't meant to be secret, why didn't your name appear on a single public document?

Why didn't you reveal your interest when the property came up for rezoning? Why didn't you reveal your business relationship with Padreda when the gun-range contract was ratified?

Why did you lie about the land deal when first asked by reporters?

These are obvious questions, but most of the commissioners didn't want to ask. They wanted to talk, and their comments ranged from the inane to the incoherent.

"As far as I'm concerned, there is no crisis," said Barry Schreiber, whose former bond-issue connections make him an expert on conflict of interest.

From Mayor Steve Clark: "(Pereira) could have a problem in the future, but that's neither here nor there."

Beverly Phillips said county government is "nearly paralyzed," but didn't have much else to add.

Jim Redford took a ramble down memory lane, recounting some long-ago stint as a reporter. He concluded by likening the current Pereira scandal to "underwear." Mercifully, he did not try to clarify.

George Valdes made an impromptu speech about the $9,400 desk Pereira ordered when he first took the job, about how it wasn't really Sergio's desk but it belonged to all the people. I swear, he really said this.

Barbara Carey, who's been griping about the land deal for the last five days, instead wondered if Sergio couldn't do something to get better coverage in the media.

Sherman Winn struggled to put the mess in perspective: "Sure, there are ongoing investigations. I guess there are ongoing investigations all over this world." He then paid Pereira the ultimate tribute by comparing his situation to that of Ed Meese.

For a fleeting moment, Harvey Ruvin tried to dig out an actual fact. He asked if zoning applicants are required to divulge the names of all property owners. A simple question, but the county attorney said he couldn't answer it.

Of all the commissioners, only Clara Oesterle came out and said what thousands of Dade County residents have been thinking: Nobody just "forgets" a $127,000 windfall.

When Oesterle began to speak, you could see the dyspeptic expressions settle over Clark, Schreiber and the other apologists.

The thing they had most feared was coming to pass: Somebody had the guts to put Pereira's feet to the fire. Somebody had actually bothered to study the numbers.

Now, instead of simply bashing the press, Oesterle was demanding more documents from the manager—more tax returns, a full list of real estate holdings. She even asked for an outside auditor.

At this point, the well-organized Sergio Fan Club—mostly pals and county workers—shifted uneasily in their seats. When Oesterle suggested that Pereira temporarily step aside, the grumbling began.

Imagine—a commissioner who doesn't approve of a county manager breaking the law! The gall of it.

But the moment passed quickly. Valdes took the microphone and everyone breathed a sigh of relief. Good government was safe again.

OB should fence off VIP seating

August 10, 1988

You often hear people asking why anybody in their right mind would run for public office in South Florida.

Finally we've got an answer: They get swell seats for the Orange Bowl game.

It turns out that the organizers of the annual Orange Bowl Classic make tons of good tickets available for sale as early as August, four months before the big game. The only hitch is, you've got to be a local politician to get dibs.

This interesting arrangement came to light during a Miami Commission meeting in June, when Commissioner Miller Dawkins complained about the location of his seats for last year's game. Dawkins began whining just as the city was debating whether to spend $16 million to refurbish the old stadium.

"How come I got such bad seats for the Orange Bowl game?" Dawkins asked Orange Bowl Committee President Jim Barker.

Barker replied, "I will be more than happy to sit down and work something out . . ."

Dawkins cut in: "No. If you want my vote, you will work it out now." Lo and behold, two weeks later the commissioner was offered 34 seats on the 50-yard line. So what's a little extortion among friends?

True, every bowl game in the country offers VIP seating. It would be naive to imagine that UM President Tad Foote, or TV star Don Johnson, or the publisher of this newspaper couldn't scare up decent seats to the Orange Bowl game. This might not be fair, but it happens.

When it comes to politicians, we're not talking about a few measly seats under the press box. Last year the Orange Bowl offered 519 seats for sale to Miami city commissioners and the mayor. The big winner was City Manager Cesar Odio, who was allotted 270 seats worth $8,185. With that many he could bring the entire Miami Rowing Club.

The Orange Bowl's generosity spills beyond Miami's city limits. Last year each of the Metro commissioners was allocated 24 tickets, while Mayor Steve Clark got 64. For reasons equally mysterious, 48 seats were set aside for the Coral Gables commission and another 138 for its city manager, who must have a very large family.

Even the Miami Beach city commissioners, whose importance in the Orange Bowl festivities remains unclear, were allowed to buy 30 seats (one of the commissioners, Stanley Arkin, griped that the best he could do was the 35-yard line).

All tickets must be purchased at face value and are not to be resold for a profit. This is called scalping, and it is against the law. I can't imagine any of our loyal public servants stooping to such a thing.

The chairman of the Orange Bowl ticket committee, Bill Cullom, said there's nothing wrong with offering primo seats to politicians. "Professional courtesy," he calls it.

There's another name for it, Bill, and I think we all know what it is.

Why should some meathead commissioner be entitled to better seats than a loyal UM fan who stands three hours in line in the hot sun? No less disturbing is the manner in which these seats are distributed in blocks throughout the stands, with no warning to regular Orange Bowl spectators.

Say you and the family drive all the way from Nebraska just to see the Cornhuskers play on New Year's Day. Upon arrival, you discover that your seats are located in section T of the south stands—a teeming nest of local commissioners and their chums. Talk about a vacation nightmare.

If the Orange Bowl feels obliged to suck up to officeholders, then at least it should take precautions to protect the general public.

One idea is to seat all politicians in the same section of the stadium. The end-zone bleachers might be an appropriate place. Rope it off and mark it clearly, so the rest of the fans know to stay away.

Then again, maybe that's not such a great plan. You let that many politicians sit together (even at a football game), bad things are bound to happen.

The whole county could be rezoned commercial by halftime.

Lobbyists could try semaphore

May 15, 1989

A grave new crisis awaits the Metro Commission when it meets Tuesday.

Telephones.

Specifically: Should private lobbyists be allowed to call commissioners during the meeting and instruct them how to vote?

You remember four weeks ago when poor Mayor Steve Clark screwed up and voted the wrong way on a big airport construction project. No sooner had the mayor opened his mouth than his phone started to beep.

On the other end was lobbyist Eston "Dusty" Melton, the mayor's chum, ghostwriter and moral compass. Melton is to Steve Clark what Edgar Bergen was to Charlie McCarthy.

It just so happened that Melton was also a paid operative for the construction firm that stood to gain an extra $220,000 from a favorable vote on the airport project.

Apparently the mayor was reminded of this connection during the frantic phone call. He immediately arranged a new vote, absented himself (as originally planned), and the airport funding squeaked through.

Unfortunately, the mayor forgot to turn off his microphone when he took Melton's call. To complete the spectacle, a video monitor captured every moment of Clark's chagrined retreat ("Yes . . . No . . . I can't change now!")

Later the mayor said he didn't recall any of this. Then he remembered the phone call, but not who made it. Melton wisely refused to confirm or deny his half of the conversation, which probably went something like this:

"You !&*%! bozo, can't you get anything right!"

In the ensuing furor, Commissioners Joe Gersten and Larry Hawkins said lobbyists should be barred from calling during the commission meetings. Barbara Carey even ordered her phone disconnected.

And, just last week, the mayor's telephone suddenly vanished from his desk on the dais. Clark probably feared that some wise guy would publish the number (375–2400), thus inviting input from hundreds of lowly, garden-variety voters.

You might wonder why a developer's lobbyist should be able to call the mayor (375–2400) in the middle of a commission meeting, when that same privilege is not extended to the people who elected him. This is an excellent question, and the source of the commission's current agony.

To deprive lobbyists of their private touch-tone tickler is to invite mayhem. Without a phone, you can't be sure the commissioners will stick to the script. Mayor Clark is simply not as adept at memorizing his instructions as some of the others.

Tuesday's meeting requires special orchestration. On the agenda is a fancy condo project planned for smack dab in the middle of the Oleta River State Recreational Area.

The condo developers want to put in a marina. Environmental groups, joined by some county staffers, say a marina would threaten the river's population of manatees.

It promises to be a tense battle, and a controversial vote. Guess which lobbyist is pushing hard for the developers: Dusty Melton.

Now, what's Mayor Clark to do without a phone? What if he gets flustered again? What if he just plain forgets what to do? DUSTY! HELP!

The options are limited. Melton could scribble his orders on the cuffs of the mayor's shirt sleeves (a technique favored by many actors who can't remember their lines). Or maybe he could train a little parakeet to land on the mayor's shoulder and squawk in his ear before every vote.

Commissioner Charles Dusseau jokingly suggests that lobbyists bring megaphones to the meetings and holler their advice. Actually, sema-phore flags would be less disruptive, or signal lights mounted in the rear of the chamber—one blink means vote "yes," two blinks mean "no," and three blinks mean, "Go home sick, we've got our quorum."

Who knows what will happen on Tuesday. The Oleta River project is a hot one, and the stakes are high.

Maybe the mayor will put back his telephone (375–2400). Maybe he'll just change the number.

Or maybe Melton and the other high-priced schemers will bring flashcards and hope for the best. There's always more than one way to reach out and clout someone.

To Dawkins, black isn't always black

March 16, 1990

Poor, confused Miller Dawkins.

Last week the Miami commissioner raised a ruckus when a man named Mario Williams was nominated for a position on the Bayfront Park Management Trust.

Williams is a black lawyer who happens to have been born in Costa Rica. Dawkins seemed unable to accept the concept. "He's a Hispanic," Dawkins said. "He's not black."

The profound ignorance of this remark would have been stunning had it come from anyone else.

The fellow who nominated Mario Williams insisted that he was indeed black, but it was to no avail. Ultimately the appointment was deferred. Meanwhile, Commissioner Dawkins has demanded a letter from Williams stating that he is, in fact, a black American.

Williams, a Harvard graduate who has lived here since the age of 10, says Dawkins is a bigot.

That might be one explanation for the commissioner's behavior. Another might be that the man is just hopelessly dim.

Dawkins (a) doesn't understand that there are black Hispanics, (b) doesn't consider black Hispanics to be black Americans, or (c) doesn't believe that a black of Hispanic heritage can fairly represent the race.

We don't know precisely what Dawkins meant because, as usual, he didn't explain himself. Assuming he was simply trying to gain a balanced representation on the Bayfront Park Management Trust, he couldn't have done so in a more degrading manner.

The panel has seats set aside for blacks, whites and Hispanics—a situation that creates obvious overlap because Hispanics can be black or white. Theoretically commissioners could challenge every Latin appointment as taking up a seat reserved for another ethnic group. At some point, common sense must be applied.

In a community where racial tensions run high, the flaming leadership of Miller Dawkins has been something to behold. There was his legendary threat to burn down a Hispanic-run AIDS center if it opened in a black neighborhood.

Then, last year Dawkins pitched a fit when a white person representing the NAACP appeared before the City Commission. Dawkins seemed flabbergasted by the apparition, and refused to discuss the NAACP proposal unless the organization sent a black to the meeting.

And when a young Haitian-born lawyer was nominated to the same Bayfront Trust, Dawkins similarly questioned the color of his skin. Eventually he was satisfied that the man was black enough to deserve the job.

It would be refreshing to hear Dawkins ask about a person's education, experience or expertise. What he seems to care about most is pigmentation.

Try to imagine what kind of letter Mario Williams must write to convince Dawkins that he's qualified:

Dear Commissioner,

I know the name "Mario" is confusing, but let me assure you that I am black. Really! How black am I? Well, how black do you want—black as night? Black as tar? How black is black enough?

With all due respect, I know what I am. This morning I checked in the mirror, just to make sure.

The fact of my Latin heritage doesn't change the color of my skin, or lighten the struggle of being a black man in America. I am as wounded by racial hatred as any person, whether they were born in Overtown, Kingston or San Jose.

I'm black, commissioner. Trust me on this.

Certainly Dawkins wants to make sure that minorities are represented in all municipal endeavors—cities often need to be pushed, shamed and bullied into racial fairness.

However, in his quest Dawkins implies that some blacks are more deserving than others. Those with recent roots in Haiti, Jamaica, Nicaragua, Cuba or Puerto Rico are suspect, and must undergo scrutiny and interrogation about their true cultural identity.

To be so humiliated by anyone, much less an elected official, is an insult. It's only exacerbated by the irony that Dawkins himself is black.

At least he says he is.

This junket stinks to high heaven

April 4, 1990

From the Thick-as-a-Brick Department:

Metro Commissioner Larry Hawkins flies on a developer's private jet to New Orleans for wine and brunch at a fancy restaurant.

Days later, back in Miami, the commissioner votes in a way that would have helped that same developer build luxury homes on an old Indian burial site.

Noooooooo problem. The junket had no influence on Hawkins' vote—and he makes the argument with a straight face.

He sees no conflict of interest in accepting a free whirlwind day trip from a developer, then voting on a matter that directly affects that developer's fortunes. The commissioner says he has a right to a private life, and that his friendship with developer Lowell Dunn does not sway his judgment as a public servant.

Sure, Larry, and we still believe in the tooth fairy, too. It's merely coincidence that when Dunn wants something—whether it's zoning protection, or a big county construction contract—Hawkins votes to give it to him.

Whatever the commissioner lacks in common sense, he makes up for in style.

Many politicians would have settled for dinner at Cye's, or a pair of skybox tickets at Joe Robbie Stadium. Not this guy. He goes all the way to New Orleans for authentic Cajun ambience.

And he doesn't fly commercial, either. We're talking the big L—a Lear. Seats that swivel. Cute little curtains on the windows. Plus you don't have to rent the earphones.

And when Commissioner Hawkins arrives, a private limousine awaits to carry him through the historic Garden District to that elegant eatery known as Commander's Palace—jeepers, if only we'd alerted Robin Leach . . .

Nobody would begrudge Hawkins a little glamour and adventure on his day off, but the Louisiana excursion wasn't the most brilliant move he's ever made. It gives not only the appearance of impropriety, but the stench of it.

Even the most chowderheaded officeholders know that, like it or not, they are judged by the company they keep. Friendship is one thing. Voting in a way that shovels money in your friend's pocket is something else.

Believe it or not, Dade County has a Code of Ethics. I'm not kidding.

It's an actual law that says Metro Commissioners can't accept gifts from anybody who does business with the county—"whether in the form of money, service, loan, travel, entertainment, hospitality, item or promise in any other form."

The Code of Ethics has been a source of much befuddlement to the county attorney, especially when commissioners get caught in egregious escapades. The Hawkins case is no exception.

A fourth-grader can look at the ethics ordinance and know that Hawkins broke it (note the terms travel and entertainment) but the language remains strangely impenetrable to County Attorney Robert Ginsburg, who declared: "We will not comment on things that have already taken place . . . and we don't engage in speculation."

Or enforcement, for that matter.

By his bizarre utterance, Ginsburg seems to be saying that commissioners can do whatever they please—just don't tell him ahead of time. After it's happened, he's not interested. Perhaps the State Attorney's Office can pick up the slack.

While Hawkins insists he's done nothing wrong, it's worth noting that he didn't go out of his way to publicize his trip with Lowell Dunn. Obviously the commissioner knew it would look like a stinky deal, which it does.

Dunn owns 60 oak-shaded acres known as Madden's Hammock, an old Tequesta village and burial ground. The county staff wanted the land declared a protected parkland, which would limit development. Dunn wanted to build houses there.

Two days after returning from New Orleans, Hawkins voted in Dunn's favor, and lost 5–3. The developer says it proves he gained nothing from wining and dining a Metro commissioner.

Others might say it proves only that he needs a bigger airplane.

The dock, Mayor Daoud and Centrust

April 13, 1990

The CenTrust slime trail now yields the pawprints of Miami Beach Mayor Alex Daoud.

Federal investigators have discovered that Daoud received at least $35,000 in checks from CenTrust corporations soon after voting to approve a large dock at the swanky island home of CenTrust chairman David Paul.

Daoud's attorney insists that his client got the money in exchange for legal services—which is exactly what any creative defense lawyer would say, given the circumstances.

But what an odd way for the mayor to receive legal fees. At least $10,000 was sent to his home instead of his law office, and the senior partner in the law firm says Daoud never mentioned getting any money from CenTrust. Perhaps the $35,000 slipped the mayor's mind.

Another peculiar detail about the payments: A fat chunk, $25,000, came from a Kansas City insurance company that is a subsidiary of CenTrust. A former executive of that firm has told bank examiners that he received numerous directives to send $5,000 checks to Daoud.

When the insurance executive objected to these requests, he said, David Paul personally phoned and told him to pay the mayor or "jobs would be terminated," according to investigators' reports.

Kansas City does seem like a weird route for those legal fees. A suspicious person might wonder if somebody was trying to bury the paperwork. (Daoud recently produced a retainer agreement with the insurance firm which was dated May 1988; bank examiners have questioned its authenticity.)

Never known as a shy man, the mayor has been conspicuously un-available in the days since the *Boston Globe* broke this story. Presumably he is busy scouring his files for some shred of evidence—a billing notice would be nice—proving that the CenTrust money was a legal fee and not a payoff.

Don't be surprised if something turns up. Daoud has already produced an "attorney's letter" describing legal work supposedly performed for CenTrust. Bank examiners said they couldn't verify most of the services. They also said Daoud's letter had not surfaced in a May 1989 bank audit, as it should have.

Again, perhaps it was only an oversight.

It is unusual, though, for the mayor of a major city to take such an ardent interest in a private citizen's boat dock. The fact that the citizen happened to be a wealthy campaign contributor probably had nothing to do with it.

In 1987, David Paul had wanted to sink 20 pilings into Biscayne Bay and build a teak landing for a 94-foot yacht. Some of his La Gorce Island neighbors fought back.

Ultimately Paul agreed to build a less ambitious dock, and the Miami Beach City Commission decided to give him a variance. Voting in Paul's favor was Mayor Daoud—but he never mentioned doing any legal work for the S&L. Under state law, he was required to disclose any potential conflict of interest.

Nine days after the vote, Daoud began receiving the CenTrust corporate checks. Later he made an unusual appearance before the Metro Commission to show his support for Paul's dock application. The structure was approved.

This interesting chain of events would never have been connected had not CenTrust gone belly up. That's when investigators got a look at the books. They said the payments to Daoud "are suspected of buying favorable consideration from the mayor with regard to Mr. Paul's attempts to gain variances which would allow him to build a massive dock . . ."

It will be intriguing to hear Daoud's explanation for his failure to reveal his CenTrust income before the vote. Perhaps it was yet another innocent oversight.

And perhaps the mayor has a dream of a kinder, gentler Miami Beach where every citizen with a 94-foot yacht gets a chance to have a teak boat dock.

To paraphrase another visionary leader, some men see things as they are and ask why.

Others see things that might be and ask: How much?

Wanted: Real job for Metro commissioner

July 18, 1990

It's rough when even the politicians can't get a job.

This is the plight of Metro Commissioner Jorge (No Visible Means of Support) Valdes.

He claims a net worth of $357,581, drives a Mercedes-Benz, owns a big house and two boats . . . and is unemployed.

Times are hard, but Valdes is resourceful. His family works, and he relies heavily on the kindness of friends. Many of these friends conduct regular business with Dade County, and appear before the County Commission to seek favorable rulings. Valdes often votes for his friends' projects—but not, he insists, in return for personal favors.

Sure, a county contractor catered his daughter's wedding. And it's true that he used the legal services of a heavyweight zoning lobbyist for a private land deal in Key Largo. And Valdes doesn't deny that he has supplemented his commissioner's income by working for firms connected to the Latin Builders Association, a group frequently appearing before the Metro Commission.

Says Valdes: "It's hard for the public to understand. Personal contacts make people friends. Who are you going to ask to help you?"

In a way, it's refreshing to find an elected official who makes absolutely no attempt to conceal obvious conflicts of interest. Valdes, in fact, seems unfamiliar with the term.

Facing re-election this fall, he ought to think about lining up a real job, pronto. He can't afford the poignant delusion that all these folks are showering him with generosity simply because he's a nice guy, and not because of his position. If Valdes gets voted out of his office, his pals in the building industry won't be nearly as helpful.

No one can possibly live on the $6,000 that county commissioners are paid annually, but it's supposed to be a part-time gig. Most commissioners at least go through the motions of finding other employment. Mayor Steve Clark, for example, is part owner of a travel agency—although he doesn't spend a great deal of time at the office booking Disney tours.

Many politicians claim to be lawyers even if they have no clients and, in some cases, no office. It's a convenient occupation because people expect you to dress nicely and eat well. When you drive up in a fancy car, everybody assumes you made the dough from your law practice and not bribes.

Another occupation often claimed by elected officeholders is "consultant." The beauty of this job is that it sounds important but, at the same time, no one knows what it means.

Unfortunately, Commissioner Valdes currently isn't in a position to do much consulting. And he doesn't have a law degree, so that's out, too.

Still, there must be something that suits his skills. All over Dade County, men and women of his age put in a full day of good honest work. The classifieds are full of interesting opportunities, if Valdes would only look.

We're talking hundreds of jobs—auto mechanics, typists, medical assistants, accountants, computer programmers, bartenders, truck drivers, salesmen, cashiers . . . OK, scratch that last one. It's probably not a brilliant idea for a county commissioner to be handling money.

But there's this ad for what seems a good match: "CLOWNS WANTED. NO EXPERIENCE NECESSARY. WILL TRAIN." I called the number and told Fran Bombino (of the Bombino Brothers) that Commissioner Valdes needed work. Bombino said Valdes would probably make a wonderful clown, once he learns how to juggle and ride a unicycle.

For a less strenuous vocation, a Dade beauty shop is advertising for a professional hair weaver—a craft that Commissioner Valdes could probably pick up, with a little practice. Also, there'd be lots of time to visit leisurely with his constituents.

If it's solitude the commissioner wants, the Rivero funeral home is looking for an embalmer—a peaceful respite from the turmoil of county government. Best of all, there's virtually no chance of a future conflict with Valdes' official duties, since dead people seldom ask the commission for favors.

From pathetic to revolting, our leaders run gamut

May 29, 1994

Local Leaders on Parade:

First comes Carlos Valdes, state representative and volunteer field-tester for the Magic Marker company. A hidden camera caught this bonehead scribbling on the wall of a Miami Beach condominium.

Valdes says he and his mother, with whom he lives, are locked in a nasty quarrel with the condo association. Recurring vandalism near Valdes' unit caused the management to install a hidden video camera.

Catching the culprit didn't take long. The surveillance tape shows Valdes sauntering down the hall and squeaking a black marker across the paint. Then the 43-year-old juvenile delinquent scurries back to his apartment.

Prosecutors charged Valdes with criminal mischief and he doesn't deny that he's the guy on the tape. While conceding his action was "unacceptable," he says it stemmed from the legal dispute which he's waging "on behalf of my 77-year-old mother."

That's real class. Lay it all on dear old Mom.

If only she were more spry, she'd fight her own battles. But what's a good son to do? Gimme the Magic Marker, Ma. I'll take care of this!

It's a good thing Valdes doesn't live in Singapore or he'd be in prison today with stripes on his butt and Mom waiting at the gate with a jumbo tube of Desitin ointment.

From the pathetic to the revolting, we turn to the latest installment of "Larry Hawkins' Favorite Pickup Lines."

The Metro commissioner recently resigned from the board of a national veterans' group after a staff member complained that he frequently sexually harassed her and once exposed himself. The woman put her charges in a sworn affidavit.

It's not the first time. Last year, two of Hawkins' former secretaries told a state attorney that he'd hassled them with lewd remarks and raunchy overtures.

Although prosecutor Joseph Centorino declined to file charges, he concluded that Hawkins "may have engaged in a pattern of offensive conduct toward female staff members, including unwanted sexual advances, crude and suggestive language and conduct, all of which constituted a form of sexual harassment."

The names of five additional women allegedly harassed by Hawkins were provided to Centorino. He gave the case to the state Ethics Commission, which is famous for doing nothing. A hearing is set Thursday.

Hawkins won't discuss the new accusation and denies the rest.

There's probably a perfectly logical explanation: All these women—some of whom don't even know each other—have banded together in a diabolical conspiracy to destroy the political career of a wheelchair-bound Vietnam veteran.

Right, Larry. And they hatched the plot in Dallas, hiding on the grassy knoll.

Being a pig around women isn't against the law, but using one's position for sexual intimidation is a cause for legal action. There's nothing worse than a boss with runaway hormones, and juries can penalize such antics with hefty judgments.

For voters, the issue isn't financial liability so much as character. Do you want a lecher on the county commission? If so, they'll need a telephone hotline to handle the complaints.

Hawkins can deny it until he's purple in the face, but only gullible fools would believe that several different women could misunderstand his sense of humor or concoct the same terrible lie about him.

Don't expect the Ethics Commission to do much but ruminate. That agency was invented by politicians to investigate politicians and therefore was given no teeth.

Voters will be the ones to get rid of Larry Hawkins, or let him continue his quest for Bob Packwood's world title.

Homestead's sneaky deal raises hackles

December 3, 1995

A month before the final vote, Metro commissioners are catching heavy flak for their outlandish giveaway of Homestead Air Force Base.

Hundreds of South Dade residents appeared at a public hearing last Wednesday to protest the county's furtive move to lease 1,800 acres to a group called the Homestead Air Force Base Developers, Inc.

HABDI wants to turn the hurricane-battered base into a commercial airport with shopping, offices, apartments and an industrial park.

It's an ambitious plan, especially coming from local home builders who've never before developed an airport.

But these aren't just any builders. HABDI's principals are also big shots with the potent Latin Builders Association, whose members donate large sums to Metro Commission candidates.

HABDI's top man is Carlos Herrera, president of the LBA. Other partners in the Homestead project include two former LBA directors and a vice president.

Their 45-year lease agreement was quietly being maneuvered through the commission when details began leaking. No sooner did neighbors begin raising objections than HABDI started braying about discrimination.

That's what happened at Wednesday's hearing, too. HABDI's Camilio Jaime and others staged a walkout, charging that opposition to the airport is being led by anti-Hispanic racists.

Which must come as a surprise to project critics such as Metro Commissioner Maurice Ferre and former Miami mayor Xavier Suarez, who happen to be Hispanic.

HABDI isn't fooling anyone. Its accusations are a smoke screen contrived to obscure a land deal that stinks.

It began when the U.S. government decided to close most of Homestead Air Force Base and turn it over to Dade County.

Oddly, the county never advertised that the base property was available to private interests. There was no public meeting, no competitive bidding.

Yet, nine days after receiving HABDI's written proposal—a proposal kept secret, at HABDI's request—Metro aviation officials offered the group a lease.

Acting against staff recommendations, county commissioners in July 1994 voted to give HABDI first dibs on the air base. Another developer made a pitch, but was rejected.

True to form, Dade officials endorsed the HABDI lease without researching the feasibility of putting a big air park in South Dade. Some question whether it can compete with a newly expanded Miami International Airport.

Another question is the risk to taxpayers, if the project flops. The agreement calls for the HABDI partners to invest a minimum of $16 million the first seven years. But most of the development money—an estimated $500 million—would come from other investors, still unnamed.

The county would contribute $10 million worth of roads and improvements. Meanwhile HABDI would pay no rent on undeveloped property.

County Manager Armando Vidal says he's confident the Homestead deal is solid, and the public's interest will be protected. Commissioners will take a final vote Jan. 11.

Many who live near the base—Anglos, blacks and Hispanics alike—are justifiably suspicious and upset. It's not that they don't want the place developed; they just want to make sure it's done fairly, and with the best chance of success.

They don't want a sneaky political deal shoved down their throats, which is what's happening.

Time will tell if HABDI can make good on its grandiose promises for the old air base. What's disgraceful is that nobody else is getting a chance to bid, so people in South Dade will never know if something better could have been done.

Greenpalm: A true-life tale of bugs and rats

September 22, 1996

You've probably heard of Howard the Duck. Now meet Howard the Rat.

That would be Howard Gary, former Miami city manager and now a star informer in the Operation Greenpalm corruption probe.

While Howard the Duck was merely a lame movie character, Howard the Rat is a true-life crook. He got caught trying to squeeze a $2 million "consultant" fee out of Unisys, a computer company seeking contracts with the city of Miami.

Unisys executives, it seems, weren't in the mood for a shakedown, so they told the feds about the outrageous money demands made by Gary and his corrupt cohort, then-Miami Finance Director Manohar Surana.

Both men were soon visited by FBI agents, who apparently explained with excruciating clarity what lay ahead. Both Gary and Surana agreed to cooperate in the hopes of avoiding prison.

Before long, the men were wearing electronic bugs and chatting up dirty deals. Implicated so far are ex-City Manager Cesar Odio, City Commissioner Miller Dawkins, County Commissioner James Burke and other players to be named later.

Odio has been charged. Burke hasn't. Both men claim they were set up, although they'll have a tough time explaining some of what they say on the secret tapes.

A brief history is helpful: After being fired as city manager in 1984, Gary opened a municipal bond firm. His old chums in Dade politics steered lots of business his way, and the firm prospered. In 1993 alone, it was involved in $2 billion worth of deals nationwide.

Bond issues are a convenient way for politicians to repay favors and reward big campaign contributors. Law firms that are appointed local bond counsels receive absurd fees for minimal work. Likewise, home-town bond companies often get a juicy cut of the sales while New York underwriters do the heavy lifting.

The best part is it's perfectly legal. Usually. The FBI and SEC have been sniffing around Dade's queerly allocated bond packages for several years.

Gary entered the business at a time when it was finally opening up to minority underwriters. "I don't think it's bad getting in because of politics," he once said. "I think it's bad if you get in the door and don't do your job."

Or, say, get busted.

Once the feds had him by the shorts, Gary offered to share some tricks of the trade, Miami-style. Wearing a wire, he approached Commissioner Burke, who chairs Metro's finance committee.

Gary offered Burke up to $100,000 if Gary's bond firm got a piece of a major deal—a $183 million refinancing of Dade's recycling plant. Sources say Burke agreed, and shortly thereafter Howard Gary and Co. was listed as a last-minute addition to the bond management roster.

Burke insists he didn't get, or ask for, any money. But he conceded: "There were some conversations which I shared with [Gary] that there was something I wanted . . . some things we were going to do together. They were personal."

Translation: It might sound like a bribe on tape, but it's really just two guys, talking about guy stuff.

Howard the Rat's role in the blossoming scandal is particularly odious because of the way he's traded on his firm's status as minority owned. His crookedness is a slap in the face of every honest black businessman who's tried for a public contract.

Ironically, Gary probably wouldn't be in trouble if he'd been content with the fortune he's making with bonds. But no, he had to go try a $2 million rip-off of Unisys.

It's nothing but greed, which remains a serious character flaw among rats. That's how they always get caught.

Take over city; commissioners won't notice

December 1, 1996

With Miami auguring toward bankruptcy, state authorities are poised to snatch control of the city's mucked-up finances.

But Gov. Lawton Chiles made a strategic mistake by announcing his intentions ahead of time. He easily could have seized Miami's reins without forewarning the city commissioners.

They'd probably never have noticed.

When it comes to taxpayer money, these characters are so dependably inattentive that they wouldn't know what questions to ask, much less of whom.

For years the cookie jar was controlled by the slippery-fingered duo of City Manager Cesar Odio and Finance Director Manohar Surana. Unfortunately, neither fellow demonstrated the fiscal expertise to manage a Crandon Park hot-dog stand, much less a $275 million budget.

They were able to hold their jobs mainly because the politicians who hired them remained, conveniently, uninterested in simple arithmetic. As long as a few bucks were left lying around for pet projects, commissioners were content to let Odio and Surana juggle the numbers.

Evidently they took advice from the distinguished accounting firm of Deloitte, Cheech and Chong.

For example, the city for years failed to collect millions of dollars in overdue lease payments. In real-estate parlance this is called "getting stiffed by your tenants," a technical concept that someday may be explained to the commission.

It took a bribery scandal and a slew of felony indictments to reveal that Miami is sinking into a $68 million sludge pit of debt. Wall Street seems ready to downgrade the city's bond rating to "J," for joke.

Bottom line: If something drastic isn't done immediately, Miami will run out of dough in March or April. That could mean no cops, no garbage pickup, no firefighters, no pay.

So the commission, faced with the gravest crisis in its history, of course has done zilch. Commissioners continue to balk at doubling garbage rates, which would gain a few months of solvency.

Under Florida law, the state can take over a city that's going down the tubes. A special oversight committee can be appointed to handle its finances in an emergency.

That's what Miami Mayor Joe Carollo wants, and no wonder. It'll get him and his pusillanimous pals off the hook. Let somebody else hike fees and take the other painful, unpopular steps necessary to save the city.

The commission's lack of spine provides more ammunition for Miamians seeking to have the municipality dissolved. While those petitions circulate, Gov. Chiles should move ahead swiftly with a state takeover of the budget.

And there's really no need to notify the commission. Nothing would have to change down at City Hall.

Commissioners can continue to hold regular meetings, just as they do now. Pass a few meaningless resolutions. Honor a few good Samaritans. Name a few streets after their campaign contributors.

Somebody can even jot down the minutes. Televise it, too, just for giggles.

Carollo can continue as make-believe mayor. Ed Marquez can be the make-believe city manager. As a lark, somebody can even serve as make-believe finance director.

And the rest of the commissioners can sit on the dais and pretend they're doing a job, pretend the city is in good hands, pretend somebody honest is handling the budget.

The same as they've been pretending all along.

Only this time they officially won't have control of the taxpayers' money.

But if nobody tells them, it'll probably take years before they figure it out.

So, ssssshhhhhhh.

Miami's fiscal crisis: Look at the bright side

December 5, 1996

An Open Letter to America from the City of Miami:

As everybody knows, our city is in the throes of a financial crisis. The media coverage has been so gloomy that tourists, newcomers and investors are being frightened away.

It's time to clear the air, set the record straight and take the bull by the horns. The bad news: Miami is so broke that the state of Florida has stepped in to try to stave off bankruptcy.

The good news: Our days of harebrained spending, bumbling management and corruption are temporarily over, because there's basically nothing left to waste, misspend or steal.

Heck, we're in the hole by 68 frigging million bucks—who'd try to rip us off now? Which brings up the first of several ugly misperceptions that must be addressed.

• Misperception 1: The entire city is corrupt.

Flatly untrue. Not one current Miami commissioner or administrator is under indictment, house arrest or the regular supervision of a parole officer—a record we're darn proud of.

Most city employees are honest and hard-working, except for a few deadbeat relatives and cronies of politicians. So what if there's an ongoing criminal investigation. Don't tell us the FBI never body-wired any informants at your city hall!

• Misperception 2: The city infrastructure is a disaster.

To begin with, "disaster" is a relative term. Miami hasn't been flooded by a hurricane or leveled by an earthquake. Most nights it's not even on fire.

And if it was, we've still got plenty of skilled firefighters on the payroll, at least until March or possibly April.

• Misperception 3: The city is a dangerous place to live.

Oh, come on. If Miami was so unsafe, would Madonna and Sly Stallone own homes here? No way. Not even with their high-voltage fences and beefy bodyguards.

And don't forget Pat Riley. He could've coached an NBA team any place he wanted, but he chose Miami. Why? Not just because of the incredible contract he got, but because he wanted to be in a city that offered his family the very finest selection of high-voltage fences and beefy bodyguards.

• Misperception 4: The city is unsafe for visitors.

Contrary to what you've heard, the streets of Miami haven't been overrun by gangs and drug dealers—well, most of the streets haven't. Pat Riley's, for example.

And we've still got hundreds of experienced police officers on the payroll, at least until March or possibly April.

• Misperception 5: The city is a risky place to invest money.

Once more, "risky" is an awfully broad term. Perhaps you just like adventure. Maybe there's some riverboat gambler in your blood. Come on down and take a chance on Miami.

Given the negative publicity, it's understandable if major corporations and commercial investors are apprehensive about the city's ability to provide basic services, such as garbage pickup.

Be assured we've got some of the most efficient garbage collectors on the whole Eastern seaboard, at least until March or possibly April.

• Misperception 6: The city is about to be abolished.

Again, the word "abolished" can mean so many things. Remember that Miami is more than just arbitrary boundaries on a road map—it's a state of mind.

Say, for the sake of argument, that the city charter is dissolved. The magic wouldn't die. Miami wouldn't suddenly disappear. It would still be right where it is today, smack dab between the airport and the beach.

Which means you suckers still have to drive through the place, regardless of what happens in March or April.

Suarez's act won't play on Wall Street

December 4, 1997

Miami Mayor Xavier Suarez is in New York today, still trying to convince Wall Street that the city is in tiptop shape. Before he comes home, he should drop by Bellevue for a checkup.

Because the mayor is either certifiably nuts or seriously undermedicated.

In only a few short weeks, he has single-handedly managed to undermine both Miami's image rebuilding and its fiscal recovery, which were well under way before he took office.

First, Suarez dumped the well-regarded city manager, Ed Marquez. Then he declared war on the state oversight board that essentially had saved Miami from bankruptcy.

No wonder Moody's Investors Service, an important bond-rating firm, warned that the mayor's actions "have introduced significant uncertainty" about Miami's future, and "could disrupt or even reverse [the city's] recent progress toward fiscal recovery."

The firm added: "There does not appear to be any financial experience at the helm right now." In other words, the inmates are running the asylum.

Suarez's transformation from a reasonably bright, thoughtful guy to a babbling fruitcake has been both astonishing and sad to watch. Erratic, impulsive and imperious, Suarez has morphed into the delusional loner we once predicted of his predecessor, the tightly wound Joe Carollo.

Ironically, it's Carollo who has behaved for the last year like a grown-up, making levelheaded decisions and cooperating with the rescue panel appointed by the governor.

Meanwhile, Suarez campaigned on the theory that the city's $68 million budget shortfall was fabricated for political purposes by Carollo, abetted by the state, this newspaper and other nefarious interests. Never mind that capable, independent persons who examined the city's books concurred that disaster was imminent.

Once elected, Suarez strolled into City Hall and began firing people. More incredibly, he talked of lowering taxes, a rather unorthodox approach to a cash shortage. He didn't even show up at the last commission meeting, choosing instead to hunker in Nixonian seclusion inside his office.

With each new day, Suarez gets loonier and Carollo looks more like Alan Greenspan.

The mayor's paranoid rant is playing poorly in all venues north of Flagler Street. He got a frosty reception in Tallahassee this week when he tried to convince lawmakers (one of whom he bizarrely addressed as "Senator Cabbage") that Miami doesn't need any more help.

As proof, Suarez proudly pointed to the city's current $13 million surplus—money, he might have added, that exists only because of cost-slashing measures imposed by the oversight board.

It takes a certain type of person to boast about somebody else's hard work, then try to get rid of them. A crazy person is what it takes.

As shown by Moody's preemptive strike, Wall Street will be an even tougher audience for the mayor. His conspiracy theories are bewildering enough, but wait until he tries to explain his choice of Humberto Hernandez as chairman of the City Commission.

As a rule, legitimate bankers and brokers shy away from accused money launderers. Suarez's appointment of the federally indicted Hernandez has done nothing to inspire Wall Street's confidence.

In fact, you'd have trouble finding any experts who would heartily recommend investing in Miami. Even before the election, the city's general obligation bonds were considered "junk," with an anemic double-B rating from Standard & Poors.

But don't underestimate Mayor Suarez. By the time he's finished campaigning, Wall Street could be inspired to create a whole new category for Miami bonds: Triple D, for deranged.

Breakthrough at City Hall

August 16, 1998

An otherworldly event occurred Friday at Miami City Hall. Commissioners actually did something brave.

OK, "brave" is overstating it. But they did do something—proposed raising fire-rescue fees, garbage fees and the millage rate, with a novel goal of balancing the budget.

A big question is whether the commissioners are serious or faking it. As Miami spirals toward insolvency, they've done little but bicker, posture and stall. They are decisive only on the issue of when to meet again, for further bickering, posturing and stalling.

Another question is whether the proposed fee changes add up. Experts will be double-checking the city's accounting methods, which are often highly creative.

In July, the governor's Financial Oversight Board got another five-year recovery plan from the city, and found it so defective as to be insulting.

For example, Miami had included among projected revenues $3.2 million in federal grants that hadn't been approved by Congress. Another whimsical entry was $1 million from a lease that hadn't even been signed.

Members of the oversight board couldn't contain their frustration. Still, the commission's three biggest wimps—Willy Gort, J. L. Plummer and Tomas Regalado—continued to grandstand as champions of regular folks who can't afford to pay more for trash pickup.

What they really can't afford is more bad theater at City Hall.

Last week's vote was a result more of intimidation than courage. After a year of bewilderment, ineptitude and cowardice, the commissioners knew time was running out.

Gov. Lawton Chiles appears ready to stop the carnival, and is empowered to suspend the whole bunch. Monday is the deadline given for a new plan.

Faced with losing their jobs, commissioners reluctantly recommended doing what analysts have long advised—raise fees to enhance cash flow (cash being somewhat necessary to pay police, sanitation workers and other municipal employees).

The city says the higher rates would cost the average Miami homeowner an extra $92 in fiscal 1999, rising to about $181 by 2003. It won't be popular with residents, who already pay hefty taxes for mostly crummy service. But the alternative is worse—chaos and decay, if the city goes broke.

It's possible that Miami's budget has been a hoax for so long that nobody at City Hall remembers how to put together a real one. When Cesar Odio was city manager, he and his crooked budget chief, Manohar

Surana, would fill gaping holes in the ledgers with silly made-up numbers.

And it worked for a while, because commissioners could be relied upon not to ask many questions. It took a corruption scandal to reveal the extent of deficit scamming.

The Securities and Exchange Commission is investigating whether the city fictionalized its finances on three bond offerings. The SEC is wondering how Miami "balanced" its 1995 books by listing a $9 million lump sum of U.S. crime-fighting funds—money that in fact would be distributed incrementally over several years.

Other unusual projected revenues included $3 million from the sale of fill for which nobody had offered a penny.

Today the game's over, and Miami's slag-heap bond rating elicits giggles on Wall Street. Investigators might be encouraged by talk of raising municipal fees, but remember that Friday's vote was preliminary. Commissioners have plenty of time to chicken out.

In which case Gov. Chiles should act swiftly to rescue Miami's long-suffering residents by decommissioning the commission and putting the city in responsible hands.

Stormy Weather

'Tis the season some builders get generous

December 16, 1987

Once again it's that merry season of the year when contractors all around Dade County are racking their brains and wondering: What do I give the building inspector this Christmas?

Good news! Cash is "in" again, and it's perfectly safe—judging by the courthouse results of that big Metro police undercover sting.

Posing as a county inspector, detective Alex Ramirez collected almost $6,000 from builders in just four months. Driving from site to site in West Dade, Ramirez seldom got through a day without somebody slipping him wads of money, food, fine wine or a bottle of booze.

Typical was this exchange between the undercover cop and a building foreman, recorded by a hidden microphone:

Ramirez: "You know, you don't have to give me anything."

Foreman: "No, I don't have to give you anything, but in life, don't I leave a tip when I eat in a cafe or a bar?"

Twenty-five people were ultimately indicted in the sting, and 15 of those pleaded guilty or no contest. All received small fines and probation, and all but one had the incident wiped from their permanent records. Nobody went to jail.

In dishing out such punishment, the Dade judicial system sent a message loud and strong: Payoffs are no big deal. Don't sweat it.

A welcome sentiment—and just in time for the holidays!

Believe it or not, the custom of secretly purchasing the cooperation of public servants is still regarded as controversial. In some parts of the country it is referred to as "bribery"—and judges actually put people in jail for it.

Fortunately, many of the indicted Dade contractors were able to convince our courts that the cash wasn't a bribe in the naughty sense—but rather a "tip," or lunch money, or just an innocuous gesture of friendship. Some opted for the business-as-usual defense, with uncanny results.

An attorney for Hector Brito Jr., who had paid $50 to detective Ramirez, insisted that it wasn't really a bribe because Brito didn't specifically ask for something in return.

"It was more of a thank-you, which is very common in the business," the lawyer explained. (Circuit Judge David Gersten threw out the case.)

Similarly, a jury acquitted carpenter Jorge Gonzalez of bribery after he admitted giving Ramirez $20 "for lunch" on three occasions. Gonzalez's attorney said his client was not seeking special favors, but gave the cash merely because Ramirez "arrived promptly and had been a gentleman."

Untouched by the police sting were those few inspectors who make a practice of shaking down Dade builders and contractors. Since these greedy little suckers are still on the loose, they'll probably be expecting stocking-stuffers for the Yule season.

A word of caution: If you're giving cash, don't go over $100 per bribe. In fact, the less you give, the more innocent it looks.

Whenever possible, avoid cramming the money directly into the inspector's palms. Instead, place it in an unmarked envelope and leave it in a clever place where he's sure to find it—taped to the hood ornament of his El Dorado, for example.

When paying off an inspector, don't ever demand something in return. Even though both of you know perfectly well what the money is for, don't come right out and say it. Not only is it rude, it's risky.

You never can tell when some run-amok jury might misconstrue the meaning of: "Hey, Mac, here's the 50 smackers for the plumbing inspection."

Should you have the misfortune of bribing an undercover cop, don't panic. Just tell the judge you thought the guy was collecting for United Way. Tell him the cash had nothing to do with the fact that the guy inspected your entire 600-unit apartment building without ever leaving his car.

The court will understand. Some old scrooges might call it corruption, but down here we call it the spirit of giving.

Shhhhhh! Let the inspector get his sleep

June 4, 1990

When investigators tailed Dade building inspectors on daily rounds, they saw: a roofing inspector who never climbed a ladder the whole time; an electrical inspector who goofed off at a bowling alley; an elevator inspector who spent county time napping at the library.

Construction was certified on some projects using the convenient drive-by method, so the inspector never had to leave the comfort of his car. Other work was approved, site unseen.

The Dade grand jury says the Building and Zoning Department is often more devoted to helping the construction industry than protecting the public from sleazy contractors. It's virtually the same conclusion that another grand jury reached in 1976.

Nothing ever changes. Only four years ago, an undercover cop posing as a building inspector collected thousands of dollars in "gifts" from local contractors. Detectives said it was business as usual.

Efforts to weed out the crooks and deadbeats have been stymied. Just last week, prosecutors mysteriously declined to provide the names of those few inspectors whose antics were exposed in the most recent probe. This means they're still on the job—or at least pretending to be.

If only they kept a journal . . .

8 A.M. Drove out to Old Cutler Shady-Lakes-On-the-Bay Estates for a thorough inspection. The cement is still slightly mushy, but what can you expect after only six weeks? When I got back to the car, I discovered

someone had dropped an envelope with $500 on the front seat. Must be my lucky day!

8:07 A.M. Drove out to New Cutler Meadows-Near-the-Bay to check on complaints of substandard work. Everything looked jim-dandy to me. I leaned my golf bag against several walls, and not one fell down. While I was checking the place over, someone put two first-class plane tickets to Bermuda on the windshield of my car. Some sort of sweepstakes, I guess. Talk about luck!

9–10 A.M. Stopped by library to check the stocks in the *Wall Street Journal*. Blue chips look strong, but I'm thinking about dumping IBM while it's riding high. Also, I wonder if I went too heavy into tax-free munis.

10:15 A.M. Drove out to Green Cutler Gardens Somewhat-Near-the-Bay to check on reports of inferior drywall. Another false alarm: Every wall I inspected was dry as a bone. When I got back to the car, I found a new gold Rolex Submariner on the front seat. Too bad I've already got one.

10:30–Noon. Stopped at the bowling alley to see how the ceiling struts were holding up after 23 years. Just by coincidence, the All-Dade Hooters Waitress League was having a tournament, so I stayed to watch—just to make sure they weren't injured by any falling beams.

12:15 P.M. Ran into the new guy, Mario, on a site for that new nursing home. Get this—he was actually up on a ladder, checking out some piddly leak in the roof. A ladder! I nearly busted a gut laughing. Told him he should've been a fireman.

12:30 P.M. Tried to inspect the New World Old Cutler Financial Plaza-In-the-Bay, but traffic was lousy and it started to drizzle. Just so happened I could see the structure perfectly from Hooters, where I'd stopped for a late lunch. So I used my binoculars to count the floors: forty-two, right on the button! As I was phoning in my inspection, somebody broke into my car and left a deed to a three-bedroom condo in Cozumel. Not only that, they were considerate enough to put it in a third-party offshore trust!

1:55 P.M. Went out to Rolling Cutler Hills Nowhere-Near-the-Bay Estates for a final inspection, and all 1,344 units checked out fine—at least they looked pretty darn nice from the car. As I drove past, someone lobbed a tooled-leather valise in the front seat. Just a guess, but it looks like it might contain $25,000 in nonsequential unmarked bills. What a day I'm having!

2:11 P.M. Holy cow, where did the time go? The wife is probably worried sick. Still, I ought to swing by the bowling alley once more to double check those struts.

Now, perhaps, we'll develop with more care

August 27, 1992

OK, God, you got our attention.

Heck, you've eighty-sixed an entire U.S. Air Force base. Who wouldn't be impressed?

And about that South Florida Building Code—well, maybe it's not as tough as they promised us. Or maybe it's not being enforced with what you'd call unflagging diligence. Sure seems peculiar that so many older homes survived your Hurricane Andrew with little or no damage, while newer subdivisions exploded into match sticks.

God, was this hurricane a pop quiz on survival?

Because if you were testing courage and compassion, you won't find more of it anywhere. Heroes walk every street, or what's left of the streets. The valor on display in South Dade makes Desert Storm look like a Tupperware party.

But, God, if you were testing us on how wisely we've cared for this astonishingly fragile peninsula, then we failed. We've done some dumb things, starting with reckless planning and manic overdevelopment.

In our lust to carve up this place and hawk it as a waterfront paradise, we crammed four million people along a flat and vulnerable coast. It's complete lunacy, of course. We haven't been able to employ them all, protect them from crime, properly educate their children or even guarantee the most basic of human needs—drinking water.

And, as we've seen this week, we certainly haven't provided safe housing. Thousands and thousands of families are homeless and heartbroken this morning. The rest of us, blessed by capricious luck, finally have time to reflect.

We thought we were ready. Honest, we knew the drill. Who hadn't seen the harrowing footage from Donna, Camille and Hugo? By the time the TV weather people told us to worry, we were worried. We collected our D-cell batteries and our Sterno, our duct tape and our plywood, and then we watched Andrew march due west. We waited hopefully for the Big Swerve, but it never came.

Six hundred thousand souls who had never been through one of your hurricanes actually evacuated when they were told to do so. Elsewhere that might be routine behavior, God, but down here it's close to a miracle. Moses himself would have a hard time rousting the rollerbladers from South Beach.

All that valiant preparation—and still the community lies devastated. What did we expect? Aim a hurricane's fury at four million people and the only possible outcome is a horror.

We had been warned, again and again. The people who should've been listening were too busy counting their campaign contributions from big developers. Now, as always, the suffering is heaped on the most helpless—those whose only sin was buying into the Florida dream.

The only good to come from Andrew would be a resolve not to let it happen again. We can't change the course of hurricanes, but we can damn sure build houses with walls that don't disintegrate and roofs that don't peel like rotted bananas.

It's been about 30 years since South Florida got nailed by a big storm. You probably figured we needed a reminder. Next time, don't wait so long. Send us a modest, midsize hurricane every couple of years, and soon Florida will have some of the world's sturdiest and most sensible housing developments.

Thirty years was plenty of time for us to screw up. We got lax, we got greedy. We quintupled the population and idiotically called it progress. Now it's a disaster area.

God, please don't say you told us so. We got the message.

And thanks for not making it worse.

Blustery talk about Andrew is all hot air

October 18, 1992

Don't buy the breathless hype that Hurricane Andrew was "The Big One." It wasn't, not by a long shot.

The Big One won't strike the most thinly populated stretch of South Florida, the way Andrew did. The Big One scores a dead hit on downtown Miami, Hialeah or Fort Lauderdale.

Unlike Andrew, the Big One won't blow through in a few frantic hours. It parks on top of us for two or three horrifying days, dumping enough rain to flood most neighborhoods to ruin.

And the Big One won't be a tightly packed storm, the way Andrew was. It'll be huge and rambling, like Camille, and its path of total destruction will breach three counties.

Not that Andrew was a pussy cat; it was a swift, powerful hurricane. Those who've had their lives shattered cannot imagine anything worse, and there isn't.

But to propagate the melodramatic notion that Andrew was a once-in-a-century catastrophe is not only scientifically wrong, it's morally reckless.

Understand that certain folks—politicians, developers and the building lobby—have a vested interest in promoting the myth of the Big One. They want you to believe that Andrew was a freak storm with satanic powers, and that nothing could have prevented the mass destruction.

Rubbish. The only freakish thing about Andrew was that it hit us, for a change. It did what all Category Four storms do—tore the hell out of everything in its way. Another one equally fierce could hit next week, next month or next year.

The other day, the Latin Builders Association took out a full-page ad to whine about all the bad press that the construction industry is getting. The LBA implied that shoddy workmanship wasn't widespread, that Andrew's supernatural gusts were humanly unstoppable.

Especially if your contractor didn't bother to fasten your roof to your house.

Lennar, Arvida and other developers also are pitching the myth of the Big One: Hey, we sell sturdy homes. Nothing could have survived Andrew. (Except the low-cost houses built by Habitat for Humanity.)

While the companies try to cover their butts, homeowners are filing richly deserved lawsuits. A grand jury is convening (yes, again). Even the State Attorney's Office is on the prowl for indictments. More shocking revelations are sure to come.

Andrew exposed, at a terrible human cost, what happens when a system meant to protect citizens is poisoned by greed, politics, corruption and ineptitude.

Failure occurred at every step. The vaunted South Florida Building Code deliberately was weakened to allow faster, cheaper work. Staples instead of nails? Great idea! Waferboard instead of plywood? Hey, give it a try. What next—Lego blocks?

What were these idiots thinking? Clearly no one—from the builders to the inspectors to the buyers—had ever experienced a major hurricane. Responsible tradesmen warned of disaster, but nobody listened. Politicians such as Mayor Steve Clark sat zombielike while the regulations were neutered. Why bite the hand that bankrolls your re-election?

County Manager Joaquin Avino was in charge of building and zoning when some of the crummiest developments were approved. When an NBC reporter recently asked about those projects, Avino experienced a bout of prime-time amnesia. It was truly pathetic.

Andrew revealed the system for the incestuous charade that it is, and now the guilty parties are scrambling for cover. It's not our fault, they cry, it's Nature! Two hundred mile-per-hour winds! The Big One!

The Big Lie is what it is. So much preventable damage, so much unnecessary misery—it's not the storm of the century, it's the crime of the century.

Happy ending slow to come at country walk

May 6, 1993

Hi-ho, hi-ho.
It's off your roof did go.
We don't care if your house ain't there.
Hi-ho, hi-ho.

Once upon a time, there were 70 or 80 dwarfs who built a place called the Village Homes of Country Walk.

Some of the dwarfs were good workers, but others weren't. The bad dwarfs had names like Lazy, Dizzy, Drowsy, Greedy, Clumsy, Careless and Sleazy. They worked for a company called Walt Disney, which had a snow-white reputation.

One summer night, a fierce hurricane came from the sea. It huffed and it puffed and blew lots of houses down. The people of Country Walk were very surprised, for the dwarfs had promised that the condominiums were built solidly and would not fall apart in a strong wind.

After the storm, the residents went through the rubble of Country Walk and discovered many bad things about the way the dwarfs had built the homes. There were masonry walls with no steel bars for reinforcement, and sometimes no cement! There were wooden posts that hadn't been anchored to the foundations. There were roof trusses that weren't properly attached.

Country Walk was a disaster area, but it wasn't the only one. Across the land, people who lost everything in the hurricane were learning terrible facts about how poorly their houses had been constructed. Soon those people hired lawyers, who began to sue.

At first, the home-building companies said they didn't do anything wrong. They blamed all the damage on the hurricane, which they said was the most powerful storm in the history of the planet! But scientists who studied the hurricane, and engineers who studied the wrecked homes, disputed the builders. They said most damage resulted from cheesy construction.

Facing expensive and embarrassing trials, two companies did something very smart: They caved in, agreeing to give money to those who'd lost their homes in the storm.

A company called Lennar gave $2.4 million to customers in several neighborhoods where houses had disintegrated like match sticks. After deducting legal fees, each owner got about $3,800 from the settlement—a bargain for Lennar, which was one of the most profitable developers in the whole United States.

In the place known as Country Walk, a company called Arvida/JMB Partners agreed to give $2.74 million to the owners of 135 condos that were damaged or destroyed by the hurricane. In exchange, the customers promised not to sue Arvida, and thus spared the company months of humiliating public disclosures about the shabby quality of its Country Walk homes.

But one company that didn't make peace with its customers was Walt Disney, which was more famous for entertaining children than for building condos. Disney had put up 209 units at Country Walk. Many were ruined by the storm that blew in from the sea.

The people in the condos wanted Disney to pay $5.9 million, to make up for the many mistakes made by the bad dwarfs. But the company offered only $2 million, insisting that its homes were nailed together just fine.

So the owners went to court. Suddenly Disney found its snow-white reputation in jeopardy. Several of the bad dwarfs got subpoenaed to testify. Lazy, Clumsy and Careless were the first to snitch.

When Disney's lawyers read the dwarfs' depositions, they became very, very worried. They faxed the Country Walk homeowners and offered lots more money to forget the whole thing. The homeowners accepted the deal, put new roofs on their condos and lived nervously ever after.

Especially during hurricane season.

Slow to act? No, state was setting trap for builders

July 29, 1993

This week, the Dade State Attorney's Office and the lieutenant governor announced an ambitious plan to crack down on crooked builders.

Gee, what's the big hurry? It's been only 11 months since the hurricane. South Dade residents have only lost millions of dollars to swindlers, licensed and unlicensed, who have taken the money and left the houses in shambles.

But authorities aren't waiting for something really serious to happen. They're leaping into the fray now, four whole weeks before the first anniversary of the storm.

A press conference put out the word. The state attorney is hiring three new prosecutors, an investigator and two secretaries. The state's Department of Business and Professional Regulation is adding a dozen investigators, plus five persons to help take complaints from the public.

Everybody knows the task force that calls itself "We Will Rebuild." This one could be called "We Will Indict."

Lots of folks in South Dade aren't too impressed. They think something should have been done even sooner about crooked builders—before the evidence was trucked off to the dump.

True, Hurricane Andrew's wreckage revealed widespread illegal construction practices and egregious nonenforcement of the building codes. True, these were crimes inflicted on thousands of homeowners, crimes that have caused horrible suffering and financial ruin.

And, true, not one contractor responsible for the damage has lost his license. Not one inspector who approved the shoddy work has been punished.

But that's only because authorities decided to set an ingenious trap, one that required patience.

Sure, it would have been easy to rush in and prosecute a few lousy builders after their Tinker-Toy subdivisions blew apart in the hurricane. It would have been simple to collect the defective trusses and holey shingles, and then show a jury the right way to put on a roof.

It would have been easy, all right. Too easy. And it would have spoiled the secret plan.

Think about it. Indicting crooked builders too soon after Hurricane Andrew might have scared off many of the thieves and con men masquerading as legitimate contractors who stampeded Florida to cash in on the storm.

So authorities shrewdly decided to lie low and pretend they weren't interested in what was happening in South Dade. They knew it would soon be a bonanza of sleaze. They knew that there weren't enough honest builders to go around, that people desperate to have their homes rebuilt would eventually turn to unscrupulous strangers.

And they were right. Each day since Andrew has brought new reports of outrageous rip-offs and incompetent workmanship. Many homeowners have lost all their insurance money to fly-by-night vagabonds. Since August, the DPR's Miami office has logged a 1,800 percent increase in complaints against contractors.

For state investigators, the waiting has paid off. They now have a much larger number of cases to choose from, and therefore a much better chance of actually winning one or two.

Unfortunately, it won't help the thousands of people fleeced by shady operators during the last 11 months. Thousands more won't realize that they also have been conned until another hurricane hits and their roofs fly off like a bad hat.

But don't worry. When that happens, the state of Florida will be there again, ready to swoop in with crack investigators and prosecutors. You might not see them for, oh, the first 10 or 11 months after the disaster, but that doesn't mean they don't care.

No, they're just lying low, waiting for the trap to spring.

Government can't be trusted to enforce codes

December 30, 1993

Finally, thanks to Hurricane Andrew, an insurance company gets wise.

United States Fidelity and Guaranty (USF&G) has announced that it will begin inspecting every home it insures for potential storm losses. In other words, company-paid experts will do the job once entrusted to local building officials.

It makes good sense, given the scandal of Andrew. The wonder is that more insurance companies aren't doing the same thing.

The hurricane tragically confirmed that government cannot be relied upon to enforce building codes, especially in areas of uncontrolled growth. Andrew turned South Dade into a panorama of devastation, much of it caused by lousy construction and a lack of competent code enforcement.

The insurance industry took its worst beating ever, paying out $16.5 billion in claims. We know what happened next: sharp rate increases, and attempted mass cancellations of Florida policies. Most insurers have restricted or even stopped insuring new homes in coastal regions.

That's one way to cut losses, the cold-blooded way. It unfairly punishes people with well-built houses and also punishes honest home builders. The USF&G experiment is more humane and ultimately smarter for the industry: Its own inspectors will rate the houses.

Consider how fussy these firms are about auto insurance. The annual premiums on a new Ferrari are thousands more than those on a 5-year-old Tercel. Why? The sports car is a bigger investment, and statistically a bigger risk.

It seems logical, then, that insurers would view a high-risk house with even greater concern. A house, say, built with no hurricane straps. Or too few nails in the shingles. Or defective gables.

But until Hurricane Andrew, insurance companies seldom asked questions about the quality of construction in most subdivisions. As long as a house passed local inspection, getting a policy was virtually automatic. Everybody made money, everybody was happy.

Andrew spoiled the party. The insurance industry was shellshocked by the extent of unnecessary destruction, and by its own studies predicting losses would be three times higher if a storm hit Miami directly.

It was evident that Dade County had failed, spectacularly, to make sure its housing was safe from hurricane winds. In several areas, code enforcement had been a costly charade.

One way to avoid future failures is for insurance companies to do the inspections themselves. The advantages are obvious. Private inspectors wouldn't have the ludicrous quotas imposed on county inspectors, nor would they be subject to cronyism and political pressures. Many homeowners would welcome a visit from an independent expert.

Not long after the hurricane, a State Farm executive told me that hiring its own inspectors was a good idea, but too expensive. It's hard to imagine anything more expensive than Andrew.

Say State Farm spent $20 million a year on building inspections. That's only 1/170th of the $3.4 billion that the company shelled out in hurricane claims. In retrospect, inspectors would have been a smart investment.

While USF&G insures less than 1 percent of Florida's homeowners, its new inspection policy covers all customers around the country. If other insurers tried the same program, the quality of coastal construction might improve dramatically. Who's going to a build a house that can't be insured?

The key is incentive. Insurance companies have the most to lose when the next hurricane hits—and the strongest motivation to make sure history doesn't repeat itself. If that means climbing a few roofs and counting a few nails, it's a small price to pay.

How soon we forget what these storms do

June 9, 1994

The governor's special hurricane committee has warned that Florida is flirting with "great loss of life and property in coming years" unless strict construction laws are passed.

The committee's chairman made "an urgent plea that this report not be put on a shelf and forgotten."

The governor was LeRoy Collins. The year was 1960. The hurricane was Donna. Everyone wanted to make sure such needless destruction wouldn't happen again.

But time passed, and people did forget. Just like today.

A hearing examiner says the only Metro building inspector fired in the aftermath of Hurricane Andrew should get his job back—a poetic beginning to the new hurricane season.

It was a foregone conclusion that nobody of consequence would be punished for the crimes exposed by Andrew. The builders who slapped together the lousy houses, the developers who sold them and the inspectors who rubber-stamped them had little to worry about from Dade prosecutors, or anyone else.

What modest progress is being made to prevent another disaster comes against powerful opposition. Even now, special interests are trying to weaken hurricane reforms before they take effect.

From a pessimistic Herb Saffir, engineer and nationally recognized expert on hurricane damage: "The only thing I can say is, I hope we don't get an Andrew-type storm coming through the populated areas of Miami."

After Andrew, public outrage and press scrutiny forced the Metro Commission to review building practices and enforcement. The Board of Rules and Appeals, a lap dog of the building trades, was supplanted by a more independent Building Code Committee.

To the surprise of no one (especially those living at Country Walk or Naranja Lakes), the panel found that much of Andrew's devastation was the result of poor housing designs and flawed construction. Yet virtually every worthwhile reform faced opposition. The industry's recurring argument was that home buyers won't pay a little extra for better shutters, stronger windows and nailed-down roofs. Total nonsense.

Eventually, new standards were approved. Shutters, garage doors and windows would be required to withstand higher winds, high-speed impacts and cyclic "loading"—the push and pull of hurricane gusts.

The Metro Commission's reaction? Delay, delay, delay.

The latest date for the new safety standards to take effect is Sept. 1, a week after Andrew's second anniversary. But some members of the code committee fear the commission will bow to pressure and stall the deadline once again.

If that happens, says engineer Jose Mitrani, "then it's a joke, a fraud being perpetrated on the people of Dade County."

Some builders have taken the initiative, producing solid, medium-priced homes designed to weather most hurricanes. Others prefer to keep cutting corners, pushing Metro commissioners to help the industry regain control of regulation. Hefty campaign donations help.

Each summer that passes without a new hurricane dims the public's memory, and emboldens commissioners to roll back reforms. Many experts fear that if a Category Four storm slams us this year, the damage will be worse than it was in August 1992.

Mitrani advises home buyers to hire their own experts to make sure the construction is sound. The alternative is to entrust your family's safety to politicians concerned mostly with pleasing big campaign contributors.

It would be inexcusable if the dire post-Andrew warnings are "put on a shelf and forgotten." Apparently the only event that will stop that from happening is another terrible storm.

Just the fittest will survive next hurricane

August 25, 1994

Charles Darwin believed that species evolve by survival of the fittest. His theory, slightly updated, will be put to the test when the next hurricane hits.

The smartest will do fine. The not-so-smart will be scrounging for roofers.

Everybody knows what happened two years ago this week, when Andrew ripped South Dade: Many thousands of homes went to pieces.

Lousy construction, inferior materials, poor engineering and a weakened building code all contributed to the devastation.

Aerial photographs told the story: one subdivision in ruins; across the street, another development barely damaged. Facing Andrew's fiercest gusts, some houses held strong; in the storm's weakest wind bands, other houses mysteriously disintegrated.

It wasn't fate. It was the difference between good and bad construction.

On Sept. 1, tougher building regulations take effect in South Florida. Windows and shutters on new homes must be stronger. Roofs will require more straps and heavier trusses. Plywood sheathing will be thicker.

To no one's surprise, some builders are rushing to get permits before the new rules take effect. They say there's a shortage of the new approved materials, and they can't afford delays. Others complain that the hurricane reforms will force them to raise prices on homes, and they'll lose customers.

This, from a developer in Pembroke Pines: "For something that happens once in 35 years, you are charging the public a lot of money."

Now that's the kind of responsible builder I want—someone so ignorant of Florida history that he thinks hurricanes come ashore every three and a half decades. Forget the many destructive storms of the '20s, '30s and '40s. Forget the pair that hit in 1950, and Donna 10 years later.

Go on and cut corners. Why fret about the lives and safety of your loved one, and the security of all your earthly possessions, when you can save a few hundred bucks by using ½-inch plywood?

This is where Darwin's theory kicks in. Government can do only so much to save people from their own stupidity. Then Mother Nature takes over.

As hurricane survivors can attest, the price of a house isn't nearly as critical as its structural integrity. For smart home buyers, the priority is finding a place that won't crash down on their heads.

After Andrew and the scandals it exposed, anyone who buys a crackerbox house or condo or trailer surely must know they're in temporary housing.

Believe it or not, Florida has many conscientious builders who make solid homes that stand up well to hurricanes. Finding one takes time, and possibly an independent engineer to help you decide.

If it costs a little more than the houses across the street, so what? The houses across the street will probably be rubble in a Category Four storm.

For those who endured Andrew in shabbily built houses, there's no excuse for making the same mistake twice. For those new to Florida, there's no excuse for not knowing what happened to thousands of unsuspecting homeowners in 1992, and why.

Which leads back to the building reforms that take effect Sept. 1.

Smart people—the fittest, in the Darwinian lexicon—would demand housing made to the stronger specifications. They wouldn't hire a builder who's racing a deadline so he can save on materials.

But not everyone is smart. In each herd are the strong and the weak, the survivors and the doomed. Darwin understood Nature's dramatic style of choosing.

One way is a hurricane.

When homes collapse, best course is court

April 16, 1995

We didn't need Nostradamus to predict this one:

After 2½ years of so-called investigation, the Dade State Attorney's Office has found nobody to prosecute for the shabby construction of the Country Walk subdivision, blown to twigs by Hurricane Andrew.

Residents are disheartened but not stunned, given the state's record in ducking these cases.

Lennar Homes similarly was let off the hook for its crackerbox construction. Now it's Arvida/JMB Partners and the Walt Disney Co., which owned Country Walk when much of the subdivision was built.

Goofy, Pluto and the other construction supervisors are yukking it up today.

Who can forget Country Walk, Land of the Flying Gables—trusses without braces, braces without nails, corners without brackets. Of 184 homes, 147 were deemed uninhabitable after Andrew.

Initially, Arvida blamed Mother Nature, the standard alibi following the hurricane. Yet independent reviews of the destruction in South Dade cited shoddy work, dumb designs, substandard materials and lax code enforcement.

Still, nobody is going to jail. The State Attorney's Office says it cannot prove criminal wrongdoing at Country Walk, though the term "insufficient evidence" seems hollow to those who were knee-deep in it on Aug. 24, 1992.

The companies probably lost no sleep worrying about an indictment. What really grabbed their attention were the lawsuits.

These days it's fashionable to rail about runaway litigation. A key conservative plank is "tort reform," meant to discourage private citizens from suing big companies.

Yet that was the only remedy for customers of Lennar and Arvida who were wiped out by the hurricane. Suing was the only way to get compensation, and settlements provided that.

Insurance companies are also in court with Arvida and Disney over the Country Walk debacle. This is good if it discourages flimsy house building. The larger the cash penalty, the greater the incentive for companies to be more diligent next time.

Eventually, corner-cutting developers will sit down with a calculator and figure out that Andrew was bad for the bottom line. While it's great to sell scads of houses, it's not good business when scads of customers and their insurance companies sue your pants off.

Homeowners were left with few options. The building industry obviously didn't police itself, while government failed at every step in its obligation to protect consumers from such a preventable tragedy.

Plied by campaign donations from developers, Dade politicians made scarcely a peep as the South Florida Building Code was watered down. Even then it wasn't well-enforced. And those who violated or corrupted it seldom got punished.

So that left the civil courts as the only forum where Arvida, Lennar and the others could be held accountable.

The State Attorney's Office admitted as much. In explaining why it took so long to complete the Country Walk probe, the lead investigator said he was "waiting to see if the civil litigation revealed any smoking guns."

Good thing they don't handle murder cases that way.

For home buyers, the lesson is simple but cynical. If you're looking for a safely built house or condominium, expect no trustworthy safeguards from the state or county. And expect no action when gross abuses come to light.

The way to avoid heartache in the next hurricane is to avoid living in cheesy cardboard subdivisions. Judging by the houses that endured Andrew's worst winds, good builders are out there. The trick is finding them.

Start with the ones who aren't tied up in court.

Novel approach: We build it, we approve it

May 11, 1997

This week's Bureaucracy-Buster Prize goes to Carlos Valdes, chief building inspector for Dade County.

For five years Valdes moonlighted as a roofer and repairman, pulling 31 construction permits from the same agency for which he worked. Twice he inspected his own jobs, and gave final approval on both of them.

At first glance, this seems to be an outrageous conflict of interest, particularly if you're a competing contractor.

And for a building department pilloried after Hurricane Andrew for lax enforcement, it might seem slightly . . . well, irregular for an inspector to be approving his own construction work.

But from Valdes' perspective, you could make the case that he was merely trying to streamline a cumbersome bureaucratic process.

Call it Carlos' One-Stop Roofing—the guy who lays your shingles also inspects the job. For customers in a hurry, it was a nifty arrangement:

Valdes: I'm all done with your roof, Mrs. Smith.

Customer: Fantastic, Carlos . . . oh, but now I'll have to wait weeks for those chowderheads at the building department to come out for an inspection.

Valdes: No, you won't, Mrs. Smith. See, I'm also a building inspector! Let me climb up there right now and check it out.

Customer (elated): Oh, Carlos, you think of everything!

Imagine the relief of home builders and owners, who no longer had to fret about their roofs passing muster. Suddenly it was a done deal.

If Valdes didn't personally do the inspecting, his co-workers did. According to county records, fellow inspectors once flunked a Valdes roof—then Valdes himself signed off on the final papers, saying the problem was fixed.

Quick and efficient. Isn't that what we all want from local government?

Unfortunately, there's some silly rule against Dade building inspectors part-timing as builders. Valdes has been suspended with pay while an investigation is conducted. That's the price of being an innovator.

Anyone who's tried to get a house built or repaired in South Florida since the big hurricane knows how exasperating it can be. Often there are long delays between inspections, because building departments are so short-staffed and overworked.

The Valdes approach was a marvel of simplicity: We build it, we approve it.

It's the sort of idea that would appeal to some Metro-Dade commissioners, who seem primed to cave in to industry pressure and roll back post-Andrew reforms.

Heck, go for broke. Why not deputize all contractors as county building inspectors?

You'd save lots of time and paperwork. You'd save wear-and-tear on county vehicles. And you'd save a fortune on ladders, because builders usually provide their own.

Last, but not least, you'd eliminate the corruption problem. Under the Valdes system, there'd be little reason for unseemly cash payoffs.

Honest builders would do honest inspections. As for the crooked builders, whom would they bribe—themselves? That seems unlikely, even in Miami.

To be sure, a one-stop permit-and-inspection program would have drawbacks. A careless contractor probably isn't the best qualified to say whether his construction methods are sturdy or not.

But look on the flip side. After the next hurricane hits, we'll know precisely who's competent and who isn't. Builders won't be able to blame inspectors, and inspectors won't be able to blame builders . . . because they'll be one and the same.

It'll be so darn simple that maybe, just maybe, the state attorney might be able to indict some of them.

Cyberfraud simplifies corruption

August 7, 1997

No anniversary of Hurricane Andrew would be complete without a scandal in Dade County's building department. This time it's cyber-corruption.

Somebody logged onto the master computer and typed in phony inspection approvals for hundreds of construction projects. Many homes and buildings might need to be reinspected and repaired.

In some cases, roofs that flunked repeated on-site inspections were mysteriously approved later, by computer. Most entries were traced through a password to a former building department clerk, Pablo Prieto, who denies any wrongdoing.

Whoever the phantom hacker was, the implications of his scheme are far-reaching for development in South Florida. If computerized corruption is perfected, it will revolutionize bribery as we know it in municipal building departments.

The customary method is an all-too-familiar charade. A crooked inspector gets into a county truck, drives out to a construction job, maybe even climbs up on the actual roof for a minute or so, if it's not too hot.

Afterward, resting in the air-conditioned comfort of the truck, the inspector might find a $100 bill tucked under the visor, or tickets to a Dolphins game on the seat. That's when he writes up his report, approving the roof as sturdy and up to code.

As graft goes, it's fairly uncomplicated. However, it's also time-consuming, wasteful and increasingly risky.

Computers could streamline the whole corruption process from start to finish, paradoxically benefiting taxpayers as well as dishonest builders.

If a bad roof can be "fixed" with a few surreptitious strokes on a keyboard, there's no point in sending a shady inspector to a site. Think of the money the county would save in one year on gasoline, tolls and wear-and-tear on its vehicles. Think of what it would save on stepladders.

In fact, if the chore of falsifying building records can be handled more efficiently by cybersavvy clerks, it renders crooked inspections obsolete. Why even bother?

For an unscrupulous builder, computers would take the guesswork and seedy melodrama out of bribery. Never again would you be made to wait around all day in the blazing sun for a roof inspector, in the hopes he was one of those who would take a payoff. Most won't.

Imagine a day in the not-so-distant future when all you do is call the building department and speak to your friendly hacker-on-the-payroll. He pulls up your company's file, taps a few words on the screen and, presto!—all your roofs are instantly inspected and approved.

Before the lid blew off at Dade's building department, cybercorruption was spreading rapidly. Investigators are examining 3,000 cases for clues of electronic tampering, and there are plenty.

For instance, the county's computer lists 18 air-conditioning jobs inspected on a Saturday. The only problem is, air-conditioning inspectors don't work on Saturdays.

If the hackers weren't especially careful, they probably knew they didn't need to be. Officials who uncovered the fraud waited more than a year before notifying the police.

With that kind of ragged oversight, and some clever software, it's conceivable that an entire subdivision could be cleared, built, sold and occupied without a single legitimate inspector setting foot on the property.

The people who bought homes there would never find out the truth, unless a hurricane came and blew off their roofs and knocked down their walls.

In which event, Dade building officials better pray the storm is big enough to knock out the computer's memory, too. That's the one thing that could byte them where it counts.

Storms ahead if construction bill is passed

April 27, 1997

With only five weeks to hurricane season, the Legislature has taken the first step toward weakening some important post-Andrew construction reforms.

The House has given preliminary approval to a mind-boggling law that would prohibit local governments from imposing some building rules stricter than those required by the state.

They ought to call it the Roofers-from-Hell Relief Act.

It's aimed largely at Dade County, which had (for obvious reasons) imposed tougher regulations for overseeing construction.

Dade had taken the radical position that people who put houses together should know what they're doing, or have a supervisor who does. For instance, the county now requires one licensed journeyman for every three unlicensed workers on a job.

Builders didn't like the rule, so they enlisted two friendly politicians to shoot it down—Sen. Fred Dudley of Fort Myers and Rep. Carlos Lacasa of Miami.

Remember those names the next time you open your homeowner's insurance and wonder why the premium is so high.

Perhaps Lacasa and Dudley didn't read the Dade grand jury's report on Hurricane Andrew, but you can bet State Farm did. Among the panel's recommendations were stiffer qualifications for construction workers, to help weed out incompetents.

Lacasa says Dade's journeyman rule is burdensome and unnecessary, because plumbers and electricians—the trades most affected by it— weren't responsible for buildings blown apart during Hurricane Andrew.

He's right, but those who were responsible should be equally tickled by Lacasa and Dudley's legislation. If it passes, local communities will find it hard, if not impossible, to independently crack down on unqualified roofers, masons and carpenters.

That's because the proposed law would block Dade and other counties from adopting any "professional qualification requirements relating to contractors or their work force. . . ."

Parroting industry lobbyists, Lacasa blames a flawed code—not crummy construction—for Andrew's devastation. This guy should be a poster boy for short-term memory loss syndrome.

Does the name Country Walk ring a bell? Among the rubble of that development was ample evidence of slipshod and reckless work— trusses without braces, braces without nails, and more.

In fact, serious construction mistakes were documented at virtually every subdivision that had been leveled by the storm. While the building code wasn't perfect, at least it called for roofs to be strapped securely to houses—an inconvenience, apparently, for a few builders.

So widespread was the problem of bungled workmanship that hundreds of Dade homeowners sued, and some of the area's largest developers agreed to settle out of court.

None of this escaped the notice of insurance companies, which had taken a $16 billion hit from the 1992 hurricane. Some firms pulled out of Florida, and those that stayed raised their property rates astronomically.

Dade's building reforms came after lengthy public hearings with plenty of expert testimony. Even the politicians seemed to understand that a stronger, better enforced code not only would save lives and property, it could lead to lower insurance rates.

Don't get your hopes up now. Lobbyists for the home-building industry are pushing Metro to roll back some of the post-Andrew changes, and to weaken the code enforcement office.

Similar forces are behind the foolish Lacasa-Dudley bill. How dare Dade try to protect people from construction rip-offs! That's a job for the Legislature.

Which clearly needs some firsthand experience with hurricanes. On the eve of a new season, we can only hope.

Tax Dollars at Work

Dade taking furniture flap sitting down

January 27, 1986

A true news item: In only five months, Dade County Manager Merrett Stierheim and his successor, Sergio Pereira, spent $63,674 furnishing the same office twice.

Harry Hassock, Dade County's newly appointed Curator of Fine Furniture, was steamed.

"Why do you people keep picking on us?" he screeched, waving the newspaper.

I could barely see the man over his teakwood desk, which was nine feet high and tastefully trimmed with polished emeralds.

"Mr. Hassock, we're not picking on anyone," I shouted up to him. "It's just that the taxpayers are getting upset. They see Mr. Pereira running all over town preaching for a sales tax hike and warning that Metro is going broke. It's hard to take him too seriously after he spends $9,000 on a sofa."

"The man needs a place to nap!" Harry said, peremptorily.

"But for that kind of money you could feed and house a homeless child for a year."

Harry Hassock winced. "Please, we're talking leather here. The finest leather from the finest cows in Argentina. And get your notebook off of there—that's a $9,999 coffee table!"

In exasperation I said, "One more time, explain to me why Sergio needed to buy an expensive round desk instead of keeping Merrett's expensive rectangular one."

"Because there was chewing gum stuck under all the drawers," Harry said. "Besides, Sergio is a round thinker. You can't put a round thinker at a rectangular desk—it would be disaster. Hey, what's that crud in my ashtray?"

"Looks like ashes," I said.

"Ashes! Who'd dump ashes in a beveled diamond ashtray? Have you any idea what that ashtray cost?"

"Probably $9,999."

Harry Hassock eyed me suspiciously. "How did you know?"

"Wild guess," I replied. "Sergio's desk set cost nine grand. So did his credenza. All this stuff seems to run about nine grand. Why is that?"

"Because," Harry said, dropping his voice to a sly whisper, "if it cost any more, the Metro Commission would have to vote on it. In public, for God's sake—can you imagine?"

"Talk about problems."

"You bet your burlwood bookcase," Harry said. "To dodge that silly $10,000 rule, I advise county bigwigs to buy their fine furniture in $9,000 pieces. In fact, we have a little saying around here: Nine is fine, ten is trouble."

"Seems pretty sneaky," I said.

Harry Hassock rolled his eyes. "Next thing, you'll be asking why Sergio doesn't pay for this stuff out of his own pocket."

"Why not? He makes $99,500 a year."

Harry sighed impatiently. "What the public fails to understand is that in order for government to function smoothly, it must function in comfort. Comfort requires fine furniture."

Harry climbed off his desk, descended a rosewood stepladder and sat next to me on a $9,999 ottoman. "The more comfortable your government is, the more efficient it will be," he said earnestly. "Simply stated: Government needs a soft place to put its tush."

Somewhere on his colossal desk a magnesium telephone began to ring. Harry scrambled up and answered it.

"Curator of Fine Furniture," he said. "Yes—oh hello, Mr. Manager. Thanks, I knew you'd like it. What! Who said that? Well, it's not Day-Glo marble and you tell 'em that's not the least bit funny."

As Harry spoke, he expertly squirted a can of Lemon Pledge at a thumb smudge on his mink-lined credenza.

"But, Sergio, what's wrong with the desk chair you've got? Hmmmm. I see." Harry cupped a hand over the phone and asked me to step out of the office. "Just for a second," he whispered, "and try not to drag your shoes on the Burmese carpet."

Harry Hassock went back to his phone call. "A throne?" I heard him say. "What kind of throne are we talking about, Sergio?"

Metromover's new legs would be very shaky

July 2, 1986

The same wizards who gave us Metrorail now want to spend $240 million to expand the peoplemover to both ends of downtown Miami.

They foresee a day when the cute little tram is packed to the gills with commuters and shoppers. They foresee a time in the next century when future Dade Countians will look back and marvel at what visionaries we were.

More probably, they will look back and wonder: What kind of mushrooms were those folks eating?

The logic of taking an underutilized rail system and making it bigger is baffling, to put it kindly. Since the collective memory of the political establishment seems so short, let's re-examine Dade's sterling record of mass transit (using the term loosely).

Born of the best intentions, Metrorail is a proven Megaturkey. "The laughingstock of the nation," says Harvard transportation expert Jose Gomez-Ibanez. Building it cost $250 million more than promised; operating it now threatens to break the county budget. The ridership, though improving, remains a pitiful one-seventh of projections.

It's a clean, fast system but—for a variety of reasons—commuters avoid it in droves. This year taxpayers spent $32 million running a train for a measly 14,000 daily two-way riders.

If Metrorail were a horse, it would be shot.

Enter the Metromover, inaugurated to run a loop through downtown Miami and boost (we were promised) Metrorail's popularity. It's an adorable toy, except for one problem: Only 4,500 of 60,000 downtown workers are riding the darn thing.

You'd think we'd learn our lesson. Think again. Rep. William Lehman (normally a rational man), the Metro commission and downtown property owners (surprise!) love the idea of extending the Metromover south to Brickell Avenue and north to the Omni Mall.

What we now have is a government fully mobilized to turn disaster into catastrophe.

If you were a merchant and somebody offered to run a spiffy tram to your doorstep, wouldn't you say yes? Of course you would, especially if the state, the city and the feds were sucking up 90 percent of the tab. What's another $240 million when we've already spent four times that much on Metrorail?

Forget the fact that our buses are falling to pieces. Forget the fact that routes from needy neighborhoods have been cut back, thanks partly to Metrorail's huge deficits.

The trouble with the Metromover is that it benefits the downtown lunch crowd more than the people who truly need mass transit. It will make it convenient for some of us to hop a tram from the office to the Tofutti parlor, but meanwhile thousands need reliable transportation from their neighborhoods to their jobs.

In a strategic move to derail the Metromover expansion, the head of the U.S. Urban Mass Transit Administration, Ralph Stanley, said last week he would be willing to let Dade County spend its Metromover funds on buses.

It's an unprecedented offer, and a smart one. Buses are the first crucial link of any urban transit system; almost seven times as many people ride them as ride Metrorail. The $102 million already set aside for the Metromover extension is enough for 728 buses, a whole new fleet. This would be a radical step in the county's transportation saga—spending money on something people would actually use.

In defense of the dream, Metromover's proponents say the new downtown legs are necessary to meet the needs of future growth. Planners predict 25,000 peoplemover riders by the year 2000.

Only two things are certain about such predictions: If it's the cost, they underestimate. If it's the ridership, they overestimate.

They've never been right. They've never even been close.

But let's say this time they are. Twenty-five thousand riders for $240 million—this is a bargain? Maybe so, if you own a bank on Brickell Avenue; maybe not, if you're standing on a hot street corner, hoping for a bus, any bus, that runs on time.

Paint Rosario nattily naïve, fiscally fickle

February 2, 1987

This week's Most Frighteningly Dumb True Quote comes from Miami City Commissioner Rosario Kennedy, when informed that it had cost $111,549.71 to renovate her office at City Hall:

"Nobody told me anything about a budget. I was not involved in it at all. I was involved in the colors."

Now, then, isn't this the kind of eagle-eyed public servant you want playing with your tax dollars? Where did Mrs. Kennedy think the money for the new furniture was coming from, Publisher's Clearing House?

It's quite a feat to out-Sergio our county manager and his $9,000 desk, so let's look at some of the goodies in Mrs. Kennedy's den.

You've got your pewter-gray light fixtures ($2,144), your striped pumice-colored lounge chair for $1,056 (and don't ask me what "pumice" looks like), your three gray desks ($3,625) and your 257 yards of wallpaper ($2,380). Then you've got your striped bench seat for $1,134, your six slabs of marble for $320 and your dove-colored carpet for $1,958.16 (and no, I don't have the faintest idea whether dove goes with pumice).

Add to that your six pieces of framed artwork ($959.24), your three dove-gray file cabinets for $2,299 (I wonder what the regular gray would have cost), and your standard Vegas-style mirrored wall for $505.

The Rosario hit parade continues with air-conditioning at $4,769.68. That's for one office, folks. You can install central air in a nice-sized house for about half as much. Are we talking solid-gold thermostats or what?

Then there's the little matter of "parts" for $6,602.24 (probably truckloads of Windex for all the mirrors).

And let's not forget labor: $63,401.74 worth, all performed by faithful city employees who have nothing better to do, since the rest of Miami is in such tip-top shape.

It all adds up to more than $111,500—a mere five times what the city's crack fiscal wizards estimated it would cost. This might seem incredible to you and me, but none of our highly paid government watchdogs at City Hall is the least bit concerned.

City Manager Cesar Odio, for instance, said he wasn't aware of how much was spent on Commissioner Kennedy's new office. But when told (and this is our Second Most Frighteningly Dumb True Quote of the Week), the city manager replied: "I think that's an acceptable figure. . . . I don't know much about costs."

EARTH TO CESAR: That's your job, buster.

While some of the commissioners are more prudent about office expenses than others, the obscene profligacy at City Hall is not Mrs. Kennedy's alone. The city paid an interior decorator $4,000 to pick out the colors (red and gray) for Miller Dawkins' office, and to design a clever mural made out of travel posters. I know a high-school art class that would have done it for free.

By contrast, it's more amusing than infuriating that Joe Carollo spent $92.70 on a security door chime that alerts him whenever someone walks into his office. The purpose, we can only surmise, is to give the commissioner that vital extra half-second to dive for his Uzi, if necessary.

Conveniently, most of the commissioners' pillaging of city coffers is never discussed at public meetings. See, the city has this nifty little deal where purchase orders for less than $4,500 don't need the approval of the full commission. That way commissioners can submit reams of invoices for $4,499 and get instant approval—without clogging up the city's very important public agenda.

It's true that Miami City Hall is a creaky old dump in need of repair and renovation, and it's also true that city commissioners deserve offices that are decent and attractive. The sum of $111,549 is neither. It seems beyond belief that careless nitwits could spend this kind of dough and claim not to know about it.

From now on, if any commissioner demands to sit on pumice, let it be the real thing.

For city execs, all work, no play pays off

April 10, 1987

The hottest vacation package in Florida is being offered by the city of Miami, which is paying its top brass big bucks to stay in town.

It's such a good deal that you wonder why every little kid doesn't want to grow up and be a faithful public servant.

The trick is to store up as much "accrued vacation time" as possible. The longer you do this, the more money you get at retirement. Why? Because the city, in all its fiscal wisdom, will pay you for any unused vacation hours at your current top salary scale.

It doesn't matter if you piled up the time 10 years ago while making $10 an hour. If you're now earning $20 an hour, that's the rate at which you get reimbursed.

How bighearted can a bureaucracy be! This vacation gig is better than an IRA account. Throw in pensions and sick time and you've got yourself a healthy nest egg.

With this kind of incentive, it's no surprise that so many city executives claim they go for years without taking time off. You've got to feel sorry for these tireless souls, toiling at their desks day after day while each summer their pals trundle off to Disney World or Six Flags or Knott's Berry Farm.

As a matter of fact, it might be instructive to locate and publish the time sheets of these working-class heroes—not to test their memories, mind you, but merely to give inspiration to new employees.

The all-work, no-play mentality is so pervasive at City Hall that Miami now has $9.5 million of accrued vacation time on its payroll. Alarmed, the city manager wants to pay some of this in lump sums now, instead of letting the money build up until workers reach retirement.

Under this voluntary payback program, the city has already delivered some handsome checks. Assistant budget director Frank May got $25,085 for 894 hours of unused vacation—110 days, 109 nights in beautiful Miami.

Deputy City Attorney Robert Clark cashed in 100 hours at more than $45 an hour. Finance director Carlos Garcia collected 263.5 hours at more than $36 an hour. And budget director Manohar Surana got about $42 an hour for 286 hours of unused vacation. (His $87,000-plus salary is almost as high as that of his New York City counterpart.)

One of the biggest winners was internal audit director Sujan Chhabra. For 18 weeks of vacation time he received nearly $30,000, which, city officials say, he needed for a new house.

Interestingly, only Miami's highest-paid honchos are eligible for this exciting program. City sanitation workers are limited to 100 hours of accrued vacation while many other general employees are allowed no more than 180 hours.

City Manager Cesar Odio himself has racked up 11 weeks of unused vacation during his seven years as a Miami employee. If he elected to cash in now (which he says he won't), Odio would be paid at his current salary rate of about $44.23 an hour—or $20,125.

However, if he waited 10 years and retired from the same job at the same pay, his accumulated vacation time could be worth $45,000 cash, or more.

If, as Odio says, the early vacation payback will save the public money, then perhaps he ought to set an example by doing it himself. As long as it's optional, some employees will continue to hoard their hours and cash out at retirement.

What would really save money is to require workers to take all their vacation the year they earn it. This radical policy is enforced at most private companies because the other method is not only ridiculously expensive, but counterproductive to healthy work habits.

Some people might even say it would be more sensible if all city workers with accrued vacation (no matter how much) were forced to take it right now—say, starting this morning. Just hop a plane and go away for a while. Don't come back until your vacation is used up.

But think of what this would mean: The big shots at City Hall would be gone for weeks and weeks. Why, there'd be no one to sit around and dream up these rackets.

How would we ever get by?

City flushes $101,000 right down the john

January 19, 1992

When I heard about the $101,000 latrine, I had to see for myself.

The concept staggered the senses. I've been privy to some fancy bathrooms, but nothing that cost a hundred grand. That's what Dade County spent on a new public restroom at Indian Hammocks Park.

How was it possible? I didn't know. Maybe they let David Paul design it.

In any case, a $101,000 bathroom was bound to be something special—the Taj Mahal of all toilets.

Excitedly I drove to Kendall. My imagination was racing. Surely the urinals would be carved from the finest Italian marble; the toilets, thronelike. Silk towels would come from sterling dispensers. And the soap—perhaps a Parisian blend, lightly scented with tulip petals!

I arrived at the park in midafternoon. Leaves whispered. Birds sang. Children frolicked. It was lovely.

The first restroom I found was in melancholy condition. Witless graffiti artists had defaced the walls. The drain on the drinking fountain appeared to have been clogged since the Eisenhower administration. Puddles at the door suggested a grim scene within. I fled.

The search led to a simple, one-story building that looked discouragingly like Restroom No. 1, sans graffiti. It had a shingle roof and concrete walls. The architecture is best described as Neo-Modern Toolshed. I thought: Not even Metro could spend $101,000 here.

But I was wrong. This was the place. The only outward signs of extravagance were the royal blue restroom doors. Obviously the big money was spent inside, on the fixtures.

Two workers were busy in the utility area. They said the men's room was fully operational. Being a taxpayer, I felt obliged to check it out. And what a letdown: one toilet, two sinks, two urinals and an ordinary towel dispenser (no towels, naturally). There wasn't any marble or gold or sterling silver. It was a very routine restroom. At least the men's half was.

Somewhere in that latrine was $101,000, and I couldn't figure out where. Home Depot (I swear) is selling commodes for $49. Bathroom sinks start at $25.66. It didn't add up.

Let's say the county went hog-wild and ordered Super Deluxe Model everything. That still left about $97,000 lying around for the structure, electrical wiring and plumbing. They build houses for less than that.

Where did the money go? Then I remembered: The parks department said the new restrooms cost so much because they're made to be "almost vandal-proof."

Ah! I started testing for high-tech security gadgets. I touched the wall in a mock graffiti attack. No laser rays zapped my hand, no alarm bells sounded. I could've scrawled all of *The Canterbury Tales* in Day-Glo paint, without interruption. Next, I approached the john in the stealthy manner of a pathological toilet clogger. Again, no Mace, no shocks, no sirens. Nothing would have prevented me from flushing a load of stolen laundry down the crapper.

Vandal-proof? The $101,000 shrine is about as vandal-proof as a subway car. It would've been smarter to build a $30,000 latrine and spend the rest on security guards.

The problem with public restrooms isn't the equipment, it's the maintenance. Toilets get built and then forgotten. Using them becomes an act of courage, or perversion. One of Dade's most infamous facilities graces the boat ramp at Crandon Park. Here you can always spot the tourists—they're the ones innocently strolling toward the restroom. Those who make it out are dazed and reeling.

It would be sad if the same thing happened at Indian Hammocks. The county seems determined that it won't. The other day, when the workers finished at the new john, they tried something that certainly should thwart vandals. They locked the door.

Which is the only way to protect a $101,000 investment.

Metrorail: The bigger it grows, the more it loses

May 26, 1994

All aboard! Today Miamians can actually ride an elevated tram from the Omni Mall to Brickell Avenue.

You might wonder, why would I do that? Answer: Because you're paying for it through the caboose.

Building Metromover's two new extensions cost $224 million in federal, state and local funds. Like all of Metrorail, the Brickell and Omni legs are expected to lose tons of money.

Naturally, a big party is being thrown to celebrate the occasion. Everyone hopes the new routes will attract thousands of loyal riders, reduce traffic congestion downtown and revive the flagging Omni and Bayside shopping areas. In other words, everyone's hoping history won't repeat itself.

The Metro-Dade Transit Agency says the Metromover legs will boost daily boardings from 6,800 to 13,000. If MDTA is right—or even close—it will be an historic event.

Metrorail has bled red ink for a decade. Originally, officials predicted daily ridership of 101,000 round-trips. Today, an average of 25,000 people use the trains for round-trip commutes to work, shopping and special events. Annual operating deficit: about $34 million.

Every county resident is paying for a railway used by a tiny minority. Anti-tax crusader Richard Friedman says an MDTA study forecasts that, even with $466 million in committed subsidies, Dade's entire transit program will suffer a $148 million shortfall between now and 1999.

Undeterred by failure, the Metro Commission wants more federal funds to extend Metrorail as far north as Joe Robbie Stadium and as far south as Homestead—a plan as audacious as it is deranged.

Metrorail will always lose money. The bigger we make it, the more it will lose. Every 50-cent round-trip on the new Metromover links is estimated to cost taxpayers an embarrassing $29.90.

Miami's fiasco isn't unique. All over the country, mass transit loses big bucks. The most heavily traveled subways in the nation—New York's—are also the most heavily subsidized.

In a sensible world, suburban commuters would abandon their gas-guzzling cars for an inexpensive, hassle-free train ride. Unfortunately, it hasn't happened here or anyplace else.

Maybe Metrorail will look like a shrewd move in the event of another global oil crisis. For now, though, it's a staggering drain of precious funds that would be better spent on patching roads or expanding the bus system.

A $4.7 million Metromover station is planned here at 1 Herald Plaza, even though a gorgeous facility just opened across the street at the Omni. The Herald's parent company is paying for part of the new building, while the feds supply $3.5 million.

(How a train stop could cost as much as Madonna's mansion is a mystery, but we're hoping for crystal chandeliers.)

Transit officials say the Herald station is needed to serve the newspaper's 2,000 employees and will be closer (by at least a twentieth of a mile) to the proposed Performing Arts Center.

I admit the new station will make my life easier, especially at lunchtime. Instead of trudging two whole blocks in the broiling sun to catch a tram at Omni, I can board at the Herald's front door and ride all the way to Tobacco Road.

Since $4.7 million is a rather large sum for such a seemingly small convenience, I personally want to thank each and every taxpayer for his contribution. We promise to keep our new Metromover station bright and spiffy for future opera buffs and ballet patrons.

For that kind of money, it's the least we can do.

Falling down just part of the job in Miami

December 19, 1996

The revelation that nearly one of every three Miami city employees files for workers' compensation statistically means they're either the clumsiest bunch in the country, or the most brazenly dishonest.

With new injury claims pouring in at 1,000 per year, Miami has become a Banana Peel Republic. If you work for the city, falling down on the job often is part of the job.

Among the chronically accident-prone are 254 employees who've made more than 10 claims apiece, and who ought to be wearing bubble wrap to work.

Menace looms in seemingly harmless situations. Since 1979, according to a Herald computer survey, 123 city employees have received workers' comp for falling out of (or into) chairs.

Ninety others were injured in encounters with dangerous desks, 11 were felled by computers, 15 were waylaid while lifting (or watching) TV sets, another seven were incapacitated by paper cuts, and two others were alleged victims of candy (one chipping a tooth on a Snickers bar).

Outside of the office, city workers constantly come under attack from the animal kingdom. Since 1979, 281 have been paid for injuries caused by dogs (often their own), while three others got money for feline-related incidents.

One police officer received $214 after cutting his hand while opening a can of cat food, most certainly in the line of duty.

Meanwhile, insects mowed down 126 unsuspecting workers at a cost to Miami taxpayers of $36,000. That's lots of bees in lots of bonnets.

But the most perilous employee activities are, in order, driving a city vehicle, hauling garbage—and sports. Workers are incredibly unlucky when it comes to sports.

After firefighter Kim Robson went down playing basketball, the city of Miami agreed to an NBA-style compensation package worth almost $213,000.

Robson was one of 143 city employees who've been hurt on the basketball courts, which suggests a dire need for helmets, cups, instructional videos and Nerf balls.

Most Miamians don't mind paying for a groin pull suffered during a five-alarm fire or a SWAT raid, but a botched rebound is something else.

Police, fire and other departments promote sports for physical training, but the frequency of claims indicates no surplus of fine-tuned athletes. Volleyball proved too much for 96 workers, jogging hobbled 82 more, softball claimed another 32, while 31 were disabled in tennis matches.

Three employees managed to hurt themselves playing catch, while one poor soul suffered an injury at badminton. Perhaps an errant shuttlecock is deadlier than we think.

In all, 634 alleged sports mishaps drained $1.6 million from city coffers since 1979. For insurance purposes, workers are statistically much safer at their desks, trying not to fall out of their chairs while watching TV, munching Snickers bars and opening cans of Little Friskies.

Many city employees believe it's wrong to take advantage of workers' comp and won't file unless their injuries are serious and legitimate. But those who do file usually get paid, even if the claim is outlandish.

That's because Miami slashed its overworked risk management department so severely that it can no longer afford to contest most injury claims. Four adjusters are handling nearly 2,700 open cases.

Consequently the city seldom says no. In 1995, workers' comp cost taxpayers $9.3 million. It's like a broken ATM machine that just keeps spitting out cash, except now it's nearly empty.

Either Miami employs too many klutzes or too many fakers. In any case, the result is an excruciating fiscal hernia.

The city has fallen and it can't get up.

Officer Romeo makes out big in sex scandal

May 9, 1996

When the cop car's rockin', don't come knockin'.

That's the message from Metro commissioners, who voted to richly compensate a policeman who got caught having sex in a parking garage.

For his bare-bottomed indiscretion, Jesus "Romeo" Bencomo will now receive $180,000 and a pension of $50,000 a year. Talk about an afterglow.

The moment of rapture occurred on March 21, 1994, when a security guard at Miami Children's Hospital spotted a black Chevrolet shaking back and forth. The guard feared a rape was occurring and called for help.

An off-duty Metro detective pulled his gun and approached. Inside the car, a man and woman were carnally entwined. The detective recognized the man as Bencomo, a division chief for the department.

When disciplinary charges were filed, Bencomo offered a chaste version of the incident. He said he'd met a woman dressed in white and offered her a lift. He said they'd had an innocent chat in the front seat of his county Chevy, but no nookie.

The best part? He said he never got the woman's name.

A police review panel was not persuaded by Bencomo's yarn and sustained charges of using a county vehicle for personal business and conduct unbecoming a police officer—engaging "in open lewd and lascivious behavior."

Metro Police director Fred Taylor demoted Bencomo to major in December 1994.

After such a dumb screwup, most cops would've been thrilled to still have a job, especially one that paid $93,000 a year. Not our Romeo. He claimed he was the target of a political vendetta.

He sued the police department. He sued the detective who caught him in the act. He even went to a federal agency and charged he was the victim of anti-Hispanic discrimination.

Seriously, that's what the man said.

Could Bencomo prove that black cops and white cops are allowed to have sex in police cars, while Hispanic cops are forced to use their own personal vehicles? We'll never know, since the case isn't going to trial.

This week the Metro Commission decided to pay Bencomo off, in exchange for his dropping all claims. Taylor and a majority of commissioners said settling the case now was cheaper than litigating it for years.

While the move saves the county some legal fees, it also spares the police some unwanted embarrassment. Bencomo's lawyer had hinted that, after 28 years on the force, his client had lots of fascinating anecdotes about the antics of other officers, as well as prominent politicians.

It's unknown whether the allegations would have involved sex in squad cars, paddy wagons, helicopters or body armor.

In any event, a mud bath is being avoided at a public cost of $180,000. With such a windfall, Bencomo should be able to afford a motel room the next time lust overcomes him.

Ironically, the precedent set by the settlement ultimately could offset any short-term savings. The county might end up paying out a fortune if other cops in disciplinary trouble use the Bencomo case as a blueprint for counterattack:

Sue everyone in sight, threaten to smear the department and then demand an obscene settlement.

Given the Metro Commission's willingness to cave in, risk-management experts should consider a new policy:

If you see a parked police car rocking like crazy, assume the officer is testing the shock absorbers. Don't investigate—it's too expensive.

For Bencomo, his interlude in the county Chevy undoubtedly will be his most memorable ever. Not only did the earth move, so did the blood pressure of a million taxpayers.

Bullet train would shoot state budget

January 12, 1997

Get ready for The Great Train Robbery, Florida-style.

The loot is $6.5 billion, and the robbery victims are you, me and every other taxpayer.

The Department of Transportation is pressing ahead with fanciful plans for a "bullet train" connecting Miami to Orlando and Tampa. It's not only the worst boondoggle to come out of Tallahassee in years, it promises to be the longest-running.

Building the bullet train will cost billions more than its backers predict, almost nobody will ride it, and it'll lose money forever.

Otherwise it's a terrific idea, especially for FOX, the consortium of companies that got the nod for the project. Forget the bullet, this train is pure political gravy.

Last week DOT Secretary Ben Watts made his pitch to state lawmakers, some of whom have taken generous campaign contributions from FOX interests.

Watts wants a mere $40 million for planning next year. Not building the bullet train—planning it.

This year's tab is "only" $9.5 million, three-quarters of which is paid by the state while the rest comes from FOX.

Expenses include $435,000 for lobbyists and a $2.3 million ridership survey. (We know all about ridership surveys, especially those commissioned by the same folks who are boosting the project.)

Here's the amazing part: The DOT now says the state should budget $6.5 billion over the next 40 years for the bullet train and the bonds required to support it.

The bond payments are to be guaranteed by future revenues from ridership, which is a complete joke. That's why the train can't get rolling unless the U.S. Congress agrees to repay the bond debt if ridership lags.

Meaning all U.S. taxpayers will get soaked, not just Floridians.

DOT insists a 200-mph train is a smart investment, and will eventually turn a profit.

Oh, absolutely. Just like Metrorail turns a profit. And Tri-Rail. And how about Amtrak?

Find a passenger rail system in this country that makes money on its own, without subsidies. Yet we're assured the bullet train will be a lucrative exception.

That's the word from DOT, which hasn't been right yet. It hasn't even been in the ballpark.

Initially Watts predicted the project could be propped up with $2.2 billion over 30 years. Now the price tag has tripled, without the first rail spike being driven.

How can such a half-assed plan pick up steam? Politics.

Designers, contractors and land brokers know the windfall comes when Tallahassee first opens the vault. Once construction begins, nobody will dare pull the plug no matter how bad it gets.

Bet on the usual long delays and huge overruns. Then, when the monstrosity finally is finished, the state will be stuck with what's essentially a multibillion-dollar ghost train.

Because it'll still be cheaper, faster and more convenient for passengers to catch a nonstop jetliner from Miami to Orlando.

A caboose full of drunken monkeys couldn't have devised a more foolproof formula for failure than the bullet train. Yet it got a warm reception by members of the House Transportation Committee, who apparently are bored spending tax dollars fixing roads and bridges.

To their credit, other legislators refused to be dazzled by the high-tech imagery, or suckered by DOT's groundless optimism.

What if the ridership falls short? State Sen. John Ostalkiewicz of Orlando asked Watts. "Who will repay the debt? The public is going to be on the hook for over $6 billion?"

Replied the DOT secretary: "Yessir."

See, it's not just a train ride. It's a stickup.

Miami port's generosity runs too deep

May 22, 1997

The bad news: Vanquished Port of Miami chief Carmen Lunetta will receive a golden parachute of $328,501 cash, in addition to his $113,000-a-year pension.

The good news: Some lawyer will probably get most of it.

Lunetta leaves the busy cruise port awash in a $22 million red tide and a stinking scandal.

His hefty cash severance includes unused sick pay, vacation and holidays accrued over Lunetta's 38 years with the county. If he'd spent less time at the office, perhaps the port wouldn't be in so much trouble.

Lunetta hastily resigned Friday after the Herald obtained records detailing one of the artifices through which Dade taxpayers were robbed.

For years, a stream of public funds was routed through a company called Fiscal Operations, which controls the port's gantry cranes. The firm was headed by Calvin Grigsby, a rich San Francisco political wheeler-dealer.

It turns out that Miami's port paid for Calvin's California yacht, and maid service to keep it spiffy. The port also paid for Calvin's Super Bowl seats, country club membership and symphony subscription.

It even paid a parking ticket.

The port not only gave Calvin a $75,000 salary as president of Fiscal Operations, it paid him $300 an hour to give legal advice to his own company. Then it paid the company a $150,000 "management fee."

Meanwhile, Fiscal Operations secretly funneled thousands in campaign funds to Democratic candidates and local commissioners.

Along the way, the crane-operating firm fell behind on $24 million in payments and interest to the port—money that will never be collected. This sheds fresh light on the agency's embarrassing debt.

All these Grigsby boondoggles had to be approved by port boss Lunetta. The mystery is: Why was he so generous to Calvin, and what did he get in return?

Some inquiring soul ought to pose those questions today, if Lunetta appears as scheduled before the Metro Commission.

Lots of cash went streaking through Fiscal Operations, and investigators might never be able to track it all. The probe is another unhappy tiding for Grigsby, already implicated in the Operation Greenpalm corruption investigation.

The FBI has videotape of Grigsby and Metro Commissioner James Burke, allegedly chatting about a $300,000 kickback. Agents believe the payment was to be made in exchange for Burke steering a piece of Dade's municipal bond business to Grigsby's investment firm.

As expected, both fellows heartily deny any wrongdoing. Grigsby has retained the services of O. J. Simpson defense ace Johnnie Cochran. Lunetta ought to take a cue.

Lots of big-name lawyers would be be eager to offer counsel, especially after ogling that humongous severance package. When $328,000 is on the other end of the line, even F. Lee Bailey picks up the phone.

The size of Lunetta's golden parachute shows he was assiduous about logging his own attendance at work. If only he'd been half as careful with the port's budget, the place might actually be turning a profit.

Lunetta had help with the ransacking. Dade commissioners regularly dipped into port funds to pay for pet projects.

Still, it isn't easy losing money on the world's busiest commercial sea harbor. You've really got to work at it.

Records show that Lunetta put in for 301 accumulated sick days, 500 hours of unused vacation and salary for showing up on 68½ county holidays.

Who knows how much of that time was spent serving the port, and how much of it was spent disbursing the public's money to Calvin Grigsby and other secret pals.

Odio's exit a bargain for taxpayers

June 5, 1997

With so many corruption scandals breaking out, Florida will soon need a special pension formula for crooks in public office.

In some cases, it might be cheaper to offer them a cushy, corporate-style retirement than to keep them hanging around, so they can continue pilfering from government coffers.

Cesar Odio, the former city manager of Miami, is the most recent example. Although he pleaded guilty last week in an illegal kickback scheme, he now seeks his pension, sick leave and unused vacation pay.

State law requires officials convicted of corruption to forfeit their retirement benefits. However, the crime to which Odio copped out—obstruction of justice—isn't specifically mentioned in the statute.

Odio's supporters claim he therefore should be entitled to a full pension, because of his years of unselfish service. Others say he shouldn't get a dime, because he betrayed those he'd sworn to serve. The dispute appears headed to court.

If Odio's lawyers are crafty, they'll point out how much dough taxpayers will ultimately save by getting rid of him now.

His controversial pension package begins to look like a pretty good deal when compared to how much of the city's money he already squandered, and how much more he was planning to steal.

For example, the bribery plot for which Odio was indicted would have paid him a $5,000-a-month kickback from a municipal health insurance contract. That's $60,000 a year in purloined public funds.

Do the math: Odio's annual pension computes to only $58,166—a net saving to taxpayers of $1,834 yearly against his future bribes. (And those are just the future bribes we know about.)

Now, factor in the thousands upon thousands of dollars in city funds that Odio gave to cronies, pet causes, political supporters, even sympathetic "journalists." The man was a human ATM.

Small wonder that Miami's budget was such a mess—a fact that raises even a more dramatic, though no less cunning, argument in favor of giving Odio a pension:

By leaving when he did, he likely spared the city from certain bankruptcy.

It's not a fanciful hypothesis. After 11 years with Odio and his cohorts at the helm, Miami was a boggling $68 million in the hole.

A smart lawyer could contend that, indicted or not, the ex-city manager should be rewarded for quitting—and thus "saving" Miamians the $6.2 million a year in deficits that was averaged during his tenure.

Stacked against those kinds of figures, a $58,166 send-off seems almost stingy.

On the other hand, if taxpayers had known City Hall was being run like a traveling flea market, they wouldn't have waited for Odio to be busted for corruption. They would've demanded he be canned for incompetence.

That fear is perhaps what Odio had in his mind when, in 1994, he persuaded commissioners to give him a "phantom" salary increase that existed only on paper. The sole purpose of the bogus raise was to inflate his future pension benefits to $76,635 a year.

The tricky ploy was later scuttled, but in retrospect it might have been worth a shot. Maybe it would have inspired Odio to retire a bit sooner.

Numbers don't lie. An earlier exit by the city manager would have been a bargain to taxpayers, at almost any price.

In these shady times, we need creative ways to entice other felons to leave office, preferably before they get arrested. Too many of them are doing worse things than Odio did, and taking more of the public's money.

Maybe they wouldn't steal so much if they knew it was coming out of their own nest eggs.

Ralph Sanchez and Other Subsidized Sports

City gave away park to get rid of problem

February 21, 1986

This weekend thousands of Grand Prix fans will pay big-ticket prices to visit a park that already belongs to them, sit in bleachers they already own, and watch a road race that their tax dollars have subsidized.

You've heard of Live Aid and Farm Aid; this is Ralph Aid.

Ralph Sanchez is a terrific promoter, a magician when it comes to raising money. For instance, after the inaugural Grand Prix got rained under three years ago, state legislators agreed to help Ralph out of the hole by buying the bleachers for $500,000.

Our generosity didn't stop there. This year Tallahassee kicked in another half-million bucks to Ralph's races, while the county agreed to pony up $350,000 to cover any deficits. And the city of Miami—well, the city not only put up $250,000 for the new racetrack, but loaned Sanchez the same amount, interest free, to pay his share.

If all businessmen had pals like these, we could board up the bankruptcy courts.

The new Grand Prix course snakes through 35 acres once known as Bicentennial Park. It's not a park anymore, of course, it's an asphalt racetrack with two baseball diamonds stuck between the curves. How it got that way is an interesting story.

The Grand Prix got shoved out of south Bayfront Park because some big developer needs the land for fancy restaurants and macrame shops. The city of Miami felt so crummy that it agreed to "compensate" Sanchez by paying him $350,000 and annihilating a suitable stretch of Bicentennial Park to augment the race course.

All this happened very fast and very quietly—the paving, especially. If only the Department of Transportation crews could work so quickly.

When folks started asking about why the city paved the park—a public park purchased with bond money—everybody stuttered a little until they came up with one of the craftiest excuses I've ever heard: Basically, they said, we did it to get rid of the winos.

To hear Grand Prix boosters tell it, the winos of Bicentennial Park are the urban equivalent of the Viet Cong. Apparently the only thing to dislodge them is a Porsche bearing down at 140 miles per hour.

In defense of plowing the park, supporters recited all the nasty things that have happened there since it opened in 1977. Rapes, murders, muggings, assorted corpses. No wonder hardly anybody goes there.

Some cities would've taken a slightly different approach to these problems. Some cities might have opened shelters to get the winos off the streets. Maybe put more cops in the park, installed brighter lights, improved the parking, added tennis and racquetball courts. Bulldozed that stupid San Juan Hill of a berm that blocks the bay from the boulevard.

Other cities might have done more to save the park, but what Miami did was to give up, and give it away.

It's true that for two whole weekends the Grand Prix draws thousands of fans to downtown Miami, which is swell if you happen to own a hotel or parking garage. It's also true that the TV coverage gives the city lots of valuable exposure, providing the sun is out.

And it's true that one of the prime missions of the Grand Prix is to make some bucks for Ralph Sanchez. Nothing wrong with that. ,

But carving up the park?

I guess the city commissioners couldn't help themselves. They saw this luscious hunk of bayfront not making money, just sitting there being a park, and they couldn't stand it. The shakes set in, then drooling; an uncontrollable urge to bulldoze. Apparently shrubbery was not the kind of green that Bicentennial Park was meant to sprout.

The giveaway occurred so swiftly that critics have questioned its legality. The city's staff says everything is proper because the racetrack technically is a "park amenity."

A country mile of four-lane blacktop—some amenity. What does that make the Palmetto Expressway, a national shrine?

The Indy races to put Metro in debit dust

July 18, 1986

First there was Hands Across America. Then Farm Aid II.

Brace yourself, South Florida. Now comes Ralph Aid II.

In a heartrending gesture of charity, the Metro Commission is considering bailing out auto racing impresario Ralph Sanchez with $5 million over 10 years.

In return, Sanchez promises to give the county 17 percent of the "adjusted gross income" from his Indy races at Tamiami Park.

What a deal. Except for one glitch: The Tamiami event lost money last year. A ton of money—$1.3 million, according to Sanchez.

On a similar note, this season's Grand Prix, held at the mutilated Bicentennial Park, lost $652,000—that, after getting a $350,000 subsidy from the tourist tax.

Isn't government wonderful? Used to be that when a private entrepreneur couldn't turn a profit, he or she was doomed to a cold fate. Going out of business, it was called. Used to be that the idea was to take in more money than you spent.

Apparently this isn't always possible when you're trying to put together a "world-class event," whatever that might be. Costs add up—you know, little things, like $23,500 for your lobbyist's new Mercedes-Benz.

Can't have a world-class event without a world-class lobbyist. God knows what Ron Book would have gotten if the Grand Prix had actually made money—maybe Sanchez would've sprung for a Rolls.

The architect of the latest giveaway is County Manager Sergio Pereira, who—invoking the Miss Universe Pageant Boondoggle Theorem—says the TV exposure makes the road races worth every nickel, tourist-wise.

Pereira selflessly took it upon himself to review the ledgers of the Tamiami affair, and concluded that Sanchez needs help.

Right now he gets a piddling $100,000 a year for the Indy race. Pereira wants to increase the stipend to $500,000 annually for the next decade. What a guy, and what a grand gift at a time when Dade's economic condition is so bleak!

It seems like just last week that Pereira asked for property tax increases of 12 percent in unincorporated neighborhoods.

It seems like just last week that he proposed raising water and sewer rates, and cutting funds for meals for the elderly.

And it seems like just last week that the cost-conscious county manager declared an urgent need to wipe out the Dade Consumer Advocate's Office, as well as the Fair Housing and Employment Appeals Board. Citizens, he said, would simply have to go elsewhere with their job and housing discrimination complaints.

Pereira computed that these last two budget items would save the county a whopping $303,000 next year. Why, that's almost enough to pave another park and put in a race track.

The question is, would anyone show up?

Contrary to rosy press reports at the time, only half the expected crowd turned out at Tamiami, according to Sanchez's own estimate. We may never know the true attendance because, he says, he didn't bother to use the turnstiles for two days.

Such casual bookkeeping doesn't seem to disturb Commissioner Barry Schreiber, content with Sanchez's assertion that "we fill hotel rooms." Others, such as Commissioners Bev Phillips and Clara Oesterle, have expressed serious doubts about Pereira's plan.

Since the races are partly bankrolled by the city of Miami, Dade County and the state of Florida, taxpayers might be interested in details about the bottom line, which currently is red. Call us nosy, but we'd sure like to see the books before donating another half a million bucks.

Next week the county's finance committee will consider whether or not to set aside its fiscal worries, dig into your pockets and give generously to this sporting cause.

Considering his track record with the county commissioners, it's no wonder that Ralph Sanchez is back at Government Center, a pit stop in more ways than one.

Track developer now charity case for Homestead

August 1, 1993

For those wondering how long it would take the new Metro Commission to start throwing money away, the wait is over: $20 million for auto racing in Homestead.

The 11−1 vote came last Tuesday at midnight, when public attendance was conveniently at a minimum. It brought to $31 million the total that Grand Prix hustler Ralph Sanchez has charmed from the county commission since October.

It's his biggest jackpot ever. Who needs telethons when you've got such softhearted politicians? Sanchez and Homestead City Manager Alex Muxo had no trouble selling the outlandish proposition that South Dade's hurricane recovery should be anchored by a private racetrack, to be used for only three or four major events a year.

Behind-the-scenes players included two longtime Sanchez cohorts, lobbyists Ron Book and Sergio Pereira. Pereira is an old hand at frittering public funds. As county manager, he once spent $9,400 on a new desk.

The Sanchez giveaway comes from a sports tax on hotel beds. Muxo raided the same kitty before; the result is an empty $12 million baseball stadium. Now Homestead wants racing, even though Sanchez's track record is an 11-year skid of red ink.

While claiming his races are a hit, Sanchez remains mysteriously dependent on the dole:

• 1985. Despite receiving more than $1 million in public subsidies, Sanchez says his races lost more than $2 million. Nonetheless, he manages to find the money to pay for a new Mercedes-Benz for his lobbyist, Book.

• February 1986. Ralph Aid I: Miami paves Bicentennial Park into a grand prix track. The city also gives Sanchez $250,000, plus an interest-free loan. That's added to the $800,000 he's already gotten from the county and the state.

• July 1986. Ralph Aid II: Sergio Pereira, then county manager, decides Sanchez needs more. He proposes a $5 million bailout over 10 years. The Metro Commission pares the handout to $200,000 a year, plus a $368,000 payment for "unexpected" costs.

• 1987–1988. Still itchy, Pereira and Sanchez hatch a scheme for Metro to buy out Sanchez's operations, and move the races to the Opa-locka airport. That nutty idea costs taxpayers $300,000 in consultant fees. The plan is dropped when Pereira quits as county manager, after he's caught lying about his secret involvement in a land deal.

• 1992. Miami gives Sanchez his customary $200,000, plus $300,000 in fire and police services. Not enough! He wants to move the Grand Prix to Munisport, a toxic dump in North Miami. Residents protest, saying they'd rather have a quiet dump than a noisy racetrack. Sanchez turns to Homestead . . .

And Homestead is ripe for the picking. Flattened by the storm, vacated by the Air Force, jilted by the Cleveland Indians, the city is frantic for a boost.

Disguising Ralph Relief as hurricane relief worked brilliantly. Commissioner Larry Hawkins played everything but the violin, and Sanchez got his racetrack without putting up a penny. The public got a $20 million lube job.

Like the ballpark, a track will bring temporary construction jobs to South Dade. But after it's built, then what? For all but a few weeks each year, the place won't draw flies, much less tourists. (Muxo says Homestead police might use the new track for training, making it the world's most expensive driver-education course.)

If the Grand Prix can't turn a healthy profit on prime downtown bayfront, Sanchez stands no chance in the distant fields of South Dade.

The only winners in this deal are the taxpayers of Miami, who will be spared their annual $500,000 bailout of Ralph's party. Now he is Homestead's charity case.

Let Lipton thrive or fail on its own

July 25, 1990

Another brainy idea from the county manager: using a tourism tax to build a tennis stadium on Key Biscayne.

Yes, folks, the happy Lipton giveaway continues. In his zeal to keep the International Players Championships at Crandon Park, County Manager

Joaquin Avino wants tax dollars used to help pay for a permanent $16.5 million stadium.

This is the very same stadium which, only a few years ago, promoter Butch Buchholz had promised to build with private funds. Not a penny of public money would be spent, he said.

What happened? We got stuck again, that's what. The Lipton is costing county government plenty, and it's about to get much worse. Having been clobbered once in court, the county charges onward heedlessly, making the same mistakes. It is certain to be sued again.

Undaunted, the commission on Tuesday accepted Avino's tennis-tax plan, allowing him to begin negotiations. Short-term memory loss apparently afflicts some of the commissioners, who only two years ago vowed to spend no more public funds on the Lipton.

Hailed by supporters as a booming triumph, the tennis tournament nonetheless loses money year after year. Most private businesses, faced with such chronic deficits, would either reorganize or go bankrupt. Not the Lipton, which has been a special charity case from Day One.

First the county handed over a big chunk of a public park. Then it financed a $1 million clubhouse. Then it paid for the parking lots. Then it sweet-talked the state out of a cool $1 million or so. Now it wants to tax tourist motels to bankroll a new stadium.

Which brings up another mystery. For months we've been warned that the Lipton would abandon Dade County for greener pastures if a permanent 12,000-seat stadium weren't constructed. Then an appellate court ruled that the tournament violates the deed, as written by the Matheson family when it donated the unspoiled property half a century ago.

Suddenly the ultimatum for a 12,000-seat stadium disappeared. Planners emerged with a new scheme for a smaller, 7,500-seat stadium with more public parking. It was put forward as a "compromise" to please worried Key Biscayne residents—but the real effect was to dodge the South Florida Regional Planning Council, which must review and approve large projects. Supporters defend these tactics by saying the Lipton is good for Florida, good for Dade County, good for Key Biscayne. They claim a positive economic impact of $111 million annually—an unsubstantiated puffery based on some of the wildest calculations you ever saw.

Ralph Sanchez and Other Subsidized Sports

Certainly this is a fine tennis tournament, but it ought to succeed or fail on its own. To use millions in tax money to prop up a private sports enterprise is reckless. To use a public park for it is a disgrace.

There's nothing to stop the promoters from buying their own land and developing their own tennis stadium—people in South Florida would cheer for its success. As it now stands, every taxpayer in Dade County should get free admission to the Lipton tournament, since they've paid for so much of it.

Even if the commission votes for the tennis tax, there's an excellent chance the stadium will need a new location. If the Matheson property isn't used exclusively for public park purposes, the deed allows the family to invoke a "reverter" clause to take the land back.

Which is exactly what they're contemplating.

If the Matheson heirs choose to reclaim the donated property, it will be a lacerating embarrassment to the county. The family could give the Crandon tract to either the state or the federal government for preservation as a park. That means no tennis stadium, no retail shops, no tournament.

The county will fight it, of course—spending hundreds of thousands more tax dollars on what could easily be a losing cause. And a misguided one.

Parks shouldn't be used to fill private coffers

April 19, 1992

All parks officially are up for grabs. Dade Circuit Judge Gerald Wetherington has ruled that putting a 14,000-seat tennis stadium in Crandon Park is no big deal.

The pioneer Matheson family, which donated the land, has been fighting the proposed Lipton tennis center. The Mathesons say the property wasn't meant to be handed to a private sports promoter. The 1940 deed gave the land for "public park purposes only."

In a decision that warmed the hearts of would-be developers, Wetherington said: "As times have changed, the concept of public purpose has changed."

Twisted is more like it. The term "public purpose" now means taking public land for the purpose of enhancing private pocketbooks. It's a broad concept that benefits entrepreneurs who are too cheap to buy their own property.

The Lipton technically leases part of Crandon, but the tournament remains heavily subsidized with public funds. Naturally, the new stadium will be built with tax dollars.

Fifty years ago, the Mathesons never imagined that the county would give away the park. When donating the land, they composed the deeds in language that seemed straightforward.

Understandably, family heirs were upset when the county allowed a private sports venture to take over part of Crandon. They've argued adamantly that the tract wasn't intended for commercial exploitation and that the original deed prohibited it.

By ruling against the Mathesons, Judge Wetherington essentially announced that it didn't matter what the family might have intended—a tennis stadium would be built. No clearer message could be sent to future donors of public parks. The county will betray you in a flash unless the deed is airtight:

"I, (YOUR NAME), hereby give and bequeath the property located at (LEGAL DESCRIPTION) to Dade County, for use exclusively as a park. This deed shall hereby exclude the following commercial events: tennis tournaments, automobile races, soccer, skeet shooting, rodeos, croquet, lacrosse, monster-truck pulls, Wrestlemania or any Battle of the Network Superstars.

"For the purposes of this deed, the term 'public park' strictly shall be defined as a place for public recreation and enjoyment at all times. Turnstiles are forbidden."

Miami lawyer Dan Paul, who helped write the county charter, favors an amendment that will protect the parks from Lipton-type development. Under his proposal, no park could be leased, built upon, or turned over to a commercial enterprise without a countywide referendum.

Ironically, Judge Wetherington's Crandon giveaway came on the same day that plans were revealed to turn Miami's troubled Bicentennial Park into an enormous dock for cruise ships.

It won't be the first time the place is remodeled in the name of private profit. The city previously leased Bicentennial to promoter Ralph Sanchez, who paved it for a Grand Prix. (He'll soon be getting $9 million of tourist tax money to upgrade the racetrack, which is used exactly twice a year.)

Now Carmen Lunetta, czar of the Port of Miami, wants to expand Bicentennial and adjacent property into a fancy harborage for cruise liners. New shops and restaurants would be featured (even though nearby Bayside is gasping for survival). To keep Sanchez happy, Lunetta is tossing in an extra 6,000 seats for the Grand Prix.

Voters bought the Miami waterfront for use as a park, not a commercial port. But, as Judge Wetherington says, times have changed. What's a park these days without taxis, buses, jillions of harried cruise-ship passengers and the occasional nine-pound wharf rat. I'm already packing my picnic basket.

If Lipton should fall, let Avino's crew shovel it

May 10, 1992

The Lipton tennis boondoggle is in deep trouble, all of it self-made.

On Friday, Dade Circuit Judge Jon Gordon halted construction of a tax-funded, $16.5 million stadium on Key Biscayne. In an emphatic ruling, Gordon said the land was deeded for use exclusively as a public park, not a commercial tennis operation. The decision was a victory for the Matheson family, which donated the tract 52 years ago.

Dade officials appear typically numb and bewildered. County Manager Joaquin Avino is moaning that Gordon's decision will cost taxpayers millions of dollars.

That's not the fault of the judge or the Mathesons. It was Avino and that sorry crew of commissioners who recklessly launched construction of the Lipton stadium, knowing that the project faced stiff court challenges.

Whether it was arrogance or sheer stupidity, the county blew it. They gambled and lost. Now, having squandered tons of tax money, the county's legal wizards are forging blindly ahead to squander even more. Yes, folks, they're trudging back to the courthouse for another try.

None of this nonsense was necessary. From day one, Dade officials knew they were on shaky legal ground by putting the Lipton in Crandon Park. They'd privately taken their plans for the tournament to the Matheson heirs, who objected strenuously. The family saw the Lipton center as unadulterated commercialization, which it is. They threatened to sue to enforce the deed.

At that point, the tournament, the stadium and millions of bucks could've been saved by relocating the Lipton to another site. Nothing prevented promoters from buying their own tract and putting up a first-class facility wherever they wanted.

But that's not how it's done in Dade County. Why pay for something out of your own pocket when taxpayers will do it for you? The lure of free Key Biscayne real estate was impossible to refuse. Behind the scenes, high-priced lobbyists and political power brokers worked to keep the Lipton on the island, despite the opposition of many residents.

Brushing off the threat of lawsuits, the commissioners giddily pressed ahead with the tennis extravaganza. Anything promoter Butch Buchholz wanted, he got—including public financing of the stadium he once promised to build with private funds. Meanwhile, the county was spending a fortune on legal fees—again, your money—to fight the Mathesons.

Avino acted as if the family was just a pesky annoyance. The possibility of losing the case didn't seem to cross his mind. Talk about cocky: Bulldozers went to work on the 14,000-seat stadium on April 1—three weeks before Circuit Judge Gerald Wetherington was scheduled to hear the lawsuit.

Though Wetherington ruled in the county's favor, he abruptly changed his mind and took himself off the case. Construction on the Lipton proceeded as if nothing were amiss.

For developers, it's the oldest trick in the book. The more you can build and the faster you can build it, the harder for opponents to get it torn down. That's Avino's woeful defense: Dade taxpayers have invested so much in the Lipton that it's too expensive to turn back. Gee, Joaquin, whose fault is that?

While the county fights Judge Gordon's decision, the digging and destruction will likely resume on Key Biscayne. Drive out there and take a look—after all, you're paying for it.

But remember that if the Mathesons prevail (and there's a good chance they will), the stadium will come tumbling down. If that happens, shovels should be distributed immediately to the county manager and each gung-ho commissioner. Bus them to Crandon Park and make them clean up their mess.

Sort of an old-fashioned groundbreaking, in reverse.

Metro tumbled into sand trap with golf club

June 26, 1994

If P. T. Barnum were alive to watch the Metro Commission in action, he'd probably revise his famous axiom. Not only are suckers born every minute, they invariably get elected to political office.

Dade politicians are big suckers for sports. They've got a history of blowing public funds on extravaganzas that fail to produce the windfall promised by hungry promoters. The most infamous entitlement programs are the Lipton tennis tournament and the Miami Grand Prix.

Now another sport is sucking precious dollars out of the county coffer: golf. So far, unsuspecting taxpayers have forked out $8.9 million on the Golf Club of Miami. That's not a typo: $8.9 million—with about $8 million more to come.

Even using silk flags and the lushest Bermuda grass, it hardly seems possible to spend so much to spruce up a few fairways.

Here's what happened. Five years ago, the county contracted with the PGA Tour to rejuvenate the Golf Club of Miami in North Dade. The courses had gotten ratty, and worried neighbors voted to tax themselves to purchase much of the property. The county had the rest.

The PGA Tour eagerly offered to run the place and touted itself as capable and experienced. The prestige of attaching the Tour's name was supposed to attract a luxury hotel and hordes of golf-crazy tourists.

As it turned out, a bunch of chimpanzees couldn't have negotiated a worse contract than the one approved by Metro commissioners. Ironically, the only one opposed to it was then-Mayor Steve Clark, the county's undisputed authority on all golfing matters. Clark said the Golf Club of Miami deal was no good, and he was right.

Oh, the courses are in better shape today, and they're finally making a modest profit. Unfortunately, the county's seeing little of it; $500,000 annually comes off the top, for the PGA.

How bad was the contract? Item: new cart paths. The Tour's price tag: $558,000, or about three times the going rate. The Caddyshack Commission said sure. Since 1989, the Golf Club of Miami has drained a small fortune from the county's general fund, including $863,000 a year in bond payments. We're stuck with those until 2004.

Of course, the big luxury hotel never materialized, costing Metro another $4.2 million in bed taxes to repay investors. Incredibly, the Parks Department also "loaned" the golf club $4.1 million to construct a third course, an executive-style par 62. Not only was the price higher than many first-class par 72s, but the short course lost a tidy $460,000 in its first two years.

The county claims all of that money eventually will be paid back out of future revenues from the golf club. Sure. When they raise the greens fees to $2,000 a day.

In addition to the $8.9 million in general funds, the Golf Club of Miami has received much more from other public sources. Metro commissioners grabbed $3.5 million from the sports-franchise bed tax and built a new clubhouse dedicated to one of their own, Sherman Winn. His name on the building is a fitting reminder of the suckers who paid for it.

Defending the project, county officials say the funds spent on the Golf Club of Miami aren't a total waste. Said one: "At least we've gotten into public ownership three pretty nice golf courses."

And a dandy bargain it is. Let's see . . . 54 holes at a minimum final cost of $24.6 million. That comes to about $455,555 per fairway.

From now on, golfers will have an option of replacing their divots, or listing them with Century 21.

Wayne skating on thin ice of fan loyalty

July 23, 1995

Wayne Huizenga says he's moving or selling the Florida Panthers if somebody doesn't build him a new arena. Gonna get the puck out, he says.

The announcement came at a press conference during which a testy Huizenga expressed no fondness for Broward officials, who'd rejected a tax on tourists or restaurants to finance a new $165 million hockey rink.

Instead, the county had rashly suggested that Mr. Blockbuster himself should pony up a heftier chunk of the arena money—an option no self-respecting sports tycoon likes to contemplate.

The common philosophy is that sports fans should be so darned grateful to have a big-league franchise that they ought to subsidize it with taxes.

It's not enough to pay for overpriced parking, overpriced tickets, overpriced junk food and overpriced souvenirs. No, you should pay for the overpriced facilities, too.

Happens all over. That's how St. Louis lured the Rams from Los Angeles: new stadium, sweet deal. For many owners it's proved a successful extortion: Build me a new place to play, or I'll take my team elsewhere.

When the ungrateful citizenry of Broward balked at bankrolling a hockey stadium, Huizenga stomped off. Even if the county comes crawling back, he declared, the deal's off.

So there. Nah, nah, nah.

Huizenga says he needs help because the team is losing $1 million a month by sharing the Miami Arena with the Heat. He wants a new ice palace tiered with posh, high-priced skyboxes.

Not so long ago, politicians would've bellied across broken glass to appease Huizenga. The mood today is slightly less worshipful, and the reason is simple. Voters are tired of using public monies to enrich millionaire sports owners.

South Floridians have contributed heavily, if not knowingly, to the downtown arena, as well as a private Grand Prix track and a tennis stadium. It's welfare for the rich, disguised as civic boosterism.

Huizenga's grim account of the Panthers' finances is troubling. Here's a team (unlike other local franchises) that plays to 97 percent capacity, yet still manages to bleed red ink. That's quite a trick.

How did such a sharp businessman fall into such a stinky deal? Clearly, Huizenga agreed to share the arena only because he was sure he'd be getting a new one soon, courtesy of some hockey-crazed municipality. Unfortunately, he misjudged.

His assertion that more luxury skyboxes will save the Panthers is equally suspect, considering that the relatively few skyboxes in the Miami Arena aren't sold out.

One positive thing to come from Huizenga's tantrum is a possible partnership with Heat owner Micky Arison, also in the market for a new venue. Together, they've got more capital to invest, and a better chance of turning a profit.

A similar joint deal worked well in Chicago. There, the basketball and hockey teams split both the cost and revenues from the new $175 million United Center. Both teams are making money.

But here's the real shocker: The Chicago arena was constructed largely with private funds. The owners, not taxpayers, picked up the tab. What a radical concept.

Unfortunately, building a new arena here would kill the old one, which isn't that old and wasn't so cheap. It would be better if Huizenga and Arison joined forces (and bankers) to refurbish the current Miami Arena in the high style they desire.

Right now, the most valuable part of the Panthers franchise is fan loyalty, but that can change quickly. An owner's ultimatum for luxury skyboxes cuts no ice with the folks in the cheap seats.

Let Broward have its arena—and the debt

February 1, 1996

Dade taxpayers should breathe a collective sigh of relief this week. They might be off the hook for a new sports arena.

Broward County has impulsively offered to build a basketball-hockey emporium to keep both the restless Miami Heat and the money-losing Florida Panthers in South Florida.

Price tag: $212 million, minimum. Most of the dough would come from a 2 percent hotel-bed tax, backed by county bonds.

Broward voters haven't been asked for their opinion, as a public out-pouring of skepticism might discourage Heat owner Micky Arison (who has already threatened to move his team) and Panthers owner Wayne Huizenga (who's supposedly trying to sell his).

By a 5–1 vote, Broward commissioners vowed to spring for a new arena if the teams sign in advance and agree to share revenues with the county. The deal is far from sealed, and Dade officials are hurriedly polishing a new pitch of their own.

Only in the irrational realm of big-league sports can two of the richest guys on the planet sit back and watch suckers plead for the privilege of building them a palace.

In Broward, three cities have hurled themselves worshipfully at Arison's and Huizenga's feet. Fort Lauderdale has a downtown site off Interstate 95. Pompano Beach is pushing a parcel near the harness track. And Sunrise has property located near West Broward's social and cultural shrine, the Sawgrass Mills outlet mall.

The Sunrise Heat? The Pompano Panthers? These days anything is possible—witness the Mighty Ducks of Anaheim.

Backers say a sports arena will bring to a neighborhood great jobs, economic prosperity, national prestige and immeasurable civic pride.

Sound familiar? These are the same promises heard when basketball promoters lobbied for the building of the Miami Arena, which has not exactly revitalized the downtown area.

In fact, a new fiscal study of 35 major sports facilities finds little positive economic impact on the communities that turned cartwheels to attract them. Arenas and stadiums are strictly designed to make money for the team and its owners.

There's nothing wrong with the Miami Arena. It's not old, it's not falling apart, and it's not too small—in fact, on some nights it's downright cavernous for the crowd that shows up.

Sure, it's in a tough neighborhood, but that's true in other basketball and hockey cities. It's not the fans who are complaining loudest about the facility, it's Arison and Huizenga. They want more seats and more luxury skyboxes, which are hugely profitable.

Sports owners all over the country engage in the same strong-arming of loyal fans and local taxpayers: Give us what we want, or we'll bolt. And too often they do.

That's because there's always another town with an inferiority complex and gullible politicians willing to put up somebody else's money. It's not about economic betterment, it's about egos. Every place lusts for its own pro sports team.

Listen to what Fort Lauderdale's city manager said about the benefits of a new arena: "This will bring Broward County out of the shadow of Dade."

A baffling remark, considering that Broward is already growing much faster than Dade, and is internationally perceived as a safer and more desirable place to live.

The only shadow Broward residents ought to worry about is the one made by a tower of debt, which is what they'll be trapped under if Arison, Huizenga or some future sports tycoon gets antsy again in a few years.

Which seems to be the nature of the game.

A rejected rough draft of the latest Letter of Intent to move the Heat and the Panthers from Miami to Broward County: "And whereas we could move to Boca Raton"
March 24, 1996

"Whereas we, Micky Arison and Wayne Huizenga, the owners of the Miami Heat and the Florida Panthers, respectively, are committed to terminating our leases at the present Miami Arena, (hereinafter referred to as 'The Dump');

"And whereas neither of us intends to finance, wholly or in large part, the construction of a new sports arena, despite the fact we're both stupendously wealthy, and could probably pay for the whole darn thing out of our personal money-market accounts;

"And whereas the prospect of losing basketball or hockey has spurred local politicians to a burst of fiscal cleverness hitherto unknown in more mundane crises, such as juvenile crime or classroom overcrowding;

"And whereas the Broward County Commission has expressed verbally and in writing an almost pathological eagerness to construct a new sports arena for us, at considerable expense and public risk;

"And whereas said Broward Commission (hereinafter referred to as 'The Big Suckers') have acquiesced on numerous key points concerning the division of future arena revenues, including ticket sales, luxury box leases, food and souvenir concessions;

"And whereas, in the face of such blind generosity, we'd have to be out of our cotton-pickin' minds to fork out a nickel from our own pockets;

"We therefore declare our intention to move the Miami Heat and Florida Panthers to Broward County, providing all parties agree that:

"(a) This Letter of Intent shall be entirely nonbinding (hereinafter referred to as 'worthless' or 'not worth the paper it's printed on').

"(b) This Letter of Intent shall not deprive us of our right to jerk Broward County around while we wait for other offers.

"Such jerking around (hereinafter referred to as 'thoughtful reconsideration') shall include but not be limited to postponing or ignoring agreed-upon deadlines, making coy and ambivalent public statements about where the teams wish to play, and generally stalling whenever it suits our purpose;

"And whereas, to our vast amusement, civic leaders and elected officials in Dade County have recently expressed an almost desperate desire to keep the Heat and/or the Panthers;

"And whereas we'd be foolish not to sit back and watch Dade and Broward compete like little children for the privilege of building us a brand-new $200 million arena;

"And whereas we don't particularly care where the money comes from, as long as it's not ours;

"And whereas Dade authorities appear every bit as gullible and easy to intimidate as those in Broward;

"And whereas while we find it hard to believe that local politicians are goofy enough to build two new arenas, we cannot rule out the intriguing possibility;

"Therefore each of us individually retains the right to pretend this Letter of Intent to Broward commissioners is a gag, and to continue negotiating for an extravagant new arena with Dade officials (hereinafter referred to as 'Even Bigger Suckers');

"Such negotiations with Dade may continue until the very day that construction on the Broward arena is completed. At that time one or both of us will sign an Amended Letter of Intent, allowing the Heat and/or Panthers to play in Broward County until something a little better comes along.

"Your pals, Wayne and Micky."

Team rebates send tax money down the drain

March 16, 1997

Wayne Huizenga is about to pick our pockets for another $60 million. But don't fret, it's all for a good cause: spiffy new toilets at the former Joe Robbie Stadium!

Huizenga believes that all Florida taxpayers—most of whom have never brought their bladder to a football game—should subsidize renovations such as upgraded concession stands, concourses and restrooms.

This, after they've already bankrolled the conversion of JRS into a baseball park. Huizenga glommed the first $60 million on behalf of the Florida Marlins. Now he wants an identical handout for the Dolphins.

Is the Legislature slutty enough to roll over twice for the same smooth-talking billionaire? Not only is it possible, it's virtually a sure bet. (He's getting another 60 mil for the Panthers' new arena.)

The money is a massive rebate of sales tax revenues—spread over 30 years—which would otherwise be frittered away on extravagances such as elementary schools. And, after all, what's more important to Florida's future—new textbooks for kids, or new chili-dog stands for Wayne?

See, up in the Capitol, them boys loves their sports.

In 1988, they approved a tax kickback to lure big-league franchises from other states. Since then, the loophole has been enlarged to funnel millions to pro teams that are already here, but have threatened to defect.

Huizenga isn't the only tycoon to cash in. Owners of the Tampa Bay Bucs and the Orlando Magic have also taken advantage of the exemption. And Micky Arison is using his $60 million rebate to help finance the new arena for the Miami Heat.

But only Wily Wayne has tried to double-dip from the same jackpot. He figures he deserves a capital improvement subsidy for every sports team he owns, even if two of them happen to play in the same ballpark.

But just to show what a big heart he's got, Huizenga promises not to use any tax money to doll up the exclusive private suites and corporate skyboxes.

According to Wayne's lobbyist Ron Book (and we know he would never lie), the rebate will be spent "only in the areas that are accessible to the general public."

That means you'll be able to admire firsthand the gleaming new porcelain in your favorite fixture—for which you'll be paying, along with your game ticket, parking fees, programs, cheese nachos and the beer you're now getting rid of.

It's a swell deal for Huizenga. But as long as elected lawmakers do what billionaires tell them, billionaires will continue to ask for outrageous favors.

Ordinary folks needn't bother. Nobody who runs a mom-and-pop diner could con the state into buying them a new Mr. Coffee, much less a wall-to-wall renovation. Nor would they dream of trying.

Then again, ordinary folks can't afford to shower politicians with the hefty campaign donations that Huizenga spreads around. That's how votes are bought, and that's how these boondoggles are orchestrated.

If Stadium Giveaway II sails through the Legislature as expected, as much as $120 million in public funds will have been earmarked for improvements to JRS. That particular crater in the state's tax booty will be filled with other money—yours, mine, the folks with the diner.

To help groveling lawmakers defend their obeisance, Huizenga's forces have provided a sheath of hilariously inflated statistics about how much the Dolphins' eight regular-season home games contribute to South Florida's economy.

Think about that when you visit one of Wayne's new toilets.

You could flush yourself silly, but you'll never catch up to them boys in the Capitol.

Speedway lessees race to the bank

April 13, 1997

When Ralph Sanchez and Wayne Huizenga joined forces at the Homestead motor speedway, you knew good things would happen.

To Ralph and Wayne, of course. Not necessarily to Homestead.

Sure enough, Sanchez and Huizenga are about to roar away from the troubled racetrack with at least $10 million each, while the flat-broke city limply waves a checkered flag.

Sanchez claims the place can't make it without hosting the popular

Winston Cup stock car races—something that won't occur unless he and Huizenga sell out to NASCAR impresario Bill France.

France didn't want the track unless the lease was watered down. Last week the city obliged.

"I walked out of the council chambers sick to my stomach. They gave away the farm," says Steve Losner, a lawyer whose family has been in Homestead for 70 years.

It was as predictable as it is pathetic. The 65,000-seat motorsports complex was built with public funds, including $31 million from county tourist taxes and bond sales. How much will Dade get from the Sanchez sellout? Zippo.

Homestead itself has spent $8 million on the track, and is in debt for another $25 million. Its take from the new deal: nada. Amazing, considering that the city is deeply in the red, and that workers are being laid off.

Meanwhile, Wayne and Ralph can peel rubber on their way to the bank. It was a match made in heaven, two masters of finagling public funds for private projects.

By selling his share of the Homestead lease, Sanchez would maintain a perfect record: In 15 years he's never operated a racetrack that made money. Oh, he made plenty—but not the races, and not the municipalities that subsidized them.

After skipping out of downtown Miami, Sanchez found fresh suckers in hurricane-battered Homestead. True to form, he miscalculated the cost of the new speedway by about 500 percent, and his lofty promise of reviving South Dade's economy turned out to be hot air.

Even the track itself has been a headache, beset with costly design flaws that cast large doubts upon Sanchez's touted racing expertise. Huizenga came in as a partner by loaning $20 million for new construction.

Now Sanchez says the racetrack is "overbuilt." Seriously, that's what he says. He told New Times: "If I didn't have to sell I wouldn't sell, but this is the reality of the situation."

Here's the reality: He and Huizenga are making out like bandits, while taxpayers are once again eating dust.

Of all Sanchez's failures, Homestead will be his most lucrative. In a meeting with South Dade business leaders on April 3, he admitted that he and Huizenga each will receive about $10 million if France buys them out.

Which seems likely, since the track's new tenant is no longer required to share race profits with the city—one of several outlandish concessions approved by council members.

The hosing was orchestrated by none other than Alex Muxo, who did plenty of damage as Homestead's city manager. Now conveniently employed by Huizenga, Muxo met individually with council members at the racetrack.

His message: This thing won't ever fly without a Winston Cup weekend.

In other words, forget the Indy cars. Forget the Jiffy Lube. Forget everything Sanchez promised four years ago.

Many folks in Homestead won't forget. Neither will some of the politicians who gave him that first $31 million. As former Metro Commissioner Maurice Ferre lamented: "I still wonder how we could have allowed this to happen."

Join the club.

Choked on Growth

If three's a crowd, what is 5 million?

September 13, 1985

Something dismal to contemplate next time you're stuck in highway traffic:

This week the National Planning Association predicted that Florida will have 5.7 million more residents by the year 2000 than it had in 1980. The Census Bureau forecasts 7.7 million, though this is considered high. And the University of Florida's Bureau of Economic and Business Research conservatively puts the growth at 5 million.

Which is still equivalent to absorbing the entire population of Missouri. Or, put another way, if the number of new people invading Florida during the next 15 years formed their own state, it would be more populous than 38 other states.

Incredibly, there are those walking among us who think this is wonderful news, and who are busily restructuring their banks, mapping new condominium clusters and dreaming up bigger and better trailer parks.

Meanwhile, growing numbers of dispirited Floridians wonder where it will all end, and worry about already-frayed quality of life.

"You're talking about a 50 percent increase in a 20-year period. In terms of numbers of bodies, it's a tremendous increase," says Stanley K. Smith of the University of Florida.

Among the fastest growing counties are Palm Beach, Lee, Collier, St. Lucie and Martin. Broward is still growing, though not nearly as fast as before, while Dade County is stagnant, its new arrivals nearly matched by those packing up and heading north.

As expected, most newcomers hail from places that are either cold, crowded, dirty or economically depressed. By the turn of the century, they will have enlarged our numbers to 14.7 million.

As John D. MacDonald has observed, almost everyone who moves down here wants to slam the door behind him. This might be selfish, but it's also understandable: It doesn't take a disciple of Thoreau to notice the loveliness of Florida wane in direct proportion to humanity.

"At some point," Smith says, "it's possible that the quality of life will become so unattractive that no one will want to move here. That'll solve your growth problems. But that's like cutting off your arm to save the whole body."

This year the Legislature passed a "growth management" law, supposedly to impose order on the state's tumultuous development.

Frankly, the notion of "orderly growth" is about as tangible as the tooth fairy. Growth that is orderly would break a century-old tradition of lust, greed and wantonness. Already three Florida counties (Palm Beach, Broward and Dade) hold more human beings (3.5 million) than the states of Mississippi or Colorado or Oregon or Oklahoma, to name a few.

No governor in our history has voiced as much concern for the trampling of Florida as Bob Graham, but I doubt that even he has the clout to put on the brakes. He is considered bold for endorsing "growth management," but he'd be laughed off his lectern for suggesting a growth cap.

So we're stuck with this stampede.

Developers along the Palm Beach and Treasure Coasts can salivate at the good fortune coming their way, but those living there might ponder the lesson of boomed-out Dade County.

Dade has stopped growing because it is perceived as crowded, volatile, crime-ridden and racially tense. It is seen less as a community than a newly urbanized war zone; a place with too many people, too many problems and too few opportunities.

Broward, fast bloating, will be the next to bottom out. In a few years Palm Beach County will probably follow.

By the time it all goes sour, when even Disney and sunny beaches can't trick people into coming, the big-money boys will have made their killing and hustled elsewhere along the Sun Belt.

Leaving everyone else to stew in traffic, and try to remember why they moved here in the first place.

Highway opens one of last frontiers to overgrowth

July 16, 1986

The Romans managed to build 53,000 miles of road without once celebrating the achievement by dressing up in frog costumes.

Things have changed since 312 B.C. The roads are better, but the PR is worse.

Thursday brings another official opening of the Sawgrass Expressway in West Broward County. This opening—marked by the imposition of a $1.50 toll—should not be confused with two previous official openings, at which great political merriment and self-congratulation occurred.

The highlight of these seemingly endless festivities has been the introduction of Cecil B. Sawgrass, a grown man dressed like a frog. Cecil B. Sawgrass is the expressway's official mascot. If you live in Broward, you got postcards in the mail with Cecil's green likeness inviting you to try the new expressway. "Hop to it!" Cecil implored. And, sure enough, if you drive the Sawgrass you'll see dozens of Cecil's little frog cousins squashed dead on the fresh asphalt.

The Romans had too much class to invent animal mascots for their roads. Of course, they never had to sell a $200 million bond issue either. These days, we are told, highways must be promoted like breakfast cereal, imprinted on the public consciousness. This is especially true when the highway doesn't really go anywhere that the public wants to go.

The Sawgrass Expressway is a 23-mile incision that runs near the Broward-Palm Beach boundary, then jogs south along the westernmost fringe of civilization. It runs parallel to the dikes that contain the submerged Everglades conservation areas, vital South Florida watersheds. Someday the Sawgrass will link with I-595.

There's not much to see on the highway now, and that's the beauty of it. There are cattle grazing in open fields, hawks circling in the sky, and bass hitting in the canals (at least the canals that weren't grossly over-dredged by road contractors). Across the dike are breathtaking waves of sawgrass and virgin wetlands.

It won't stay this way long, which explains all the celebrating. The sound of bulldozers is the sound of money.

Don't think for a minute that this road was built in 15 months because thousands of commuters were begging for it (try to get a pothole plugged that fast). And don't think it was built to ease the deadly chaos of I-95, because it runs nowhere near the interstate.

The Sawgrass was built for one reason only: to open the last frontiers of Broward County for rapid development. The value of sodden rural property tends to appreciate when somebody graciously runs an expressway to it. It's like Christmas in July.

It's just progress, right? If you like truck routes, it's progress.

Twenty-five years ago Dade County planners exulted in the opening of what was then called the Palmetto Bypass. The highway's purported mission was to carry motorists on a western loop around Miami's congested central core. Within months of its inaugural, the sparse Palmetto had attracted a bottling plant, three industrial parks, a machine shop, a metal shop, and a tractor plant. The rest is traffic history.

Today, if you were choosing the most unsightly, treacherous and truck-heavy highway in America, the Palmetto would be in the running for grand prize. It's a mess.

Well, guess what's already happening along the perimeters of the Sawgrass Expressway? Coral Ridge Properties just gobbled up 610 acres. Gulfstream Land is planning 29,000 residential units. Stiles Development Corp. is promising 6 million square feet of office and industrial space—as much as all downtown Fort Lauderdale.

The hype is that the Sawgrass was built to alleviate future traffic. The opposite is true. The plan is for more, not less. The plan is a new western front ripe for malling and townhousing.

The plan is to scour every last available acre.

Funny how nobody wants to come right out and say it. Instead they send a frog to do a buzzard's job.

Buying a piece of Florida? See it like a native

February 16, 1987

Forgive a little boosterism, but I'm getting sick and tired of people casting aspersions on the land-sales business here in the Sunshine State. Geez, some customers want everything their way.

Last Friday's front-page story about the mammoth General Development Corporation was the last straw. To summarize, over the past three years GDC has received more than 400 complaints from dissatisfied land and home buyers, many of whom say they didn't get what they paid for.

Well, PARDON US FOR LIVING, OK? I mean, this is Florida. There's a certain, uh, image to uphold.

As you know, GDC is one of these megacompanies that gobbles up tracts of real estate and turns them into "planned communities" that are all named Port Something-or-other, but aren't really ports at all.

Flying over a planned community, you marvel at how the miracle of geometry allows so many houses to be squished onto so many side-by-side lots. This stylish platting technique is modeled after the marine barracks at Camp Lejeune.

Such developments have attracted thousands of new residents to Florida, most of whom would never dream of griping. They're just mighty glad to be here.

As a convenience for out-of-state customers, GDC's mannerly and low-key sales force is scattered throughout the country. What happens is that you go into the land-sales office and a very nice man or woman helps you pick out a lot—thus saving you the hassle of flying all the way down here, renting a car, buying a map and trying to locate the darn thing yourself—and the bugs! Forget it.

You'd think buyers would be grateful for this service, right? Wrong. Some crybabies have had the gall to complain that the land they ended up with wasn't the land they meant to buy. Some lots turned out to be worth only a fraction of the purchase price, and one customer said a canal near his lot turned out to be a "swamp."

Talk about picky. Hey, pal, ever heard of a canoe?

Customers who buy GDC land site-unseen are offered a company-paid trip to visit their new property. By taking the trip, however, they waive their option to cancel the sales contract. Some might say this policy is unfair and defeats the whole purpose of the trip, but look at the other side. Think of how many freezing snowbirds would try to weasel a free vacation to Florida this way!

Then there's the recurring problem with property appraisals. It seems that when residents try to sell their GDC lots or homes, the appraisals sometimes come up just a tad short of what was originally paid. One couple purchased a house for $65,000 in 1984; just a year later, an independent appraiser valued the place at $40,500. Another woman bought a house at Port Malabar for $67,000, and eight months later it was appraised at $43,000.

I'm sure there are excellent reasons for these minor discrepancies. So much can happen to a new house in eight months or a year—the paint can fade, the dog can mess up the carpets, the sprinklers can turn the sidewalks orange. Fifty bucks here and there, and before you know it, you've got $24,000 worth of serious depreciation.

More to the point, why would anyone want to sell their lovely GDC home anyway? The whole idea is to move to Florida and spend eternity in paradise, assuming the roads eventually get paved.

Instead of whining about it, I say we applaud GDC for goosing up its prices and discouraging resales. Florida needs citizens who stay put, not buy-and-sell vagabonds who disturb the stability of a carefully planned community.

Even more important—and forgive us for getting a little misty-eyed—is preserving Florida's glorious tradition of hawking itself as shamelessly and profitably as is humanly possible. If someone sells you swampland, it's because someone sold swampland to their fathers, and perhaps even to their grandfathers before that.

Maybe it's in our blood, or maybe it's just something in the water, but it is part of our heritage. Thank heavens it's still alive.

Maybe first Thanksgiving soured early

November 24, 1989

A University of Florida historian reports that, contrary to American folklore, the first Thanksgiving did not take place in 1621 after the Pilgrims' arrival at Plymouth Rock.

Rather, the original feast supposedly was held 56 years earlier at St. Augustine when Spanish explorer Pedro Menendez de Aviles invited the Timucua Indians to dinner. The prayerful gathering was called to celebrate the Spaniards' safe landing on the Florida coast.

If true, this revisionist account of the holiday raises important historical questions. Why did tradition embrace the New England Thanksgiving instead of the original Florida Thanksgiving? What really happened on that autumn evening in 1565 when the Spaniards and the Timucua broke bread? Did something go terribly wrong to spoil the occasion? Perhaps it all went sour on the day after the big cookout, when . . .

"Chief, you look awful—what's the matter?"

"It's those damn garbanzo beans. I should never have let Pedro talk me into a second helping."

"Speaking of Pedro, he and his men were up at the crack of dawn this morning. They chopped down many of our finest trees, and now they seem to be building something on our beach."

"I wondered who was causing all that racket. What are they making, another one of those ugly forts?"

"Not exactly, Chief. Pedro calls it a high-rise."

"I don't understand—what is that word, 'high-rise'? How would we say it in Timucuan?"

"Literally, it means Tall Box Full of Noisy Strangers."

"But why would Pedro put such an unnatural thing on such a beautiful shore!"

"He says he had a spiritual vision, Chief. He says that thousands upon thousands more settlers will soon be coming to Florida, and they will all need a place to sleep and eat and give thanks."

"What's he got against good old-fashioned thatched huts?"

"Pedro says the new settlers will want something fancier than palmetto. He says they'll be willing to pay major trinkets and beads to live in a high place with a good view of the ocean."

"This high-rise—exactly how high will it be?"

"Higher than the tallest pines, Chief. Higher than the eagles soar."

"Ha! I think our friend Pedro had a little too much grape last night."

"He seems quite sober, Chief. And his men are swift carpenters. I don't mind telling you, the rest of the tribe is very concerned."

"I, too, am worried—and surprised. They seemed like such nice fellows, these explorers. Much friendlier than the French. I can't believe they'd want to build a giant box on our beach and fill it with noisy strangers. What're we going to do?"

"Well, Chief, we could always eat them. Like we did with those Huguenots."

"Yeah, and we all had the trots for a month afterward, remember? Let's try to think of a different way to discourage Pedro."

"We could pass some tough coastal zoning ordinances."

"Naw, that'll never work. Pedro's lawyers would find a loophole somewhere."

"Chief, wait, I've got an idea! You know those funny little mushrooms that grow down by the creek? The ones that make the armadillos bark like coyotes?"

"Yes, the magic mushrooms."

"Well, suppose we invited Pedro and his crew back to dinner tonight. This time it would be our treat, a second thanksgiving."

"Hmmmm. A garden salad would be lovely for starters. Coonti roots, garnished with mushrooms."

"Yes, a bounty of mushrooms, Chief. And, later, cream of mushroom soup. Then, for the main course, wild buzzard stuffed with mushrooms."

"That should do the trick."

"After such a meal, Pedro and his men will totally forget about building anything on our peaceful beach. No more conquering, no more pillaging. All they'll want to do is run with the rabbits and fly with the hawks."

"Which reminds me, you'd better lock up the livestock."

"Good thinking, Chief. These men have been at sea for a long, long time."

Retail flops fail to stop mall frenzy

February 8, 1989

This is a terrible time for mall freaks.

First, Branden's announced it was closing. Not only was this bad news for Branden's employees, but also for several South Florida malls which had counted on the big department store as their "anchor" to bring in customers.

Four—The Promenade, Town & Country, Colonial Palms and The Fountains in Broward—are suddenly stuck with about a jillion square feet of retail space, of which there is already a gross surplus.

In South Miami, the long-troubled Bakery Centre was clobbered by the abrupt closing of the Bodyworks spa and adjoining Sports Rock Cafe. Certainly it was an interesting idea while it lasted: Presumably you were supposed to pig out on the cafe side, then burn off the fat at the gym. Only in America, and only in a mall, could such a concept be born.

The shutdown of Bodyworks was the final blow to the Bakery Centre, which has announced that it's converting from retail to office space. Meanwhile developer owner Martin Margulies and the bank that loaned him the dough are suing and countersuing each other over why the loans aren't being repaid.

A new fire station that Margulies had promised to build in exchange for the mall approval is still just a sketch on paper. Gee, what a surprise.

The Bakery Centre fiasco is not a unique story. All over South Florida, shopping malls are in trouble for the simple reason that there are too many of them. A recent study showed a glut of 25 million square feet of shopping space in Dade, Broward and Palm Beach counties. Vacancy is high, tenant turnover is high, foreclosure is high.

Still they build more and more of these megaturkeys—a mystery, unless you understand the symbiosis of greed. Developers usually don't lose a dime on dead malls—they get their money from the banks. The ones who really take it on the chin are the small, independent shop owners trying to make the rent in an air-conditioned ghost town.

Yet zoning boards lustily endorse mall after mall, seemingly oblivious of the fact that many of these projects have no prayer of financial success.

A perfect example: A few years ago, an economic study done in Broward reported that there was so much empty retail space that it couldn't all be filled until well into the 21st century.

Officials conveniently chose to ignore the experts, and continued to rubber-stamp every shopping mall that came up on the drawing board. Their groveling allegiance to developers is best manifested along a two-mile segment of University Drive in Plantation, where there are now no less than five malls and shopping centers.

If the Russians ever decide to bomb us, this particular stretch of sub-urban claptrap is where they'll start. The aerial resemblance to a muni-tions dump is uncanny.

Any idiot could have predicted that not all these malls could make money—any idiot except the ones who approved them; the elected ones.

Here's one idea you won't hear from government planners: Don't build any more shopping malls until the ones we've got are at least 90 percent occupied—and the stores are actually making a profit.

There's a radical notion. No one suggests such a thing because it means saying no to fat-cat developers and their lawyers. Saying no to a mall is like saying no to growth, and saying no to growth is like spitting on the flag.

Why, what would we do without another multiplex cinema—a dozen theaters, each no bigger than a tollbooth! Where else but a mall could we buy our apricot bagels? Where else could our daughters get their ears pierced?

And, most of all, what would we do with all that open space if there were no more shopping malls? Oh, I suppose you could plant some trees, put in a playground or maybe a ballpark for the kids.

But what neighborhood would ever go for something so dull when it could have its very own J. C. Penney and Wicker World and Orange Julius and parking lots as far as the eye can see.

We're talking quality of life.

A message to outsiders: Florida's full

January 5, 1990

The latest census figures show that the 1980s was a decade of astound-ing migration to the South and the West. Florida continues to draw new residents like a dead marlin draws flies. Between the 1980 census and July 1, 1989, the state's population grew from 9.7 million people to an estimated 12.7 million people—an increase of 31 percent.

Anyone who says this is good news needs to have his head examined. It's a disaster in the making, an avalanche of humanity with which our state has no prayer of coping. As it is, we don't have enough roads, schools, police, water, affordable housing or health care. We apparently don't even have enough electricity to operate our toasters during a cold snap.

Yet still they come to Florida, in hopeful hordes, at a rate of about 900 a day. What accounts for this lemming-like behavior? More to the point, what accounts for our welcoming them so cheerily?

To hear some civic boosters talk, we should all be proud that so many folks are dying to be our new neighbors. It's as if we've all pitched in to make this a little slice of paradise, with lots to offer.

Hogwash. We had nothing to do with it. People move to Florida for the same reasons they've always moved to Florida: to get warm and stay warm. No matter how crowded or crime-ridden this state becomes, it'll always look better than a dying factory town on the shore of Lake Erie in the dead of winter.

Florida is where folks come when things get unbearable back home. It's been that way ever since they invented air-conditioning and bug spray.

Only three states grew faster in the 1980s: Arizona, Alaska and Nevada. None is in any immediate danger of becoming urbanized; Arizona's entire population is no more than that of Dade, Broward and Monroe counties together.

It's more reasonable to compare what's happening in Florida with the trend in other populous states. In the 1980s we absorbed more new residents than New York, Pennsylvania, Illinois, Ohio or Texas. Only California (which has considerably more space) took in more people than we did.

Every year Florida's population grows by about 320,000—that's an entire city larger than Tampa. Every single year.

This must stop if the place is to be saved. Stanching the flood will require higher taxes, tougher laws and a few courageous politicians who aren't afraid to say enough is enough. Try to find just one.

Not that the cataclysm has been ignored. The 1980s was the decade in which state legislators embraced the term "growth management" and passed important laws to try to improve local planning. Not a week goes by that some university scholars or blue-ribbon panel aren't conducting a symposium on growth and all its implications—social, economic and environmental.

Some of the brightest people in Florida are hot on the case. The problem is, the faucet is still running.

And too many people are getting rich off the migration to admit that it's a peril. The money that fuels political campaigns tends to come from people who prosper from rampant growth and development. They cannot conceive of a place where these things would be controlled or, God forbid, halted.

Ironically, many who are suggesting such remedies were once migrants themselves. They see Florida becoming a place very much like the one they fled, and they'd like to prevent that from happening.

So now you want to slam the door? reply the guys in the suits; now that you've got your piece of paradise, you want to lock out the others, is that it?

Exactly. Because the alternative is to be overrun, choked and bankrupted; to destroy the very natural beauty that attracted all these people in the first place; to let the hordes keep coming until there's nowhere to put them—and then let our children and grandchildren worry about what to do next.

Damn right we should slam the door, or at least put a shoulder to it.

Gas-tax veto wisely brakes development

May 9, 1990

Lots of people are lambasting Gov. Martinez for vetoing the proposed four-cent gasoline tax, which would have provided several hundred million dollars for road projects.

The critics say the governor's veto was irresponsible. They say it will hurt the economy by obstructing "growth management."

Translation: Without new roads, it's harder for developers to get new projects approved. It's no mystery why the most vocal supporters of the gas tax were road contractors, builders and chambers of commerce.

Maybe the governor didn't believe Floridians wanted the tax, or maybe he truly felt the money would be spent "unwisely and inappropriately." Either way, the veto was the right thing to do.

In what dream world do the gas-tax proponents dwell? It must be a fairy-tale place, where all construction contracts are awarded wisely, where the work is completed within budget, without scandal and always on time.

Where is this magical land? It's not Florida, that's for sure.

The Department of Transportation has suffered through some inglorious budget screwups. In 1988, $700 million in projects had to be canceled or scaled down. Last year the department came up $116 million short for purchasing rights-of-way. The Martinez administration deserves blame for chaotic mismanagement, but at least the governor this year had the sense not to give DOT more money to lose.

It's bad enough that most projects cost millions over budget, and drag months and even years past deadline. The worst part is: By the time these roads get finished, they are already obsolete.

For example, we've been dourly forewarned that the interminable widening of I-95 will be hopelessly inadequate, and that shortly after the highway's completion motorists will again find themselves mired in truck traffic. Wonderful.

Sure, many roads already are perilously congested. And yes, some of the bridges are falling down. Is more money the answer? Not if it goes for highway projects designed to fuel more growth—because growth is the root of the problem.

Florida has too many people in too many cars, and the numbers swell by nearly 900 a day. Until we do something drastic to reverse this trend, there's no hope of having a modern, efficient road system. Government is incapable of keeping pace with such an insane migration.

Some of the projects in the doomed transportation bill undoubtedly would have improved transit, cut down on auto pollution and saved lives. Few would argue the need to widen bloody U.S. 27 in Palm Beach County.

However, prudent taxpayers might question other big-ticket items that would have received funds from the gas tax. For example, would the city of Fort Lauderdale really grind to a halt if A1A were not rebuilt to accommodate commercial development along the beach? This seems an odd priority, considering the plight of less glamorous neighborhoods where people can't even get a simple pothole patched.

Another dubious item was the state's plan to purchase the Sawgrass Expressway, which (like Metrorail) is now being called successful because it's losing fewer millions of dollars than it once did.

Having paid for the Sawgrass once (and for the criminal prosecutions that followed), Broward residents would have been forced to pay again with the gas tax, this time joined by other drivers. That's not progress, it's larceny.

If the Martinez veto ultimately means less road construction for a while, that's not so bad. The worst traffic jams in Florida are caused by road projects that never seem to end.

All of us love to drive on fast-moving, freshly paved freeways, but they don't stay that way very long. They fill up, slow down and clog. The gas tax would have accelerated, not halted, this phenomenon.

Besides, there is something to be said for sitting bumper-to-bumper and contemplating the mess we've made of this state. The real problem isn't roads, and most people know it.

Finally, a leader admits growth is choking state

September 4, 1991

Last week, Lt. Gov. Buddy MacKay uttered one of the most stunning comments ever to exit the lips of a Florida politician.

"In the past," he said, "we've had a policy of trying to stimulate growth. We measured our success by the numbers of people who moved into the state. We can no longer continue to do that."

What refreshing blasphemy! Finally, somebody in elected office has the guts to admit that Florida is drowning in its own humanity.

Every crisis facing the state—water, pollution, crime, health care, traffic, and budget—is the result of too many people, too few resources and gutless leadership. The quality of life is deteriorating in direct correlation with population growth, but until lately you could find only a handful of Florida politicians willing to come out and say so.

More was always better. To challenge that philosophy was to jeopardize hefty campaign contributions from banks, builders and utilities. Unthinkable! That's why officeholders always talk about "managing" growth instead of stopping it.

With the state government practically broke, the Chiles administration is promoting the theme of "growing smarter." Translation: Help! What do we do now!

The statistics are chilling. Each day, more than 900 people stampede to Florida, and that's not counting illegal aliens. Think of it as adding two entire cities the size of Hialeah every year.

Every day, more than 300 acres of green space are paved for shopping malls and subdivisions. Planners say that keeping up with such expansion requires two new miles of road, two new classrooms, two new prison beds, two new cops and two new schoolteachers hired each day.

In other words, there's no way to keep pace. Nine hundred newcomers a day is insane and ultimately suicidal. Stopping the flow will take imagination and a radical change in the way we promote the state.

Pro-growthers say Florida's got plenty of space to grow—just look out the window when you're on an airplane! And it's true, you can actually see some empty green patches in the center of the state. Unfortunately, that's not where most new residents want to go.

Until now, people who've migrated here were foolishly allowed to settle any place they wanted. Not surprisingly, the coastal cities were overrun—first Jacksonville, Miami and Fort Lauderdale, now Boca Raton, Tampa and Fort Myers. A big mess. Glorified human ant farms.

One smart way for the Chiles administration to modify Florida's metastatic growth is to channel it—by decree—toward more thinly populated areas. Absolutely nobody else should be permitted to settle in Miami until North Florida fills up. It's only fair.

Consider that the density of Pinellas County (anchored by St. Petersburg) is about 3,055 people per square mile, the worst in the state. Broward is second with about 1,026 people per square mile, and Dade is third at 958 per square mile. No wonder the homicide rate is so high.

Now think of Liberty County. Tucked snugly in the Panhandle and bordered by the misty Apalachicola River, Liberty County has the lowest density in Florida—about six people for every square mile. Paradise!

Or Lafayette County, kissed by the quiet Suwannee—and only 10 human beings per mile of riverside. Or spring-fed Gilchrist County, which grows some of the world's juiciest watermelons, and does it with only 22 people per square mile.

Why do they deserve all the peace and quiet? It's time for rural Florida to carry an honest share of growth's burden. Think of it as a redistribution of wealth.

Starting tomorrow, Liberty County should take at least 100 of Florida's 900 daily new arrivals. Sprinkle the remainder in Lafayette, Gilchrist, Wakulla, Calhoun, DeSoto and so on.

Give those folks a taste of what we're experiencing down here, and you won't hear any fuzzy debates about "growth management." They'll vote to close the borders.

Guns-for-all law one way to end congestion

May 20, 1993

Rep. Al Lawson sparked a small uproar last week by proposing that every household in Florida should be required to have a gun, and that every Floridian should be trained to shoot.

The man seemed dead serious. He talked of introducing a guns-for-all law during the upcoming special session on, fittingly, prisons. "I don't see any option for the people but for them to bear arms," he said. "Every house would have a gun."

Obviously Lawson isn't from South Florida (he's from Tallahassee), but it's still hard to understand how an elected official could be so grossly uninformed about the demographics of crime. Miami has armed itself to the teeth, but only occasionally does a citizen manage to shoot a criminal. Usually it's a spouse, child, neighbor or pal who gets wasted, in moments of anger, drunkenness or stupidity.

My hunch is that Lawson knew the homicide stats very well, and that we underestimated him. Nobody could be daffy enough to believe that saturating rough neighborhoods with more guns will reduce crime. I think Lawson's true aim was to reduce population, a worthy goal.

Florida's got too many people, yet continues to grow at an insane pace. Virtually every major social crisis stems from overcrowding— crime, pollution, gridlock, failing schools, you name it. The state's going broke trying to provide for its 13 million residents, and the thousands more who arrive permanently each week.

Nothing seems to scare them off, either. Not the publicity about drugs and street violence. Not the specter of another killer hurricane. Not even the fact that Madonna and Mickey Rourke both live down here. People keep coming anyway.

Most politicians are resigned to the notion that Florida will grow until it bursts at the seams, and nothing can be done. Lawson is different. He's come up with a surefire way to thin the herd. Putting a gun in every home would be radical, but effective.

Now embroiled in controversy, Lawson is backing off. An aide insists that the lawmaker was misunderstood: He doesn't really think everybody must have a gun, especially if they don't want to.

Lawson shouldn't give up so quickly. A guns-for-all law could be promoted politically as helping the average Joe fight back, where the cops and the courts have failed. Among crime-weary citizens, the plan would strike a patriotic chord. A chicken in every pot, a Glock in every nightstand!

Conservatives from both parties would rally to Lawson's side. The NRA would canonize him. He'd get invited on *Rush Limbaugh*. The Legislature, cowed by Lawson's newfound celebrity, would probably ignore the pleas of police organizations and pass the law.

The results would be instantaneous. With a gun in every house, the murder rate would skyrocket, eventually offsetting the influx of new residents. Lawson's firearms-training program would pay dividends, too, as Floridians would be shooting each other with unprecedented accuracy.

The bloodbath would make headlines worldwide, putting a minor dent in our tourist trade. However, that would be balanced by sunny economic news: Funeral homes, casket makers and florists would enjoy a sales boom.

Undoubtedly, Lawson's gun policy would make Florida a much less congested place. Traffic would improve dramatically, as would highway etiquette. Those long lines at the post office would be a thing of the past. And it would get much easier to find good seats at the Marlins games.

For years, the Legislature has unsuccessfully tried to cope with Florida's population explosion. Why not let Al Lawson take a shot at growth management?

Overcrowding solution: Pay folks to leave

September 8, 1994

The nations of the world are meeting in Cairo to tackle the crisis of global overpopulation. Here in Florida the problem isn't the birth rate, it's the arrival rate.

No matter how crowded and crime-ridden the place gets, people keep coming. That's because most of them are leaving places that are equally crowded and crime-ridden, but without the sunshine and beaches.

Currently Florida's population is growing at a net rate of about 753 persons per day, which is manifestly insane. These aren't rafters or boat people, but American migrants in U-hauls and station wagons and minivans.

Most of them will end up working the popcorn machines at Wayne's World, or in some other low-paying, service-sector job. But still they come.

Each year Florida gets enough new residents to fill a city more populous than Tampa. Not even sky-high homicide rates put a dent in the problem. The challenge is to offset the unending influx of arrivals by aggressively encouraging others to move out.

One way of spurring departures is to scare the pants off people, but that's the job of the media, not government. Besides, residents of Florida aren't nearly as intimidated by crime as are tourists.

A juicier incentive (and a time-honored ritual in Tallahassee) is to give money away. Lawmakers do it routinely for special interests—this time they could do for the good of the whole state:

Pay people to move out.

Why not? When a plane is overbooked, the airline offers free tickets to anyone willing to give up a seat. Works like a charm.

Imagine Florida as a humongous jumbo jet, packed with 13 million restless passengers. Plenty of families would deplane if we made the right offer—say $10,000 cash. Call it a buyout, residential severance or a "relocation bonus."

Here's how it might work: After moving elsewhere, mail a copy of your Florida driver's license to Tallahassee, along with proof that you've bought or rented a place in another state. Presto—Florida cuts you a nice fat check.

If 275,000 folks were persuaded to depart annually (to match the 275,000-plus new arrivals), the payout would total $2.7 billion. That's expensive, but in the long run it's a tax saver.

Think of the future expressways, airports, transit systems, hospitals, schools, jails and landfills that won't need to be built if Florida's population levels off. Think of the resurgence of tourist dollars, once we get a handle on growth-related social problems.

Politicians won't admit Florida is overpopulated. To do so would offend too many campaign contributors—developers, bankers, real-estate firms—who make their fortunes drawing new settlers here in the largest possible numbers.

More is better, growth is good! In no region is the credo more religiously followed than South Florida, which has become so urbanized and perilous that tourists stay away by the millions, and longtime residents bail out in droves.

The rest of the state faces the same gloomy fate, if drastic measures aren't taken soon.

Clean high-tech industries aren't attracted to places with runaway crime, bursting schools and a steadily declining quality of life. Corporate recruiters already have a devil of time selling Florida to young executives with families.

Depopulation is the only answer—not kicking people out; rather, presenting them with a generous opportunity to leave.

Ideally, we'd combine the relocation bonus with a stiff entry cap: Nobody gets across the Georgia border until somebody else leaves.

We'd "wait-list" newcomers, just like the airlines do.

More crime, traffic jams? Bring 'em on!

February 4, 1996

Weird but true: In Jacksonville, an extravaganza called "Millionth Mania" was recently held to "celebrate" the area's one millionth new resident.

As if this were a good thing, something to be desired.

South Floridians can only shake their heads in puzzlement. We stopped celebrating about three million newcomers ago. Today, ascending population in Dade, Broward and Palm Beach are curtly noted and often received with quiet dismay.

In Jacksonville, they shot off fireworks on the river, while Barbara Eden and Frankie Valli entertained. But not everyone was jumping for joy.

Mike Webster, a native Miamian, fled to North Florida in 1980. Now 39, the Jacksonville yacht broker is a founding member of a small but feisty cell of objectors called the Florida League Against "Progress."

FLAP has no dues, no officers, no membership rolls and no meetings. What it does have is a blunt and plainly articulated position:

That growth for growth's sake is reckless, and that all Floridians are paying the price in a declining quality of life: crime, traffic gridlock, overcrowded schools, more taxes.

Years ago, FLAP gained modest attention by distributing delightfully seditious bumper stickers that said: LEAVING FLORIDA? TAKE A FRIEND!

Understandably, Webster was chagrined when his adopted hometown began to boast about swelling to one million residents. It was the same greed-head mentality that had turned South Florida into a parking lot.

So fervid was Jacksonville's yearning to reach its "magnificent milestone" that the city fudged the numbers. Duval County, which defines metropolitan Jacksonville, has only about 700,000 people. Therefore, promoters of "Millionth Mania" were compelled to include in their arithmetic the combined censuses of Duval, Baker, Nassau, Clay and St. Johns counties.

Technically, it was "northeastern Florida" that two weeks ago welcomed its one millionth resident. Mike Webster says he was no less alarmed.

He banged out an irreverent press release that was pretty much ignored by the region's mainstream media. That's too bad, because in it he enunciated what many frustrated Floridians are feeling.

"For places like Jacksonville," Webster wrote, "the question of growth is not one of right or wrong, but rather of addiction. We have worshipped the lord of growth. We have multiplied, now we must become fruitful."

Webster is no New Age granola-head. A self-described conservative Democrat, he was until recently a loyal member of the NRA. He doesn't worry about endangered panthers so much as farmers, river men and others whose futures are jeopardized by overdevelopment.

"Much of what passes for progress isn't," Webster says. He includes himself among the threatened: "If our marine resources collapse, the bottom falls out of the boat business."

And while FLAP stops shy of advocating a cap on growth, Webster has dryly suggested that Florida ought to start "depromoting" itself to slow the influx of new arrivals.

Which got me thinking: What better way for a city to spook prospective residents than to publicize (with fireworks!) its own overcrowding.

Is it possible, I wondered, that FLAP infiltrated Jacksonville's chamber of commerce? Was Webster himself secretly responsible for the big "celebration"?

Though he denies involvement, the phrase "Millionth Mania" certainly has the sly ring of parody. Perhaps it wasn't the hokey, misguided boosterism I first thought. Perhaps it was a prank—a perversely brilliant prank—meant to scare people away from Duval County.

And it'll probably work.

Court's message to home buyers: Trust no one

April 18, 1996

By overturning the fraud convictions of four developers, a U.S. appeals court this week affirmed a common-law doctrine of Florida land sales known as Fornicat Emptor:

Let the buyer be screwed.

The court dismissed the case against former executives of General Development Corp., one of the state's most prolific land-scamming operations. Judges said there was insufficient evidence the men broke federal law.

Which is ironic, considering that GDC had long ago pleaded guilty, and two of the four indicted big shots had tried to do the same.

"Construing the evidence at its worst . . . it is true that these men behaved badly," the appellate court wrote. "[But] the fraud statutes do not cover all behavior which strays from the ideal; Congress has not yet criminalized all sharp conduct, manipulative acts, or unethical transactions."

Not exactly a ringing character endorsement, but a legal victory nonetheless.

The core of the case dates to the '70s and '80s, when GDC was vigorously marketing Florida property to out-of-state buyers. In its heyday, the company sold thousands of homesites and tract houses in "planned communities" such as Port Malabar and Port St. Lucie.

GDC's scurrilous sales techniques became legendary. Bare lots were sold to aspiring snowbirds for three to five times the true resale value. Waterfront sometimes meant swamp front.

And when customers asked to see their land, the company invited them down for a free tour—but only if they first signed away their right to cancel the contract.

GDC's most ambitious swindle targeted home buyers. The company used its own appraisers to jack up the value of its houses. Customers, most of whom financed through GDC, didn't learn about the price gap until they tried to resell.

Couples who'd bought a retirement home for $65,000 found out the hard way that its market value was $40,000. Complaints began piling up.

Finally the feds indicted the company in 1990. GDC pleaded guilty to conspiracy and pledged restitution. Chairman David F. Brown and President Robert F. Ehrling also agreed to plead guilty.

Within a month, GDC filed for bankruptcy, but the case wasn't done. U.S. District Judge Lenore Nesbitt surprised prosecutors and defendants by rejecting the original plea deal, and a subsequent one. She wanted tougher sentences and stronger terms of restitution.

Trial began in 1991. Nine months later, a Miami jury convicted Ehrling, Brown, Richard Reizen and Tore DeBella. Nesbitt sentenced them to prison, and ordered each to pony up $500,000 to defrauded GDC customers.

What seemed like a victory for the little guy didn't turn out that way. Many home buyers who'd sought compensation ended up with a small check and securities.

Meanwhile, the ex-executives appealed their convictions, leading to Tuesday's dismissal by a three-judge panel in Atlanta.

While agreeing that GDC had overvalued its homes, the judges ruled that "people of ordinary prudence" could have investigated the marketplace before purchasing.

In other words, the customers were at fault—not GDC's bosses. It's a coldhearted view, but the reasoning has logic.

Basically, the judges are asserting what many of us have known for generations: that anyone buying real estate in Florida should trust no one and assume the worst.

Lawyers for the defendants have tried to put a more positive spin on the court's ruling, claiming it vindicates the late GDC as a fair and honorable firm.

And never mind about those guilty pleas.

A gift for dad who has it all in his backyard

December 8, 1996

If you live in a Lennar development, here's the perfect holiday gift for Dad: a shiny new backhoe, so he can find out what's buried in your yard.

The residents of Hampshire Homes in Miramar already have watched as 260 truckloads of tires and trash were hauled out of the infamous sinkhole that opened up there.

Now, three former subcontractors for Lennar Homes have come forward claiming that company officials told them to bury illegal trash at 19 construction sites in Dade, Broward and Palm Beach counties.

According to the subcontractors, the debris included household appliances, auto parts, batteries and even a fuel drum.

Last week, the president of Lennar Homes said the company never ordered anyone to bury junk beneath its developments, because that would've been against the law! "Some fuel drums might have been buried," Stuart Miller said, "but it was not done under company direction."

For alarmed homeowners, the most pressing issue isn't who ordered the trash buried, but what exactly got buried where.

Lennar doesn't offer random excavations of its subdivisions, although the company promises to haul off any unsightly debris that might surface unexpectedly.

That's fine if your dog happens to dig up a rusty Maytag near the hibiscus or a seeping 12-volt Delco under the swing set. But what if the junk is buried too deeply for Fido?

The former Lennar subcontractors say washing machines and other secret goodies are interred beneath FPL power lines in the upscale Coral Springs developments of Turtle Run and Whispering Woods.

At Tamarac's Kings Point, they said, the mother lode of debris is entombed within the banks of lakes.

And somewhere beneath the Images of Pembroke Pointe is the not-so-scenic image of a buried fuel drum.

Even if your hobby is archaeology, you probably wouldn't buy a house if you knew it was built above or even adjacent to an underground dump site.

But more than a few Florida developments are. The law allows limited on-site disposal of lumber, tree stumps and nonhazardous construction materials, but some builders bury all sorts of nasty stuff. It's cheaper than paying hauling fees, plus you get to keep the fill.

The sneaky practice was widespread in years past, and almost never disclosed to potential buyers. Lennar would've sold very few houses had Hampshire Homes been straightforwardly advertised as Tierra del Tire Dump or Sinkhole Estates.

Recent headlines have piqued the interest of hundreds of other Lennar customers, who now wonder what's percolating beneath the surface of their neighborhood. Also curious is Florida's attorney general, who has subpoenaed records from all Lennar developments dating back to 1980.

The company president says the files weren't always meticulously maintained. That could make it difficult to determine which subdivisions are at risk.

For concerned homeowners, even a small backhoe would be a big help. Lennar should provide them free to anybody brave enough to buy one of its houses.

That way there will be no guesswork or suspense. Once you notice the shrubs blackening or the patio furniture starting to melt, you can dig up the lawn and find out what the heck's buried down there.

Apparently Lennar isn't that eager for you to know. So, at least for this season, it's up to Santa to bring Dad that backhoe—and maybe a lightweight metal detector for Mom, too.

And don't forget the kids. Just imagine the joy on Christmas Day if they woke up to find cute little Geiger counters in their stockings!

Our dream, our nightmare

September 13, 1998

The least startling headline of the last few days: The Sierra Club has rated South Florida one of the most blighted places in the country for unchecked urban sprawl.

Among the major metropolitan areas, Broward County ranks ninth nationally in annihilating of wetlands, farms and forests since 1990. That statistic is surprising only because Broward didn't take first place— imagine eight other regions actually doing a worse job of planning.

Elsewhere in Florida, Tampa ranks 14 and Miami-Dade is 18 on the Sierra list. Nationally, the top spot for runaway urban sprawl is fast-mushrooming Atlanta.

Losing land to development was only one factor considered by the Sierra Club when evaluating the impact of metropolitan expansion. The group also looked at pollution, water consumption, traffic congestion and population.

The critical yardstick is density, the ratio of people to land mass, and few places are as densely packed as South Florida. Nowhere is the ugliness more evident than southwestern Broward, where a drive along I-75 reveals little but rooftops, as far as the eye can see.

If the torrid pace of paving continues, Pembroke Pines, Coral Springs and other hot spots will eventually make Hialeah look like the Garden of Eden.

According to census data and University of Florida economic research, by 1997 Miami-Dade's population added up to 2,070,473 people living in an area of 2,109 square miles—or about 982 persons per square mile.

By contrast, Broward had 1,439,663 residents living within a much smaller area, 1,220 square miles. That works out to a nerve-jangling 1,180 persons per square mile, the human equivalent of living in a beehive.

The true elbow-to-elbow density of both counties is actually higher, when you eliminate their vast, unpopulated Everglades acreage.

Only one place in the state is more statistically overchoked: Pinellas County, the St. Petersburg/Clearwater area, where more than 2,700 people are shoehorned into every square mile. If they were rats, they'd probably be gnawing each others' limbs off.

Inevitably, growth has slowed dramatically in Pinellas, as it has in Miami-Dade—not only because these places are running out of room, but because people are running away. In large numbers, they're fleeing the woes and headaches of rapid urbanization—crime, traffic, taxes, sardine-can classrooms.

Where are the disenchanted going? Broward, according to population experts. Then Palm Beach, Martin and St. Lucie along the east coast; Lee, Collier, Charlotte and Sarasota on the west coast.

That's the great, bitter irony. About 800 people a day move to Florida in pursuit of a dream that's being obliterated by their own footprints. It's a dream they're destined to chase from one end of the state to the other, trying to escape all the other dreamers.

Thousands have fled Miami-Dade for Broward, and now Broward is more densely congested than Dade. In a few years, the same thing will likely happen to Palm Beach County, and hordes will flee there in search of someplace more sane and livable.

An advanced civilization might produce leaders who would learn from the foolhardiness of others and take steps not to inflict the same ills on their own communities.

This doesn't happen in South Florida, where politicians customarily cave in to developers at the expense of wise long-range planning. The result is what you see, an unbroken panorama of greed.

Palm Beach County is destined to become another Miami-Dade, just as surely as Collier is destined to become another Pinellas. Nobody has learned a damn thing, which is symptomatic of another type of density crisis.

The density of certain skulls.

Vanishing Florida

The bombs of progress blast crater in nature

August 6, 1985

From the road you can't even see it.

The buffer is North Key Largo hammock, dense and darkly tangled, quiet on a summer morning. The mosquitoes are exuberant, and there are also snakes, so it is best to keep walking.

Suddenly, the pristine tamarind and mahogany end, and the sun strikes the eye harshly. Ahead the land is bare, bleached and broken, as if a giant's claw had raked away a hundred acres of forest.

It looks like a bomb exploded here, and it did. It was called Port Bougainville.

Three years ago the fancy advertising promised "the romance of the Mediterranean and the freedom of the Florida Keys." There would be a yacht club, beaches, lakes, a shopping plaza, a hotel, more than 2,500 condominiums, all with "the charm of a painting by Cezanne."

Try Salvador Dali on a bad day.

What you see now is an obscene moonscape of pits and boulders. The sales models are boarded up, the quaint unfinished plaza is a pastel ghost town. The bulldozers have been towed away, and some of the trucks and trams are up on blocks. Castor bean and other garbage weeds flourish where hardwoods once grew.

Construction ceased on Port Bougainville more than a year ago when its financing collapsed. The work that began here was mostly done by dynamite, blowing craters in the hammock to create phony lakes upon which to sell "waterfront units."

Touring the 406 acres now, one might guess that the controversial mega-condo has gone belly-up. The polite term is that the project is "in receivership."

The bank foreclosed on the developer and the developer sued the bank and now there are lawyers crawling all over the place, which means we're talking about a serious, long-term mess.

Ironic, considering the development's history—approved after months of scandalous publicity, bureaucratic hand-wringing and celebrated compromise. While environmentalists battled stridently in court, everyone else signed off on Port Bougainville—the state Department of Community Affairs, the South Florida Regional Planning Council and, of course, Monroe County's zoo of a planning department.

The project is fine, they said. A boon for the economy, they said. Environmentally sound, they said.

A darn big improvement, they all said.

Now they say: Hey, we did our best. Nobody dreamed the deal would disintegrate.

But don't think for a minute the project is dead—this is Florida, remember? This type of development is like the Frankenstein monster, a lurching clod kept on life support forever. Every so often, a new genius shows up with a new scheme for resurrection.

Ten years ago, Port Bougainville was known as Solarelle—another developer, another failure. Years from now, after the current fiasco is sorted out, the project probably will have a new owner and a new name and a new theme. Today the Mediterranean, tomorrow Venice.

And, as always, an elaborate public show will be made of trying to save as many trees and birds and butterflies as possible, which is not easy when you're using dynamite.

On Sunday, a single snowy egret searched for minnows from the shore of a jagged, blasted-out creek. A ground dove pecked for berries on a disused limestone roadbed. Yellow butterflies darted above the remaining buttonwoods but veered clear of the gashed land.

Nobody wanted Port Bougainville to turn out this way, but it did. Nobody in government had the guts to say stop.

It's classic for South Florida. Where else would they even agree to stick one of the largest-ever condo projects between a national wildlife sanctuary and the continent's only living coral reef?

Each officious drone who said yes to this extravaganza ought to be forced to spend a day on North Key Largo, walking the property with his own children.

Explaining the scars, the rubble, the whole atrocious legacy.

Pristine oasis may go to waste in trash crisis

November 8, 1985

As the last wild traces of South Florida disappear under the dredge and bulldozer, it's a good time to weigh the fate of the Pond Apple Slough.

That such a place has survived the blind rapacity of Broward County's development is both a marvel and mystery. Stubbornly it thrives, a steamy oasis wedged between two of the busiest and ugliest thoroughfares ever built, State Road 84 and U.S. 441.

Perhaps one thing that has saved the 200-acre gem is its invisibility not only from the roads, but from the South New River Canal, which forms its southern boundary.

Hemmed in, shut off, nearly forgotten, the freshwater swamp and its adjacent cypress forest is one of the most pristine Florida habitats left on the peninsula. Beyond the drooping pond apples are royal palms, coco plums, leather ferns and sprawling ficuses, ancient giants draped with moss, wild orchids and airplants.

Penetrable only by canoe and foot, the Pond Apple Slough is a refuge for bobcats, raccoons, squirrels and gray foxes; snakes, alligators and endangered crocodiles; hawks, ospreys, kestrels and other birds of prey. The animals have adapted remarkably well to the swamp's clamorous borders, and even to the roar of 727s passing low on approach to the Fort Lauderdale-Hollywood airport.

But soon there will be new neighbors: Interstate 595, arcing high overhead, and a massive garbage incinerator, with two enormous land-fills. The highway is an aesthetic nuisance but nonintrusive; the incinerator is something else.

The battle has been predictably emotional, with homeowners and environmentalists on one side, county officials on the other. Beginning Tuesday at the Davie-Cooper City Library, state officials will hold nine days of hearings about the new garbage plant, and one of the main issues is its effect on the rare slough.

The swamp itself is on state property, technically protected. But one of the landfills is planned for 200 acres of county property, now sawgrass, which borders the tall cypress. Environmentalists fear poisonous runoff from the ash and refuse will decimate the swamp.

George Fitzpatrick, chairman of Broward's Environmental Quality Control Board, says the landfill "will have a very negative effect. . . . You shouldn't build incinerators with landfills in a swamp."

Adds naturalist Woody Wilkes: "It will destroy this whole area. There's no way to get around it."

Faced with a mountainous garbage crisis, Broward is determined to build new incinerators; it's already issued $521 million worth of bonds to finance two of them.

Tom Henderson, director of resource recovery, says the county has spent a fortune studying the pond apple habitat and is committed to saving the slough and restoring long-lost waterways near the dumps.

"The area's going to be much better than what's there," says Henderson.

He also says the dump site nearest the Pond Apple Slough won't be needed until the turn of the century, if ever, and that all ash would be deposited on a thick layer of plastic to prevent leeching into the precious groundwater.

Opponents say that's not enough. They view the incinerator as a fountain of rancid air, and they want modern emission controls on its smoke-stack. They also want its ash and rubble trucked out west; in other words, no landfills near the swamp.

The classic problem with dumps is that nobody wants one in their own backyard. Trouble is, this just isn't any old backyard; it's one of the few remaining glimpses of Florida as it was a century ago, a gentle canoe trip into the past.

Surely the state can settle this controversy by demanding strict, enforceable measures to save the Pond Apple Slough and the air it breathes. A dump is one kind of political legacy; a wilderness is another.

It would be a tragedy to lose it to a 40-foot hill of burnt slop.

Sewage charges latest outrage at ocean reef

December 16, 1985

The idea of dumping raw sewage into the waters of the John Pennekamp Coral Reef State Park is so vile that it makes the blood boil.

This month, the wondrous park's 25th anniversary, the Ocean Reef Club in North Key Largo was indicted on 346 counts of allegedly emptying its toilets straight into the ocean over the continent's only living coral reef.

If the charges are true, this is by far the worst in the club's long history of flagrant abuses. Of all the developments in the Florida Keys, Ocean Reef Inc. has been the most prolific violator of environmental laws. Its motto might as well be: Let's do it until we get caught.

The place is legendary: Canals appear overnight to create instant "waterfront" lots; protected mangroves vanish in the darkness. The investigatory files on Ocean Reef stuff several drawers at the state Department of Environmental Regulation and the U.S. Army Corps of Engineers.

Yet sanctions against the resort have, until now, been laughably weak. The largest fine was $50,000 stretched out to five payments in five years—hardly the sort of penalty that teaches a lesson.

Much is made of the fact that Ocean Reef is a haven for the rich and famous. Wealthy or not, the people who live there had nothing to do with the sewage scandal. In fact, their complaints helped trigger the investigation by the Environmental Protection Agency.

"We're shocked by what happened, and we're angry," says Barrett Wendell, president of an Ocean Reef property owner's group. "The reef is too valuable an asset to be treated this way."

"We're the victims—not the people perpetrating this," adds Charles Howell, another resident.

Ironically, Ocean Reef homeowners had been negotiating with the developers to buy out the utilities, including the long-troubled sewage system. Last summer a tentative agreement was reached, but suddenly Ocean Reef Inc. changed its mind and decided to keep the sewer plants.

For many homeowners, this month's pollution indictment was a bitter and shameful moment. "We felt like we were indicted, too," Howell says. Some members fired off a letter to financier Carl Lindner, the principal owner, condemning the company for such a "despicable" act.

Says resident Clayton Kolstad: "We think it stinks."

And stink is the word for it. According to the indictment, raw fecal matter was purposely spewed into a slender waterway known as Channel Cay. From there tidal currents swept the putrid effluent into the Atlantic and out over the endangered offshore reef.

The dumping allegedly took place between Nov. 1, 1982, and Nov. 10, 1983, but several residents claim it actually went on much longer. Ocean Reef Inc. has declined to discuss the charges.

Up to now, the club—whose membership is full of political heavyweights—has treated the state and Army Corps like pesky gnats.

But the EPA is the big league, and this indictment is criminal. Ocean Reef's president, vice president and utilities director face a possible year in prison for each of the 346 counts, while the development conceivably could be hit with an $8.6 million fine.

If the club has a lick of common sense, the case will be settled before it ever gets to trial. A fine will be paid, nobody will do a day in jail, and the company will get back to the business of squeezing every square inch of profit out of its North Key Largo holdings.

Ocean Reef Inc. can afford a hefty fine: A couple of years ago, one undeveloped waterfront lot sold for $900,000.

Prosecutors ought to shoot for a seven-figure settlement. Big money is the only thing that gets arrogant polluters' attention, and it's the only thing that will make them think twice before opening a "magic valve" again.

As one furious Ocean Reef resident put it: "I don't know what kind of mind would pump raw sewage into a canal where children swam and snorkeled and boated. It's horrible."

Margaritaville marshlands: Wasting away?

October 27, 1986

The most tranquil part of this crazed island is unknown even to some of the locals—407 nearly virgin acres of mangrove, mahogany and marshlands. The Salt Ponds.

In a place where real estate is as precious as Mel Fisher's gold, it would seem a miracle that the ponds haven't already been drained, dredged, paved and plastered. Unfortunately, that sad day might be coming. A developer named Larry Marks has fought an extended court battle for the right to put up 1,100 units here, and he says he'll do it.

In the old days, a familiar corps of tenacious environmentalists would have stood alone against the development, and probably lost. This fight is different. Opposition to the Salt Ponds project is broader, and it includes a famous voice that carries clear to Tallahassee.

Jimmy Buffett can look out at the ponds from the porch of his home. He has explored by canoe and found egrets, herons, ospreys, even an eagle. "It's beautiful in there," the singer says.

Buffett doesn't think this is a suitable location for a thousand condominiums or apartments. "Affordable housing," the developer calls it. "Monstrosity" is the term preferred by critics. The Key West City Commission meets Tuesday to discuss the plan. Tonight Buffett will sing at a "Save the Salt Ponds" rally at a restaurant on Duval Street.

This is not the best of news for the developer; Buffett is a popular fellow with a huge following here. The singer already has angered Larry Marks by suggesting that one of Marks' other big condo projects should be used as a bombing target by the Navy.

Though he usually avoids Key West politics like a tropical plague, Buffett says the Salt Ponds are too important to ignore. "We've got enough condos. I mean, how many people can live on this island?"

The strategy to save the Salt Ponds doesn't include another prolonged legal slugfest with Larry Marks—except as a last resort. The new plan is to get the state of Florida to purchase the wetlands outright. There are many who think that Marks would be willing to sell his portion, for the right price. Both the City Commission and the Florida Audubon Society say it's a good idea, and last week the state took the first step toward placing the Salt Ponds on its list of lands to be acquired for preservation.

The problems are time and money: It might take years before the funds are available. In the meantime, the bulldozers could roll.

Because the Salt Ponds are so remote—a verdant pocket near the airport's runway, far from the Conch Train's view—most tourists and many Key Westers have never visited the beautiful tidal marsh. Buffett says it can't be saved until people know what they're saving.

"It's the same ploy we used with the manatees," he says. "Nobody knew what manatees were, seven years ago."

Buffett's importance in a local controversy like this is inestimable. No other personality is so instantly identified with Key West; no one has done more to popularize the island's charms. If anyone can mobilize Margaritaville, it is he. High-rises have no place in Buffett's lyrical view of paradise.

"If you want to make it look like Fort Lauderdale," he says, "then, hell, go live in Fort Lauderdale."

Still, it's one thing to pick up a guitar and quite another to stalk into City Hall and make a speech. "I promised my grandfather that I would never get into politics," he says with a groan.

With enough attention, the Salt Ponds can be saved. All it takes is money. The 407 acres are divided among more than two dozen land-holders, all of whom deserve compensation. Exactly how much compensation will be a matter of some dispute.

The crucial thing is for the city to keep the ponds just as they are until negotiations begin. Buffett, who knows the Keys too well, has a good idea: "They should have Vanna White come down and all the developers gather around the Wheel of Fortune—and we'll all play."

If only it were that easy.

Feds must save wetlands from development

November 19, 1986

The destruction of West Dade's wetlands has been momentarily slowed by a bunch of pesky federal bureaucrats who seem to think water quality is more important than new strip malls and townhouses.

At issue is the fate of the Bird Road Everglades Basin, a dozen square miles of marsh along Krome Avenue west of Kendall.

For a long time developers have been slobbering over the prospect of invading and paving this preserve—a notion recently endorsed by county commissioners, who once again have rolled over compliantly at the whiff of money.

This time the money came in hefty election-time checks from developers, their attorneys and members of the Latin Builders Association—those who most eagerly want to bulldoze the wetlands.

To no one's surprise, the landowner's attorney insists that West Dade's Glades aren't worth saving because the land has little environmental value. That this unsupported assertion contradicts the view of virtually every expert public agency doesn't seem to matter to the county commission, which never lets facts get in the way of a favor.

The Bird Road basin and surrounding wetlands feed the Biscayne Aquifer, which filters and supplies our drinking water. Originally the area was closed to development under the county's master plan. Last summer, heavily lobbied by building interests, the commission voted to open several tracts.

Leading the charge was Commissioner Jorge Valdes, who's never met a developer he didn't like. The developers like him, too. Building interests contributed heavily to Valdes' $471,000 re-election campaign this year.

In an inspired, if not transparent, bit of strategy, the commissioner lobbied to build a new high school in the Everglades basin.

It's one thing to indignantly fight the construction of a shopping center, or a high-rise, or a tacky warehouse—but a school? A school is for children. A school is patriotic. Who could argue that we don't need new schools?

No one, certainly. The question is: Of 95 possible sites for the high school, why was the Bird Road Everglades Basin chosen?

The answer is easy—to open up the protected wetlands. You can't have a school in the middle of a marsh. Think of the mosquitoes. Think of the snakes. Think of all that green space just sitting there, not making money.

No, once you have a school, you need a neighborhood to go with it. And you can't very well have a neighborhood without houses and apartments and gas stations and burger joints. This is the history of growth in South Florida.

Proposing a new high school is just a ruse to unlock new territory. It also gives Mayor Steve Clark and other county commissioners something respectable to hide behind when explaining their votes. What's harder to explain is why they ignored the advice of their own environmental staff, and waived all the usual requirements for the new school site.

Luckily, the future of the Glades does not ultimately rest with politicians who obediently kiss the rings of big-time zoning lawyers. It rests with federal officials who take a broader and less predatory view of Florida's withering resources.

The Environmental Protection Agency says the Bird Road basin is a lousy site for a new school. The U.S. Fish and Wildlife Service agrees. So does the National Marine Fisheries Service. They say that the basin, while not pristine, is important enough not to be disturbed.

The issue has gone to the U.S. Army Corps of Engineers, which can kill the project outright, or demand an environmental study that might take years to complete.

As you might suspect, a thorough scientific survey is the last thing county administrators want to see. They've asked the Corps to please just skip all the environmental stuff and approve the new school as fast as possible.

And, just to be sure its letter made sense, the county cleverly let the landowner's lawyer write it.

Ill-conceived landfill plan begets smoke

April 6, 1990

In North Dade, the Munisport landfill is burning, and has been for weeks.

The city of North Miami can't put the fire out because it doesn't have a fire department. Dade County, which has the trucks, apparently doesn't do underground fires.

The adjacent city of North Miami Beach, which is getting smoked out, is now considering a lawsuit to force somebody to extinguish the blaze. It doesn't seem like too much to ask, but this is Munisport, where nothing is simple.

To begin with, it wasn't supposed to be a dump.

Twenty years ago North Miami bought a 350-acre tract from the county with the promise that the land would be used for public recreation. The purchase was financed with a $12 million bond issue, which the taxpayers of North Miami are still paying off.

The original plan called for a swimming pool, tennis courts and two municipal golf courses—rolling emerald hills. Trouble was, no natural hills could be found. So North Miami agreed to allow the developer, Munisport Inc., to dump so-called "clean" fill to raise the elevation to a level suitable for golfers.

As it turned out, what got dumped in the landfill was not always clean—acetone, hospital waste, veterinary remains, chemical drums and, by some accounts, Freon and asbestos.

The perils should have been obvious. Munisport sits next to Florida International University and the Oleta River State Recreation Area. Heavy rains could leach toxins from the landfill into public waters—and that's exactly what happened.

Dumping continued day and night, and hills of waste rose majestically. Years passed, but not a single verdant fairway materialized.

In March 1976, Munisport and the city of North Miami received an after-the-fact permit from the U.S. Army Corps of Engineers to fill 291 acres for a "recreational" facility. Mangroves were to be destroyed. Garbage was to be piled in 103 acres of wetlands.

Lots of people in North Dade got upset. So did the Environmental Protection Agency, and in 1981 it vetoed the Corps permit.

Later Munisport was found to be so contaminated that it was placed on the EPA Superfund cleanup list, and that's where the battle has simmered for years.

The city of North Miami—whose negligence and bungling created the fiasco—has insisted the landfill really isn't so bad. A high-powered Washington law firm was hired to lobby congressmen into pressuring the EPA to lay off.

North Miami said the state was perfectly capable of cleaning the dump without federal supervision. City officials wanted Munisport "delisted" from the Superfund so it could be sold and developed. Yes, developed.

At City Hall there was talk that Hyatt was interested in building a high-rise hotel on the Munisport site (probably as soon as they finished the Hyatt Chernobyl).

Meanwhile the EPA was reporting that the lakes on the dump site showed excessive levels of cyanide and ammonia. The mangroves were tainted with lead and silver. The fish had arsenic and PCBs in levels that posed a cancer risk to human beings. Aquatic life in north Biscayne Bay was threatened by the contaminated runoff.

North Miami's answer to this nauseating litany was to threaten to sue EPA.

On March 18, EPA finally recommended a plan to remove the ammonia from the wetlands at Munisport. Some environmentalists say the proposal is inadequate because it leaves the state with the most crucial task—cleaning up the landfill itself.

Before that can happen, somebody will have to get a hose and put out the fire.

Everyone agrees that Munisport should be cleaned up immediately. The questions are: Who pays for it—and who decides when it's really safe.

Maybe some day it will be a golf course, just like they promised 20 years ago. They can always sell gas masks in the pro shop.

Key plan shows just how low developers go

February 13, 1991

The battle to save Soldier Key isn't finished.

Faced with a rejection by the National Park Service, developers seeking to convert the tiny islet into a pseudo-tropical tourist trap are appealing their case to Washington.

The group includes the folks at Blockbuster Entertainment, who have attached the company's name, logo and slogan ("Wow! What a Difference") to this abominable scheme for exploiting the island.

Though privately held, Soldier Key is located in the protected waters of Biscayne National Park, a few miles south of Cape Florida. The government has tried to purchase the island before, but the owners have always held out for more money. Last year they turned down Uncle Sam's offer of $135,000 and instead sold the option to a Fort Lauderdale-based tour operator, Florida Princess Cruise Line. Initially, the project called for shore-to-shore cabanas, ersatz beaches and a gift shop to sell the sort of tasteful merchandise that heatstroked, booze-addled tourists seem to favor. In the face of a decidedly unenthusiastic response, the developers slightly scaled down their plans for a Soldier Key resort, though it would still be a blight on the bay.

Forget pelicans, porpoises and sea breeze; think cocktail bars, steel drums and limbo madness.

Park superintendent James Sanders has officially notified the promoter that he opposes the day-cruise project for several reasons. A rare sea turtle, the hawksbill, successfully nested on Soldier Key last year for the first time since 1981. The presence of five hundred carousing beachcombers might discourage future visits from the shy, endangered animals.

Beyond the turtle problem is the impact of cruise parties upon the whole park, one of the most ecologically sensitive marine preserves in the country. Soldier Key is the first link in a delicate necklace of small islands that the National Park Service has been acquiring for preservation. Tom Brown, the park system's associate regional director for planning, says that Soldier Key should be "maintained in its natural condition."

Which doesn't include the concrete swimming pool now planned for construction. Opponents, including Everglades Earth First!, plan a protest regatta to the island Feb. 23.

Recently the government substantially hiked its cash offer for Soldier Key, but the option holders didn't accept. Through congressional channels, they are quietly trying to persuade high officials in Washington, including Secretary of Interior Manuel Lujan, to overrule the park service and allow the island to be developed.

Such a reversal would be unusual, but not unprecedented. Blockbuster Entertainment chairman Wayne Huizenga is a wealthy Republican campaign contributor whose phone calls would probably be swiftly returned, were he to express a personal interest in getting the Soldier Key project approved.

Three and one-half acres isn't much to work with, but promoter Robert F. Lambert hopes to make the most of it. An optimistic brochure for

Blockbuster Cruises invites travelers to "our private island in the Bay" for a day of sailing, sunning, swimming, snorkeling and "live calypso music."

Finally! Something to drown out the cries of those pesky seagulls.

The nighttime excursion sounds even more enchanting. I quote from the brochure: "Sailing south through the Biscayne Bay, witness a beautiful sunset as the moon rises over Miami."

That will be a neat trick, getting the moon to come up in the west. We can hardly wait. But there's even more tropical excitement after our ship drops anchor off Soldier Key: "Ashore, guests will be treated to a sumptuous Island luau under the skies and a live native review. Dance to the sounds of our steel drums or see 'how low you can go' in our limbo contest."

How low, indeed. Take a perfectly lovely island and turn it into the Tiki Bar from Hell.

All things considered, we'd rather stay home and rent a movie.

Pipeline crisis could turn Bay into cesspool

June 13, 1993

Think what would happen if your toilet somehow started flushing into your swimming pool. Bubble, bubble, bubble—until the pool was up to the brim: 15,000 gallons of you-know-what.

Now picture 6,000 swimming pools full of the rancid stuff, and imagine that much—90 million gallons—pouring into Biscayne Bay every single day.

That's what will happen if the old sewer pipe running underwater from mainland Miami to Virginia Key breaks. The bay will turn from blue to brown, and we're not talking pastels.

Fearing a Chernobyl-under-the-palms, the Environmental Protection Agency has sued to force Dade to rebuild its disintegrating sewers as soon as possible. Local and state agencies belatedly began brainstorming the crisis a few months ago, but the feds aren't waiting. The situation is that dire.

Two good things might come from the lawsuit. First, a new cross-bay pipeline could be built in time to avoid the catastrophe that would result from the old pipe fracturing.

Second, prosecutors could block most new construction while the sewer system is being rebuilt. Theoretically, more hookups wouldn't be permitted until more capacity is added. At least for a while, growth in Dade might slow to a healthier trickle.

A few no-growth years is the best thing that could happen here. Breathing room is what people need, especially the thousands still struggling to rebuild after Andrew.

Reckless, runaway expansion is what caused the system to fail in the first place. Faithful to the developers who bankroll their campaigns, past county commissioners approved one subdivision after another—tens of thousands of new toilets—even as sewers began to burst, literally.

Thanks to a few corrupted bums, we're now facing a septic eruption that will do for Miami's tourism what Exxon did for bird watching in Alaska.

Disaster could strike any time. The 72-inch pipe across Biscayne Bay is aged and perilously overloaded. Hydrogen sulfide gas (an aromatic product of human waste) is aggressively eating the metal from the inside out.

Much of Dade's waste is treated at Virginia Key so it travels silent and deadly across the bay. In 1992, the grand jury said the Biscayne sewer line was "a time bomb."

For years, the county environmental office has badgered the Water and Sewer Department to start work on a larger pipeline. And, for years, the Water and Sewer people have pondered and hypothesized and written reports on the problem.

Meanwhile, the building frenzy continued. The sewers got more full, and the pipes got more fragile. The most recent failure occurred at Easter, tainting the water from the Julia Tuttle Causeway to the Rickenbacker. And that was a relatively piddling leak, only 20 million gallons.

When the mother lode ruptures, forget about diving, sailing or swimming. Forget about the fish and the manatees. Biscayne Bay will look, and smell, like an immense tropical cesspool.

Fact: Fecal contamination is very bad for tourism. Fact: A moratorium on sewer hookups will be costly to powerful builders.

For one or both of those reasons, a new sewer line will be built across the bay. Pray that the old one holds out until the new one is finished. In the meantime, enjoy the lull.

Because when the new pipe is done, developers will stampede the county seeking thousands and thousands of new sewer hookups. And the commissioners will say . . . yes, yes, yes!

Same old story. Same old you-know-what.

'Revitalization' a threat to Virginia Key

April 3, 1997

The cash-starved city of Miami is again trying to deliver Virginia Key to favored developers and concessionaires.

Under the pretense of "revitalization," nine parcels currently marked for conservation are proposed for rezoning. The result could be hotels, marinas, shops and even houses.

Planners insist the zoning changes are technical corrections that won't affect the character of the island, but there's no reason for optimism. The stewardship of Virginia Key has been one of bungling, neglect and political favoritism.

Practically everything the city touched has turned to failure. The Marine Stadium has been a wreck since Hurricane Andrew. The beach and park on the Atlantic side—refurbished a few years ago at great expense—is now closed, supposedly because of the budget crisis.

It's as if Miami purposely abandoned Virginia Key and let it crumble, in order to stir support for development.

Mayor Joe Carollo has grandiose dreams for reviving the bayfront lagoon area by the Marine Stadium: hotels, restaurants, shops and a Jet Ski extravaganza that would bring needed lease revenues to City Hall.

At least, that's the pitch. In reality, the "technical" rezoning opens the door for transforming the island into another Dinner Key—an aesthetic calamity, and a grab bag for political cronies of commissioners.

For years the city has been aching to carve Virginia Key into a resort. The chief obstacles have been public opposition, and a large, odoriferous sewer plant.

In 1995 commissioners endorsed a preposterous proposal to put an RV park on 153 acres. The "ecologically sensitive" project included 300 motel units, a convenience store and miniature golf.

Voters, who weren't fooled by the city's tree-hugging hype, killed the plan.

This time around, commissioners don't want the public mucking up their big ideas for Virginia Key. Conveniently, rezoning can be accomplished without referendum.

Miami planning chief Jack Luft says there's no reason to worry. The changes, he says, actually will help preserve the island's unspoiled stretches.

Removing the "conservation" designation seems an odd way to protect land, but the city does many odd things at Virginia Key.

Twenty years ago the city leased out prime bayfront to the private Miami Rowing Club. Price: a whopping $100 annually.

Eventually the rowers built an 11,000-square-foot clubhouse, a swimming pool, a banquet hall and bar. In 1987 it was revealed that the club was renting out the facilities, and in one year had collected $147,000.

Guess how much the city got. And when the rowers needed storage space, commissioners generously let them fence off 10,000 square feet of land.

At the time, beet-faced officials denied any connection to the fact that then-City Manager Cesar Odio was a former president and life member of the rowing club.

Another funny coincidence: According to members, security services at the club once were provided by a firm owned by a young city commissioner named Carollo. Small world, isn't it?

Ironically, Miami wouldn't be broke today if it hadn't mismanaged city holdings and given away so many costly favors; if it had collected reasonable rents and leases (not to mention a few debts).

It would be good if the ghost-town lagoon area could be "revitalized" without ruining the rest of Virginia Key, but promises of preservation seem far-fetched. The city can't take care of a beach, much less an entire island.

Rezoning is just the first step toward another giveaway, and you don't need to be downwind from the sewer plant to smell the truth.

Explanation for road widening quite a stretch

June 15, 1997

By a slim vote, the South Florida Water Management District last week launched one of the nuttiest schemes in its long nutty history:

Widening the 18 miles between the mainland and the Florida Keys from two lanes to three, with a fourth phantom lane to be prepared but left unpaved.

The new paved lane will be northbound, ostensibly to improve hurricane evacuation. The unpaved Mystery Lane will run southbound, and nobody in authority has convincingly explained its purpose.

Why scrape an extra swath along sensitive marshlands if it's not meant to be paved? Because it is meant to be paved, as soon as local opposition dies down.

Widening the so-called Stretch isn't about hurricane egress or driver safety, it's about cramming more warm bodies into the Keys. It's about selling more rum runners, T-shirts and time shares.

And, most significantly, it's about boosting road capacity to allow a wave of new construction along the islands.

Those most eager for the project are commercial interests and land speculators in the Middle and Lower Keys. The people most adamantly against it are those who live in the Upper Keys and, ironically, drive the hairy Stretch more than anyone.

Originally, the plan called for widening the entire 18-mile leg, which is now two-laned with intermittent passing zones. Opposition to four-laning was so fierce that planners devised a bizarre alternative—two lanes north, one lane south, and the unpaved "footprint" of another southbounder.

In case of what? Unless you're traveling to the Keys by horseback or by wagon train, an unpaved lane is of little use.

Nobody down here was fooled by the phony "compromise." Opponents remained vocal, but the county pushed ahead.

A state hearing officer eventually approved the project. Incredibly, he ruled that expanding the main corridor into the Keys would have no secondary effects; not on the environment, not on growth, not on the quality of life.

Just as Alligator Alley hasn't had an impact on traffic and crime in Naples and Fort Myers. Just as the Sawgrass Expressway hasn't disastrously urbanized northwest Broward. Much.

Safety is a bogus issue. Widening a fast highway always draws more cars, and more cars mean more serious accidents.

Supporters of a new Stretch also invoke images of hurricane stampedes as a reason to widen the road—a groundless argument meant to mask the true agenda: to bring in more people.

The Mystery Lane is no mystery at all. Paving it at a near-future date will be easy, because the water management board will say yes. A slave to politics, the board virtually always says yes.

For folks who live in already-crowded Key Largo, and who don't especially want the Turnpike in their front yard, the last hope lies with two men—Col. Terry Rice of the U.S. Army Corps of Engineers, and former U.S. Attorney Dexter Lehtinen.

Lehtinen, a longtime advocate for the Everglades, plans to appeal the state's decision, on behalf of Keys conservation groups. He'll argue that four-laning the Stretch will imperil the water and wildlife of the islands.

In the meantime, construction cannot begin without a green light from the Army Corps. Rice, the agency's chief troubleshooter on Everglades restoration, has serious concerns about the far-reaching effects of expanding the entry to the Keys.

Rice is also curious about why the state agreed to the weird idea of a phantom southbound lane. "Why should we fill wetlands," he asked, "to make a lane they say they aren't going to pave?"

Sounds like a ploy to run a big-city freeway straight into Key Largo, but maybe it's not. Maybe it's just the world's most expensive jogging path.

The Everglades
and Big Sugar

Tainted bass a warning for all of us

March 10, 1989

What a winter for the Everglades. First the sawgrass catches fire, and now the fish are contaminated.

Health agencies have warned anglers not to eat any largemouth bass or warmouth caught in Conservation Areas 2 and 3. They've also suggested reduced consumption of bass pulled out of the Loxahatchee National Wildlife Refuge.

The reason: Samples of these fish show high and potentially harmful levels of mercury.

Such a warning is unprecedented for any freshwater species in Florida. When bass (the state fish) are in jeopardy, it's a startling signal that something very bad is happening out in the black muck of the Glades.

The story goes way beyond the culinary concerns of weekend fishermen. What's happening—invisibly, bewilderingly—is the poisoning of the source of our water and of the food chain that it supports. Animals that ingest mercury don't necessarily die, but they sometimes stop reproducing.

The sprawl of the contamination is boggling. They're not talking about a backyard pond or a patch of marsh or even a whole creek. The danger zone encompasses more than 1,200 square miles of vital watershed.

Tainted bass have been found as far north as Loxahatchee and as far south as the L-67 canal in Dade. The fish, about 70 in all, were collected with electronic stunning gear. They weighed between 2 and 8 pounds each. Experts were shocked at the amounts of mercury discovered.

The government considers any level exceeding .5 parts per million to be cause for concern. Anything over 1.5 is unfit for human consumption.

No wonder health workers were alarmed, then, when one of the sample Everglades bass tested at 4.4 parts mercury per million. Some sites yielded fish with levels averaging 2.5.

Much has been made of these statistics because people want to know how much mercury is safe to eat. Fact: Bass aren't supposed to have heavy metals in their flesh.

In humans, mercury poisoning can damage the central nervous system. The most famous and tragic outbreak occurred in the 1950s, when mercury-laden effluent from a factory contaminated the fish in Minamata Bay, Japan. Thousands of people who ate the fish suffered severe mercury poisoning that led to blindness, paralysis and birth defects. More than 300 died.

The Everglades scenario is not so extreme. The average person would have to eat a mess of tainted bass to be affected, but the health risk is larger for pregnant women and nursing mothers.

Actually, the edibility of these fish is the least of concerns. The more urgent riddle is where the pollution is coming from and what it portends for the ecology of South Florida.

"There is no theory at this point," says Frank Morello, a biologist with the Game and Fresh Water Fish Commission. "It's just a mystery."

The possibilities are far-ranging. Mercury can travel airborne from coal-burning power plants. It's also a common residue of agricultural fungicides, which have been known to be flushed into the Glades.

Over time mercury accumulates in living tissue, and the high levels found in the bass suggest a serious long-term pollution. Sediment samples might provide some clues, if not answers. The trick is tracing the source of this slop and identifying the offenders.

In a way, the invisible nature of the mercury threat makes it easy to underestimate. It's not like a red tide or a chemical spill. You won't see lots of bloated bass or dead panfish floating around the docks; in fact, you won't see much of anything.

A sudden fish kill looks more dramatic, but it tends to be brief and contained. The slow poisoning of an entire ecosystem is more sinister and potentially more catastrophic.

The hushed beauty of the Everglades is deceiving. It is so rich with life that we naturally assume all the life to be healthy.

For now, mercury and all, there are plenty of lunker largemouth bass to be caught. But the way it's going, someday we'll be fishing for them with magnets instead of worms.

News isn't so sweet for Big Sugar

March 5, 1990

The sugar industry, despoiler of the Everglades, got some not-so-sweet news last week.

Powerful federal agencies have come down strongly on the side of U.S. Attorney Dexter Lehtinen, who is suing to make Florida clean its water.

A report of the U.S. Department of Interior, U.S. Army Corps of Engineers and the Environmental Protection Agency says Everglades pollution is at "crisis proportions," and the state's plan to stop it is too weak.

The prime pollutants are phosphates, and the chief culprit is Big Sugar. Because cane companies donate lots of money to politicians, their disgraceful irrigation techniques have been overlooked for years.

Lehtinen ruined the party with his unprecedented lawsuit, which was filed 18 months ago. It charged the South Florida Water Management District with pumping filthy farm runoff into Everglades National Park. And it charged the state Department of Environmental Regulation with doing virtually nothing to stop it.

The message of the suit was so simple: Make the growers quit fouling our water. It hardly seemed like too much to ask.

But it was. The great state of Florida has spent more than $1 million in legal fees to fight the case. Makes you proud to be a taxpayer, doesn't it? The lawyers get rich while the water gets worse.

All sides agree that the public will be better served if an agreement can be reached out of court. As usual, politics is mucking up the priorities.

Gov. Martinez wants the lawsuit to disappear because it's politically embarrassing. The board of the water district (which Martinez loaded with farmers and developers) wants the lawsuit to go away because it could cost Big Sugar a fortune.

Florida had insisted it would come up with a comprehensive plan to save the Everglades, if only the feds would back off. Given the sorry history of water management, it was difficult to be bubbly with optimism.

Sure enough, the district's new Surface Water Improvement and Management plan was greeted by environmentalists with resounding derision. SWIM would give Big Sugar until the year 2002 to clean up its act, using 40,000 acres of public wetlands as filtering pools.

Water managers said they didn't know what SWIM would cost, or how much of the expense would be borne by agriculture. Big Sugar's response: We'll be happy to help clean up our slop if Uncle Sam pays every penny of the cost.

What a deal. It's like emptying a septic tank into your neighbor's bathtub, then demanding money before you'll mop it up—and finishing the job 12 years later.

The sugar growers' arrogance is well-founded. Thanks to the state, they get all the fresh water they want. Thanks to the feds, they can sell their crop at artificially inflated prices.

It isn't farming, it's glorified welfare. Naturally Big Sugar wants the public to pay for its pollution remedies—we've been paying, one way or another, for everything else.

State agencies always had the power to halt the polluting, but never had the political spine to do it. The staffs of the water districts are handcuffed because board members are political appointees who know more about irrigating campaign treasuries than vegetable fields.

The great thing about the U.S. attorney's lawsuit is that it forces the issue: Why should the Okeechobee growers be allowed to do what no other private industry can?

Knowing what we now do about the slow death of the Everglades, it's appalling that the sugar debate has lasted so long. The ultimate price of such cowardly politics could be a future of rationed, tainted drinking water for our kids.

We owe the Big Sugar companies zero; they owe us. They should filter the runoff on their own land, at their own expense, starting now.

But they won't do it, and the state won't make them. That's why Lehtinen sued.

It certainly got everyone's attention, and not a moment too soon.

New wetlands plan rooted in bad policy

May 20, 1991

In a political retreat that could mean disaster for parts of South Florida, the Environmental Protection Agency is proposing new rules that would allow massive development of once-protected swamps and marshlands.

Under pressure from developers and farmers, the EPA recently redefined "wetlands" in a way that excludes up to 10 million acres nationwide. If the new definition is adopted, it could abolish federal protection for large sections of the East Everglades, and for thousands of acres of marshes bordering the conservation areas in southwest Broward.

Developers have been drooling lasciviously over these unspoiled tracts, and now they'll be gassing up the bulldozers. The EPA says the definition of "wetlands" should be narrowed to meet three guidelines:

• The land's soils must be composed of muck or peat;

• The surface must be flooded by tides, or saturated by rains for more than 14 consecutive days during the growing season;

• More than half of the plants growing in the area must be among the 7,000 species commonly found in wetlands.

Unfortunately, those criteria can no longer be applied fairly in South Florida. Here, pristine wetlands have been invaded by melaleuca, Brazilian pepper trees and other water-guzzling exotics. Areas once rich in peat and soggy underfoot are now parched.

Paving is no solution; replenishing is a better idea.

The necessity of saving wetlands is so obvious that George Bush made it a campaign issue, and pledged there would be "no net loss" of marshes and swamps during his administration. It's distressing, then, to see the EPA, the Department of Agriculture and the Army Corps of Engineers all cave in.

The political pressure is overwhelming. In many places, the feds are the only serious obstacle for run-amok developers. Look at Broward. To describe the county's land-use policy as spineless would be kind; even calling it a "policy" stretches the definition. Anything developers want, they usually get. The Sawgrass Expressway is a shining example.

When the government announced tough wetland rules two years ago, powerful people were upset. It screwed up their plans to turn the marshes and wet prairies of southwest Broward into a vast panorama of cheesy condos, strip malls and high-density housing developments. The holy mission to make Broward uglier and more crowded than Dade was temporarily put on hold.

Now the feds have gone soft. Bowing to complaints that the current definition of "wetlands" includes land that isn't very wet, EPA chief William Reilly last week said: "We're only interested in saving genuine wetlands. There was a backlash over the previous policy because of what appeared to be overreaching . . ."

Needless to say, the "backlash" didn't come from the masses. It came from folks with connections.

Before the weaker definition of wetlands takes effect, the White House must approve it. Significantly, the Interior Department refuses to endorse the EPA's recommendation.

In South Florida, the dynamics are simple. Developers are running out of land, and they will fight for every acre. Land-use attorney Don McCloskey beautifully articulates his clients' selfless philosophy: "Government cannot use my private property to save the world."

So much for the Everglades, and for the underground aquifer that gives us water.

The EPA's logic is politically convenient: Marshes that already are damaged don't deserve protection. To be deemed valuable, wetlands had better be wet, and free from foreign vegetation.

The irony is classic Florida. Melaleucas originally were imported in a grandiose scheme to suck the Everglades dry. Though that plan was thwarted, it looks as if the stubborn exotics finally will get their revenge. The trees won't have to drink a drop, they'll just have to stand there.

Developers gleefully will be counting them, one by one, to prove that their land isn't worth saving.

Glades need a hero before options dry up

January 12, 1992

Big Sugar might help save the Everglades, in spite of itself.

The longer that cane growers refuse to clean up their waste and the more unfiltered scum they pump into the watershed, the greater the public backlash. No cause has so enlarged and galvanized the conservation movement.

Cheers went up when acting U.S. Attorney Dexter Lehtinen sued Florida for letting growers pollute Everglades National Park. More cheers went up when Gov. Lawton Chiles recently settled the case.

The agreement called for a modest cleanup that gives Big Sugar years to comply. The industry's arrogant response: 18 lawsuits against the Department of Environmental Regulation and state water managers.

People got mad—even people who didn't fish or hunt, who didn't care much about alligator nests or the sight of wild flamingos at sunrise. People who simply knew a scandal when they saw one.

Big Sugar gets all the water it wants for practically nothing, dirties it with tons of phosphates, then spits it back at nature. That's not the only reason the Everglades is in trouble, but what's wrong can't be fixed until the cane growers get on board.

"What we're talking about," said DER chief Carol Browner, "is a significant replumbing of South Florida."

When the Everglades Coalition met this weekend in Key Largo, the conference drew nationally known conservationists, biologists, planners, lobbyists and water experts. There were lawyers, too—mean, tough, hungry lawyers. That's what it takes these days to battle the special interests.

The mood was sober because the situation is dire. Half the original Everglades has been lost to drainage and development. Fish and mammals are dying from mercury poisoning. The number of nesting wading birds is down to 7,000 annually (in 1931 it was 100,000). Brazilian pepper trees have devoured 100,000 acres of native vegetation.

Everyone agrees the Everglades is dying from pollution, droughts and urbanization. The worst predictions are coming true at the worst possible time. Just when Tallahassee awakens to the crisis, the state finds itself broke and panicky.

Without heroes in the Legislature, there will be no money to clean up the Everglades. No money to find out where the lethal mercury is coming from. No money to purchase endangered wetlands. "It's kind of scary," said Lt. Gov. Buddy MacKay. "The economics of growth may now be coinciding with the politics of decline."

That's an amazing admission from a Florida politician, and maybe MacKay wouldn't have said it at a convention of home builders. But he's absolutely right.

For 40 years the natural marsh was diked, dammed and diverted to benefit farmers and developers. Today 4 million people in Dade, Broward and Palm Beach counties rely on the Everglades system for their drinking water. Nature's plumbing can't handle it.

Big Sugar can be blamed for stubborn avarice, but the industry makes one irrefutable point: Overdevelopment has done more to destroy the Everglades than all the cane and dairy farmers put together.

Cleaning agricultural runoff isn't hard, it's just expensive. The people problem is not so easy to clean up. MacKay wonders what happens when South Florida's 4 million becomes 6 million, and the 6 million becomes 8 million. Where will they get their water?

They probably won't. The plight of the Everglades has transcended images of panthers and bald eagles. Now it means something even the most thickheaded legislator can understand: no water. Suddenly growth management is more than a slogan, it's an imperative.

In his speech, MacKay compared Florida to a big gangly teenager. "We don't have the foggiest notion of what we want to be when we grow up."

Unless other politicians start listening, the one thing we'll definitely be is thirsty.

Big Sugar's sly cleanup plan is dirty pool

April 12, 1992

The Florida Sugar Cane League, not famous for its environmental conscience, suddenly has unveiled a plan to clean up the Everglades.

A late April Fool's joke? Nope. Big Sugar says it's serious.

The huge corporations that grow cane finally admit they shouldn't dump so much scummy fertilizer into South Florida's drinking-water supply.

To prove their deep concern for the public welfare, they've offered to reduce by 151 tons the amount of phosphorus being pumped off the farmlands into the Everglades. The only catch: Big Sugar, not the state, would be in charge of the anti-pollution efforts.

How considerate of the cane growers, not wishing to trouble government with the task of enforcing its own laws. Instead, we all should just relax and rely on the sugar barons to make the water clean and safe. That's about as likely as Lake Okeechobee freezing over.

Big Sugar's newfound commitment to the environment is explained in one word: fear. First, the U.S. attorney sued Florida for allowing the Everglades to be polluted. After a lengthy legal battle, both sides settled on a $400 million cleanup program that requires cane growers to pump dirty farm runoff into large filtration ponds.

Sugar companies say the plan will tie up valuable land and cost agriculture 20,000 jobs. Led by U.S. Sugar and Flo-Sun Inc., the industry has fought back with a hail of lawsuits. Big Sugar has steadfastly resisted all previous attempts to make it pay for its own putrid practices. A Greek chorus of expensive PR men and lobbyists have insisted the phosphorus in farm runoff is as harmless as rain.

That nonsense won't wash anymore, and Big Sugar knows it. By offering their own cleanup plan—"an olive branch," in the words of one sugar executive—the industry is making a last-ditch effort to appear reasonable and to keep control of its own drainage pumps.

Says Joe Podgor, of Friends of the Everglades: "It's like a traffic cop has pulled you over, and now you're trying to sweet-talk your way out of it."

Fittingly, the latest stall tactic came in the same week that the Everglades was named one of the 10 most endangered rivers in North America. A national conservation group, American Rivers, blames agricultural pollution and urbanization as the major threats to the vast shallows that provide fresh water for about four million South Floridians.

Some respected conservation groups aren't wild about the state's plan or Big Sugar's self-serving alternative. Friends of the Everglades, for instance, favors a complete scientific remapping of South Florida's plumbing, combined with "hard-core enforcement" of existing pollution laws.

Profitable habits are hard to break, and the sugar industry has long enjoyed a sweet deal: cheap water, migrant labor, government-inflated price supports—and the Everglades as its backyard cesspool.

The arrangement is cemented each election year by generous contributions to pliant politicians. According to the Center for Public Integrity, 17 sugar PACS gave $2.6 million to congressional campaigns between 1985 and 1990. Money doesn't just talk, it shouts: Of 29 U.S. senators who got $15,000 or more from Big Sugar interests, 85 percent voted to keep the price subsidies.

It's no wonder that cane growers, coddled for years, were stunned by the federal lawsuit over pollution. And with little experience at (or need for) compromise, it's no wonder that Big Sugar's counteroffer is so weak.

Backs to the wall, cane growers miraculously discover a way to keep 151 tons of phosphorus out of the Everglades!

Incredible. When these guys aren't flushing fertilizer, they're shoveling it.

Future of keys rests in the fate of Florida Bay

February 21, 1993

If you went to the Keys this weekend, you probably noticed that the once-clear waters of Florida Bay have turned the color of bile.

A vast and destructive algae bloom has floated out of the backcountry and settled in near Islamorada. Looking northwest from the Overseas Highway, you saw a milky green-brown soup surrounding the mangroves, a perverse parody of Christo's decorated islands. Crossing the tall arch to Long Key, you noticed a foul-looking stain stretching gulfward to the horizon.

What you saw is Florida Bay dying.

It started with the turtle grass, essential cover for shrimp, baby lobsters and small fish. In 1987, the grass turned brown and began falling out in clumps, then strips, then acres. The dead grass rotted in the warm water, releasing nutrients that fostered algae. Meanwhile, where the lush grass once grew, the bay bottom turned muddy and barren.

Today the die-off is so huge that between 300 and 400 square miles of Florida Bay is called the Dead Zone. Scientists say its effects are spreading, and the prospects are dire: The collapse of a uniquely bountiful estuary, and the potential crippling of a multimillion-dollar tourist and fishing economy.

There's no quick answer. Grass beds are sensitive and slow-growing; replenishment takes a long time. Part of the problem lies miles away, in the Everglades.

For centuries the southward flow of fresh water emptied purely into Florida Bay. Then the geniuses who manage our canal systems began diverting water to benefit developers and farmers. That folly was implemented under the guise of "flood control."

With its flow of fresh water disrupted, Florida Bay got saltier each season. The hypersalinity, combined with drought, caused drastic changes. Some biologists believe additional harm came from fertilizers and pesticides which flushed through the Everglades into the bay.

What you now see out your car window is unlike anything that's happened before. From an airplane, the sight is even more dramatic and dismaying.

In past years the blooms were smaller, localized. They came and went in a couple months. This one was born in October, and continues to spread like an 80-square-mile amoeba.

Chilly weather hasn't killed it, only moved it from the remote middle part of the bay—Everglades National Park—toward the populated islands. Each night at the fishing docks, backcountry guides grimly exchange information on the movement of the algae; on some days it's a challenge to find clear water.

The cloudy bloom not only looks like sewage, it blocks out vital sunlight, causing marine life to flee or perish. Sponges are dying by thousands—clots of them can be found bobbing in the algae. That's bad news for future lobster harvests; the juvenile crustaceans require healthy sponges for food and protection.

Even more alarming is that strong winter winds have pushed broad streaks of the algae out of the bay through the Keys bridges, into the Atlantic. The offshore reefs, already imperiled, could suffocate if the microbic crud thickens.

Imagine what would happen to the boating, diving and fishing—in other words, the entire Keys economy. Disaster is the only word for it, like an oil spill that won't go away.

This weekend the nation's top environmental groups are gathered in Tallahassee for the annual Everglades Coalition. The task is to devise a way to remap South Florida's plumbing to repair the Everglades.

Incredibly, it's the first time that the agenda includes a serious scientific discussion of the fate of Florida Bay. Pray that it's not too late.

Douglas would trade medal for preserved Glades

December 2, 1993

A bone-numbing north wind blew across the breadth of Everglades early this week. At the farthest tip, near Cape Sable, the sky flashed with wild birds: herons, curlews, ibises, blue egrets, white pelicans, sandpipers and a few roseate spoonbills.

They swarmed to the mud banks and oyster beds as the tide ran out, diving, wading, and wheeling overhead in such numbers that one could hardly imagine the place is dying. It is.

A long way off, an amazing woman named Marjory Stoneman Douglas was sleeping at the White House as an honored guest of the first family. On Tuesday she received the Presidential Medal of Freedom for a life's work trying to preserve the Everglades.

Medallions are nice, but Mrs. Douglas probably would trade hers in an instant for one solid promise from Mr. Clinton. Water is what the Everglades needs—a restored flow, streaming pure from Lake Okeechobee to Florida Bay. The way it was 103 years ago, when Marjory Stoneman Douglas was born.

That any of her Everglades remains untouched is the miracle. What Mrs. Douglas and her colleagues accomplished will never be done again. Not a chance.

Look at a map. The entire southwest thumb of Florida is a park—2,300 square miles that can't be malled, dredged, subdivided or plowed into golf courses. President Harry Truman made it official in 1947, the same year that Mrs. Douglas came out with her masterpiece, *River of Grass*.

Originally the park was 460,000 acres, a small piece of the total Everglades. The remainder was to be channelized by the Army Corps with the unabashed mission of conquest. In 1950 the park doubled its size, and has since grown to 1.5 million acres.

Saving so much raw real estate from the clutches of banks, developers, and speculators would be impossible today. Even if such a vast spread existed, the forces of greed would never surrender it for preservation.

The creation of Everglades National Park culminated a crusade that began in 1927, when Mrs. Douglas was just one voice on a local committee pushing for it. She admits that she knew "next to nothing" about the Everglades. When she started researching her book, she'd visited the place only a few times.

Today she is its patron saint. Ironically, her highest honor comes when her beloved Everglades is most imperiled. Although it can't be paved, it is being starved. Man-made canals with man-made faucets govern the ebb of its lifeblood; decisions rest with bureaucrats sympathetic to special interests.

The headwaters of Mrs. Douglas' river are spoiled by the sewage of millionaire sugar barons. What moves south is siphoned to suburbs, cities and a handful of vegetable farmers. The water that reaches Florida Bay is an anemic trickle—a 10th of what it once was. The bay, muddy and algae-clogged, languishes.

Those grand birds that rise from the mangroves on a wintry breeze are but a fleeting fraction of what once thrived here. Yet it would be untrue to say that the sight isn't a cause for hope. Given half a chance, nature rebounds swiftly.

Soon the Clinton administration will reveal more details of its controversial Everglades restoration plan, which includes a cleanup settlement with Big Sugar. At stake is more than bird life. It's our water, our economy, our whole future.

For political impact, the Everglades deal will be promoted as tough, bold and urgent. It had better be exactly that, or Mr. Clinton will have to contend again with Mrs. Douglas.

She might not be the type to return a presidential medallion, but she could definitely hang him with it.

Sugar bosses fight to keep real sweet deal

April 30, 1995

Powerful politicians want to spoil Big Sugar's sweetheart deal by eliminating the program that artificially props up the price.

Sugar barons hate the word "welfare," but that's what it is: guaranteed income, at the expense of foreign growers and American consumers.

Last week a congressional subcommittee meeting in Belle Glade heard from scores of regular folks who said that wiping out federal price guarantees would wipe out their way of life.

The sugar companies say so, too: They just can't hack it in a free-market economy.

Judging from all that whining, you'd think they were barely scraping by—U.S. Sugar, Flo-Sun and the other growers. You'd think their saga was one of a small farmer, struggling to eke a living from the fickle soil.

That's the image being peddled these days, as Big Sugar lobbies to keep its place on the federal gravy train.

And it's impossible not to feel sympathy for the working people of Clewiston, Pahokee and Belle Glade, who rely on the industry's prosperity. Those folks are truly scared, and they made an impression on the visiting congressmen.

Big Sugar's other face was not so visible. Take the Fanjul family, for instance, which owns 170,000 acres of Okeechobee cane. Its tale is not such a humble tearjerker.

As heads of Flo-Sun, brothers Alfie and Pepe Fanjul have gotten grossly wealthy because the U.S. government lets them charge eight cents per pound above the world price for sugar, and imposes strict import quotas on foreign competitors.

Forbes magazine estimates the program enriches the Fanjuls by $65 million a year. Their combined fortune is said to exceed $500 million. They live luxuriantly in Palm Beach, and contribute heavily (and, up to now, productively) to both Democrats and Republicans.

Interestingly, the Cuban-born brothers have never applied for American citizenship. They keep Spanish passports, which means their foreign assets aren't subject to U.S. estate taxes.

Oh, it gets better.

Recently the Fanjuls discovered the benefits of minority set-aside programs. They own most of a financial company, FAIC Securities, that's getting a cut of the juicy municipal bond business from Dade and Broward.

Set-asides were conceived to help local minority-owned firms compete with underwriting giants such as Merrill Lynch. Broward finance director Phillip Allen told *Forbes* it was "irrelevant" that the Fanjuls were noncitizen multimillionaires.

It's naive to think that the anti-sugar sentiment in Congress was born of righteous indignation. The impetus for "reform" comes mainly from candy makers, soft drink companies and other commercial users of sugar.

Big Sugar's supporters contend that eliminating price supports won't help consumers, and they're right. Coca-Cola isn't famous for passing its savings along to shoppers.

The best argument for axing the price supports is fairness. If Congress is slashing welfare, the blade ought to come down as brutally on corporate moochers as on social programs.

The sugar barons always howl about doom and disaster. They cried the same way when they were told to clean up the water they dump in the Everglades.

The truth is, they won't go out of business unless they choose to. A glimpse of the Fanjuls' lifestyle is glittering proof that Big Sugar isn't a struggling, shoestring operation.

Killing the price guarantees undoubtedly would have a major impact, and probably lead to a radical paring of expenses. For starters, the sugar barons could save millions by cutting back on lawyers, lobbyists, yachts, polo ponies.

Whoa. Now we're really talking disaster.

Sugar barons' campaign: Not sweet but low

November 10, 1996

Big Sugar did a masterful job of crushing the penny-a-pound tax amendment. All it took were $24 million and a stupendous pack of lies.

With ammo like that, it would be possible to convince a majority of voters that dogs have wings.

Political campaigns are often orgies of deception, but the battle over Amendment 4 set a grimy new benchmark. Twisting the truth is commonplace in election years; abandoning it completely is unusual.

That's what happened when the sugar barons decided their only hope of victory was to scare and confuse the public. The best way to do that was to make stuff up, and they did a brilliant, if despicable, job.

As a result, there are people walking around Florida today who actually believe they would have paid the penny-per-pound sugar tax instead of the growers.

Because that's what Big Sugar told them over and over on TV. It was the largest of many lies aimed at a stratum of voters who might be charitably described as impressionable.

The manner in which the sugar industry defeated the penny-tax proposal is relevant only for what it means to the Everglades, which would have been the beneficiary of Amendment 4.

Since the referendum, which cost a stupefying $36 million, both sides have been talking vaguely about mending fences and getting down to the urgent task of cleaning up South Florida's water.

U.S. Sugar, in particular, has indicated a willingness to move ahead in harmony with conservationists. It would be great news, if it were true. The question is, how can you believe a word these guys say?

Look at the execrable campaign they just ran. Look at the avalanche of lawsuits they've unleashed to block or delay key facets of Everglades restoration.

On the other hand, you've got to wonder if the sugar barons are tired of being portrayed as the Antichrists of the environment. These aren't stupid people. Cynical and ruthless, to be sure—but not stupid.

They know most Floridians want their wetlands pure and protected. The lopsided vote in favor of Amendment 5, which requires polluters to pay for Everglades cleanup, was a sharp reminder of the public's passion on that subject.

As a matter of fact, environmentalists hope to use Amendment 5 to pry more money out of the sugar industry. At the same time, EPA Chief Carol Browner says the feds want Big Sugar to fork over a bigger share.

Last week's impressive victory at the polls didn't get the sugar barons out of the political woods, nor did it improve their image. If they hope to hang onto their lucrative price supports, they need to appear more concerned about their waste water. They need to appear more reasonable and responsible.

And they need to make more friends. Cooperating actively with the Everglades cleanup would win them many.

Conservation groups should be similarly motivated to sit down at the bargaining table. The first incentive is economic—lawsuits and political campaigns are a drain of precious resources.

The second incentive is time, which is running out for our watershed. The sooner the replumbing begins, the better the chance of a successful restoration.

Many environmentalists acknowledge that nobody wins if Big Sugar bails out of Florida. Properly filtered, agricultural runoff is less damaging to the Everglades than the fallout from urban encroachment.

There's no reason why the farms can't stay and the great river can't be repaired and replenished. Let's hope the next $36 million is spent on the water, not on television commercials.

Everglades National Park 50th Anniversary
Homage to a magical place

October 19, 1997

The cabin hung on wooden stilts in a marsh pond, the stilts rising up through lily pads as big as hubcaps.

Getting there was tricky but my friends Andy and Matt knew the way—gunning a johnboat down subtle and sinuous trails, the sawgrass whisking against the hull. If you were foolish enough to stick out your hand, it came back bleeding.

The stalks were so high and thick that they parted like a curtain when we plowed through. The boat's bow acted as a scoop, picking up gem-green chameleons and ribbon snakes and leopard frogs. By the time we reached the cabin, we'd usually have spider webs on our heads, and sometimes the spiders themselves.

We were kids, and it was fantastic. It was the Everglades.

One night we stood on the canted porch and watched tiny starbursts of color in the distant sky. At first we couldn't figure out what they were, and then we remembered: It was the Fourth of July. Those were fireworks over the city of Fort Lauderdale.

But we were so far away that all we could hear was the peeping of frogs and the hum of mosquitoes and the occasional trill of an owl. We didn't need to be told it was a magical place. We didn't need to be reminded how lucky we were.

I don't know if the old shack is still standing in Conservation Area 2B, but the eastward view certainly isn't the same. Instead of starlight you now get the glow from the Sawgrass Mills mall, a humongous Ford dealership and, absurdly, the crown of a new pro hockey arena.

We wouldn't have thought it possible, three teenagers gazing across wild country that swept to all horizons. Ice hockey on the doorstep of the Everglades! We couldn't have imagined such soulless incongruity and blithering greed.

Fortunately, somebody was smarter than we were. Somebody 30 years earlier had realized that the most imposing of natural wonders, even a river of grass, could be destroyed if enough well-financed intruders set their minds to it.

And somebody also understood that Dade, Broward and Palm Beach counties would inevitably grow westward as haphazardly as fungus, and with even less regard for their mother host.

So that, politically, the only part of the Everglades that could be set aside for true preservation was its remote southernmost spur, and not without a battle. As impenetrable as the area appeared, speculators nonetheless mulled ways to log it, plow it, mine it or subdivide it.

That the U.S. Congress and state Legislature ever went along with the idea of an Everglades National Park remains astounding, 50 years after its dedication.

Nature helped its own cause. Hurricanes hammered South Florida in the 1930s and 1940s, so most land grabbers weren't in the market for more submerged acreage. It was hard enough hawking the soggy, stamp-sized lots they already had.

Seasonal flooding and fires had become such a threat to coastal development that extravagant technology was being directed toward a radical solution: containing and controlling all water near the farms and newly sprouted towns.

Thus preoccupied, most entrepreneurs remained wary of the buggy, moccasin-infested wetlands below the Tamiami Trail. That particular wilderness was, if not unconquerable, presumed not worth the high cost of conquering.

So in 1947 there came to be a spectacular national park, 1.3 million acres and destined to grow.

Ironically, it wasn't long afterwards that the rest of the Everglades, an area five times the size of the park, came under attack from the dredge and the bulldozer—a methodical and arrogant replumbing. Hundreds of miles of canals and dikes were gouged through the sawgrass meadows, pond apple sloughs and cypress heads.

Once the big "water management" project got under way, not enough people considered what might happen to the park itself, to the south. Too few understood its vascular, life-or-death connection to the sugarcane fields of Clewiston, the limerock mines of Medley or the tomato farms of Homestead.

As a consequence, hundreds of millions of dollars are today being requisitioned to undo the damage and "restore" both the flow and purity of the Everglades. Nowhere in the world has such a massive, complex hydrological repair been attempted. If by some miracle it succeeds, your children and their children probably will never run out of clean water.

And, as a fine bonus, they might get to see a healthier Everglades National Park.

As vulnerable and anemic as it is, the park remains impressive and occasionally awesome; still rightfully mentioned in the same breath with Yellowstone and Grand Canyon.

Visually, its beauty is of an inverse dimension, for the Glades are as flat as a skillet, the trees mostly tangled and scrubby, the waters slow and dark. The monotony of its landscape can be a deception, as endless and uninviting as arctic tundra.

But for anyone finding themselves on that long two-lane road to Flamingo when the sun comes up, there's no place comparable in the universe.

True, the Everglades have no regal herds of elk or buffalo to halt tourist traffic—you might briefly be delayed by a box turtle plodding across the blacktop, or by a homely opossum. Yet for the matchless diversity of its inhabitants, the park is truly unique.

That's because it is essentially the tailing-out of a great temperate river, transformed on its southerly glide from freshwater prairies to an immense salty estuary, Florida Bay.

Entering by canoe at Shark River, you would be among woodpeckers and mockingbirds, alligators and bullfrogs, garfish and bass, white-tailed deer and possibly otters. Most of them you wouldn't see, but they'd be there.

And by the time you finished paddling—at Cape Sable or Snake Bight or the Ten Thousand Islands—you would have also been among roseate spoonbills and white pelicans, eels and mangrove snakes, sawfish and redfish and crusty loggerhead turtles.

Buffaloes are grand, but name another park that harbors panthers at one end and hammerhead sharks at the other. Name another park where, on a spring morning, it's possible to encounter bald eagles, manatees, a jewfish the size of a wine cask, an indigo snake as rare as sapphire, and even a wild pink flamingo.

I feel blessed because the park's southern boundary reaches practically to my back door. One June evening, I walked the shore of a mangrove bay and counted four crocodile nests; in a whole lifetime most Floridians will never lay eyes on one. Another afternoon, in July, I helped tag and release a young green turtle, a seldom-seen species that once teetered toward extinction.

And only weeks ago, near Sandy Key, I saw a pod of bottle-nosed dolphins doing spectacular back-flips for no other reason but the joy of it. Nobody was there to applaud or snap pictures; the dolphins were their own best audience, exactly as it ought to have been.

Such moments are remarkable if you consider what has happened to the rest of South Florida in the past half a century. It seems miraculous that the Everglades haven't been completely parched, poached or poisoned to stagnation by the six million people who've moved in around them.

The more who come, the more important the national park becomes—not only as a refuge for imperiled wildlife but as a symbolic monument for future human generations; one consecrated place that shows somebody down here cared, somebody understood, somebody appreciated.

A fantastic place from which your children and their children will, if they're lucky, never see the lights of an outlet mall or a car lot or a ridiculous hockey stadium. Just starburst glimpses of birds and baby gators and high-flying dolphins.

Lawmakers sell Glades down river

May 7, 1998

To cap off the most worthless legislative session in recent memory, Florida lawmakers passed two last-minute bills that could sabotage Everglades restoration.

They rammed one through under the phony banner of property rights, but it's not your property or your rights they care about. It's Big Sugar's.

The new law substantially jacks up the cost of the Everglades project by requiring land purchases to be negotiated under the state's condemnation law, instead of the U.S. government's. That lets large landowners stiff taxpayers for attorney fees, consultants and witness expenses.

Many millions of dollars will be added to the price of land needed to reconstruct South Florida's freshwater drainage system. The chief beneficiary of this latest gouging would be Flo-Sun, the sugar conglomerate with vast holdings near Lake Okeechobee.

A relatively small chunk of cane acreage is essential to the Everglades puzzle, which is why water managers want to purchase it. Thanks to lawmakers, Flo-Sun now stands to make an even fatter-than-usual killing.

The rip-off has a perversely splendid irony. Big Sugar spent decades using the Everglades as its toilet, and receiving U.S. subsidies all the while. Now that it's time to help clean up the mess, the sugar barons don't want to play by Uncle Sam's rules.

Oh, they're happy to take federal bucks for their property, but they don't want the feds to limit how much.

So: First we pay the sugar tycoons while they're polluting our water supply. Then we pay them even more for selling us back what they screwed up in the first place. And who says welfare is dead?

The Flo-Sun bill is such egregious larceny that it has been attacked by two local congressmen, Democrat Peter Deutsch and Republican E. Clay Shaw, who both fear it will drive the cost of Everglades restoration so high as to cripple it.

The last hope lies with Gov. Lawton Chiles, who with a stroke of the pen should snuff the Flo-Sun giveaway, along with another disastrous bill pushed by U.S. Sugar and adopted in the Legislature's final craven moments.

That measure gives lawmakers a virtual item-by-item veto over all future changes to the Everglades project, even if no state funds are involved. It's plainly designed to subvert the comprehensive study of South Florida's watershed now being completed by the U.S. Army Corps of Engineers.

Remember that the Corps and the South Florida Water Management District were empowered by Congress to replumb and repurify the Everglades—an enormous engineering project to which every taxpayer in America is contributing.

The last and worst thing to happen would be another layer of interference—not just extra bureaucracy, but grubby political meddling that could bring the restoration process to a grinding halt.

It's no surprise that Big Sugar, like Big Tobacco, is scared by what's happening lately in Washington, D.C. It's also no surprise that cane growers are turning for a bailout to their favorite slobbering lapdogs, the state politicians in Tallahassee.

Historically, the Legislature has been a faithful friend to Big Sugar and most major agricultural interests. Anything they wanted to dump in our drinking water or spray on the ground was pretty much OK with lawmakers, which is one reason our rivers, bays and estuaries are so sick today.

Allowing the Legislature to now appoint itself chief caretaker of the Everglades would be like putting Ted Kaczynski in charge of the postal service.

If Chiles doesn't do something, the Everglades Forever Act is doomed to be another hollow promise. They'll need to rename it Big Sugar Forever.

Masterpiece foretold a legacy

May 17, 1998

It was the first Friday this century that the Everglades awoke without Marjory Stoneman Douglas. In the bay where the great river empties, the sun rose vermillion over the Calusa Keys and hung there fixed like some holy ornament, ember-bright in a lavender rim of haze.

Near Whipray Basin an osprey enthroned on a wooden stake flared its wings and scanned the shallows for breakfast. Snowy egrets and blue herons high-stepped grassy banks in search of shrimp. Lemon sharks and spinners prowled the channels.

Closer to the mainland, at a place called Snake Bight, lives a flock of rare wild flamingos, pink and skittish confetti in the mangroves. Not far away a creek mouth is patrolled by several lean alligators and a single plump crocodile. At times the mullet run so thick that the water froths with predation.

Such spectacular eruptions of life and death—all flowing from one river that's a choking wisp of its old self; a river that by every scientific measure is dying itself. It might have been dead already, dried up and perhaps even plowed, were it not for the ardor of Marjory Stoneman Douglas.

You know about her book; a monumental book, *The Everglades: River of Grass*. But how many important books are published, acclaimed and then forgotten? For Douglas, her masterpiece wasn't the culmination of a life's work, but the beginning.

The book came out in November, 1947, a month before the dedication of Everglades National Park. What a park, too, the entire lush tip of the Florida peninsula, preserved forever! How easy it would have been for Douglas and her cohorts to congratulate themselves and let it end there, with that grand achievement.

But she was unlike many journalists. She owned a grown-up attention span. Even after the book became celebrated she remained not only intrigued by her subject, but passionate about it.

And she knew from science and common sense that the park alone wasn't enough, and would in fact be reduced to baked tundra and slime ponds if the rest of the Everglades was not similarly protected. She kept writing books, of course, but she also sent letters and made speeches and generally raised hell.

Long crucial years went by when not enough folks took notice, particularly those in Tallahassee and Washington. Meanwhile, the Everglades went from fire to flood to drought, and more and more of its water was siphoned for new cities, subdivisions and farms.

Douglas was discouraged, but never beaten. The older she got, the stronger and more insistent her voice became. Finally in the '70s, when water woes began to jeopardize development, politicians discovered the Everglades.

And here's what they learned: A broad and avid constituency already existed, thanks to some blunt-spoken, floppy-hatted old woman who wrote a book a long time ago. Lots of people, it seemed, already cared about the Everglades. They wanted very much to save it.

So suddenly every Tom, Dick, and Gomer who ran for office in Florida was waxing lyrical about Mrs. Douglas' river of grass. In shirtsleeves they pilgrimmed to Coconut Grove for a prized private audience and, if they were lucky, a photograph.

Because a photograph with the famous lady herself was worth votes. This they'd figured out, these genius politicians: People really loved those Everglades. How about that?

Douglas, naturally, used such occasions to make plain her skepticism. Do more, she would say. Do it faster. Being an icon was tolerable only because she could be an icon with teeth.

So part of her must have been pleased, after half a century of gnashing, when billions of dollars finally were pledged to fix the whole works, from Lake Okeechobee to the Ten Thousand Islands.

Can they be "restored?" Impossible. Patched up, cleaned up, rejiggered—maybe. Shamefully little has been done so far, but Douglas leaves vocal legions who promise to keep the heat on.

She wasn't a misty-eyed dreamer but a wary realist. She understood the slagpit of politics, and what was needed to make a ripple. And she would not have continued fighting to the age of 109 if she'd believed the cause was lost.

Undoubtedly she would have found pleasure in the warmth of Friday's teasing sunrise over Florida Bay, and in the skittering baitfish and aristocratic wading birds and all-embracing solitude. But she'd also have reminded us that what we were seeing, no matter how singularly exquisite, was but a waning shadow of what existed not so long ago, in the slow blink of earth-time.

The last chapter of Marjory Stoneman Douglas' book is called "The Eleventh Hour," and in it she warns of time running out. "There is a balance in man . . . ," she wrote 51 years ago, "one which has set against his greed and his inertia and his foolishness; his courage, his will, his ability slowly and painfully to learn and to work together."

To do more, in other words. To never give up.

Wild Kingdom

Dateline: Big Pine Key
Deer poachers' tactics show true cowardice

August 20, 1985

This is how the brave hunter works.

He comes at dusk and parks by the side of the road, where he waits with a rifle across his lap.

As night falls, a delicate silhouette slips out of the pinelands and crosses the pavement. The deer is graceful and small, no larger than a golden retriever. It is not afraid of the car or the man, because each evening now there are cars and people.

This is the place they come to feed the rare Key deer.

It is illegal to do so, but the tourists come anyway, with their Toll House cookies and stale Doritos and picnic leftovers. They bring the kids to see Bambi close up, not understanding how easy they make it for the brave hunter.

Because the deer are losing their fear of man.

And the brave hunter is clever. He also brought morsels tonight, something the animals will like.

The brave hunter holds the goodies out the window of the car and, sure enough, the deer stops its crossing. Its velvet nose twitches, the ears flutter.

The man speaks softly, just like the cooing tourists. The deer takes one tentative step toward the car. Then another.

The brave hunter urges the deer to come, take the food from his hand. So the deer, not knowing any better, approaches the car.

And when the animal is very close, perhaps no more than eight feet away, the brave hunter raises his rifle and fires, killing the tame quarry with one or two or even three shots.

Since the Key deer is protected by law, and since the brave hunter is not quite brave enough to do time in a federal prison, he must be cautious. He quickly skins out the deer and finds a place in the car to conceal the venison, which is easy because there is hardly enough for steaks. Then the brave hunter escapes down U.S. 1.

The Key deer are slowly dying off.

Only 250 to 300 adult animals are left. Deborah Holle, manager of Key Deer Refuge on Big Pine Key, already has found 25 dead this year, most the victims of roving dogs and careless drivers—the cost of the rapid development of Big Pine.

The poachers' toll is high but unknown, for the evidence vanishes with the culprit. The preferred weapon is a gun, though Holle says knives, bludgeons and even more ghastly methods are used to ensure a silent kill. A few months ago she picked up a discarded garbage bag and inside found a severed doe's head, one leg, a tawny hide and a man's sandal.

Sadly, the deer are not wise enough to know the difference between a goofy camper handing out Pringles and a poacher handing out death. Rangers warn visitors not to feed the deer and signs are posted to trees, but nothing works. "For the deer's sake," Holle says, "we have to keep the wild in them."

Two weeks ago, a pregnant doe was slaughtered after dark on nearby No Name Key. A Monroe County sheriff's deputy chased and finally stopped four men in a pickup truck.

Three of them escaped into the mangroves, where we can only hope they were ravaged by billions of bloodthirsty mosquitoes, or worse. The Florida Game and Fresh Water Fish Commission (1–800–432–2046) is offering $1,000 for information leading to their capture.

The fourth man in the pickup was arrested. Authorities identified him as Gerardo Blanco, a Mariel refugee living on Stock Island in Key West. So far, he has been charged with one misdemeanor violation of the Endangered Species Act, for which he could spend a year in jail and get a $10,000 fine.

At a hearing Blanco told a U.S. magistrate that he knew nothing of the dead doe stuffed behind the seat of the truck, or of the .22-caliber rifle allegedly used to shoot the animal at extremely close range.

Then there was the odd matter of the carrots.

"There were carrots in the vehicle," Deborah Holle says, fresh carrots to entice the deer.

This is how the brave hunter works.

Manatees still hapless victims of area boaters

January 8, 1986

She floated clockwise in the current.

That she could move at all was miraculous, but every few minutes a whiskered nose poked through the surface to take a breath. She drifted in a special tank hidden from the Seaquarium's main attractions; not far away, people clapped for the killer whale show.

Dr. Jesse White, a veterinarian, studied the manatee and said, "What amazes me is that she can still move the back of her tail. There's four, maybe six major lacerations of her back, then one big chunk. The propeller had to be at least 20 inches in circumference—that's from a Cigarette boat on up."

The boat ran her down last Thursday in a Stuart waterway. The props shredded the animal's tail to raw pulp and tracked an awful spiral trail across her flesh. The folks who did this certainly knew—the impact would have been comparable to smashing a 900-pound log. Yet they sped away, leaving the young manatee spinning in a cloud of her own blood.

Amazingly, she was able to swim, and for some reason went south. By late Friday she made it under the Hobe Sound Bridge; by Saturday morning, Jupiter Inlet. At dusk Sunday she was spotted offshore at Juno Beach.

By dawn Monday she lay dying in the warm waters of Florida Power & Light's Riviera Beach power station. She had traveled more than 30 miles before the Florida Marine Patrol and rescue workers could get a net on her. By this time she was too weak to struggle.

Back at the Seaquarium, Dr. White cut away strips of dead and rotting flesh. Using a seven-inch needle, he gave the manatee two enormous injections of antibiotics. Afterward the doctor stood by the tank and stared at the wounds. "Damn," he said, under his breath.

The seasonal slaughter has begun. Cold weather has driven the slow-moving sea cows to warm water, where mindless boaters run them down. Last week three manatees in South Florida were killed this way.

You'd have to live under a rock not to know better. Jimmy Buffett sings songs and Gov. Graham goes on TV, and warning signs are posted throughout the inland waterways. The law is tough and the fine for speeding in protected waters is steep, averaging $119.

Still, boatloads of morons don't care. Go out any Sunday and watch them tear through the cooling canal at Port Everglades.

Sgt. Royce Hamilton of the Marine Patrol helped with the Riviera Beach rescue. This time of year he writes a lot of tickets to boaters speeding through manatee zones.

"We've had people tell us that manatees are like dinosaurs, and nobody misses them. We get that all the time. I had an attorney who I arrested last year who said he hadn't seen a manatee in five years. As I was writing the ticket one surfaced right by his boat! That shut him down real fast."

It would be easy to blame the snowbirds for the mayhem against the manatees, but Hamilton said this is not fair. Most of those arrested, he noted, are year-round Florida residents, "the ones who should have the most concern."

At the Seaquarium, Dr. White pointed at the drifting manatee and said, "The third cut is so deep it hit the spinal cord longitudinally . . . the only wounds I've seen worse than this are on dead animals."

Up close she looks as if she's been chewed by a threshing machine. Odds of survival: "Very slim."

Somehow the manatee made it through Monday night. On Tuesday morning she got another jolt of antibiotics. Dr. White talked more hopefully of saving the animal and including her in the Seaquarium's captive breeding program, saying, "We keep putting babies back in the world to take the place of the ones they keep killing."

Next month the first captive bred-and-born manatees, named Sunrise and Savannah, will be released into the Homosassa River.

The Seaquarium's newest manatee has no name. Dr. White said it was too soon for that. It's a lesson he's learned over the years—if you name them right away, it hurts even more to watch them die.

A loud cry for the state's wild panther

September 5, 1988

Last summer, in a pine hammock north of the Big Cypress Swamp, a rare Florida panther was released to the wild.

The big charcoal cat, known as No. 20, had been hit by a pickup, rescued and nursed back to health. To those of us who watched it dash into the wilderness, the animal looked awesomely fit and unconquerable.

But two weeks ago, the radio collar around No. 20's neck emitted an alarm from a device known as a mortality switch. The signal meant that the panther had not moved its head in several hours. No. 20 lay dead in the scrub.

Experts were deeply worried. Within days, three wild panthers would die from a population of only a few dozen. Another captive animal would die of liver disease. Tom Logan of the Game and Fresh Water Fish Commission: "When you're dealing with low numbers to start with, any loss makes you pucker up a bit."

The deadly streak began in mid-June, when the only breeding female in Everglades National Park was found lifeless. Panther No. 15 had recently given birth, but the kittens were missing. It is believed they were killed by a predator, possibly a male panther.

A necropsy noted wounds on the female's forearms, but the cause of death remains unknown.

Another collared panther was struck by a car near Homestead and suffered a severely broken leg. A juvenile found starving on an island near Shark River was flown to Gainesville for emergency treatment. Both cats are recovering, but it is not certain when, or if, they can be safely freed again.

Outside the park, August was the killer month. No. 24, a 126-pound male that roamed Highlands County, died for reasons that will never be known. A faulty mortality switch on its collar prevented biologists from finding the body before it decomposed.

Days later, another young male cat, No. 25, died near Alligator Alley after being badly bitten in a fight with another panther. The wounds resulted in a bacterial infection that raced fatally to the animal's heart.

Before the tests, though, state game officials wondered if it could be more than grim coincidence that so many panthers were dying in such a short time. "A very bad week," said biologist Sonny Bass. Experts speculated about a mystery virus.

So far, there is no evidence of it. Tom Logan believes a combination of things contributed to the death of No. 20 near Immokalee. The animal had a heart murmur, first diagnosed after the truck accident. While in captivity, the cat also broke all its canine teeth, which veterinarians painstakingly recapped before its release.

But the dental caps came off in the wild, making it difficult for the panther to take large prey such as deer and wild hogs. No. 20 had lost 33 pounds in the months before it died.

The deaths have rekindled the debate over the state's radio tracking program, with critics suggesting that the collars inhibit breeding and possibly harm the cats.

Bass, Logan and others disagree. Radio telemetry has enabled rescuers to locate several panthers that had been struck by cars and would have died without help. As for the mating cycles, biologists have tracked one family of collared cats through three prolific generations.

Already in peril, the panther's future would seem especially bleak after such a bad summer: six animals (four dead, two injured) removed from a total wild population that might not exceed 30.

Yet state biologists are not ready to panic. Far-ranging and fiercely territorial, the panther is subject to a natural mortality, even among younger animals. When two cats meet and battle in the wild, there is nothing that man can do.

"These losses appear to be tragic," Tom Logan says, "but they really are a part of what goes on."

Where there is death in the Big Cypress, there is also hope for life. Panther watchers are currently tracking three separate litters of healthy kittens—and hoping that enough of them will survive to carry on the species.

Watering down of rules throws sharks to wolves

December 24, 1992

One of the great indoor sports for Floridians is browsing our souvenir shops, to see what tourists are buying.

Once I found a shark embryo in a jar. No joke: A store in Key West had an entire shelf of real shark embryos, bottled like dill pickles. This was promoted as a clever memento of one's tropical vacation.

These days you won't find so many baby sharks, on land or sea. We've done quite a job of slaughtering them.

Some of the killing occurs in the name of sport, because shark are fine game fish. Ernest Hemingway sometimes machine-gunned his initials into their heads. As a kid, I killed a few myself, though not so exuberantly.

In those days we never dreamed the ocean would run out of sharks, but that's what is happening. The big money is in the fins, which are sold in Asia for expensive sharkfin soup.

It's an obscene reason to annihilate the planet's most important wild predator. Without sharks, the complex ecology of the sea will go haywire. This year Florida adopted a good law stopping commercial shark fishing within the three-mile state waters. It also limited the sharks taken by recreational anglers to one per day. (Some days, you'd be lucky to see that many.)

The U.S. government became so alarmed by the decline of sharks that it proposed similar restrictions in national waters, up to 200 miles offshore. It also sought to ban the barbaric practice of "finning"—hacking the fins off live sharks and tossing their maimed bodies overboard.

Weeks before the shark rules were to become law, a campaigning-President Bush announced a 90-day moratorium on all new federal regulations. Now, with the election over, the National Marine Fisheries Service has presented a revised shark plan, which goes into effect in January. It's not nearly as tough as the original.

"An unmitigated disaster," says Dr. Sam Gruber, a University of Miami biologist who's been studying sharks since 1960.

Though live finning is outlawed, the new guidelines still allow commercial fishermen to take 2,436 metric tons of coastal sharks annually—

lemon, bull, tiger, nurse and several other species. Each recreational boat can kill four.

"It's a joke," says Gruber. "It legalizes the wholesale slaughter of these things, for no reason."

The fisheries service insists the regulations will reduce the harvest enough that shark populations will resurge. Some marine biologists are skeptical. Unlike most fish, sharks take years to mature, and reproduce in small numbers. It worked for 4 million centuries, but not so well in the last decade.

Gruber has watched the change. In 1986, he began studying the life cycles of 140 lemon sharks in a secluded bight near No Name Key. The next year, only 90 of the sharks remained. By 1989, all were gone.

Divers and charter captains report similar observations along the Gulf and Atlantic coasts. Some commercial boats have gone out of business or moved to North Carolina, where sharks migrate in concentrations along the continental shelf.

Sure, sharks have a PR problem. Bumblebees kill more humans, but sharks get the bad press. And TV is always a sucker for dockside footage of a dead Great White, rotting ferociously in the sun.

Scary or not, sharks play a critical role in keeping the seas bountiful. It's not easy to kill off a creature that's survived 400 million years, but we've found a way. The rich folk do like their soup.

Meanwhile, I'm steering clear of tourist shops, in case somebody gets the bright idea for manatee steak.

A regular at saloon, popularity killed her

April 6, 1995

"El Presidente" died last week. Bullet in the head.

Those who loved her might have loved her too well.

El Presidente was an alligator who lived by the Last Chance Saloon in Florida City. She was eight feet long, half-blind, a favorite with bar patrons.

They thought she was a male, hence the nickname. Attempts at gender verification were deemed unwise.

Laura Dryer, who runs the Last Chance, says El Presidente was a fixture for 12 years. Never bothered anybody but the garfish.

Wildlife officers say she had become a threat because people came to feed her in the canal, which flanks busy U.S. 1. They feared a tourist or small child would tumble down the bank and get chomped.

Two citizen complaints were filed with the state Game and Fresh Water Fish Commission. Lawmen visited the scene. The verdict: El Presidente had to go.

"It met every criteria for a dangerous nuisance alligator," says Todd Hardwick, the man assigned to the capture. "It was 10 feet from U.S. 1, and a few feet from a bar where people were drinking."

One-eyed alligators and bleary-eyed partiers probably ought not to commingle, but through the years El Presidente and her fond admirers had no problems.

However, once branded a "nuisance," she was doomed. In gator-rich Florida, only the small ones are relocated. The large ones are harvested, because transfers are costly and often fruitless.

Recently a beloved alligator named Grandpa, in a rare clemency, was moved from Big Pine Key to Homosassa Springs. Bitten and abused by resident gators, Grandpa soon died.

So El Presidente received the customary sentence: death.

Hardwick, well-known capturer and rescuer of wild critters, holds the state trapper license for Dade and Monroe. He and two assistants got the call March 30 from Game and Fish.

Snagged with a fishing rod, El Presidente proved more manageable than her fans at the Last Chance. "They were ready to lynch me," Hardwick says.

Game officers prevented Dryer and others from blocking the capture. Mouth taped, the gator was hauled away and quickly killed with a .22. In this way, 4,632 nuisance gators were taken last year. The sale of the skin, at a state auction, is the trapper's fee.

Laura Dryer is heartsick and angry about El Presidente. "There was no justification for them to pull it out of the water and shoot it!"

Says Lt. Jeff Ardelean of Game and Fish: "They signed its death warrant by feeding it."

Indeed, El Presidente was one well-nourished saurian. At her death, she weighed 270 pounds. "Obese," says Hardwick. "The fattest eight-foot-four alligator we ever saw."

The girth of her tail was a Limbaughesque 32 inches, compared to the usual 18 or 19 inches of a gator that length.

Dryer says she didn't see throngs of people feeding El Presidente. She said the canal is teeming with fish, turtles and other natural cuisine upon which the gator gorged, though it's possible that customers donated high-calorie table scraps.

Inside the Last Chance Saloon, black armbands are worn in El Presidente's memory. Mourners don T-shirts denouncing the state: "Environmentally Protected, My Ass." There's even talk of a motorcycle run, to protest the killing.

Because of death threats, Todd Hardwick's house was put under police watch. Unaccustomed to the role of villain, he says he truly understands why people are upset.

It's easy to become attached to animals, even a crusty one-eyed alligator. Sadly, in these risky relationships, it's usually the reptile who winds up getting hurt.

Wildlife losing their homes as we build ours
December 12, 1996

One day late in November, travelers on U.S. 27 in western Broward County saw an unusual sight: a wild bobcat walking dazed in broad daylight along the busy highway.

Usually the cats are nocturnal, shying from human activity. They are especially unfond of speeding automobiles.

A concerned motorist reported the animal to the Wildlife Care Center in Fort Lauderdale. The center immediately sent its ambulance and volunteers.

When they arrived at the area, just north of the Dade line, they found no sign of the cat. But after a brief search they spotted it hiding in brushy cover, not far from a cleared construction site.

The animal was weak, and put up no struggle. It died in the ambulance racing back to the Wildlife Care Center.

Rescuers had a sad mystery on their hands: an adult male bobcat about 2 years old, which should have been in its physical prime. No signs of trauma—the cat hadn't been shot or struck by a car, or mauled by another animal.

A necropsy was performed by the center's veterinarian, Dr. Deb Anderson. She found no fractures, no internal injuries, no disease in the organs.

What she did find was a shockingly emaciated animal with white gums and not an ounce of body fat. The young bobcat was all skin and bones. It had starved to death.

Starved, on the edge of the Everglades. How?

They're paving the edge of the Everglades, in case you hadn't noticed. The corridor from Southwest Broward through Northwest Dade has become bulldozer heaven.

It's the final horizon before the dikes, the last open mecca in which to slap up crowded subdivisions with fanciful names such as Big Sky North and Bluegrass Lakes. Naturally, politicians are rubber-stamping these monstrosities as fast as possible.

For humans, overdevelopment means your kids are shoehorned into classrooms and you're stuck behind dump trucks every morning on I-75. For wildlife, the inconveniences are more perilous.

Unlike scrappy opossums and raccoons, bobcats don't adapt to human encroachment—they flee from it. In fact they're so reclusive that a person could spend a lifetime in Florida and never lay eyes on one.

The cats aren't listed as endangered, but they've been pushed so far away that they're rarely encountered. Of 12,000 animals brought to the wildlife center this year, only four were bobcats.

And only one arrived dead of starvation a few days before Thanksgiving, another small casualty of "progress."

Like the much larger panther, bobcats are fiercely territorial. If a young male wanders into an older cat's range, the younger animal is attacked and sometimes killed.

Imagine what happens when one of them suddenly loses its home to machines; when the woods where it hunts small mammals and dens its kittens are flattened to moonscape.

The cat can't run east because east got paved. Can't go west because it's mostly water. Can't go north or south without battling other bobcats for a sparse, shrinking habitat.

Dr. Anderson believes the male found along U.S. 27 chose to hang tough, refusing to abandon his home range. He spent his final days running on magnificent guts and desperation, hunting himself to exhaustion in a barren future suburb of Miramar or Pembroke Pines.

Soon, on the same ground that cat and its ancestors once roamed, there will be a new condo clubhouse or outlet shops, or perhaps a multiplex cinema.

And the parking lots will fill with avid newcomers who won't know about the small wild tracks that got buried under all that greed.

'97 is already a mean season for wildlife

May 25, 1997

A few days ago, a man in Key Largo took half a raw chicken and stuck it on a big triple-barbed hook. The hook was attached to a heavy nylon rope, which was reinforced with a steel cable leader.

The man lobbed the hooked chicken into a canal and began to wait. This is exactly how a poacher would do it—"a classic set-hook for crocodilians," said reptile expert Todd Hardwick, who later was called to the scene.

Before long, something swam along and ate the man's bait. It was a male North American crocodile measuring 9 feet, 10 inches and weighing about 350 pounds.

The animal was one of a pair that lived in the waterway, not far from the John Pennekamp state park. This species has been fighting back from the edge of extinction, and South Florida is the only place in the world where it lives.

More timid than alligators, these crocs are not known to attack humans. The big one that swallowed the baited chicken had long ago been tagged by a biologist named Paul Moler, who works for the state. Moler has spent years trying to save Florida's crocodiles.

This one was No. 050358. Moler had marked it after it emerged from the nest on Aug. 9, 1982, at the Crocodile Lake National Wildlife Refuge in North Key Largo.

Its life ended only a few miles away, under a dock, where it thrashed to death on the end of a rope. Its insides were torn to shreds.

Somebody in the neighborhood spotted the carcass and called authorities, because killing crocodiles is highly illegal. Nobody has been arrested yet.

A man interviewed by wildlife officers said he was innocently fishing when the croc grabbed his bait. Wow! Fishing with a chicken on a steel cable—they must grow some damn big snappers in that canal.

It continues to be a brutal season for Florida wildlife, with jerks running amok. In March, a 30-ton Minke whale died near Big Pine Key after being shot five times by unknown persons.

Who knows why anyone would take target practice on such a harmless and elegant creature, but you can bet on a pathetic combination of boredom and stupidity. Bullets from two separate guns were removed from the dead whale.

Then, from the purely vicious to the purely greedy:

Five young sports from Hialeah were arrested two weeks ago in Biscayne National Park. They carried no fishing licenses, but had a boatload of illegal booty, including undersize and out-of-season lobster, 458 queen conchs and the remains of a rare loggerhead turtle.

The goons who butchered the turtle could get 12 to 18 months in a federal prison. A park ranger found the animal's flippers while searching the boat.

Days later, several men were busted for illegal spearfishing around Dinner Key and Government Cut. You know you've found paradise when you can poach lobsters within wading distance of the Miami skyline.

Some judges go easy on wildlife violators, and others are as tough as the law allows. Unfortunately, the maximum fines are too low and the maximum jail sentences are too light for the crime, which is nothing short of robbery.

A few neighbors on that canal in Key Largo said they were glad the croc was gone. They said they feel safer now.

That's almost understandable—it was a large, scary-looking critter. The fact it hadn't hurt anyone didn't matter. Fear is fear.

Still, some folks would like their kids one day to see a loggerhead turtle in the Atlantic, or even a wild crocodile in Florida Bay.

That No. 050358 held on for almost 15 years is a small miracle of nature, considering all the numbskulls and bandits it had to elude.

Turtle's slaying shows we need more Cousteaus

June 29, 1997

Eighty-seven years is a long time, but not long enough for Jacques-Yves Cousteau. Unfortunately, he died before his work was done.

Although his ardent writings and dazzling photography awakened millions to the world underwater, he couldn't reach everybody.

Last weekend in Marathon, a little girl named Michelle was fishing from a motel dock when she accidentally snagged a sea turtle. The child called to family members, who hurried over to investigate the commotion.

You needn't be a student of Cousteau documentaries to know that sea turtles in Florida and around the world are in danger of being wiped out. The humane response would have been to unhook the animal and let it swim away.

That's what one of the girl's relatives originally claimed they'd done. But that isn't what actually happened.

According to the Florida Marine Patrol, one of the family members grabbed a spear gun and shot the turtle as it struggled on the end of the fishing line.

Then, witnesses say, the family carried it to their boat and sped off. Other tourists, infuriated, notified authorities.

When the Coast Guard intercepted the boat in Florida Bay, officers found the deck smeared with blood, but no turtle. On shore, more blood was found in a garbage can. Samples were collected for evidence.

Killing turtles is a serious crime. The Marine Patrol has charged Rene Robinson, Carlos Robinson and Ricardo Robinson, of Miami. The federal government also might prosecute.

Officers say Rene Robinson admitted spearing the turtle and stashing it in the garbage. When another relative informed him that keeping turtles was illegal, the family allegedly decided to dump the carcass offshore.

It was quite a gruesome little tableau to unfold on a Sunday evening in a resort area, the singular attraction of which is, ironically, its unique tropical sea life.

People travel to South Florida from all over the planet to see in person what they've seen only in books or on television—the soaring dolphins, the cruising sharks, the whole teeming kaleidoscope of the coral reefs.

They certainly don't come to see a helpless creature gored by some troglodyte with a spear gun.

Killing will happen as long as there's life underwater. Sea turtles and other endangered species are regularly taken, but often it's done because people are poor and hungry—not because they're bored on their vacation.

What took place in the Keys wouldn't have surprised Jacques Cousteau, though it would have saddened him. He spent a lifetime crusading against the foolhardy and wanton pillage of lakes, rivers and seas.

He tried to teach the difference between wise harvest and reckless butchery, and tried to show why all living things beneath the water's surface, from the regal blue whale to the unglamorous toadfish, have value far beyond the dollar.

It wasn't easy to open this remote new world, or to make outsiders share his awe. In the 1940s Cousteau helped invent the first aqualung, enabling humans to breathe underwater. Thus scuba was born, and soon the oceans had a political constituency.

Judging by the millions who dive and snorkel for the beauty, and by the millions more who flock to the Seaquarium and other marine exhibits, Cousteau's legacy is phenomenal.

Largely because of his pioneering, most who are lucky enough to see a wild sea turtle don't feel an impulse to spear it. Rather, they feel what they ought to feel, what their children feel: curiosity and wonderment.

Others feel nothing, yet Cousteau never gave up trying to enlighten them. He could have used another 87 years.

Same old song: Greed drowns another species

December 28, 1997

It's a tiny wisp of a bird, the Cape Sable seaside sparrow. You probably won't even notice after it's gone.

When the floodgates crank open at a dike west of Miami, millions of gallons of water will surge south toward a remote section of Everglades

National Park, home to one of the endangered sparrow's last breeding colonies.

The birds, which nest in grasses close to the ground, could be flooded out. Many experts believe the colony is unlikely to survive.

Everglades water is watched closely by government agencies. This year the levels are high again because of abundant rain. That's usually good for birds and wildlife, but not always. This year it's definitely not so good for the Cape Sable seaside sparrow.

There's so much water in the Everglades that the folks in charge need to flush the overflow someplace. If they send it to the park's eastern marshes, it might damage some homes that were built there.

So instead they're preparing to send the water farther west, where it could wash out a few hundred olive-colored songbirds, birds so rare that most Floridians have never laid eyes on them.

Pumping, due to start last week, was postponed because of publicity. A hard rain could force the issue, a decision to be made by the U.S. Army Corps of Engineers and the South Florida Water Management District.

Officials in those agencies aren't happy about annihilating the Cape Sable seaside sparrow, but they say they've got few options. They say they're not allowed to flood private property.

That would be property known as the 8½ Square Mile Area, notable as one of the only sites west of the Everglades levee where houses went up—about 350 of them. Why that was permitted to happen is no mystery. Somebody was trying to make money.

Now, whenever there's heavy rainfall, the residents of the 8½ Square Mile Area get flooded. That's because they live in a swamp, and swamps flood; it literally comes with the territory. And when flooding occurs, the folks who live out there complain. Who wouldn't?

Allowing houses to be built on the wet side of a levee wasn't the most stupid thing Dade County politicians have ever done, but it's close. The price of that stupidity might well be the extermination of another species.

All that overflow water is being aimed away from the misbegotten houses in the 8½ Square Mile Area, and straight toward the nesting grounds of the Cape Sable seasides. Biologists say this will be the fourth consecutive season that the sparrows cannot breed in the western part of the park, leaving only about 270 there alive.

Other colonies occupy eastern marshes, but because of water diversion practices, those areas will soon be too dry for nesting. Experts believe it won't be long before all the birds die off.

The story is a bleak echo. The last U.S. bird species to become extinct was another Florida sparrow, the dusky seaside. Once thriving in wetlands near the Kennedy Space Center, the dusky was done in by overdevelopment and pesticides.

Everglades National Park is supposed to offer sanctuary from such man-made threats. Indeed, birds living within the park's vast boundaries don't see many bulldozers or crop dusters.

Water is a more inescapable presence. The stuff that could drown out the Cape Sable seaside sparrows will be pumped into the park from conservation areas to the north. Efforts to redistribute the flow more evenly will probably come too late to save the birds.

A study is being done to help decide whether all the houses and lots in the 8½ Square Mile Area should be repurchased and returned to a natural state. In the meantime, if it comes to a policy choice between soaking a bird and soaking somebody's carpet, the birds will probably lose.

Too bad they can't learn to build their nests in taller grass.

Too bad we can't learn not to build our subdivisions in swamps.

Small Victories

City gives kids a great reason to give thanks

November 26, 1986

Now it will be a good Thanksgiving at 1640 S. Bayshore Drive.

Now the kids who live there can stay as long as they need. The Miami City Commission said so Tuesday in an act of decency and wisdom.

The house is owned by CHARLEE, Inc., a nonprofit group that places abused and neglected children in foster home settings. Opened in July 1985, the home on South Bayshore operated successfully, and without controversy, until a few neighbors complained this year.

They didn't complain so much about the kids; it was the idea of such a place in their neighborhood. They said it wasn't really a foster home, but a therapeutic facility. They said it was a zoning matter.

Three years ago the city said that CHARLEE houses qualified as foster homes, and should be treated the same way. This year a different zoning official gave a less favorable opinion.

The dispute could have shut down the Bayshore house and three others in the city. Doris Capri, CHARLEE's executive director, said: "The majority of our children do not have healthy homes to return to."

Curiously, the two most prominent opponents of the Bayshore home, lawyer A. J. Barranco and County Judge Murray Klein, did not appear at Tuesday's meeting. City Hall filled with other neighbors who felt strongly both ways. An attorney for CHARLEE got up to talk about definitions. The city zoning man got up to disagree. The commissioners wrangled about concepts like "equitable estoppel."

While all this was going on, the kids were home doing their schoolwork. The house parents, Mima and Fadi Aftimos, kept it a secret that Tuesday was the big day. They didn't want the children to worry. The children have been worried most of their lives.

Some of them have been beaten and sexually molested by their real parents. The home on Bayshore is the safest they've ever known.

Back at the commission chambers, everybody was agreeing that CHARLEE was a wonderful program, and that the children now living at the Bayshore home are model kids. Even Commissioner J. L. Plummer, who wanted the issue taken to a full-blown public hearing, felt obliged to say: "I gotta tell you, I think the CHARLEE program is doing a terrific job. Let's put that in the record."

And having put that in the record, Plummer then launched into a rather odd and irrelevant inquisition into the finances at 1640 S. Bayshore—how much are the house parents paid ($9,000 each), how much the state pays CHARLEE for each foster child ($53 per day) and so on. This would have been understandable if the city of Miami were paying the bills, but it isn't. The house is owned outright by CHARLEE and every dime of expenses is paid by the state.

The real issue was not zoning, finance, or improper definitions. It was the children—whether or not they belonged.

"These are not juvenile delinquents," said attorney Gary Brooks.

Said one neighbor, "Give us some control, that's all we ask."

Said another: "Are we, the residents of this area, going to add to their neglect and abuse? . . . Let's do what is right and just."

Another man implied that he saw one of the youngsters jump from the roof into their swimming pool.

"My kids do the same thing," remarked Mayor Xavier Suarez, "and I don't even have a pool."

The house on Bayshore is only a few blocks down the road from City Hall. One of the commissioners, Rosario Kennedy, actually took the time to visit. She talked with the children and their foster parents, and even their teachers in school.

On Tuesday, after listening to nearly two hours of debate over whether the place should be zoned as a foster home or something else, Kennedy finally just said:

"All I saw was a very neat house with two caring parents . . . All I saw was a house full of caring and love."

The vote to reverse the zoning administrator was 4-1, with Plummer dissenting. Afterward Fadi Aftimos couldn't wait to get home to tell the kids they can stay. No one needs to hear it more.

Politicians waking up to the green vote

November 5, 1990

Another election season comes to an end, leaving many voters confused, disappointed, unenlightened, uninspired and depressed.

Deeply depressed. One more day of campaign commercials, and we'll all need a dose of Prozac. Bob Martinez is still rhapsodizing about the electric chair, while Lawton Chiles has enlisted the sheriff of Sumter County—Sumter County!—to tell us crime's a darn big problem.

Is there any hope for Florida?

Maybe a shred. Somehow the citizens have managed to educate office-seekers about some new priorities. For the first time, the issues of conservation and "growth management" have been pushed toward the top of the political agenda. It doesn't mean candidates must listen, but they'd better act like they're listening.

In 1986, Martinez got elected without mentioning the environment. In 1990, it's the emotional centerpiece of his re-election campaign. Television commercials show him ambling along a beach, with a dolphin splashing in the surf. All that's missing is a tame Key deer and a baby manatee.

The mood of the state certainly has changed.

The governor isn't alone in his reverie with Nature; Chiles, too, has been touting his own environmental record. It's not insignificant that both candidates have spent so much time and money trying to out-Audubon each other—the votes are waiting to be won.

In future campaigns, you'll see other politicians paddling the Suwannee and hiking the Big Cypress. Such photo opportunities will be staged to show how much these folks really truly care, which might or might not be a lie.

One thing they do care about is preserving their careers, which is why you don't hear anyone campaigning in favor of new offshore oil leases, more beachfront high-rises, or more cane fields near the Everglades.

Not so long ago, environmentalists were treated as a fringe movement to be ignored or ridiculed, depending on where you happened to be campaigning. How things have changed. Today in Dade County, an endorsement from Marjory Stoneman Douglas gets you more votes (if not more campaign contributions) than an endorsement from the Latin Builders Association.

All over urban Florida, people are upset about what's happening to the place they live. Sick of the clotted traffic, the rising crime, the overcrowded schools, the destruction of coastlines, the paving and subdividing and malling of what was once a beautiful place.

The message from the cities and suburbs is strong and clear. A threshold of public tolerance has been breached: Metastatic growth is no longer seen as necessary for prosperity. That Florida remains one of the fastest-growing states is nothing to brag about; it's terrifying, given the condition of our budget, our water supply, our highways, our schools, and our jails.

Many who moved down here are discouraged by the deteriorating quality of life and angry enough to punish those responsible. Voting is a good way to start. Consequently, politicians from Pensacola to the Keys are leaping on the Big Green bandwagon and proclaiming their ardor for tall trees and clean air and blue water. Some are sincere, and some are just scared.

The trouble is, it's hard to tell the phonies from the real thing. One clue is to check where the campaign funds are coming from—and in that department, not much has changed. The big money still flows from developers, and rare is the candidate who mails back the check.

Still, we can hope that some have gotten it through their thick skulls that it's a new day. Anti-development feelings that simmered below the surface 10 years ago are boiling over now. Lip service might get you elected, but it won't keep you there.

In the end, the private motives of officeholders aren't as relevant as their actions. If they cast one vote that saves a park or cleans up a river, it really doesn't matter if they did it out of passion, or cold naked fear. Just so it gets done.

At last, Florida has a program worth keeping

November 10, 1991

Occasionally we find intelligent signs of life in Florida government. Occasionally something actually works.

One quiet success story is Preservation 2000, an ambitious program designed to buy up endangered lands and save them from development. The first purchase occurred in Sarasota County—914 acres once marked for residential housing would instead be annexed to a state park. Since then, more than $90 million has been spent on river basins and marshes, from the Withlacoochee to the edge of the Everglades.

"It's the only happy story in Florida," says Eric Draper of the Nature Conservancy, which compiled a list of top-priority purchases for the state.

The largest land acquisition program in the nation, Preservation 2000 owes its existence to former Gov. Bob Martinez. Searching for a constituency among environmentalists, Martinez had proposed P2000 as a way to preserve sensitive lands, while ensuring that property owners were fairly compensated.

The concept got support from respected conservation groups, so the Legislature went along. "They didn't realize what a good thing they'd created," Draper says.

Currently, money for the land purchases comes from revenue bonds sold by the state, grossing $300 million a year. Half goes toward the Conservation and Recreation Lands (CARL) plan, and another 30 percent bankrolls the Save Our Rivers program. The rest goes for parks and forestry.

Working with local agencies, water districts and private philanthropists, P2000 has helped secure vital tracts along the Steinhatchee River, the Green Swamp Basin in Pasco County, and the Corkscrew Swamp. By contributing money for cleanup projects, P2000 played a role in settling the big federal lawsuit over agricultural pollution of the Everglades.

A list of areas targeted for future purchase stretches from the hammocks of North Key Largo to the pinelands of the Big Bend. Several counties have launched their own acquisition programs with bond issues approved by the public. The votes left no doubt that most Floridians will pay to protect threatened green space.

The best part of P2000 is that its bite is barely felt by taxpayers—at least for now. Unfortunately, lawmakers approved a 10-year spending project without a 10-year funding plan.

Consequently, in this season's budgetary panic, Preservation 2000 could be jeopardized—and with it, hundreds of thousands of acres of irreplaceable wilderness.

With any bond project, someone's got to pay the annual debt—about $26 million on each issue of P2000 bonds. In 1990, lawmakers got the money by raising documentary stamp taxes on liens and stocks. This year the debt service will be covered by a small hike in documentary stamps on real estate.

But what about next year? And the year after that? Each new P2000 bond carries a debt that the state must pay. For this reason, Gov. Chiles and some legislators are uneasy about issuing new bonds; rather, they want P2000 to have a dedicated source of funding.

Given the fiscal crisis in schools and prisons, it's unlikely lawmakers will simply appropriate $300 million for land acquisition. The money must come from a fresh well.

Some say bonds are still a good deal because interest rates are low, and raw land will never be cheaper. Whatever course is taken, any snag in the P2000 program would be bad news for conservation. Every lost day is costly, as illustrated by recent events near Apalachicola.

There the state had its eye on a vast stretch of swamp and pine groves called Tate's Hell. At 183,000 acres, it would have been the largest parcel ever saved from bulldozers.

But a developer with $22 million got there first. Last month the deal was signed, and soon Tate's Hell will have houses, "plantations" and a logging operation.

At least they won't have to change the name.

Proposal gives green power to the people

March 14, 1993

The days of carving up public parks for private profit might soon be over.

An amendment that appears on Tuesday's ballot would give more control of Dade's rich park system to those who own it—the people.

If the measure passes, no large commercial ventures could be launched in county parks without voter approval. That includes race-car tracks, pro tennis stadiums, flea markets and other extravaganzas that have been allowed to occupy public lands.

The premise of the charter amendment is that parks are meant to be preserved, not exploited. It's a concept that worries a few local bureaucrats, who look at Dade's shrinking green spaces and see not just trees, but money.

Piecing out park projects is a high-stakes deal; contracts and concessions often go to those with strong political connections. Letting the public get involved throws a wrench into the works. That's why Metro commissioners refused to put the Save Our Parks proposal on a ballot.

Supporters quickly collected almost 94,000 signatures on a petition, so the amendment is now on its way to voters. Meanwhile, officials in Miami and other cities are fretting aloud over the possible consequences. Imagine—allowing common citizens to decide how their parks should be used!

Politicians fear that voters might not appreciate some of their bold moneymaking schemes. Say, for example, that the city of Miami Beach wanted to build a parking garage in an oceanfront park. The uninformed masses might think poorly of the idea and vote against it, thus halting the march of progress.

Miami planners envision just such a scenario. They're trying to turn what's left of Bicentennial Park into a working annex of the seaport. If the Save Our Parks amendment passes, voters might block the expansion on the grounds that the cruise lines can damn well afford to buy their own docks. In anticipation, the city is hastily hunting for loopholes to allow the port landgrab to proceed, no matter what happens in the election.

The notion that parks should bring in revenue isn't new. It makes sense to have a bait shop at Crandon Marina, or an outdoor snack bar at Matheson Hammock. The public gets a needed service, and the county gets money from leasing the concessions.

But look at large-scale boondoggles such as the Grand Prix and the Lipton tennis tournament, which have transformed Bicentennial and Crandon parks respectively. Heavily subsidized by tax dollars, both events supposedly still bleed red ink, and each year the promoters come begging for more public money.

While the arrangement has been lucrative for Ralph Sanchez and Butch Buchholz, the county is hundreds of thousands of dollars in the hole. We're told that the deepening deficit is offset by the gazillions spent by fans attending these events, but documenting the alleged windfalls has proven difficult.

Perhaps voters will look kindly on such ambitious schemes, and eagerly surrender more local parks to private enterprise. If some dreamer wants to put a NASCAR oval in the Deering Estate—stock cars screaming around a gorgeous infield of royal palms—that's fine, as long as the voters say yes.

They probably wouldn't. Had the Save Our Parks amendment been the law a few years ago, the Grand Prix and the Lipton today might be held on private lands; same fun, different venue.

Even if the amendment passes, local government will still play the major role in initiating new projects. For once, though, the people who use the parks will get to decide whether commercializing a green space really improves it, and for whom.

If Tallahassee won't do it, voters will

December 11, 1994

If Tallahassee is the mule, then Amendment 3 was the proverbial two-by-four upside its head.

Last month, 72 percent of Florida voters approved a ban on the use of entanglement gill nets in state waters. The law took the extreme form of a constitutional amendment because it was the only way to get the issue before the people.

The governor and Cabinet wouldn't do it. Regulators hemmed and hawed. The Legislature chickened out. So a petition drive put it on the ballot.

Amendment 3's landslide passage was a powerful political proclamation: Floridians don't want their oceans and rivers raped anymore. They care passionately about conservation and will turn out in huge numbers to say so.

Was anybody in government listening? Somebody was.

"Today represents a defining moment in the care and nurture of our marine resources . . . The vote on the constitutional amendment clearly mandates that we do things differently and better."

The words come from Dr. Robert Q. Marston, vice chairman of the Florida Marine Fisheries Commission. The MFC was created in 1983 to prevent the destruction of coastal fisheries. Because of intense pressure from commercial groups, change has come slowly.

Too slowly, Marston concedes. In a new report to the MFC, the former president of the University of Florida uses uncommonly blunt language to summarize what's gone wrong.

Rather than stand up to the lobbying blitz from special interests, the state repeatedly has enacted weak conservation rules. "Such attempts have failed uniformly," Marston asserts. "Fishery stocks have failed to respond, and ultimately more stringent action is necessary."

Remember how overfishing was allowed to decimate four prized saltwater species—snook, redfish, king mackerel and Spanish mackerel—before emergency measures were taken.

Recently the MFC staff reviewed the survival prospects for 40 Florida species: 16 are considered stable, six are recovering from overfishing, and 18 "are still overfished without an apparently effective recovery plan in place."

One of those is the spotted sea trout, which has declined drastically in numbers because of heavy netting. Efforts to protect the popular food fish have been inadequate, tangled in politics and conflicting scientific data.

Even if you never touch a fishing rod in your life, Marston's call to action is a cause for hope. Wise marine management benefits not only the commercial and sportfishing industries, but every taxpayer, too.

The death of marine habitats would be calamitous for the state's economy, especially tourism. The MFC estimates that recreational fishing now brings in nearly as much money statewide as the citrus industry.

Politicians wouldn't dare stand idle if the orange harvest was being ripped off, but many have done exactly that while the fish stocks were plundered.

The MFC staff wants a streamlined rule making procedure, tougher penalties and stronger, better enforcement. Otherwise, Florida's sea waters will remain vulnerable to the same threats that have depleted two-thirds of the world's major fisheries.

Every Floridian lives within a short drive of a beach, a bay or a river. The vote on Amendment 3 proved that people have a deep affection for these places. Most biologists believe the net ban will greatly rejuvenate stocks of sea trout and other species. It's probably the most important, far-reaching conservation initiative in half a century. And the people had to do it, because the geniuses we send to Tallahassee wouldn't pay attention.

Maybe they will now. If not, there are plenty of other two-by-fours that'll do the trick.

Preserving bay today is good for the future

May 12, 1996

The most spectacular waters of Biscayne Bay are found in Biscayne National Park. This is no quirk of nature.

An unpaved swath of coastline, the last in the county, is one reason the park has stayed so healthy. The Metro Commission has an extraordinary opportunity to keep it that way for your children and grandchildren, and perhaps generations to come.

It's far-fetched, but not impossible to believe that the same political body that erected a mountainous dump on the shore of Biscayne Bay would now vote to protect the rest of it. That's what must happen, or a tragic decline is inevitable.

The southern part of the bay has been shielded from urban pollution by thousands of acres of agriculture and open green space, which acts as a filter for rainfall.

From an airplane, you can see the dramatic contrast in clarity between the water off downtown Miami and the water at the Arsenicker Keys. On some days it's the difference between chowder and gin.

To preserve South Dade's stretch of bay, Biscayne National Park Superintendent Dick Frosthas asked Metro commissioners to make two changes to the master land-use plan.

The first amendment affects 2,700 acres adjacent to the park, which now is designated for urban development. Frost believes the land provides an "essential" buffer for the bay, and should remain farms and open space.

A second, broader amendment asks the county to hold the line against any major housing projects near the national park, until the long-term impact on water quality can be determined.

Frost's recommendations were endorsed 8-1 by Metro's Planning Advisory Board, but that's no guarantee the measures will be approved. Commissioners have been known to ignore their own planners rather than rile their campaign donors.

The amendments are set for a vote Tuesday, and opponents will be out in force. Leading the fight against an expanded park buffer are Homestead City Council members, some of whom continue to invoke hurricane hardship as a justification for subdividing everything in sight.

Councilwoman Ruth Campbell complained that the park's proposal "will stymie the development at the Homestead Air Reserve Base."

A revealing remark indeed. Remember that one selling point of the HABDI giveaway was the assurance that the new airport and commercial park would be not only self-contained, but incompatible with Hialeah-type sprawl.

The proposed buffer area—lowlands between Florida's Turnpike Extension and the air base tract—faces enormous development pressure. As has been the trend in South Dade, some farm owners-turned-speculators are eager to sell.

The problem with cramming thousands of tract houses along Biscayne Bay's drainage corridor is obvious: Asphalt and concrete cannot filter water the way soil does. Instead, rain becomes dirty runoff, degrading the bay.

Those who argue that buffering the park will stunt Homestead's economy are overlooking the 500,000 visitors a year who go there to dive, snorkel and fish.

Besides the Everglades, there's no bigger tourist attraction in South Dade than Biscayne Bay. To endanger it permanently for the short-term benefit of a few powerful interests is reckless.

The superintendent said it best: "You can make a bold and daring decision today to preserve the bay and preserve agriculture in South Dade, or you can sit back and watch it disappear piece by piece.

"Then one day you look out the window and the bay is murky and dark, and you wonder how it got that way. And then it's too late."

One company had courage, fought graft

October 10, 1996

Miami's latest scandal has produced scads of villains and only one shining hero: Unisys Corp.

God knows how many companies have been hit up and shaken down by the crooks at City Hall. Unisys is one that blew the whistle.

Its executives chose not to pay outlandish bribes for the privilege of selling computers to the city. Imagine that. Imagine somebody going to the police and FBI to report a crime.

I know nothing about corporate Unisys or its reputation in the business world, but I know Miamians should be grateful. With their city government a cesspit, any such act of honesty qualifies as an act of courage.

If it weren't for Unisys, a thief-commissioner named Miller Dawkins wouldn't be pleading guilty to bribery and conspiracy, and destined for prison.

If it weren't for Unisys, a conniving bagman named Manohar Surana would still be Miami's finance director. Now a federal informant, Surana, too, is on his way to the slammer.

If it weren't for Unisys, the FBI wouldn't have been tipped to the antics of ex-City Manager Howard Gary, soliciting payoffs disguised as consulting fees.

If it weren't for Unisys, Gary wouldn't have led investigators into the murky world of the municipal bond racket. County Commissioner James Burke would never have surfaced on tape, discussing a $100,000 payment.

And if it weren't for Unisys, Cesar Odio would not stand charged with corruption. Instead, he'd still be city manager, and Miami would still be spiraling blithely toward bankruptcy.

If Unisys hadn't cracked open Operation Greenpalm, Miamians would still be under the naive impression that their city could pay its bills.

If it weren't for Unisys, Merrett Stierheim wouldn't have been deputized as acting city manager, and nobody but a handful of schemers would be aware that Miami was a boggling $68 million in the hole (give or take a few million).

Just think of what we would've missed, if Unisys had kept quiet and paid those bribes.

We would have missed the spectacle of Odio—the man who was in charge of running the whole city—asserting with that deer-in-the-headlights expression of his that, gee, nobody told him the finances were a wreck.

We'd also have missed this week's firing of the city's outside auditors, Deloitte & Touche. The firm claimed it had warned of a serious pending shortfall, but said city commissioners hadn't read either the firm's reports or the financial statements.

And, finally, we'd have missed the performance of the commissioners, who've been portraying themselves as shocked and clueless, a description with which the public can hardly quibble.

Naturally, the commissioners will blame everybody but themselves, even though it was they who let Odio and Surana run wild. The fiscal scare a few years back apparently wasn't quite dire enough to motivate the commission into paying closer attention to the books.

So, if it weren't for Unisys, nobody would have learned about the city's unique "Don't Ask, Don't Tell" policy on insolvency.

Balancing the budget will be an ordeal that hits every city taxpayer and many honest city workers in the pocketbook. Their anger and disgust is justified. They've been deceived by bureaucrats who were crooked, lazy or grossly incompetent.

As brutal as the budget crisis is today, it would be worse—maybe even unsalvageable—had it remained a secret much longer.

Which is what would've happened if Unisys hadn't done what it did, and started the dominoes falling.

Too bad it didn't happen sooner. Too bad some other company didn't have the guts.

Golden arches not welcomed in Islamorada

December 7, 1997

When the people of Islamorada heard that McDonald's was coming to town, they got mad and vowed to fight.

The prevailing wisdom said they didn't stand a chance against the corporate fast-food titan. The prevailing wisdom was wrong.

Islamorada is a sportfishing community about halfway between Miami and Key West. Busy U.S. 1 is the main thoroughfare. It runs parallel to what locals call the "Old Road," the original two-lane Highway One.

Because it's less traveled, the Old Road on Upper Matecumbe Key is a favorite stretch for bikers, joggers and rollerbladers. It's one of the few streets on the slender island where you can see moms pushing baby strollers.

McDonald's wanted to level an abandoned motel on U.S. 1 and build a restaurant/gas station/convenience store. The exit to be used by trucks, trailers and RVs would have emptied onto the Old Road.

People who lived there were upset. They hired an enthusiastic young lawyer, Frank Greenman, and collected hundreds of signatures on petitions. McDonald's insisted that it wasn't building the complex to lure passing tourists, but primarily "to serve the needs" of the local neighborhood.

Neighbors said cripes, they didn't need another gas station or stop-and-go store; Islamorada has plenty. As for fast-food joints, a Burger King stands only 100 yards from the proposed McDonald's site. Nobody saw an urgent burning need for more cheeseburgers.

But other communities have fought McDonald's, and most have lost. Nobody gave Islamorada much hope—Monroe County officials aren't famous for standing up to powerful interests. And the staff of the planning commission, which originally rejected the McDonald's proposal, had later changed its mind.

On Thursday, the planning commission met at the Key Largo Public Library to vote. Scores of Islamorada residents drove 20 miles through torrential rains to attend.

They were shown an artist's color rendering of the proposed restaurant/gas station/convenience store, lushly landscaped, and were not impressed. Once you got past the palm trees, it was still your basic high-volume gas station, convenience store and fast-food joint.

Some residents booed the drawing. They fumed as McDonald's engineers asserted that the hundreds of additional cars passing through would have "no adverse impact" on the neighborhood.

"I'm so mad. I live behind there," Jessie Wood said. She sat through much of the all-day meeting with her 11-month-old baby. "I used to ride my bike up and down that road when I was a kid. Now I have a son—where's he going to ride his bike?"

After the paid experts were done testifying, Greenman called the neighbors to the microphone. They talked about crime and noise and safety concerns, such as the nearby school bus stop. They also talked about the unique but vanishing character of the Keys.

When they finished, Planning Commissioner Lynn Mapes spoke first: "I think there are more gas pumps in this town than I've seen anywhere outside of New Jersey. I can't see any need for more gas pumps."

Commissioner Billy Gorsuch expressed other concerns. So did Commissioner Jim Aultman and Chairwoman Mary Hansley. The final vote went 4-1 against McDonald's.

A cheer erupted, hesitantly at first, because people couldn't really believe what had happened: They had actually been heard—and trusted to know what was best for their neighborhood.

McDonald's can appeal the decision, but the company will face a new hurdle next time around. In less than a month, Islamorada officially incorporates as a city.

From then on, island residents will make their own rules about density, zoning, traffic capacity—things that help determine a community's quality of life.

In paradise, that includes cheeseburgers.

Feds are right in grounding jetport project

January 4, 1998

The White House decision to delay development of the old Homestead Air Force Base has drawn instant criticism from South Dade officials, Miami-Dade Mayor Alex Penelas and even Sen. Bob Graham.

They say the delay unfairly punishes a needy community that's still struggling after Hurricane Andrew. A new commercial jetport, they say, is necessary to invigorate South Dade.

Blaming Uncle Sam for the setback is convenient. It's also a crock. The county screwed up the air-base project so badly that the feds had little choice but to step in and enforce the law.

The fiasco began when commissioners, including Penelas, chose to lease the storm-battered property to a bunch of politically connected home builders. The group, called HABDI, includes Carlos Herrera, a former president of the Latin Builders Association and a heavy Democratic contributor.

HABDI announced elaborate plans to convert the military airfield into a thriving cargo jetport. Hotels, shops and warehouses would sprout up—not to mention plenty of new subdivisions, which is what the Homestead deal is really all about.

That Herrera and HABDI had zero experience in the airport business didn't seem to bother the commissioners. They awarded the lease without considering any other bids.

Angry South Dade residents tried in vain to kill the deal. They felt like pawns in a political trade-off, and they were right. HABDI had the votes it needed.

Then somebody noticed that the group's plans for the Homestead base were far more ambitious than those originally presented to the Air Force. The number of predicted flights was doubled, and suddenly there was a drawing of a second runway.

That meant the original environmental-impact report was worthless. (On one map, for example, Biscayne Bay was labeled "The Atlantic Ocean.") Friends of the Everglades, the Sierra Club and the National Resources Defense Council demanded that the feds review HABDI's plan.

Because of its location, the Homestead jetport will have an impact on two national parks, Biscayne and Everglades. The effect of constant aircraft noise on wildlife is one issue, but questions have also been raised about potential fuel spills, air pollution and traffic.

Those concerns evidently aren't shared by Penelas, Graham or other politicians who opposed an environmental-impact statement. A new study would postpone construction unnecessarily, they insisted. The old study would do just fine.

Their argument was made at a Nov. 25 meeting between county and federal officials in Graham's Miami office. According to *New Times*, the county lamely tried to backpedal away from HABDI, saying it had not yet accepted all the company's projections.

In other words: Sure, we let 'em have the air base, but we don't agree with all their big ideas.

How's that for a cop-out? Luckily, the feds didn't buy it. On Dec. 22, the White House agreed that the revamped air base should be studied for potential environmental damage. The work is supposed to take about 18 months.

In a way, HABDI brought on the delay itself by outlandishly predicting that its airport would be a $12 billion boon to South Dade's economy. County consultants chimed in, projecting 230,000 flights a year, comparable to JFK in New York.

The price for all that wild hype is scrutiny, because the stakes are high. Industrializing a rural community shouldn't happen overnight. Nor should anyone lightly dismiss ecological threats to the Everglades, Biscayne Bay and Florida Bay—vital resources that also happen to be multibillion-dollar tourist attractions.

So the county is stuck; stuck with HABDI, stuck with the hype, and now stuck with a long delay. It's nobody's fault but the commissioners' for agreeing to such a disgraceful deal.

No wonder they're looking for somebody else to blame.

Bush listens to smart talk on environment

February 5, 1998

Jeb Bush, conservationist?

Stop laughing. The Republicans are wising up, and the Democrats had better pay attention.

A column recently appeared in this newspaper that might have made you rub your eyes, to make sure you weren't hallucinating. The headline: "Let's protect Florida forever."

The byline: Jeb Bush.

Yes, the same Bush who had no environmental platform whatsoever—no clue, in fact—when he ran for governor on the GOP ticket in 1994.

This year Bush is running again, and he's full of ideas about how to preserve wilderness and wetlands. Did he suddenly get religion, or is this an act?

It doesn't really matter, as long as promises are kept.

Bill Clinton didn't start talking like Thoreau until he ran for president, and there's no reason—based on his record in Arkansas—to believe the rhetoric came from his heart. Nonetheless, his administration has done some good things, mainly because he installed some good people.

Early in the new gubernatorial race, Bush is listening to smart talk. Republicans have a reputation as the anti-green party, and in Florida that translates into thousands of lost votes. Bush's supporters appear to have convinced him of the importance of a credible environmental platform.

The centerpiece is an extended edition of Preservation 2000, the successful land-acquisition program initiated under Florida's last Republican governor, Bob Martinez. Although Martinez made some terrible appointments to environmental watchdog agencies, he will be well remembered for pushing "P2000."

It works like this: The state issues tax-free bonds to raise money for the purchase of ecologically sensitive or imperiled lands. The benefits have been felt from the Panhandle to the Keys, wherever green space and wildlife habitat have been spared from destruction.

Preservation 2000 expires at the turn of the century, and Bush pledges to renew the concept for another decade, with $300 million a year allocated for buying and managing land.

And when a parcel is too expensive to purchase, he says, the state should secure the development rights or a conservation easement. That would preserve the land while compensating the owner for maintaining it—an approach that makes sense, as long as everyone plays by the rules.

These are interesting ideas from an unlikely source. But the greening of Jeb Bush, developer, is being guided by Martinez and his onetime running mate, J. Allison DeFoor, an attorney and ex-sheriff of Monroe County.

DeFoor is a rare breed, a Republican with solid environmental credentials. He and Martinez recently formed a GOP think tank called the Theodore Roosevelt Society. The name is meant to remind voters that the nation's most impassioned and progressive president, conservation-wise, was a Republican.

Bush is a city boy at heart, and will never be mistaken for the second coming of T.R. He's happier on the tennis court than on a mangrove island, but that's all right.

He wouldn't be the first governor, Democrat or Republican, to act out of political expediency rather than deeply held conviction. And while we can hope that Bush is losing sleep over the future of the Everglades, he's probably just losing sleep over the votes.

That's all right, too. You can't expect an overnight spiritual conversion. It'd be swell to have a governor who truly believes, but most of us will settle for one who does the right thing, for whatever reason.

Judge humbles Humberto

August 30, 1998

Thank you, Roberto Pineiro, for sparing us from another dispiriting Humberto Hernandez trial.

Taxpayers are grateful. Prosecutors are grateful. And we in the media are eternally grateful.

Pineiro is the Miami-Dade judge who socked it to Hernandez on Aug. 19 for his role in the vote fraud committed during last fall's Miami elections.

The defrocked commissioner was so crushed by Pineiro's stiff sentence—and cutting words—that last week he threw in the towel on pending bank fraud and money laundering charges.

Now there's one less cockroach in the public cupboard, and for that Judge Pineiro deserves a standing ovation.

A jury had convicted Hernandez of helping cover up phony absentee balloting. It was only a misdemeanor, and Pineiro could have let Humberto off with token jail time or a fine.

But instead he hammered him with the maximum: 364 days. Smirking Bert was smirking no more. He listened gloomily as the judge told him: "I cannot envision a more felonious misdemeanor."

For Hernandez, it was a decisively deflating moment. He couldn't endure another trial, or the prospect of a 13-year prison term. Within days his lawyer began negotiating with the U.S. attorney's office.

On Thursday a deal was announced. Hernandez pleaded guilty to one conspiracy count, for which he could get four years. He admitted his role in falsifying mortgages that ripped off banks for $2.9 million. Prosecutors say the scam also laundered a fortune in stolen Medicare funds.

Hernandez's attorney describes him as "depressed and embarrassed." Good. The idiots who voted for him ought to feel the same way.

Bert's grimy past was well-publicized before the November election. Everybody knew he'd been canned as an assistant city attorney for running a private law practice out of City Hall. Everybody knew about his abominable ambulance chasing after the ValuJet crash.

And everybody knew he was facing 23 heavy-duty charges involving bogus sales of condominiums and houses.

But Humberto easily got reelected anyway. So who could be shocked when it came to light that he was mixed up in vote fraud? What'd you expect from a crook?

And a cocky crook he was, grinning in handcuffs during his arrest. Later, hidden microphones in the paddy wagon recorded Bert and his pals joking and discussing how to manipulate talk-radio to rally support.

As for the bank-fraud charges, Hernandez vowed to win at trial. That would come after his quick acquittal in the ballot-fraud case, he predicted confidently.

Bert planned to play the "race card," to claim he was being persecuted because he's Hispanic. This despicable scheme came back to haunt him before Judge Pineiro, a former prosecutor and, like Hernandez, a Cuban American.

"Sadly, you were willing to polarize our community in order to save your political power," Pineiro said as he passed sentence. "This is unconscionable."

I don't know if the judge's stern sermon sent a message to other corrupt politicians, but clearly it sent one to Smirking Bert: Your luck's run out.

Thanks to another tough judge, Joan Lenard, Hernandez has been sitting behind bars while awaiting his federal trial. It's been lonely, demoralizing and brutally hard on his family. To risk 13 years would have been the ultimate cockiness.

Copping a plea is the first decent thing Hernandez has done in a while, but decency never comes easy to crooks. First they need to get their socks scared off.

Thank you again, Roberto Pineiro.

Glades buyout has to happen

November 15, 1998

The uprooting of 350 families in the boggy East Everglades is no cause for joy, but it's necessary, overdue and inevitable.

Last week, the South Florida Water Management District decided to buy out landowners in a sodden patch of southwest Miami-Dade known as the 8½ Square Mile Area.

Planners say the purchase is essential to restore the flow of clean, fresh water to Everglades National Park. Residents are in a furious uproar. They want to stay in the Glades, and they want government to provide new roads, sewers and drainage ditches to help keep them dry.

It's the classic Florida yarn, with villains and victims but no tidy ending.

Want to blame somebody? Start with the clowns on the old Metro Commission who allowed folks to sell "property" on the wrong side of the Everglades dike.

That's right, the 8½ Square Mile Area is west of the flood-control levee. That means—surprise!—no flood control. It's a wetland, as in: wet land.

That self-evident fact didn't discourage people from hawking lots, and nobody stopped them. This is Florida, after all, with a proud tradition of submersible real estate.

But here's the problem with living in a swamp: You live in a swamp.

Water managers have been diverting some flow from the 8½ Square Mile Area, parching the national park to benefit the homeowners. Yet every rainy season the ritual repeats: TV crews slosh out to the East Everglades to interview folks who are ankle-deep and miserable. Of course they want flood protection—who wouldn't?

It's impossible not to feel heartache for those who will be forced to give up a home, a neighborhood, a way of life. But it's ludicrous to liken—as some have—the Everglades acquisition to Fidel Castro's property confiscations.

The comparison should insult anyone who lost land in Cuba—Fidel didn't pay a dime, he just took it. Landowners in the 8½ Square Mile Area cumulatively will collect as much as $113 million, according to officials.

However, the longer the buyout takes, the more it will cost. That's a serious concern for both conservationists and budget watchers. Litigation could prolong the haggling for precious years.

Meanwhile, the park gasps for more water, and speculators snap up border tracts in hopes of gouging the government—meaning you and me—when the buyout finally begins.

But the alternative could be even more expensive. Engineers say the cost of letting people remain in the 8½ Square Mile Area and making it flood-free could reach $180 million.

Behind the scenes are a few landowners who deserve scorn, not sympathy. They want flood control not just to dry out the families, but to enable further development.

Astoundingly, these operators want more houses, more ranchettes, more farms . . . in a swamp. Swell idea: Don't fix a dumb mistake. Subdivide it.

Without a healthy Everglades, all South Floridians will face dire water shortages. The 8½ Square Mile Area is needed for re-creating an unbroken flow. It's a patch that needs to be wet. It's supposed to be wet.

If officials guarantee drainage for homeowners there, a long line of swamp peddlers would form at the water management district. Everybody who owned any wetland would demand publicly funded dikes, ditches and sewers.

The cost would be outrageous and, more importantly, the Everglades restoration project would fall apart.

It's truly a shame that people need to move out of the 8½ Square Mile Area. A worse shame is that anyone was allowed to build there in the first place.

That's why there's a law

History was made recently when the Florida Ethics Commission found an actual lapse of ethics in Florida. It's a rare instance of the system working the way it's supposed to.

The case centers on a man named Dennis Wardlow. In 1995, while mayor of Key West, Wardlow was charged by U.S. prosecutors with taking a bribe from lawyer John Bigler.

Bigler owned a company that rented Jet Ski-style water bikes to tourists on the island. He put Wardlow on his payroll for $100 a week, an arrangement that lasted 19 months. This was not disputed.

The mayor claimed he was being paid to do "public relations" work for Bigler. The feds said the money was meant to buy Wardlow's influence.

These payments came during a period when Key West officials were trying to regulate water-bike vendors. Wardlow participated in the key votes. He never told fellow commissioners or the public that he was taking money from a firm that was affected by the new laws.

It seemed like a textbook case of small-town bribery, with the facts weighing gloomily against the indicted mayor.

But this wasn't just any small town; it was Key West, where juries traditionally have a higher tolerance (or a narrower definition) of corruption. This is particularly true when the accused happens to be a native "Bubba."

Wardlow took the stand to proclaim that he was not a crook, and that he had done nothing wrong by taking the $100 payments. He insisted his work for Bigler was giving business advice, on weekends, with special attention to possible water-bike opportunities in the Dominican Republic.

As lame as that sounds, it was enough to sway jurors. They acquitted the mayor, and he went back to work. Bigler didn't fare so well. He pleaded guilty to attempted bribery, received one year's probation and gave up his law license. His water-bike business is no more.

The case would have ended, too, except for one indignant citizen named Jace Hobbs, a Key Wester fed up with graft. He wrote to the state

Ethics Commission, not the most tenacious of watchdog agencies.

"I didn't even know it existed," Hobbs said, "until a week or so before I did it."

Yet a wondrous thing happened to his complaint: It got taken seriously. The ethics panel eventually found probable cause that Wardlow broke state rules by taking Bigler's money and failing to disclose it.

True, the commission needed almost two years to reach a conclusion that most clear-thinking adults would regard as a no-brainer. Then it took another nine months to hold a hearing, and another seven months to make a ruling . . . but, hey, at least something got done. For a change.

On Dec. 3, the Ethics Commission unanimously declared that Wardlow had violated seven state rules and should cough up $12,900—a $5,000 fine, plus the $7,900 he pocketed during his so-called "employment" by Bigler.

The panel also recommended a reprimand, which won't mean diddly since Wardlow is no longer Key West's mayor. Still, with the governor's backing, the fine could send a message to politicians sniffing around for extra cash: There's a chance you'll actually get punished for it—not anytime soon but long into the future, when you can barely remember which bribe they're talking about.

Jace Hobbs was out of town when news of the Wardlow ruling reached Key West. A week later, no one had yet told him about it.

He seemed quietly pleased when he heard the outcome. When I asked why he had bothered to pursue the case, Hobbs paused for a moment, then said: "I felt obligated to the community."

That's why there's a law. Sometimes, when the stars align, it even works.

Bush on track with 'bullet'

January 14, 1999

It was the first test for Florida's new governor. Was Jeb Bush really a different breed of politician, or just another Brand X hack who knuckled under to heavyweight lobbyists?

Now we have a clue. Today Bush is expected to put a bullet in the bullet train, the most egregious public rip-off ever contemplated by the Legislature.

It was a proposed 320-mile rail link between Miami, Orlando and Tampa—a $6.3 billion boondoggle that was doomed to lose money until its tracks rusted out. Its chief selling point: a train ride that would take longer and cost more than traveling by air. All aboard!

During the gubernatorial campaign, Bush criticized the bullet train because of the immense risk to taxpayers. Beginning in 2001, the state was to begin subsidizing the Millennium Turkey to the tune of $70 million annually, escalating over 40 years to a total handout exceeding $6 billion.

And that's if everything went right.

It's nice to think Florida's worsening highway gridlock and traffic pollution could be alleviated by a railroad, but it wouldn't.

Like Metrorail, Tri-Rail and Amtrak, the bullet train would never have attracted the promised passengers. Taxpayers would have been stuck with a 200-mph rolling disaster that bled cash every time it pulled out of the station.

Bush's skepticism worried those pushing the project. The most avid shill was the state Department of Transportation, which adores expensive, endless construction extravaganzas.

The DOT's ridership predictions for the bullet train were so wacky they should have been on Comedy Central—though not too wacky for lawmakers, who had already had set aside $77 million for research.

However, a preliminary planning budget was due to run out Jan. 31, with $56 million remaining in the kitty. No more could be spent without the governor's OK.

In addition to Bush's wariness, bullet-train boosters faced a dubious upcoming report from the U.S. General Accounting Office. The GAO raised questions (surprise!) about both the estimated cost of the train and the demand.

Uncle Sam's interest was substantial because Florida had sought a $2 billion federal loan for the train, to be backed by revenues from future passenger fares. The idea transcended mere optimism, and entered the realm of the hallucinatory.

Nobody was more worried about the train's political future than Florida Overland Express (FOX), the consortium seeking to build the railway and hand it over to the state. Be certain there was a fortune to be made off the bullet train by those doing the promoting, planning and engineering. The trick was to hang taxpayers with the debt for running it.

To win over Bush, FOX hired high-profile lobbyists with strong GOP connections, including Mac Stipanovich, one of Bush's top advisors in his 1994 race against Lawton Chiles. FOX even donated $5,000 toward Bush's inaugural festivities this month.

For their efforts, company big shots got some face time with the new governor last week. Evidently they failed to change his mind.

Today Bush announces that he won't approve future funding for the bullet train. It's unlikely the Republican-led Legislature will rise up against him, so the project is as good as dead.

Had the governor caved to the lobbyists, he would have been indelibly linked to Florida's costliest transportation fiasco. Jeb's Folly, it would have been called.

But by running the bullet train off the rails now, before another penny is wasted, Bush saves future generations of taxpayers from a multibillion-dollar debacle. He also sets a promising precedent for his administration—common sense instead of common politics.

Let's hope it's not a fluke.